CHRISTIAN WORLDVIEW HANDBOOK

I know no other book that attempts to introduce the range of worldview topics covered by the writers gathered by editors David Dockery and Trevin Wax. They take care to sketch out the foundations of a Christian worldview grounded in revelation, who God is, and the nature and work of Jesus Christ and the pattern of truth in which he is embedded. Then they carefully and respectfully survey a wide array of competing worldviews, and survey numerous topics (e.g., science, education, government), some of them currently disputed (e.g., marriage, slavery, creation care). Cast as a handbook, this volume will not be read right through by many people, but it is one that we will turn to again and again.

D. A. Carson
President, The Gospel Coalition

In recent years we have become increasingly aware of the deepening struggle between the Christian understanding of reality and various religions and ideologies that oppose it. All too often Christians fail to understand how far-reaching this battle is. This timely *Christian Worldview Handbook* explores the fundamental questions at stake—the importance of objective truth, the structure of creation, the nature of sinfulness, and the uniqueness of the saving grace of God revealed in Jesus Christ. The editors and authors have given us a much-needed manual for the spiritual warfare that our generation is being called to wage and its lessons should be pondered and absorbed by all who profess and proclaim the Christian gospel today.

Gerald Bray
Research Professor of Divinity
Beeson Divinity School

I heartily recommend the *Christian Worldview Handbook* that David Dockery and Trevin Wax have put together. It covers a very wide range of topics with brief essays by an excellent team of contributors. It is precisely what it advertises itself to be—a handbook. It's a very effective, though brief by necessity, introduction to almost everything "under the sun" that relates to developing a Christian worldview in today's culture.

Scott B. Rae, Ph.D.
Professor of Christian Ethics, Dean of Faculty
Talbot School of Theology, Biola University

CHRISTIAN WORLDVIEW HANDBOOK

David S. Dockery & Trevin K. Wax
General Editors

REFERENCE

NASHVILLE, TENNESSEE

CONTENTS

Contents

PREFACE
TO THE CHRISTIAN WORLDVIEW HANDBOOK

The apostle Paul calls followers of Jesus to renew their minds and to offer themselves as living sacrifices to him (Rom 12:1–2). Similarly, the apostle Peter calls believers to prepare their minds for action (1 Pet 1:13). These exhortations form the foundation for learning to think Christianly about life and about the world. This is the beginning of worldview thinking.

Immersed in our pluralistic and secular society, Christians often find it difficult to think carefully and coherently about how the Christian faith affects all aspects of life. We fail to connect what we hear on Sunday with what we do on Monday. This disconnect especially affects our consideration of the deepest questions regarding the purpose and nature of human life. At stake is the way we understand the world God has called us to serve.

Christians around the globe recognize there is a great spiritual battle raging for the hearts and minds of men and women. Believers find themselves in a cosmic struggle between Christian truth and a morally indifferent culture. This handbook is intended to help Christians make progress in developing a Christian worldview that will help them learn to think in a Christian manner and to live out the truth of the Christian faith.

The reality is that everyone has a worldview. Some worldviews are incoherent, attempting to bring together a smorgasbord of options from a collection of different worldviews. An examined and thoughtful worldview, however, is more than a private personal viewpoint; it is a comprehensive life system that seeks to answer the basic questions of life. A Christian worldview is not just one's personal faith expression, not just a theory; it is an all-encompassing way of life, applicable to all spheres of life.

More than a century ago, James Orr, in *The Christian View of God and the World*, contended that there is a definite Christian view of all things, which has a character, coherence, and unity of its own, and stands in sharp contrast with countertheories and speculations. The articles found in this handbook are based on a Christian view of things that bears not only upon the spiritual sphere but also on the whole of life and thought.

Those who have worked together over the past five years to bring together this project join us in praying that the Lord will use this reference work to help Christians hear afresh the words of Jesus from what is known as the Great Commandment (Matt 22:36–40). In this passage we learn that Jesus calls on his followers to love God not only with hearts and souls but also with our minds. The words of Jesus refer to a wholehearted devotion to God with every aspect of our being, from whatever angle we choose to consider it—emotionally, volitionally, or cognitively. This kind of love for God results in taking every thought captive to make it obedient to Christ (2 Cor 10:5), a total devotion to Christian thinking and living. We pray that the *Christian Worldview Handbook* will serve Christians well, enabling them to see life from a Christian vantage point, thinking with the mind of Christ.

There are more than ninety contributors to this work, who serve at more than fifty different institutions, organizations, and churches. They come from North America and other parts of the globe. Coming from these diverse backgrounds, they share a commitment to the inspiration, truthfulness, and authority of God's Word as well as to the importance of developing a Christian worldview.

At the core of a Christian worldview is the truth that Jesus Christ's life and death revealed God's love for the world. Moreover, his sinless sacrifice delivered sinners from their alienation and reconciled and restored sinners from estrangement to full fellowship and inheritance in the household of God. Jesus's death on the cross for the sins of the world is the basis for the call to everyone everywhere to place their faith in him to be reconciled to God. Central to this Christian worldview message is the resurrection of Jesus Christ (1 Cor 15:3–4). The resurrection establishes Jesus's lordship and deity, as well as guaranteeing the salvation of sinners (Rom 1:3–4; 4:24–25). The resurrection provides new life for believers, enabling them to see, think, and live anew.

The contributors to this handbook also recognize that developing a Christian worldview is an ever-advancing process in which Christian convictions increasingly shape our participation in culture. Thus a Christian worldview offers a new way of thinking, seeing, and doing based on a new way of being.

The Christian Worldview Handbook, then, includes numerous articles that consider many implications and applications of the Bible's teaching for all aspects of life. These articles attempt to amplify the meaning of the biblical and theological foundations of a Christian worldview, seeking to help believers take every thought captive to Jesus Christ. They begin with the affirmation of God as Creator and Redeemer, recognizing that Christian worldview thinking is not only soteriological but also cosmological. The contributors share a commitment to the sovereignty of the triune God over the whole cosmos, in all spheres and kingdoms, visible and invisible, which is the essence of Christian worldview thinking. It is the prayer of each contributor to this project that all of us and all who read this handbook will grow in the grace and knowledge of the Lord Jesus Christ and continue to make progress in learning to take every thought captive to the lordship of Jesus Christ in order to serve and edify others, which is a high calling indeed.

We want to thank Thom Rainer and the leadership team at LifeWay Christian Resources and B&H Publishers for their support during the time this project has been developed. We express our thanksgiving and our gratitude for many through the years who have helped us develop a deeper understanding of the meaning and implications of a Christian worldview and trust that this work reflects faithfully their influence on our lives. We offer our gratitude for each contributor. Ultimately, we trust that this work will encourage and edify believers, strengthen the church, support the advancement of the gospel to the nations, and bring glory to our great and majestic God.

Soli Deo Gloria

David S. Dockery and Trevin K. Wax
General Editors

CONTRIBUTORS

General Editors
David S. Dockery and Trevin K. Wax

Essays Authors
Daniel L. Akin, President, Southeastern Baptist Theological Seminary
Jason K. Allen, President, Midwestern Baptist Theological Seminary
Bruce Riley Ashford, Provost, Southeastern Baptist Theological Seminary
Mark L. Bailey, President, Dallas Theological Seminary
Hunter Baker, Dean, College of Arts and Sciences, Union University
Mike Barnett, Former Professor of World Missions, Columbia
  International University
M. Todd Bates, Dean, School of Christian Thought, Houston Baptist
  University
Michael D. Beaty, Professor of Philosophy, Baylor University
John A. Bloom, Professor of Physics, Biola University
Darrell L. Bock, Research Professor of New Testament, Dallas Theological
  Seminary
Robert M. Bowman Jr., Executive Director, Institute for Religious
  Research
Elijah M. Brown, President, Baptist World Alliance
Theodore J. Cabal, Professor of Philosophy, Boyce College/Southern
  Baptist Theological Seminary
Justin Carswell, Dean, School of Christian Ministries, College of the
  Ozarks
Joshua D. Chatraw, Director, New City Fellows

Anthony L. Chute, Professor of Church History, California Baptist University

Erik Clary, Associate Director, Endosurgical Research, Duke University Medical Center

Graham A. Cole, Professor of Biblical and Systematic Theology and Dean, Trinity Evangelical Divinity School

C. John Collins, Professor of Old Testament, Covenant Seminary

Paul Copan, Professor of Philosophy, Palm Beach Atlantic University

Winfried Corduan, Professor Emeritus of Philosophy and Religion, Taylor University

Barry H. Corey, President, Biola University

Daniel Darling, Vice President for Communications, Ethics and Religious Liberty Commission

Jimmy H. Davis, Hammons Professor of Chemistry, Union University

David S. Dockery, Chancellor and Professor of Christianity and Culture, Trinity International University

Benjamin P. Dockery, Campus Pastor, Christ Church, Lake Forest, IL

Timothy D. Dockery, Executive Director, Principal and Planned Giving, University of Arkansas Medical College

Michael Duduit, Dean, School of Ministry, Anderson University

Jason G. Duesing, Provost, Midwestern Baptist Theological Seminary

Michael H. Edens, Professor of Theology and Islamic Studies, New Orleans Baptist Theological Seminary

William Edgar, Professor of Apologetics, Westminster Theological Seminary

Jeremy A. Evans, Associate Professor of Philosophy, Southeastern Baptist Theological Seminary

Gene C. Fant, President, North Greenville University

Nathan A. Finn, Provost and Dean of University Faculty, North Greenville University

Choon Sam Fong, Dean, Singapore Baptist Theological Seminary

Gregory B. Forster, Director, Oikonomia Network, Trinity International University

Zachs Gaiya, PhD student, Intercultural Studies, Trinity Evangelical Divinity School

Timothy George, Research Professor of Divinity, Beeson Divinity School, Samford University

Joy Greene, Assistant Dean, School of Pharmacy, High Point University

Douglas Groothuis, Professor of Philosophy, Denver Seminary

George H. Guthrie, Professor of New Testament, Regent College

Steve R. Halla, Assistant Professor of Art, Union University

Douglas V. Henry, Professor of Philosophy, Baylor University

Eric L. Johnson, Director, Society for Christian Psychology and the Institute for Christian Psychology

Stanton L. Jones, Provost Emeritus and Professor of Psychology, Wheaton College

Timothy Paul Jones, Gheens Professor of Christian Education, Southern Baptist Theological Seminary

Thomas S. Kidd, Professor of History, Baylor University

Glenn R. Kreider, Professor of Theology, Dallas Theological Seminary

Charles E. Lawless Jr., Dean of Doctoral Studies and Professor of Evangelism and Missions, Southeastern Baptist Theological Seminary

Steve W. Lemke, Provost Emeritus, New Orleans Baptist Theological Seminary

Kenneth T. Magnuson, Professor of Christian Ethics, Southern Baptist Theological Seminary

Jennifer A. Marshall, Senior Research Fellow, Institute of Theology and Public Life, Reformed Theological Seminary

Kenneth A. Mathews, Professor of Old Testament, Beeson Divinity School

Craig Mitchell, Associate Professor of Philosophy, Politics, and Economics, Criswell College

R. Albert Mohler Jr., President, Southern Baptist Theological Seminary

Russell D. Moore, President, Ethics and Religious Liberty Commission

Scott H. Moore, Professor of Philosophy, Baylor University

Christopher W. Morgan, Dean, School of Christian Ministry, California Baptist University

Paul Munson, Associate Professor of Music, Grove City College

David K. Naugle, Professor of Philosophy, Dallas Baptist University

Mark A. Noll, McAnaney Professor of History, Notre Dame University

Harry L. Poe, Colson Professor of Faith and Culture, Union University

Mary Anne Poe, Associate Professor of Social Work, Union University

Doug Powell, Christian Apologist and Musician

Karen Swallow Prior, Professor of English, Liberty University

Thom S. Rainer, Former President, LifeWay Christian Resources

Joy Riley, Executive Director, Tennessee Center for Bioethics

Read M. Schuchardt, Associate Professor of Communication, Wheaton College

Walter J. Schultz, Professor of Philosophy, University of Northwestern

Mary Jo Sharp, Assistant Professor of Apologetics, Houston Baptist University

Robert B. Sloan, President, Houston Baptist University

Kevin Smith, Executive Director, Baptist Convention of Maryland/ Delaware

Robert Smith Jr., Carter Professor of Preaching, Beeson Divinity School

John Stonestreet, President, Chuck Colson Center for Christian Worldview

Alan B. Terwilleger, Retired President, Colson Center for Christian Worldview

Felix Theonugraha, President, Western Theological Seminary

K. Erik Thoennes, Associate Professor of Theology, Biola University

Carl R. Trueman, Professor of Biblical and Religious Studies, Grove City College

Preben Vang, Director, Doctor of Ministry Program, Truett Seminary, Baylor University

Andrew T. Walker, Director of Policy Studies, Ethics and Religious Liberty Commission

Bruce A. Ware, Professor of Theology, Southern Baptist Theological Seminary

Micah J. Watson, William Spoelhof Associate Professor of Political Science, Calvin College

Trevin K. Wax, Publisher, Bibles and Reference, B&H Publishers

Stephen J. Wellum, Professor of Theology, Southern Baptist Theological Seminary

Darin W. White, Professor of Business, Samford University

James Emery White, Pastor, Mecklenburg Community Church, Charlotte, NC

Danny Wood, Pastor, Shades Mountain Baptist Church, Birmingham, AL

Taylor B. Worley, Associate Vice President, Trinity International University

Malcolm B. Yarnell III, Research Professor of Theology, Southwestern Baptist Theological Seminary

Christopher Yuan, Professor, Moody Bible Institute

Christian Worldview Formation

AN INTRODUCTION TO A CHRISTIAN WORLDVIEW

Trevin K. Wax

I can't forget the shoes. Piles and piles of them filled the room. Of all the gruesome images I saw at the Holocaust Museum in Washington, DC, that room filled with shoes from Jewish victims is the one thing I can't forget. I think about the people who once owned those shoes, and I mourn the human lives lost in a vortex of unspeakable evil.

The tragedy of the Holocaust reminds me of something I heard as a high school student: ideas have consequences. Adolf Hitler did not come out of nowhere. Before there was the Holocaust, decades of philosophical theories advocating superior races were presented, nationalistic laws were written, and the use of eugenics to weed out inferior peoples arose. Throw in a dash of "survival of the fittest" from Darwinism and perhaps the pursuit of raw power from nihilism, and eventually humankind was poised to arrive in the concentration camp—a horrifying concoction built on various falsehoods.

Ideas do indeed have consequences. But sometimes those consequences are beautiful, as in the early days of Christianity when plagues would sweep through cities in the Roman Empire. While many Roman citizens chose to abandon family and friends and flee the city to escape contamination, early Christians stayed behind to nurse the sick. Because of their belief in a Savior who sacrificed himself for others, they were content to give their lives as well.

Christianity in a World of -Isms

Capitalism. Socialism. Postmodernism. Consumerism. Relativism. Pluralism. All sorts of -isms exist in our world, each representing a different outlook on humanity, each with different opinions about the way societies should function and how people should behave. Each of these began with an idea.

Some Christians shrug off any effort to study philosophies and "isms." They say things like, "I don't worry myself with what other people think about the world. I just read my Bible and try to do what it says." This line of thinking sounds humble and restrained, but it is far from the mentality of a missionary. If we are to be biblical Christians, we must read the Bible in order to read the culture. It's important that we as a sent people evaluate the -isms of this world in light of God's unchanging revelation. In other words, we read the Bible first so we will know how to read world news next.

We also read the Bible to know how to engage people around us with the gospel. To be good missionaries, we need to have our own minds formed by the Scriptures, and at the same time, we need to understand how people think—the people we've been called to reach. That's why we need to be familiar with the big questions of life and the big debates in our world.

Three Reasons a Christian Worldview Matters

A worldview is the lens through which a person looks at the world. At the center of a worldview are the ultimate beliefs an individual holds, foundational convictions that seem so obvious that the one holding them seldom thinks much about them. Each of us has a view of the world. And so do the people around us—even if they've never given much thought to it.

I have terrible eyesight and have needed corrective lenses since I was in the first grade. Every morning I put contacts into my eyes so I can see clearly. A worldview is like a contact lens: it's the way we view the world. I don't give a lot of thought to my contacts throughout the day. I don't look at them when they're in my eyes. I look through them and see the world. Similarly, we look through worldviews and interpret the world around us.

1. A Christian worldview matters because it sets us apart from the world *(Rom 12:1–2).*

"Christians must be different from the world." Whenever we hear this statement in sermons or read it in books, we usually think about our behavior, right? We nod our heads and think, *Yes, our actions must set us apart!*

But there's another application of this statement that is equally important. Christians must be different from the world in the way we think. Our thinking must also set us apart. Yes, our actions ought to make us stand out from the world. But at an even deeper level, our thought processes should be different as well because actions follow thoughts.

Let's take a look at Romans 12:1–2, a turning point in the apostle Paul's letter to the Romans. "Therefore, brothers and sisters, in view of the mercies of God, I urge you to present your bodies as a living sacrifice, holy and pleasing to God; this is your true worship. Do not be conformed to this age, but be transformed by the renewing of your mind, so that you may discern what is the good, pleasing, and perfect will of God."

In chapter 12, Paul launched into specific instructions about how to live. In other words, in light of all that has gone before, in light of God's promises and the salvation he has provided through his Son, we Christians are told to "present [our] bodies as a living sacrifice."

You may question the use of the word "bodies" here. Aren't we talking about worldviews? Doesn't that involve our minds? Yes. And notice how spiritual transformation includes both. In verse 1, Paul wrote that we must offer our bodies. In verse 2, he wrote that we must be transformed by the renewing of our minds. Mind and matter. Physical and immaterial. Thinking and behavior. Paul didn't just say, "Think rightly." Neither did he simply say, "Behave rightly." Paul knew the gospel transforms both our thoughts and our actions.

If we are to keep from being conformed to this age, we've got to understand the connection between thoughts and deeds. Paul connected them, and so should we.

What does it look like to be conformed to this age? To think in a worldly fashion? The Bible has the answers. It shows us not only what a Christian worldview looks like but also wrong worldviews and how they lead us astray.

In the book of Job, we see how a false worldview results in false comfort. Job was a righteous man who went through a severe trial. Along the way, he was "comforted" by his friends, each of whom accused Job of having sinned. The friends shared a worldview that said, "Everything happens because of cause and effect. Do bad things, and bad things will happen to you. Do good things, and good things will happen to you." This worldview was the lens through which they viewed Job's suffering. The book of Job challenges this perspective in light of an all-powerful, all-wise God who permits things to happen that are beyond our understanding.

Consider Ecclesiastes in the OT. Much of this book expresses the worldview of "life under the sun," a life without meaning and purpose in the face of death. The author does end the book with an affirmation of a biblical worldview, but much of the poetry is written from the perspective that death is the only thing we humans can anticipate. Though he had amassed great wealth and power, the author knew everything was indeed meaningless apart from the existence of God. And in reflecting on "life under the sun," he wrote a book that helps us understand the mind-set and worldview of someone who lives as though this life is all there is.

Or consider Paul's lengthy discourse on the resurrection of Christ in 1 Corinthians 15. "If the dead are not raised, Let us eat and drink, for tomorrow we die," he wrote in verse 32. In other words, a life of hedonism—the pursuit of pleasure—is acceptable unless the claims at the center of Christianity are true. If Christ has been raised, then there is something more important than immediate pleasure and comfort. Paul contrasted a hedonistic philosophy with Christianity.

The Bible consistently presents a Christian view of the world. Along the way, the biblical authors interacted with and contradicted unbiblical worldviews. We ought to be skilled in doing the same. Developing a Christian worldview will keep us from being conformed to this world.

There is a missional orientation to our nonconformity. Worldviews matter because people matter. Seeking to understand someone with whom we disagree is a way of loving our neighbor. It doesn't mean we accept every point of view as valid, right, or helpful. Neither does it mean we paper over our differences. We must never conform. But it does mean that we will listen and learn like missionaries seeking to understand the culture we are trying to reach. If we are to "present [our] bodies as a living sacrifice," we must live in light of the mercies of God, understand our role as Christ's ambassadors to the world, and answer his call to bear witness to him and his work.

2. A Christian worldview matters because it aids our spiritual transformation *(Rom 12:2a)*.

A Christian worldview is important because it sets us apart from the world. But there's another reason why a Christian worldview matters: thinking as a Christian is part of the process of sanctification (being made holy). It is an important part of embracing our new identity in Christ. Notice Romans 12:2: "Do not be conformed to this age, but be transformed by the renewing of your mind."

This verse points us back to Romans 1, where Paul laid out the dire situation of humanity before a holy God. There he wrote, "For though they knew God, they did not glorify him as God or show gratitude. Instead, their thinking became worthless, and their senseless hearts were darkened. Claiming to be wise, they became fools. . . . They exchanged the truth of God for a lie" (Rom 1:21–22,25).

This passage shows us what happens when we exchange the truth of God for lies. Our minds are darkened, and then we engage in sinful behavior—as is evidenced in Paul's list of sinful attitudes and actions: greed, envy, murder, sexual immorality, etc. (vv. 29–31).

But in Romans 12, the situation is gloriously reversed! Because of Christ's work, our minds are being renewed. No longer are we senseless sinners living in the dark. Instead, we are redeemed people living in the light of Christ's resurrection. We also live in the light of his regenerating work in our hearts. Through the Spirit, God is changing us, conforming us—not to the world but into the image of his Son. By the mercies of God, we have been given a new identity.

What we think about ourselves matters. It also affects the way we see the world. That's why thinking as a Christian is a key part of your identity as a follower of Christ. If we have been called the children of God, then surely our new identity should affect the way we think and act.

As a parent, I am proud of my son when I see him growing and maturing. There have been times when, out of a sense of responsibility and love, he has left his toys to go check on his little sister. It warms my heart to see my nine-year-old showing signs of maturity as he grows. In the same way, God is pleased to see us thinking and acting as his children. We bring him pleasure through our obedience (Rom 12:2)—even though we often falter, stumble, and fall. It's true that we don't always think clearly. Our sanctification is indeed a process, and it is still incomplete. Yet God delights in seeing his children love him with their minds. He loves to see us embrace the new identity he has given us.

Worldviews provide answers to the fundamental questions of life. How did we get here? Why are we here? Who is in control of the world? Where are we going? What has gone wrong with the planet? What is the solution? People may not ask these questions consciously, but the way they answer such things in their own minds will shape the way they live.

Consider the example of a schoolteacher who goes to work every day convinced that the biggest problem in the world is ignorance. Lack of education leads to crime and is the source of human sorrow. If the world's biggest problem is ignorance, what is the solution? Education, of course! Salvation comes through learning.

A Christian teacher, by contrast, will see that ignorance may contribute to human suffering, but it's not the ultimate cause of the problem. According to the Bible, human sorrow comes from sin—our rebellion against God. Sin is the big problem, and salvation through Christ's atoning death and resurrection is the solution. At the end of the day, the solution is Jesus, not more education.

The answers to worldview questions lead to different outlooks on life. The way you diagnose the world's problem necessarily affects what you believe to be the solution. That's why it's important to have our minds renewed by the power of the Spirit as we study the Scriptures together. We must see the world through the eyes of biblical revelation.

The psalmist wrote, "The revelation of your words brings light and gives understanding to the inexperienced" (Ps 119:130). Ultimately, if we have understanding, it's not just because we have attained a natural level of maturity but because we've benefited from God's revelation. Being transformed by the renewing of your mind won't happen apart from God's Spirit working through God's Word. We need the Spirit to illuminate the meaning of the Bible so that we are able to find our place in God's great story of redemption.

3. A Christian worldview matters because it helps us know how to live *(Rom 12:2b)*.

Romans 12:2 makes it plain what the purpose of our spiritual transformation is. It allows us to "discern what is the good, pleasing, and perfect will of God."

I mentioned earlier how a worldview is like having contact lenses. What if I put on my contact lenses in the morning and then went back to bed to stare at the ceiling all day? That would be pointless. A waste of my lenses. The purpose of wearing contacts is to see clearly throughout the day as I go about the tasks assigned to me. In the same way, the point of developing a Christian worldview is not so I can stare into space, comforted by my good vision. The point of seeing is that I then walk in a biblical way, according to my new identity in Christ.

Sometimes Christians wish the Bible were simpler, a quick and easy guide that lays out every step of obedience. To be sure, the Bible has lots of do's and don'ts. But God didn't choose to detail specific commands for every possible situation we might find ourselves in.

What the Bible does give us is a grand narrative that focuses our attention on Jesus Christ and his gospel. In this story of redemption, we glean principles for living according to our new identity in him. Once we understand our general role in the plan and providence of God, we are called to exercise biblical wisdom in making everyday decisions.

God left us with something better than a simple list of commands. He gave us renewed minds that—through the power of his Spirit—will be able to discern what actions we should take. He is seeking to transform us so that we can determine God's will in particular situations where explicit instructions are not spelled out in Scripture.

Knowing how to apply the Bible in specific situations is one of the goals of developing a Christian worldview. We see an example of this in 1 Chronicles 12, where we find a list of King David's supporters. As the author listed the soldiers, he wrote of one tribe, "From the Issacharites, who understood the times and knew what Israel should do" (v. 32). In the context of this passage, this tribe's understanding was that David should be made king over all Israel. They knew what Israel should do because they "understood the times" and who was the rightful king.

In a similar way, we as Christians must understand the times in order to know what to do. We believe Jesus is the rightful King over all the world. And this truth necessarily influences our actions. A Christian worldview is developed in light of who God is and what he has done to reconcile the world to himself.

Conclusion

What does it mean to live according to our new identity in Christ? First, we must demolish strongholds and false ideas as we cast down the idols we make of ourselves (2 Cor 10:4–5). Then, in ongoing repentance and faith, we seek to view the world through biblical eyes. We are the citizens of Christ's kingdom. We are those who have been reborn by his Spirit and are inching ever so slowly toward maturity, driven by our hope in the final resurrection.

The more we think as Christians, the more we will have the heart of Christ. That's why we are called to summon others on behalf of the King.

TRUTH, GOODNESS, BEAUTY, AND THE GOOD LIFE

Karen Swallow Prior

In the classical tradition, truth, goodness, and beauty are seen as evidence of a form of Being greater and loftier than any other in existence. This triumvirate, according to ancient philosophers, constituted the "transcendentals," or universal, absolute ideals. Because they did not know the God of the Bible, these Greek thinkers recognized only the signs of God, not God himself; they detected the promise of his transcendence but not the fulfillment of his immanence. Yet, even within their pagan worldview, the early Greeks understood that truth, goodness, and beauty signify the existence of something beyond ourselves and the rest of the created world.

God is the source of all that is true, good, and beautiful. And he is all of these things. Human beings, being made in God's image, reflect his nature and character. Unlike other living creatures, human beings can comprehend what is true or false through the ability to reason, judge what is right or wrong through our moral nature, and recognize what is beautiful or ugly through our imaginative and creative faculties.

The development of these distinctly human characteristics cultivates human excellence, what is classically referred to as the virtues. The attainment of such virtues leads to what the ancients called the good life and what the Bible calls the abundant life. Indeed, what constitutes the good life is the question that every religion and every school of philosophy attempts to address. The Bible, of course, provides the definitive answer. In Jesus is the beautiful way, the only truth, and the good life.

11

Yet, it often seems that the abundant life that Christ desires for believers is hard to attain in this earthly realm. Much of that difficulty arises, of course, from the unavoidable effects of sin and suffering that are part of this fallen world. But some lack of abundance owes to our own inability to grasp what such a life should even look like. In his famous opening to *The Weight of Glory,* C. S. Lewis explains how our human longings can fall short:

> If we consider the unblushing promises of reward and the staggering nature of the rewards promised in the Gospels, it would seem that Our Lord finds our desires not too strong, but too weak. We are half-hearted creatures, fooling about with drink and sex and ambition when infinite joy is offered us, like an ignorant child who wants to go on making mud pies in a slum because he cannot imagine what is meant by the offer of a holiday at the sea. *We are far too easily pleased.* (p. 26)

How do we know when we are settling for less than the abundant life?

The truth is right before us in both the special revelation of God's Word and the general revelation of his creation, but our human nature resists its weight and clarity. This blindness is seen in Pilate's question to Jesus upon being brought before him before Jesus's crucifixion: "What is truth?" (John 18:38).

Such knowledge—any knowledge, in fact—begins with the fear of the Lord (Ps 9:10). God came to us as the Word so that we may know his truth (1 John 5:20). His written Word is truth (Ps 119:160; 2 Sam 7:28; John 17:17). God's commandments are truth (Ps 119:142,151), his judgments are truth (Ps 19:9), and the gospel is truth (Col 1:5). The Holy Spirit is "the Spirit of truth" who guides believers "into all the truth" (John 16:13). Yet, much about God remains unknowable, and accepting the place where human understanding leaves off and divine mystery begins is also a truth to be grasped. Knowing the truth, Jesus tells us, sets us free—free from the false visions and inadequate longings that busy us in making mud pies rather than pursuing the abundant life.

The abundant life requires more than mere knowing, however. It requires doing as well. God himself exemplifies this in his dynamic acts of creation that began in Genesis and continue in our lives and the world today. When he created the world, God declared it to be "good," and when he made humankind, it was "very good." The goodness we see in the world, even in its fallen state, is good because he made the world good. The good works we are able to do, even in our fallen human condition, are good only because they reflect his goodness. "We are his workmanship, created in Christ Jesus for good works" (Eph 2:10). Our good works give glory to God (Matt 5:16). Though this world is marked by unspeakable suffering and sin, it is filled with goodness, too, because God is good. As the poet Gerard Manley Hopkins says, "The world is charged with the grandeur of God." The good life is one that sees and celebrates the fullness of the earth and its infinite goodness.

The centrality of truth and goodness in the faithful Christian life is readily apparent. Indeed, orthodoxy (true doctrine) and orthopraxy (right practice) are the focus of most preaching, teaching, and discipleship. Beauty, on the other hand, seems peripheral, unimportant, and optional, particularly within the modern world. Beauty can even be seen as excessive or dispensable in a world rife with so many other dire wants. We need only compare the beauty of a centuries-old cathedral to that of today's car dealership converted into a church building to see how our desire for beauty has diminished today.

But the Bible tells a different story about the place of beauty in God's plan.

Throughout Scripture, we see how beauty is inseparable from truth and goodness. Truth is what God reveals of himself, goodness is why he reveals himself, and beauty is the way he reveals himself. For example, the word for "good" which God used to describe his creation refers to both moral goodness and aesthetic goodness (beauty), according to theologian William Dyrness in *Visual Faith: Art, Theology, and Worship in Dialogue.* Later, when God directed the building of his holy tabernacle, his specifications included detailed ornamentation, and he called two gifted artisans, Bezalel and Oholiab, to adorn with beauty the place where goodness would dwell. In its entirety, the Bible consists of various literary genres to express truth in Spirit-inspired language that is exquisite in its narration, exposition, imagery, musicality, and eloquence. The beauty of the Bible's language is attested in its influence on the world's greatest literature across the ages.

All that is beautiful reflects the beauty of God, and "he has made everything beautiful in its time" (Eccl 3:11, NIV). Thomas Aquinas long ago identified the properties of beauty as proportion, luminosity, and integrity. Fittingly, these qualities reflect the nature and character of the triune God as well as the abundant life we can have in Christ. The blessings proclaimed by Christ in his Sermon on the Mount are called the *beatitudes*, a word that comes from the same Indo-European root for the word *beautiful*. In *The Call and the Response*, philosopher Jean-Louis Chretien notes that the Greek word for *beautiful* is also etymologically related to the word that means *to call*. This is because what is beautiful calls and beckons us. All the beauty in the world—whether made by him or by those created in his image—beckons us to himself. God created a beautiful world that displays visibly his invisible qualities, a world that calls us to him, so that we are without excuse (Rom 1:20).

The fact that beauty calls us is a reminder that beauty is in its essence an aesthetic experience, something perceived bodily through our physical senses. A tendency to focus more on the spiritual than the physical can lead Christians to undervalue the role sensory experience plays in our formation and understanding. But God does not. Indeed, God ordained to bring salvation to humanity by taking on a bodily form in the person of Jesus Christ. When the Bible speaks of the glory of God, it is speaking of his beauty. It is his magnificence made manifest. With the coming of Christ, we can say with John that "we observed his glory" (John 1:14). The incarnation brought God to humankind in a physical form that could be seen, heard, smelled, and touched—and whose bodily death, burial, and resurrection we remember through the tasting of bread and wine. This aesthetic aspect of the truth of the gospel isn't extraneous or superfluous: it is the gospel.

And the gospel is the one story that is perfectly good, true, and beautiful.

HOW TO THINK ABOUT COMPETING WORLDVIEWS

Graham A. Cole

Our frame of reference matters. We all have at least one, or maybe bits of different ones, that we have never been able to connect up into some sort of coherent whole. Perhaps this is a question to which we have not really turned our minds in a sustained way. If we do, then the real question becomes: So where do we find a frame of reference or a worldview that tells a coherent and consistent story that really understands us and illuminates the actual world in which we live? We need—if we want to be thoughtful about it—a frame of reference that is thinkable, that is, one that is not riddled with self-contradiction. It also needs to be livable—that is, we can actually live as though this frame of reference really does correspond to the world of our experience, so that we do not have to pretend that it does. That is not to say, however, that there may not be puzzles and mysteries left unresolved. As Moses said in ancient times, there are secret things that belong to the Lord (Deut 29:29).

Questioning the Question

C.E.M. Joad made a name on British radio as a brain. He was a professional philosopher at the University of London and was on a BBC radio panel called "The Brains Trust." Listeners supplied the questions, and the panel would try to answer them and entertain at the same time. Invariably Professor Joad would start an answer to a question with "It all depends on what you mean by. . . ." He became famous for it. He was right to ask questions of the question, whether the question was stated or implied. So should we. For some, *worldview* is a term that covers a set of answers to questions about who we are, where we have come from, why we go wrong, and what we may hope for as far as change for the better is concerned. I like to call this an existential worldview because it centers on real questions about my actual existence. This understanding of worldview and my frame of reference are synonymous.

A Touchstone Proposition

What seems to be true of a frame of reference or a worldview is that some proposition or claim lies at the heart of them. One philosopher, William H. Halverson, has described such a proposition—whether that proposition is implicit or explicit—as a touchstone proposition. Examples are not hard to find. At the core of naturalism, for instance, is the idea that matter is all there is, while theism claims that there is a wise and good Creator. According to Halverson this divide between naturalistic and nonnaturalistic worldviews is the fundamental one.

Other examples include nihilism, which has at its heart the notion that nothing matters. Islam provides one more instance with its claim that Allah alone is God and that Muhammad is his prophet. But what exactly is a touchstone? A touchstone is a piece of quartz that can be rubbed against what is claimed to be gold. The chemical reaction that follows will show whether the specimen of ore is real gold or fool's gold. The touchstone proposition acts as a gatekeeper to the house of knowledge—or so it is hoped. What we count as knowledge has to pass the quality control of the touchstone proposition. Of course, and here's the rub: our chosen touchstone may be astray with the result that we are really in the dark but do not know it.

The supreme rescue story of the Bible constitutes that part of the frame of reference that helps us to understand why Jesus is so special. Further, it helps me grasp how the goodness and love of God can be believed in a world such as our own with its beauties and its terrors, its delights and its dangers. And still further it helps me to comprehend how I can find peace when I become acutely aware of my true moral status before a holy, loving God who will not overlook human wrongdoing forever, including my own. Yet God has provided through the coming and cross of Christ what I cannot do for myself: he has provided in Jesus a mediator and reconciler. Jesus lived an other-person-centered life in his humanity that should be true of each one of us but isn't. In other words, he lived the divine design for human life, love for God and neighbor. The value of his faithfulness to the divine design can be put to our account if we avail ourselves of it. He also died the death we deserve because of our wrongdoing so that we might not face God's judgment if we avail ourselves of its value. He makes an extraordinary exchange possible. Martin Luther drew an analogy for that exchange by writing of a marriage. The riches of Christ become that of his bride the church, and the great debts of the bride are swallowed up by those riches. And this Jesus is returning. Creation awaits its restoration and its King. There are limits, however, to the divine patience.

In today's world, so also in Jesus's day, there are those who give up hope of a better world beyond this one. When a teleological (goal-oriented) perspective on history is abandoned, then hedonism or apathy or despair or nihilism follows. A characteristic of the biblical story is its hopefulness. Hope, after all, is one of the great virtues alongside faith and love. Peter in his first letter writes of Christians who have been born again to a living hope (1 Pet 1:3–5). This hopefulness is founded on an astounding historical event, the resurrection of Jesus Christ from the dead and his return.

Christian hopefulness also engenders a particular perspective on human history. Unlike some other great religions of the world, especially from the East, Christians are roadies and not wheelies. Let me explain. Lesslie Newbigin sees a key divide between those who believe that the human story will be endlessly repeated like a wheel turning on its axis but not actually going anywhere (reincarnation and eternal recurrence) and those who see human history as a road. He reached this conclusion after spending many years in India dialoguing with Hindu scholars. A road has a beginning, a middle, and an end. The biblical story too has a beginning, a middle, and an end. It starts in a garden in the first book of the Bible, Genesis, and ends the human story in a city in the last book of the Bible, Revelation. In the middle is the coming and cross and resurrection of Christ. The journey is from the old heavens and earth to the new heavens and earth. Evil is no more, death is no more, tears are no more, mourning is no more. The universe is at peace; it is characterized by shalom, by God-given well-being.

Christianity has a worldview (technically, theism) but isn't a worldview. As for the Yes, there is a cluster of touchstone propositions at the heart of an intellectual account of Christianity: propositions about the Creator, the creation, the fall, the rescue, and the restoration. Moreover, as we have seen earlier, this frame of reference not only has explanatory power—that is, it makes sense of our experience—it also raises significant questions about naturalism, secularism, modernity, postmodern relativism, naïve romanticism, utopianism, nihilism, pessimism, Islam, Hinduism, and the transhuman project as alternative stories.

Evaluating Worldviews

At this point someone might respond, "OK, so Christians have a worldview. Well, so what? There is more than one worldview out there. Why settle for the Christian one?" A fair comment, for it raises the question of how we are to do quality control on worldview candidates. Let me develop further the two important criteria mentioned earlier. These criteria apply to frames of references and to worldviews.

The first criterion is whether the frame of reference is thinkable. That is to say, when articulated, does it tell a logical story in two senses of the word? Is the story internally consistent, or does it contradict itself? That's one sense. If we allow the contradictory, then anything follows. Imagine if I tried to tell someone that Christ was killed by crucifixion and that he lived to a ripe old age and had a family before passing away in his sleep. The other sense is the need for a coherent story. The elements in the story need to illuminate one another. The substories of creation, fall, rescue, and restoration throw light on one another. A frame of reference or worldview—at whatever level of sophistication—needs to be logically adequate.

The second criterion is livability. If I believe and embrace a particular frame of reference, am I able to live as though it were true to my experience of the world? Or will the living of life betray its inadequacy? This realism is what is to be expected if the Christian frame of reference with its idea of the fall and of a complete restoration to come is taken seriously.

[Portions of this material previously appeared in the Christ on Campus Initiative booklet.]

Revelation
and the Bible

GENERAL REVELATION

Bruce Riley Ashford

One powerful question underlies discussion and debate of any religious issue: what is the source of our knowledge of God? This question determines
all others because the source on which we depend—whether experience,
tradition, society, Scripture, or science—determines the questions we ask
and the answers we give. Christians believe that their knowledge of God
comes from God's revelation of himself to humanity. When we recognize
this self-disclosure and call it "revelation," we mean at least three things:

1. First, God initiates this self-disclosure freely. By his very nature, God
   communicates.
2. Second, God initiates it in order to reveal something about himself.
3. Third, he initiates it in order to display his glory and to evoke worship from humanity.

Christians usually divide this revelation into two types: special and general.
In special revelation, God reveals himself through signs and miracles, the
words of the prophets and apostles, the person and work of Christ, and the
writings of Christian Scripture. This type of revelation is special because it is
provided to particular people in specific times and places; it enables them to
come to true and saving knowledge of the triune God.

In general revelation, God reveals himself through creation, history, and the moral law he has given to all people everywhere. This type of
revelation is general because it is provided to all people of all times, and it

provides a basic understanding of God and his moral law. It establishes the facts of God's existence and humanity's moral responsibility, but is not sufficient to save fallen humans, who without exception have turned their minds and wills against God. Although general revelation is sufficient to show humans their need to worship and obey the one true God, fallen sinners ultimately reject it and reject him (Rom 1:18–32).

The Fact of General Revelation

The OT contains many passages that speak of the reality of general revelation. Genesis 1–2 teaches that God created humans in his image and likeness. When one looks at humans, one sees an image and likeness of God. Job 38–41 teaches that God has revealed himself through earth and sea, the rising of the sun, snow and hail, wind and rain, frost and ice, the constellations, the animal kingdom, and humans. All aspects of the created order testify to God's existence and character. In these chapters, Job's response to this point was worshipful silence as he recognized that he was very small indeed in comparison to our great God (Job 40:4–5; 40:15–41:34). Job's worship is particularly significant when seen in contrast to his friends' response; they looked at the created order but allowed it to confirm their false worship.

Similarly, Psalm 19:1–4 tells us, "The heavens declare the glory of God, and the expanse proclaims the work of his hands. Day after day they pour out speech; night after night they communicate knowledge. . . . Their message has gone out to the whole earth, and their words to the ends of the world." Stated differently, God's creation testifies clearly enough about God that it can be considered speech and knowledge.

The NT likewise articulates God's general revelation. In Acts 17, Paul preaches to a pagan Athenian audience on Mars Hill. In his sermon, he affirms at least six things that the Athenians could know about God by means of general revelation alone (vv. 22–31): he is the Creator and Lord of the universe (v. 24), the source of life and everything that is good (v. 25). He is entirely independent and self-sufficient (v. 25). He is the ruler of the nations (v. 26) and is intelligent (v. 26), close to them (v. 27), and greater than any other possible object of worship (v. 29).

Similarly, in Rom 1:18–25, Paul argues that all humans have a basic knowledge of God. They know that he exists, that he is Creator, and that he is powerful and worthy of worship (vv. 18–21). For these reasons, humanity is without excuse (v. 20). Nevertheless, humans respond to general revelation by suppressing the truth they know (v. 18), experiencing the corruption of their hearts and minds (v. 21), exchanging truth for a lie (v. 25), and worshipping the creature rather than the Creator (v. 25). In Rom 2:14–16, Paul also makes clear that all people everywhere have an intuitive knowledge of God's moral law.

The Content of General Revelation

These and other biblical passages establish not only the fact of general revelation but also its content. Concerning God, general revelation makes clear that he is One (Acts 17:26; Rom 1:20) and is the Creator (Acts 17:25), Sustainer (Acts 14:15–16; 17:24–28), and Ruler (Rom 1:26); that he is wise (Ps 104:24), great (Job 40:15–41:34), powerful (Rom 1:20), intelligent (Rom 1:26), immanent and active (Acts 17:24–27), just and good (Acts 14:17; Rom 2:14–15). He is worthy of worship (Rom 1:25).

Concerning God's law, God has written certain basic moral principles on the human heart. Although the Ten Commandments were crafted for the nation of Israel, the moral principles behind those commandments (Exod 20:1–17) are revealed to all people everywhere through general revelation. We are to worship God rather than other gods or idols (vv. 3–6), and we should set aside time to rest and worship him (vv. 8–11). We are not to use God's name in a careless or inappropriate manner (v. 7). We should honor our parents (v. 12) and refrain from murdering (v. 13), committing adultery (v. 14), stealing (v. 15), bearing false witness (v. 16), and coveting (v. 17). These moral principles are a universal possession of all humanity. We might not see them with perfect clarity or admit that we know them, and we might become confused about them, but we do indeed know them.

The Purpose and Limits of General Revelation

General revelation and special revelation share a common purpose in pointing to the God whom we should worship and adore. Psalm 19 instructs that general and special revelation have the common purpose of evoking worship and obedience (v. 14). Romans 1:18–34 teaches that general revelation makes clear that God exists and ought to be worshipped.

Scripture is equally clear, however, that humanity is immersed with rebellious inclinations, and for this reason it rejects general revelation. In spite of general revelation, people foolishly reject God (Ps 14:1). They suppress the truth about God, exchange it for a lie, and worship the creature rather than the Creator (Rom 1:18–32). Instead of allowing God's creation to evoke worship of God, humans take God's created gifts and make idols of them—idols such as sex, money, power, success, and approval. How often we worship them instead of worshipping the Creator.

Because humans inevitably twist and distort God's general revelation, we need a special revelation from God to help us hear God and submit to him in worship and obedience. This special revelation, which now comes to us in the form of Christian Scripture, is necessary to point us to Christ—God's ultimate revelation of himself.

SPECIAL REVELATION IN SCRIPTURE

Mark L. Bailey

General revelation and special revelation are the two ways God has chosen to reveal himself to humanity. These terms have been used to delineate the extent and purpose of revelation. General revelation refers to the general truths that can be known about God through nature. Theologians use the term *special revelation* in reference to the belief in God's intentional intervention to make his mind and will available that would not be available through general revelation alone. The distinction between natural and special revelation has little to do with the source or origin of the revelation since both come from God. Instead, the distinction has to do with the means and goals of revelation.

Special revelation is addressed to humanity with a view to their redemption and ongoing relationship with God. And it is only by special revelation that one can learn how to live a godly life and thereby glorify him. "His divine power has given us everything required for life and godliness through the knowledge of him who called us by his own glory and goodness" (2 Pet 1:3). The purpose of special revelation is the redemption of sinners and the magnification of God's glory through both his gracious act of salvation of believers and the just condemnation of those who reject him.

This level of knowledge is not universally available. Rather, it is given by God supernaturally to those who are born again by the Spirit of God (John 3:3). Paul says, "What no eye has seen, no ear has heard, and no human heart has conceived—God has prepared these things for those who love him. Now God has revealed these things to us by the Spirit, since the Spirit searches everything, even the depths of God" (1 Cor 2:9–10).

Hebrews 1:1–3 provides a succinct outline of God's special revelation: "Long ago God spoke to the fathers by the prophets at different times and in different ways. In these last days, he has spoken to us by his Son. . . . The Son is the radiance of God's glory and the exact expression of his nature, sustaining all things by his powerful word."

God's special revelation came over the course of time and therefore can be rightfully described as "progressive revelation." Each of these revelations brought a better understanding of God to people. Each biblical writer added to the treasure of knowledge about our Creator. While revelation moved from that which was partial to that which is final, it was never from the imperfect to the perfect. At every point along the way, however, all that had been revealed was fully and equally inspired.

Throughout history, God has used different means to reveal his mind and message to mankind:

1. *Special Manifestation.* The Bible records God appearing many times in physical form (Gen 3:8; 18:1; Exod 3:1–4; 34:5–7). Such an appearance is known as a "theophany." When an angel takes a physical form, it is an "angelophany." Some scholars agree that the "angel of the Lord," a figure prominent in the Hebrew Scriptures, was the Lord Jesus in his preincarnate state (e.g., Gen 16:7–13; 22:15–18; 31:11–13; Judg 6:11–23). To this may be added the testimony of Paul, who affirmed the actual presence of Christ as a sustaining companion of Israel in the wilderness of Sinai (1 Cor 10:4).

2. *Direct Communication.* Sometimes God spoke to people directly (Gen 2:16), through divinely revealed dreams (Gen 28:12; Num 12:6; 1 Kgs 3:5; Dan 2), visions (Gen 15:1; Isa 1:1; Ezek 8:3–4; Dan 7; Hab 1:1; Zech 1–6; 2 Cor 12:1–7), or divine announcements out of heaven (1 Sam 3; Matt 3:17; 17:5; John 12:28).

3. *Miraculous Demonstration.* God is also able to interrupt and supersede the natural laws of nature to make his will or power known, as in the case of the use of the Urim and Thummim (Num 27:21) or miracles, whether done directly by God—like sending hailstones and making the sun remain still in the sky (Josh 10:11–15)—or accomplished through a prophet like Elijah and Elisha (1 Kgs 17–18; 2 Kgs 2:9–14) or through the apostles (Acts 3:1–11).

4. *Personal Incarnation.* The ultimate form of special revelation is the person of Jesus Christ. Jesus affirmed, "All things have been entrusted to me by my Father. No one knows the Son except the Father, and no one knows the Father except the Son and anyone to whom the Son desires to reveal him" (Matt 11:27). The special revelation in Jesus came through his words (John 7:16–17), his person (14:7), and his works (5:17–19).

5. *Divine Inspiration.* Scripture is the written revelation of God and is the principle way by which God currently reveals himself to humans. As a result, it is the means by which all claims to truth should be evaluated.

The word *inspiration* also calls attention to the process by which the Holy Spirit superintended the production of Scripture. The term refers to that process by which an omnipotent God so guided the human authors of Scripture in the recording of his revelation so that the end product was the Word of God, exactly as God wanted to communicate it in the words of the original manuscripts.

Most evangelical Christians affirm both the infallibility and inerrancy of the Bible because God is its ultimate Author. Since the Bible is the inspired Word of God, and because God is incapable of inspiring falsehood, his Word is altogether trustworthy. Psalm 119:160 states, "The entirety of your word is truth, each of your righteous judgments endures forever." If an omnipotent God could take an imperfect person like Mary and incarnate a perfect living Word, Jesus, the Son of God, then that same omnipotent God can take a human author and produce a perfect written Word of God, the Bible, through the process of divine inspiration.

The best passages in the Bible about the Bible are found in 2 Peter 1:20–21 and 2 Timothy 3:16–17. The process of inspiration can be seen in the former: "Above all, you know this: No prophecy of Scripture comes from the prophet's own interpretation, because no prophecy ever came by the will of man; instead, men spoke from God as they were carried along by the Holy Spirit." The product of inspiration is best stated in the latter passage, 2 Timothy 3:16–17: "All Scripture is inspired by God and is profitable for teaching, for rebuking, for correcting, for training in righteousness, so that the man of God may be complete, equipped for every good work." Together these passages declare the divine origin of the Bible and its use for the adequate equipping for every work of service God desires or requires.

As the writer to the Hebrews points out, God's intention is to have all revelation find its ultimate fulfillment in his Son as seen in the complementary contrast and comparison between all previous revelation and that of Jesus Christ. In the incarnation we received the fullest expression of his Word. Jesus was and is the Word made flesh. (John 1:1,14); he spoke the words the Father taught him (12:49; 14:10), and he summed up his teaching ministry this way: "I have given them your word" (17:14).

BIBLICAL AUTHORITY

Stephen J. Wellum

Biblical Christianity has always affirmed that Scripture is authoritative because it is God's Word written, the product of God's mighty action through the Word, Jesus, and by the Holy Spirit whereby human authors freely wrote exactly what God intended to be written and without error. Why has the church affirmed this view? What is meant by the inspiration and inerrancy of Scripture?

Christians have affirmed biblical authority because of Scripture's self-testimony. As one evaluates a worldview, it is crucial to begin with the specific claims of that worldview. Thus, if we are to evaluate Christianity, we must begin with Scripture's self-attestation. We do not confer upon the Bible an authority alien to it. Rather, we let Scripture speak for itself. In doing this, we discover that it makes the staggering claim that it is God's Word written and is thus completely authoritative, sufficient, and reliable.

For example, 2 Timothy 3:16 describes OT Scripture as being "inspired by God" (an allusion to creation, where the sovereign Lord speaks the universe into being) and thus fully authoritative. So, in relation to his Word, the sovereign-personal triune God of the universe has spoken again and given us his Word through the agency of human authors (2 Pet 1:20–21). And it is precisely because he stands behind his Word as Creator and Lord—the God who knows and plans all things (Eph 1:11), who cannot lie or change his mind (Num 23:19; 1 Sam 15:29; Heb 6:18)—that we have an authoritative Scripture.

Scripture's view of itself is not found in merely one or two texts; it is found throughout the entire canon. From the opening pages of the OT, we are presented with the eternal triune God who speaks with all authority (Gen 1:1–2:3). As he enters into covenant relationship with Israel, he gives them his Word, which is to believed and obeyed (Deut 5:22,32; 29:9; 30:15–16; Josh 1:7–8). As redemptive history unfolds, the covenant-making and covenant-keeping God continues to disclose himself through the prophets. This ultimately reaches fulfillment in Christ (Heb 1:1–2).

In Christ—God the Son incarnate—God's final word is spoken (John 1:1–3,14–18). Our Lord Jesus not only fulfills the OT, but he also views it as God's Word—the standard by which we are to live and evaluate everything, alongside his own spoken words (e.g., Matt 4:4; 5:17–19; John 14:6; 10:35; cp. 2 Tim 3:15–16). In this way, our Lord authenticates the OT as God's Word, and he prepares us for the writing of the NT through his apostles by the agency of the Holy Spirit (see John 16:5–15; Eph 2:20). This is why, as the NT Scripture is being written, NT authors already view their own writings as authoritative, parallel to OT Scripture (1 Thess 1:5; 2:13). Specifically one thinks of 1 Timothy 5:18 (which quotes from Deut 25:4 and Luke 10:7) and 2 Peter 3:16 (which refers to Paul's writings); these view NT writings as "Scripture."

In all these ways, Scripture views itself as supremely authoritative precisely because it is God's Word. What Scripture says, God says; what God says, Scripture says. To disbelieve or disobey any point of Scripture is to disbelieve or disobey God. The only proper response to God's Word is to trust and obey (Isa 66:2).

It is crucial to affirm biblical authority because without it we would have no basis to affirm that the God of the Bible has spoken definitively and objectively. Without an authoritative and inerrant Scripture, we could hypothesize about God and the world, but none of our hypotheses would be properly grounded. Without biblical authority we have no foundation on which to justify our beliefs since any statement of Scripture may be false. But if this is so, then one would need an independent criterion to justify which statements of Scripture are to be judged true or false. This only compounds the problem. Not only would Scripture not be able to be used as a sufficient ground of justification, but also one must ask what exactly are the independent criteria by which we judge Scripture true or false? Would it be human reason? Religious experience? The problem with all of these so-called solutions to grounding our beliefs is that they require their own independent justification. So, in the end, without a fully authoritative Bible as the foundation for grounding our theological beliefs, we have lost the ability to do theology and know truth in a universal, objective way.

Today we face an authority crisis in every direction. Whether in issues of morality, philosophy, or religion, we live in a pluralistic age that has no grounds for saying that something is right while something else is wrong, or that something is true while something else is false. We have witnessed a massive loss of confidence in the concept of truth in the academy, on the street, and even in the pew. We have lost any sense that "God has spoken" authoritatively and definitively. Nevertheless, Scripture says the opposite. The God who is has spoken, and as such, there are universal, objective grounds for morality, human thought, and theology, rooted in Scripture as God's authoritative written Word.

BIBLICAL INTERPRETATION

George H. Guthrie

Rightly understanding the Bible is foundational for building a Christian worldview. God gave us his Word that we might "view" appropriately God's world, God himself, and God's purposes for us. He wants us to think well and live well (Deut 6:4–9; Matt 7:24), but we cannot think or live what we do not understand. Thus, sound biblical interpretation is foundational for anyone who wants to live under the lordship of Christ. In 2 Timothy 2:15 we read, "Be diligent to present yourself to God as one approved, a worker who doesn't need to be ashamed, correctly teaching the word of truth." This means that sound interpretation is laudable, that misinterpretation is possible, and that interpreters are held accountable.

Biblical Interpretation: a "Conversation"

Think of biblical interpretation as playing part in a conversation, for in the Bible God has chosen human language as the medium through which to communicate with us. John Calvin said that God has talked "baby talk" to us, getting on our level to communicate in a medium we could understand and to which we might respond. When someone speaks to us, we want to listen, understand, and respond to what that person is saying. This integrated paradigm fits well how Scripture speaks about our interaction with God's Word.

"Understanding" stands at the heart of biblical interpretation, but we are not simply after intellectual knowledge. Rather, biblical interpretation should be approached relationally, under the guidance of the Holy Spirit as we cultivate a posture of listening to God, grasping what he wants us to know, and living out his will. In Ezraa's day, when the law of God was read before the people, they "listened attentively to the book of the law" (Neh 8:3), the Levites "explained the law to the people . . . translating and giving the meaning so that the people could understand what was read" (8:7–8), and the people responded to the words of the law with mourning and celebration (8:9–12).

Learning to Listen

We must listen well, for we cannot understand or live what we do not hear. Since we are dealing with a written text, we could also use the image of "seeing" what is in the text. So biblical interpretation begins with a close reading of the text, and it helps to read a text multiple times, perhaps in various translations, to hear or see the contours, the nuances of the particulars in a passage. This means we need to slow down and read carefully. We should also pray, "Open my eyes so that I may contemplate wondrous things from your instruction" (Ps 119:18).

Understanding Words in Context

Once we have begun to hear or see the various aspects of the text, we need sound practices to understand the significance of what we are encountering, and this means we will be working with words. Since God has given us his Word in words, our interpretation will be governed in part by the way words work.

First, words work through representation, the collection of letters functioning as a symbol that represents something. For example, the Hebrew word for "bread" is *lechem*. You have to understand that that particular group of letters, in that order, refer to bread in order to interpret the word—and the passage—correctly. So as we encounter the words in a given Bible translation, we need to get at the Hebrew or Greek words behind the word or words we are studying.

Second, words are flexible. As we study biblical words (or the words of any language), we find that most words have a range of possible meanings or things they represent. This is called a "semantic range." Thus, an important aspect of biblical interpretation involves getting at the various possible meanings of a word. In English, for instance, the word "hand" has a broad semantic range: the word could refer to "help," "applause," a worker on a ranch, the minute hand on a clock, and about a dozen other actions or items. In Greek, *charis* has a number of different meanings, including "grace," "thanks," "gift," "attractiveness," "charm," or "favor." So interpretation involves seeking to understand, among the various possible meanings of a word at a particular time and place, how an author intended a word to be understood. At Ephesians 2:8, for instance, *charis* should be translated in terms of God's "grace" or "gracious care": "For you are saved by grace through faith, and this is not from yourselves; it is God's gift." We seek to grasp the appropriate meaning of a word based on how the author uses the word in context.

This brings us to a third and final point concerning how words work: words work on the basis of context. Context refers to circumstances that form the setting for a passage of Scripture by which that passage can be rightly understood. At least four types of context affect our understanding of a text.

1. Historical Context

Historical context refers to events recorded in Scripture or events that form the backdrop for the biblical story. For instance, at 2 Samuel 6, King David, along with thirty thousand warriors, is moving the ark of the covenant to Jerusalem. The ark has been placed on a cart; the cart hits a pothole; the ark begins to tip over; Uzzah reaches out to steady it; and Uzzah is struck dead by God. Read apart from historical context, this passage may lead someone to understand God as capricious for zapping a person who was just trying to help! Yet one cannot interpret well the death of Uzzah apart from the giving of the law in broader Jewish history. In Numbers 4 we read that God had given specific instructions for the transport of the ark (and other artifacts of the tabernacle), specifically instructing the priests that anyone who touched the ark would die. In short, Uzzah died because David did not know and carry out the law's clear instructions.

2. Cultural Context

Cultural context has to do with attitudes, patterns of behavior, or expressions of a particular society, which affect right understanding of a passage. In Acts 4 the priests and Sadducees confronted Peter and John because "they were teaching the people and proclaiming in Jesus the resurrection of the dead." Why was that a problem? From the broader culture of the time, we understand that the priests—most of whom were Sadducees—did not believe in resurrection. So, teaching about the resurrection contradicted their teaching and authority. No wonder they were upset.

3. Literary Context

Literary context involves how a word or passage fits and functions in a book or a group of books or in the Bible as a whole. No word works well in isolation. For instance, at the most immediate level of literary context, biblical interpretation involves dynamics of grammar and syntax. At 2 Corinthians 3:3 Paul speaks of the Corinthian church figuratively, saying that they are a "letter" of recommendation before a watching world. The Greek word *Christou* is in the genitive case and could be interpreted in various ways. Is Paul saying that the Corinthians are a letter "about Christ," or that they are a letter "of Christ," that is, with Christ as the source or originator of the letter? Based on the immediate context, the latter is probably correct since the broader passage focuses on the "production" of this letter. Good commentaries can help us understand grammar and broader issues of context.

4. Theological Context

Theological context refers to how a word or passage fits in the tapestry of theological themes in the story of the Bible as a whole. For example, when Paul says that Jesus is "our Passover lamb" in 1 Corinthians 5:7, we have to read his statement in light of the inauguration of the Passover celebration in Exodus 12, as well as Jesus's death at Passover during the final days of his ministry on earth (John 13:1).

The Goal of Interpretation

Biblical interpretation does not end with listening and understanding, for the goal of biblical interpretation has always been responding to Scripture. We are not seeking to master the text but to be mastered by it. As we live faithfully in biblical community, we are part of that extended interpretive community founded by Jesus. He taught us to interpret and live the Scriptures in light of himself, his ministry, his death, and his resurrection (e.g., Luke 24:25–27). We must read the Scriptures under the lordship of Christ, seeking to live out his purposes for us in the world.

LANGUAGE AND MEANING

Darrell L. Bock

Some people think if you know a word's definition and you know what the related grammar is, then you know the meaning. But discerning meaning involves recognizing a complex interaction between words, grammar, context, literary genre, style, background, and solid interpretive method.

The pursuit of meaning also must have the proper goal in mind, affirming the referents within the expressions of an author in the text one is studying. True meaning is not about what possible meaning a text can generate because a text without a context can generate many meanings given the fluidity of words and a multiplicity of readings. Nor is meaning about what is in the mind of the author when he writes, since meaning is not about psychoanalysis. Finding meaning, rather, is about seeking what the writer sought to communicate through linguistic signs.

Langue *and* Parole

Linguistics has long distinguished between *langue* and *parole*. These French terms designate a language system on the one hand (*langue*) and a specific utterance on the other (*parole*). An analogy used by Ferdinand de Saussure is that *langue* is like the rules of chess, while *parole* is a specific game. Thus *langue* is about possible meaning while *parole* is about specific meaning. Obviously there is an interaction between what language is capable of meaning and what a specific utterance means in a given theological, literary, social, and historical context. The process of discerning this difference involves the act of interpretation.

Meaning and Significance

It is also important to distinguish meaning from significance. Meaning is specific (even when it is intended to be generic or representative as in many psalms or proverbs). Significance can shift as it involves meaning applied in new contexts or as it is read canonically. So, certain OT texts lose their direct applicability once NT realities supersede them. Thus laws of cleanliness that once applied to God's people, especially in light of temple service, no longer apply because of how the NT no longer endorses such categories and because there is no temple to which such laws apply.

Given all of these variables, how does one work toward discovering meaning?

1. Consider what the text may mean.

One needs to be aware of what the language will permit in terms of meaning. Words and grammar can yield only so many possibilities. Commentators often wrestle with the options as they work their way toward explaining what a text means. In doing so, they are not trying to confuse people; they are recognizing what the text could be saying before deciding what it does say. Meaning is not always immediately transparent. If it were, we would not need to debate what a text means. Meaning has to be recognized and validated by discussing why certain meanings work and other possible meanings do not.

2. Literary genre, authorial style, historical background, and specific context all come into play in moving toward specific meaning.

Interpretation of meaning involves interaction between all these elements. Any one of these factors, or a combination of them, may generate an adequate interpretation.

Genre. For example, the moment we recognize we are reading an apocalyptic text, we know that the spiritual world can be depicted through symbols in that genre—which is why we get strange creatures and images in apocalyptic texts. The goal, then, is to determine what the symbol represents. A psalm or hymnic genre lifts up notes of praise, or laments particular experiences, that can give expression to the common experiences of God's people.

Style. Sometimes style is a factor for consideration. John's Gospel is known for its use of double entendre. So, when reading John, we might entertain the possibility of a double meaning more readily than when reading the work of other Gospel writers. When John speaks of being "born again" or "from above" in John 3:3 (both are possible; see CSB footnote), he may have both ideas in mind rather than intending only one.

Background. The multiple possibilities here lead to debate as to when and whether a particular background is in mind. An uncontroversial example involves Jesus's use of a little child in response to the disciples' debate over who is the greatest (Luke 9). Children had little or no social status in the ancient world. They were not valued until they were of use to the family. So, Jesus's use of the image of a child immediately communicates that a person's value is not derived from social status.

Context. By far the most important factor for determining meaning is the specific context. Context involves some of the features already noted. But beyond these are the words used, and the relationships between words, to convey meaning. When Jesus speaks of plucking out one's eye if it causes lust, it is clear he is not speaking literally. Otherwise, an individual could only lust twice before becoming blind. So the context, along with Jesus's penchant for rhetorical vividness, produces a meaning that addresses the importance of not using one's eyes lustfully.

3. The appeal to theology to determine meaning is complex because Scripture is capable of addressing topics from distinct angles and distinct contexts.

Scripture often provides complementary information rather than simply repeating itself. Thus, multiple Gospel accounts of the same event may involve different details. These details open fresh perspectives on the event. According to Mark, Jesus cries out a quote from Psalm 22:1 to express that God is forsaking him while he is on the cross. Yet according to Luke, at a later moment Jesus affirms his trust of God by appealing to Ps 31:5. In such cases one affirms the presence of Christ's varied emotions while on the cross. Another example is how Paul highlights how salvation is secured by faith without works, while James argues that works show the presence of saving faith. Since Paul and James are writing to address different concerns, we may see how the passages complement—rather than contradict—each other.

A tendency to overharmonize texts risks making each say the same thing. Overharmonization may result in eliminating a perspective. Thus, careful interpretation involves asking if each writer is making a related point or instead is addressing a question from a different angle. This means that claiming to "let Scripture interpret Scripture" can be more complex than most realize. Sometimes Scripture simply complements Scripture.

4. The interpretation that takes into account the widest array of factors in a coherent fashion is likely the best reading.

The most likely meaning emerges when a reading takes into account these various features. Such results are more persuasive than other possibilities. A text cannot mean just anything that a reader can construe it to mean. This does not suggest that we always agree on which potential meaning is most likely. This is why it is necessary to discuss why we support a given reading—to make the case that it is the most likely possibility. This is known as validation. Nevertheless, often only a handful of candidates will possibly reflect what the text means. It is important to be reflective about how we observe meaning in the text because no one is a perfect interpreter. Interpretation within community, in dialogue with others, is an important check for understanding the text.

God and
the World

THE EXISTENCE OF GOD

David K. Naugle

"In the very act of trying to prove that God did not exist—in other words, that the whole of reality was senseless—I found I was forced to assume that one part of reality—namely my idea of justice—was full of sense" (C. S. Lewis, *Mere Christianity*). This quote helps us see that there are two basic ways of seeking to establish God's existence, (1) to assume God's existence and argue from that presupposition or (2) to make a case for God's existence and argue to that belief on the basis of evidence. Regardless of approach, belief in the existence of God has tremendous Christian worldview implications.

Lewis seems to embody methods of both assuming and arguing for God's existence. So does the Bible. Both are legitimate in a Christian worldview.

Assuming God's Existence

We begin with the first of the two methods: assuming God does exist. Indeed, this is exactly what the Bible does: "In the beginning God . . . " (Gen 1:1). There is no argument for God's existence; rather, God is assumed to be there, and then he is declared to be the Creator of heaven and earth in the creation account (Gen 1:1–2:25). His existence is assumed in the entire biblical narrative of creation, the fall, and redemption.

Further supporting the assumption of God's existence is the fact that he left an abiding sense of himself in all human hearts—the *sensus divinitatis* (cp. Eccl 3:11). We are inescapably religious by nature. We all have the seed of religion (*semen religionis*) implanted within us, though idolatry corrupts it. The existence of God—Father, Son, and Holy Spirit, the One Being and three persons—makes sense of things. The lenses of Scripture add clarity and proper focus. That's why many believe we must assume God's existence in the first place. God's existence is the primary assumption or presupposition.

That's the assumption Lewis made at first, until he realized he had divinized himself in assuming or presupposing his own sense of justice as the basis by which to evaluate the rationality of the whole universe. Nevertheless, eventually he learned he needed a better explanation for justice than simply himself and his own thoughts. Hence, he later argued for God as the best explanation for all things, justice included. Many, before and after Lewis, have argued similarly in presenting evidence for God's existence.

Arguing for God's Existence
Thus we have a second method of establishing the existence of God. Rather than emphatically assuming that he is there, we make a case for God on the basis of existing things: God himself is the only adequate cause to explain the effects we find in the world. The evidence insists that God exists.

There is a biblical basis for this approach. In Hebrews 3:4, we read: "Now every house is built by someone, but the one who built everything is God." If houses must have builders, then so must everything else—including the world itself, its design, and its beauty, as well as the morality that is found in the world and in us.

This is why some have preferred to argue for God's existence on the basis of cause and effect with cosmological arguments: effects have causes (so modern science agrees), and God is the only adequate cause to explain the effect that is the entire universe. After all, "every house is built by someone, but the one who built everything is God" (Heb 3:4).

This form of reasoning leads some to prefer teleological arguments for establishing God's existence: design presupposes a designer; great design calls for a great designer, and since there is great design in this world (like male and female sexuality, eyesight, hearing, taste, DNA, the human brain, etc.), there must be a great designer behind it, and this must be God. God exists as the intelligent Designer of all things.

Still others, along these lines, have favored aesthetic arguments for God's existence: beauty exists and God is its ultimate source, whether that beauty is of natural or human origin. Consider the Rocky Mountains or Big Sur. J. S. Bach and the Beatles have produced some beautiful music. And not only are such things beautiful, but humans share the ability to perceive them as such.

For C. S. Lewis, morality, or the inherent sense of right and wrong, was the clue to the meaning of the universe. Morality (including justice) was certainly not rooted in Lewis himself (or any other human) but rather in the Trinitarian God. Often called the moral argument for God's existence, the idea is that the moral notions and motions within us (conscience) show that God—not herd instinct, not social convention, not accidental natural law, or our fanciful imaginations—must be their ultimate source. God is the cause, and morality is the effect. This is the law of human nature. As Romans 2:15 says, God's moral law is inscribed on the hearts of all, even in the hearts of those who do not know God personally.

Or it could even be that we don't need to argue for God's existence on the basis of things we find in ourselves or in the world in a cause and effect manner. Perhaps the very idea of God as an absolutely perfect being lacking nothing, including existence, must exist—necessarily. This is an example of an ontological argument for God's existence.

God's Existence and Humanity

God's existence, whether assumed or argued, is most consequential for thought and action in a Christian worldview. Ultimate reality is to be found in the one God who exists eternally as three persons: Father, Son, and Holy Spirit. He is the Creator, Judge, and Redeemer of the world.

Additionally, the world is not just nature but creation since God the Creator made it. His glory is revealed in everything (Isa 6:3). Furthermore, we humans are God's image and likeness. As a result, we possess value, dignity, and worth. All of our human powers to think, know, experience, make, imagine, choose, and love come from him. Also, God gave us an original commission to exercise dominion over the earth as its stewards, with corresponding environmental responsibilities. We are to work the earth and make something of it, and we are to watch over it carefully (Gen 2:15).

It is even possible for us to rebel against God. Yet if we do, we have to use the faculties he has given us, like reason, to try to thwart him. Of course, we cannot. Despite our futile attempts at rebellion, God in his kindness and grace has redeemed all things in Jesus Christ. Ultimately, he will complete that salvation at his second coming, though we experience it now.

He has made all things new, including his followers. He has established the church as the body of Christ in the world. In our personal lives, we have holes in our souls that only God can fill, and he will do it if we trust and believe in Jesus. As Augustine (AD 354–430) said in his spiritual autobiography *Confessions*, "Our hearts are restless [God,] until they rest in you."

Conclusion

Since God exists, knowledge is also possible, and comes in the form of gracious revelation—both natural, through nature and for all—and special, made known in the inspired words of Scripture. We, too, have the ability to comprehend this knowledge and God's truth about all things.

Morality, ethics, and beauty are objectively rooted in God's character and nature. God's existence is the "rock bottom, irreducible Fact on which all other facts depend" as Lewis argued in *Mere Christianity* (p. 184).

THE HOLY TRINITY

Timothy George

The word *trinity* (from the Latin term *trinitas*) is mentioned nowhere
in the Bible, but the doctrine of the Trinity is thoroughly biblical. The
Christian church confesses with the people of Israel, "The LORD our God,
the LORD is One" (Deut 6:4), the famous Shema Israel affirmed that was
quoted by Jesus himself (see Mark 12:29–39). Jesus believed and taught
the oneness of God as foundational to his own messianic vocation. And in
the NT the one, eternal, and living God of the Bible, the only real God, is
further revealed as three personal agents: the Father, the Son, and the Holy
Spirit. Together these agents plan, provide, and perform the salvation of
sinners.

To be sure, the doctrine of the Trinity is foreshadowed in the OT.
Genesis opens on a triadic note: "In the beginning God created . . . and the
Spirit of God was hovering over the surface of the waters. Then God said,
'Let there be light'" (Gen 1:1–3). Even the plural form of God's name,
Elohim, sometimes coupled with a singular verb, while not a proof of the
Trinity as such, does "point indirectly," as Tom Oden wrote, "to some mys-
terious plurality in the intra-subjectivity of God."

If the doctrine of the Trinity is budding in the OT, it bursts into full
flower in the New. Here, self-differentiation in God is presented with
unmistakable clarity through the incarnation. Nowhere is this more clearly
shown than in the baptism of Jesus. There the voice of the Father from
heaven identified the One being baptized by John in the Jordan as his
beloved Son, while the Spirit of God descended like a dove, attesting to

the unique Sonship of Christ and inaugurating his public ministry (Matt 3:13–17). Subsequently, Jesus commanded his disciples to be baptized in the one name of the Father, the Son, and the Holy Spirit (Matt 28:19–20). John Chrysostom put it well in writing that the NT teaches that the Father is God, the Son is God, the Spirit is God, and God is One.

The mature doctrine of the Trinity that came to full expression in the classic creeds of the fourth century was a necessary implication of Christian conversion in the first. Just as the Father sent his Son into the world, so too he has sent into our hearts his Spirit—who is the Spirit of the Son no less than the Spirit of the Father (Gal 4:4–6). It is the Spirit who places the believer in Christ, and it is the Spirit who cries out to the Father, on behalf of the believer, that special word of familial intimacy Jesus used when addressing God: "*Abba*" (Rom 8:15–17). In other words, through believing in Jesus, being baptized in God's triune name, and communing with the risen Christ in the Lord's Supper, the early Christians came to know and love increasingly the one eternal God—the Father who had sent his Spirit-conceived Son to die on the cross for their sins. This is the same Father who also sent the Spirit of his risen Son into their hearts, giving them a new life fit for eternity.

The doctrine of the Trinity is the necessary theological framework for understanding the story of Jesus as the story of God. The church's teaching about the Trinity bears witness to both the OT affirmation, "God is One," and the NT confession, "Jesus is Lord." It is not surprising, however, given the complex nature of the doctrine of the three-in-one God, that both God's oneness and his triune-ness have been doubted and denied and debated throughout the history of the church. Modalism teaches that Father, Son, and Holy Spirit are simply names or roles taken by one person at different moments in time, as if our Maker is an actor who plays three parts in a multi-act drama. Tritheism goes to another extreme, positing three deities working together in a cluster. Neither view is faithful to the Bible's teaching about God.

The doctrine of the Trinity was forged on the anvil of the church's encounters with heresy. In the second century, Marcion proposed that the entire OT be expunged from the Bible as the antiquated revelation of a Jewish deity made irrelevant by the coming of Jesus. The church of that time responded wisely, claiming the OT as Christian Scripture and by declaring that the Father of Jesus was none other than the God of Israel. In doing so, the church affirmed a fundamental connection between creation and redemption.

Several centuries later, a man named Arius denied both the lordship and deity of Jesus Christ. In AD 325 the church responded at the Council of Nicaea that the One Christians adored and loved in their worship—Jesus the Redeemer—was of the same essence (*homoousios*) as the Father.

Later, there arose others known as the Pneumatomachi, "the Spirit-fighters," who understood the Holy Spirit as a force, an energy, a power—but not God. Against those who thus denied the deity of the Holy Spirit, the church declared that God is one in essence and three in persons. The Holy Spirit is a person in eternal relationship with the Father and the Son—one God forever and ever. Edward Cooper put it this way in his 1805 hymn, "Father of Heaven, Whose Love Profound":

> Jehovah! Father, Spirit, Son,
> mysterious Godhead, Three in One,
> Before Thy throne we sinners bend;
> grace, pardon, life, to us extend.

One of the most serious challenges to the doctrine of the Trinity came with the rise of Islam. In Islam, the principle of *tawhid*, which means "unity," is defined as a kind of oneness marked by the solitary character of the being of God—that is, Unitarianism. But the unity of God cannot be reduced to a unit.

On the contrary, in the biblical view, relationship is constitutive for God himself: the Father gives, the Son obediently receives, and the Holy Spirit proceeds from both of them. John of Damascus used the beautiful Greek word *perichoresis* to describe the personality and mutuality of the three divine persons. In the eternal and blessed intercommunion of the Father, the Son, and the Holy Spirit, the one true God is united without confusion and divided without separation. The doctrine of the Trinity is crucial for understanding the biblical God of holiness and love.

The Holy Trinity is not a puzzle to be solved; it is a mystery to be adored. The doctrine of the Trinity, though infinitely complex, is not a matter for philosophical speculation but rather an essential teaching of the faith that evokes wonder, love, and praise. The doctrine should not only be believed but also taught, preached, and made central in every act of public worship.

We can never fully fathom or comprehend completely the reality of the God who is one-in-three and three-in-one; nevertheless, we can confess our Trinitarian faith joyfully, reverently, and with a sense of humility. To sing, pray, and worship the one triune God of holiness and love is to bridge heaven and earth. The white-robed throng of saints and martyrs gathered around the throne of God join their voices with other heavenly beings to sing, day and night: "Holy, holy, holy, Lord God, the Almighty, who was, who is, and who is to come" (Rev 4:8; 7:9–17). Those of us still in this world are invited to join their chorus and to add our voices to theirs, proclaiming the truths shared by Reginald Heber in his famous hymn of 1826:

> Holy, Holy, Holy! Lord God Almighty!
> All Thy works shall praise Thy name in earth and sky and sea.
> Holy, Holy, Holy! Merciful and mighty!
> God in three persons, blessed Trinity.

DIVINE PROVIDENCE AND NATURALISM

Douglas Groothuis

A common secular assumption is that natural laws displace and disallow the reality of divine providence. Natural laws are generally understood as the regularities identified in the hard sciences that govern the major areas of chemistry, biology, and physics. The law of gravity is a classic example of one such law in physics. Many hope for a "final theory" from physics that will unite all natural laws, but thus far no such theory has been identified. Things become more complex when it comes to identifying laws in quantum physics, and there is no consensus on the proper interpretation of this field.

Does the concept of natural law rule out divine providence? God's purposeful governance of all things in the visible and invisible world is his providence (Eph 1:11). Therefore, things in heaven and things on earth are under his jurisdiction and care—from the smallest particle to the most distant galaxy to the souls of men and the behavior of animals (Col 1:15–20). Nothing is excluded from God's providence. This providence is not the impersonal necessity of Stoicism or the materialistic determinism of some forms of naturalism. Nor is it some combination of chance coupled with impersonal natural laws that exist for no purpose. Unlike some Eastern religions, the Bible teaches that the space-time universe is objectively real. It is not an illusion or an extension of God's essence. God exercises his providence over creation in accordance with his divine nature (as a perfect being) and according to the nature of what he has created. God is thus neither a tyrant nor a spectator; he is active in his creation, being especially concerned with humans since they bear his image (Gen 1:26; Matt 6:26).

The Westminster Confession explains how divine providence is to be understood: "God, in His ordinary providence, makes use of means, yet is free to work without, above, and against them, at His pleasure" (V.III). In other words, God can use natural laws to do his bidding, causing the rain to fall on the righteous and the unrighteous alike (Matt 5:45; Acts 27:31). He also can bypass natural laws by directly speaking, as to Moses from a burning bush (Exod 3; also Hos 1:7). Moreover, he can go against the normal course of things by raising Jesus from the dead (1 Cor 15; see 1 Kgs 6:6; Dan 3:27).

How, then, does the secular account of natural law try to contradict the biblical view of divine providence? According to the philosophy of naturalism, God does not exist; therefore, the cosmos and human history have no divine origin, divine administration, or divine destiny. As atheist Bertrand Russell announced in his 1948 debate with Friedrich Copleston on the existence of God, "The universe is just there." In light of this, everything in the material universe (which is all that exists in this view) must be explained without a designing mind at work behind it. Divine providence is hence replaced by natural laws that are "just there." To use a philosophical term, they are "brute facts," having no explanation beyond their own existence.

Put another way, naturalism removes what Aristotle called "final causes" from the universe. While Aristotle did not possess a robust monotheism, he claimed that the First Cause endowed the world with teleology. Each thing, humans included, has a nature that moves toward an end or goal. Nothing is just there. This aligns to some extent with the biblical notion of the cosmos and history having a purpose. Each thing is created according to its kind and fulfills its role in God's personal governance of the universe.

Sadly, most of modern science is concerned only with what Aristotle called "efficient causes," or what makes something happen on the physical level. When a billiard ball hits another and causes it to move, we see efficient causation. The biblical view of divine providence requires the existence of efficient causes working on material things because the world of space, time, and matter is created and sustained by God (Gen 1:1; John 1:1–5; Heb 1:3). There is no good reason, however, to limit explanations to the efficient causation of material things. Such a limitation can be critiqued from four directions.

First, if the naturalistic account of natural law is correct, then the cosmos, humanity, and each human life are meaningless, lacking objective value or purpose. This is not a "purpose-driven" universe. All meaning is subjective, and it dies when the person dies. This worldview, known as nihilism, is counterintuitive and ultimately unlivable. We intuitively know that there is more to life than matter, chance, and brute natural laws. In part we know this because we make judgments based on objective value, such as, "Rape is always wrong." But if there is nothing but impersonal natural law governing the universe, no such judgment is possible. There is more to reality than merely physical interactions described by natural law.

Second, we have good scientific evidence from big bang cosmology that the cosmos began to exist a finite time ago. The agnostic scientist Robert Jastrow granted as much in *God and the Astronomers*:

> Consider the enormity of the problem. Science has proved that the universe exploded into being at a certain moment. It asks: What cause produced this effect? Who or what put the matter or energy into the universe? And science cannot answer these questions, because, according to the astronomers, in the first moments of its existence the Universe was compressed to an extraordinary degree, and consumed by the heat of a fire beyond human imagination. The shock of that instant must have destroyed every particle of evidence that could have yielded a clue to the cause of the great explosion. . . . For the scientist who has lived by his faith in the power of reason, the story ends like a bad dream. He has scaled the mountain of ignorance; he is about to conquer the highest peak; as he pulls himself over the final rock, he is greeted by a band of theologians who have been sitting there for centuries. (pp. 106–7)

The origin of the universe cannot, in principle, be explained by natural laws. The universe, with its laws, was brought into being by a Being outside it. Furthermore, the Being that created the universe from nothing may have a plan for it.

Third, the intelligent design movement—led by William Dembski, Michael Behe, and Stephen Meyer—has argued cogently that particular living systems and the genetic code cannot be adequately explained on the basis of natural law, chance, and eons of purposeless time. For example, the genetic code is a complex language of life containing vast amounts of information.

But all the other information about which we have knowledge, such as what you are now reading, comes from a mind. Mere natural laws may explain the current operations of life, but they cannot explain its origin. This points to design and purpose.

Fourth, the greatest reason to believe in divine providence comes from God's dealings with human history and his revelation in Scripture. God has communicated knowable truth about himself, the universe, history, morality, and salvation through the books of the Bible (2 Tim 3:15). These books form a coherent worldview rooted in history; they explain where we came from, what went wrong, how to make it right, and where we are going. In other words, we are taught the true, rational, and existentially compelling doctrines of creation, fall, and redemption (Rom 1–8). God's mission to reach out to erring mortals is culminated in the matchless achievements of Jesus Christ, the crucified and resurrected Lord of the cosmos (Rom 1:3). Since he lived a perfect life, died an atoning death, and was raised immortal, we can know that life is not meaningless. The universe is not governed by impersonal natural laws but by God's providence, which covers natural laws, teleology, revelation, miracle, and redemption through Jesus Christ, who "has revealed" God the Father (John 1:18). As the apostle Paul says, in light of the resurrection and God's past, present, and future providence, "Therefore, my dear brothers and sisters, be steadfast, immovable, always excelling in the Lord's work, because you know that your labor in the Lord is not in vain" (1 Cor 15:58).

A BIBLICAL VIEW OF ANGELS

Bruce A. Ware

Angels are created spirit beings. Some of them are holy and some are evil. The OT term for angel is *mal'ak,* and the NT term is *angelos;* both terms refer to one sent with a message or one acting as a messenger. The biblical terms for "angel" are used of human messengers in some instances (e.g., 1 Sam 23:27; 1 Kgs 19:2; Luke 7:24; 9:52) and often in the OT apply particularly to the angel of the Lord (e.g., Gen 16:7–14; Judg 6:11–14; 2 Sam 24:16; Zech 1:12–13). Most often, however, *mal'ak* and *angelos* are used for these created spiritual beings called angels or messengers (e.g., Exod 23:20; Matt 1:20; 4:11; 25:31,41).

The Origin of Angels
Because all that God creates and does is wholly good (Gen 1:31; Jas 1:17), we must understand angels, in their entire class, as created by God as good. Psalm 148:1–6 expresses praise to God for his creation of all things, and among those things specified are "all his angels" and "all his heavenly armies" (Ps 148:2). Furthermore, Colossians 1:16 makes clear that by Christ all things were created, including things "in heaven and on earth, the visible and the invisible" (cp. Rom 8:38–39). Also relevant is God's statement to Job (Job 38:4–7) indicating that angels ("sons of God") were present and shouted for joy at the creation of the heavens and earth. Angels, then, derive their existence from God, and their creation evidently precedes the subsequent creation of the universe.

A difficult question concerns how some of the good angels God created have become evil. First, we must understand all fallen angels, in their originally-created form, to have been wholly good. This was a goodness they forfeited, presumably, because of their rebellion against God. Two passages in particular lead us to think this is the case. Jude 6 and particularly 2 Peter 2:4 both speak of angels who departed from God's purposes and hence received God's judgment and condemnation. The text in 2 Peter is clear that the reason for this judgment was their sin against God. And when one adds to this the clear implication from Matthew 25:41 and Revelation 12:9 that demons are the followers of Satan, it seems obvious that these evil spirits, though created good, became evil as they followed their leader's enticement to sin against their Creator.

The Character of Holy Angels

Less is said in the Bible about the character of unfallen angels than about their activities, but some aspects of their character are evident.

1. They are personal beings, with intelligence, emotions, and volition. We receive insights about their intelligence in 1 Peter 1:12, where they long to know more of God's salvation plan; in Revelation 17:1–18, where they know and communicate God's plans; and in Matthew 24:36, where they know much, but not everything (e.g., not the timing of the second coming). Witness to their emotions is seen in Job 38:7, where they rejoice over God's creation; in Isaiah 6:1–4, where with awe and wonder they cry out "Holy, holy, holy" before God; in Luke 15:10, where they rejoice when sinners repent; and in Revelation 5:11–14, where they marvel at the Lamb who was slain and worship him. The idea that they have their own will is tied to passages such as Hebrews 1:6, where God appeals to their will to worship the Son, and 2 Peter 2:4, with its implication of some angels sinning in their choice to rebel against God.
2. They are spirit beings. Hebrews 1:14 calls angels "ministering spirits." In Luke 8:2 and 11:24 we see that demons are sometimes referred to as "evil spirits" or "unclean spirits," so presumably they are spirits by virtue of their being angels. But they can, for specific purposes, take on human form. We see this in Genesis 19:1, when the angels visit Sodom and in Hebrews 13:2, which notes that one might unknowingly entertain angels.

3. They apparently are not sexual in that they do not marry and hence do not procreate. According to Matthew 22:30, in heaven people, like angels, will not marry or be given in marriage.
4. They exist forever. Luke 20:36 states that angels cannot die.
5. They have great power. In 2 Thessalonians 1:7, angels are referred to as being "powerful." In 2 Kings 19:35 one angel sent by God destroyed 185,000 Assyrian soldiers. In Daniel 6:22 an angel "shut the lions' mouths."
6. They are holy. In Job 5:1 and Psalm 89:7 angels are called "holy ones." Mark 8:38 refers to them as "holy angels."
7. They are elected by God. In 1 Timothy 5:21 they are referred to as his "elect angels," which may refer to God's choice of them not to rebel against him when Satan and the other, non-elect angels who followed Satan rebelled and were cast from God's presence.
8. Although wondrous beings, they are not to be worshipped. In Colossians 2:18 the "worship of angels" is rejected. In Revelation 19:10 and 22:8–9, John fell down to worship the angel, but the angel said to worship God.

The Functions and Ministry of Unfallen Angels

Angels are servants of God who surround his presence (Dan 7:9–10; Rev 5:11–14) and carry out his will in various ways on earth (e.g., Gen 32:1; 2 Sam 24:16–17). Hebrews 1:14 calls them "ministering spirits." Beyond this general description, specific functions of angels are spoken of throughout the Scriptures.

1. They worship God, as seen in Isaiah 6:1–3; Luke 2:13–14; and Revelation 5:11–14.
2. They ministered with regard to Jesus during his earthly life. This is seen in Luke 1:11–20, where an angel appeared to Zacharias predicting John's birth; in Luke 2:26–38, where Gabriel appeared to Mary; in Matthew 1:20, where an angel appeared to Joseph saying to take Mary as his wife; in Luke 2:8–15, where an angel appeared to the shepherds; in Matthew 2:13,19, where an angel told Joseph to go to Egypt and then back to Israel; in Matthew 4:11, when angels ministered to Jesus at his temptation; in Luke 22:43, when an angel strengthened Jesus in the garden of Gethsemane; in Matthew 28:2–8, when an angel rolled away the stone and told the women of Jesus's

resurrection; and in Acts 1:10–11, when two angels told the disciples of Jesus's return.

3. They proclaim God's word and ordain the law. Evidence of their proclamation is in Luke 1:26–38 and Acts 27:23–24. Their work of ordaining appears in Acts 7:53; Galatians 3:19; and Hebrews 2:2.

4. They protect and deliver God's people as he directs. In Exodus 23:20–23 an angel was sent to protect Israel on entering the land. In 2 Kings 19:35 an angel struck 185,000 Assyrians dead. In Daniel 3:28 an angel delivered three Hebrew men in the furnace. In Daniel 6:22 an angel closed the lions' mouths. In Psalm 34:7 the angel of the Lord is said to encamp around those who fear him. In Acts 5:19 and 12:7 an angel delivered the apostles from prison.

5. They bear witness to and long to know more of God's salvific purposes. This is apparent in 1 Corinthians 4:9; Ephesians 3:10; 1 Peter 1:12; and possibly also in 1 Corinthians 11:10.

6. They will bear witness to Christ's confession of those who are and are not his, according to Luke 12:8–9, when Christ will confess or deny people "before the angels of God."

7. They play a role in God's reward of the righteous and punishment of the wicked before the final judgment. In Luke 16:22 angels take the poor man to Abraham's bosom. In Acts 12:23 an angel struck Herod dead for not giving glory to God.

8. They come with Christ in his return. According to Matthew 16:27, the Son of Man comes in glory with his angels. Matthew 24:30–31 states that the Son of Man will appear with his angels who carry out his will. Matthew 25:31 notes that the Son of Man will appear with all the angels with him. And in 2 Thessalonians 1:7, it's said that Jesus will be revealed from heaven with his mighty angels.

9. They gather the elect when Christ returns—as is evidenced by Matthew 24:30–31.

10. They dispense God's judgment on the wicked when Christ returns— as seen in Matthew 13:39–42,49–50. Angels will take the wicked from among the righteous and cast them into hell.

11. They are used by God to defeat evil powers and nations. This is evidenced in Daniel 10 (the message to Daniel of Michael's intervention to defeat ungodly forces). It also appears in Daniel 12:1 (Michael will rescue God's people from great distress), and in Revelation 12:7–9 (Michael and his angels defeat the dragon and his angels).

12. An angel binds Satan during the millennium, according to Revelation 20:1–3.
13. They are stationed at the twelve gates of the New Jerusalem, according to Revelation 21:12.

The Destiny of Unfallen Angels

In light of their continuous biblical role of ascribing praise to God, it stands to reason that angels will be among the great heavenly choir singing praises to God forevermore. They are present in the New Jerusalem, still ministering on God's behalf (Rev 21:12).

SATAN AND DEMONS

Malcolm B. Yarnell III

One of the most elucidating passages regarding Satan and demons is Revelation 12:9, which speaks of war in heaven and the ejection of the fallen angels: "The great dragon was thrown out—the ancient serpent, who is called the devil and Satan, the one who deceives the whole world. He was thrown to earth, and his angels with him." This text comprehensively informs us from a biblical perspective of, first, who Satan and his demons are, second, what he is currently doing, and third, it foreshadows their ultimate end. This article will summarize a biblical view of Satan and demons from that three-fold structure.

Who are they?

It must be clearly and categorically affirmed that Satan is a creature, as are all demons. He is an angelic creature, a spiritual being with great power like other angels, but he is not to be confused in any way with God himself. While Job 1:6 and 2:1 refer to Satan as coming into the heavenly throne room among "the sons of God," the phrase indicates not filial generation but fashioned subservience. To speak of the sons of God is to speak of the "heavenly army" (1 Kgs 22:19), who are also referred to as "angels" (Gen 32:1–2; Ps 103:20) and "spirits" (1 Kgs 22:21–23). The qualitative distinction between an angelic "spirit" and "the Spirit of the Lord" is both moral and dynamic (1 Kgs 22:24–25).

These angels are, on the one hand, "servants" (Ps 103:21), and, on the other, powerful beings (Ps 82:1; Isa 14:12; Ezek 28:14). Yet, in spite of being included in the "divine assembly" (Ps 82:1) or the "assembly of the holy ones" (Ps 89:5), and thus being able to appear in his presence, the distance between God and these "sons" is infinitely qualitative. They cannot even compare to the Lord (Ps 89:6), a fact that evokes great fearfulness within them. The Lord is "more awe-inspiring than all who surround him" (Ps 89:7), exceeding them in strength as well as moral virtue (Ps 89:8). The angels are limited, so any power they have is what God has given to them (Job 1:12; 2:6–7). The angels, as invisible creatures, are created through Jesus Christ and given their powers by him (Col 2:16). Of course, the use or the abuse of such grants of authority to intelligent, willing creatures are two different matters, and all authorities shall one day be corrected by Jesus Christ (1 Cor 15:24–28).

The angels in God's heaven are included within the "everything" that he has created (Ps 89:11). They are among his works over which he rules. Satan, under the type of the king of Tyre, himself is described as having been "created" by God (Ezek 28:15), and the term used here is *bara'*, which is also used in Genesis 1 to describe God's original creative activity. The "sons of God," among whom appears Satan, are specifically instructed to ascribe glory to God and worship him (Ps 29:1–2). Their desire to obtain such glory for themselves is at the root of the fallen angels' expulsion from heaven. It was such arrogant pretense to worship that prompted the final break between Satan, this rebellious one among the created servile "sons of God," and Jesus Christ, the eternally generated and subsequently incarnate Son of God (Matt 3:8–11). In falling from heaven, Satan took many angels with him. They are known under the general terminology of "demons" (Gk *daimonioi*) and are subject to the power of Jesus Christ, who in turn granted such authority to his disciples (Luke 10:17–20).

What are they doing?
The apostle John identified the apocalyptic "dragon" with the "ancient serpent" and "Satan" and "the devil" (Rev 12:9; 20:2). With a study of the occurrence of these names in Scripture alongside the apostles' overarching description of his activity as "the one who deceives the whole world," it becomes clear what Satan and his demons have been doing and continue to do.

The first appearance of this evil one in Scripture is in the garden of Eden, where he takes on the form of a serpent (Gen 3:1). His deceptive character is immediately displayed during his conversation with the woman. He first casts doubt on the word of God (Gen 3:1), then he outright denies it (Gen 3:4), and finally he does what he can to tempt humanity to rebel against God's word (Gen 3:5). While God allowed humanity to choose to succumb to Satan's deception, he promised that the seed of the woman would crush the head of the seed of the serpent (Gen 3:15). Based on NT allusions (Rom 16:20; Rev 12:9; 20:2), this promise has often been called the *protoevangelium*, the first gospel promise foreshadowing the coming of the Messiah, who would overcome the serpent and sin and death, thereby providing redemption to fallen humanity (e.g., Kidner, *Genesis*, 70–71).

The Hebrew noun, *satan*, indicates an adversary. The verb means "to accuse." In Job 1–2, Satan adopts the role of an adversary in the heavenly court to accuse Job of following God only because God had blessed Job richly. God allows Satan power, within limits, to harm Job, in order to vindicate God's claim about Job. In Zechariah 3:1–2, Satan appears again in the courtroom of God, this time in order to accuse the high priest, Joshua, of being unfit to represent the people of God.

However, in a messianic vein, the Lord calls on the Lord's own name to rebuke Satan and remove Joshua's guilt in order to give human priests a place in the heavenly court. In 1 Chronicles 21:1, Satan incited David to take a census and prompt God's anger, while 2 Samuel 24:1 says that God was behind the event. This demonstrates that although Satan and demons are responsible for their own evil, God may sovereignly use them for his own holy purposes (cp. 1 Kgs 22:19–25).

The Septuagint, the Greek version of the OT, often translates the Hebrew *satan* with *diabolos*, which means "slanderer, accuser." The NT, in almost equal numbers, either transliterates the Hebrew *satan* or uses the Greek *diabolos*, which has been translated into English as "devil." Sixteen other terms for Satan have also been discovered in the NT, including Beelzebul (e.g. Matt 12:24), Belial (2 Cor 6:15), and Apollyon (Rev 9:11). Among the terms used to identify Satan are those that imply some authority: "ruler of the power of air" (Eph 2:2), "dominion of darkness" (Luke 22:53), and "god of this age" (2 Cor 4:4) (D. P. Fuller, "Satan," in *ISBE*: 4, 342).

Jesus Christ taught that Satan ruled this world with his demons through his deception of humanity, comparing Satan and the demons to a kingdom (Matt 12:25). The devil's falsehoods were even embraced by the Israelites. Jesus divided humanity into those who believe in him as the Word of God and those who reject him. The latter are children of "[their] father the devil" who is a "murderer" and the "father of lies" because they reject the truth of Jesus as the One who is from God the Father (John 8:42–47). The kingdom of God as ruled by Christ is directly opposed to the kingdom of this world as ruled by the devil.

The proper identification of each kingdom is a matter fraught with eternal importance. The blasphemy of the Holy Spirit, an unforgivable sin, is to ascribe the work of the Holy Spirit in Christ to the devil (Matt 12:24–32). Jesus, therefore, repeatedly manifested his affinity with God and his opposition to the devil through casting out demons and healing the blind among other things (e.g., Matt 12:22–23; John 10:19–21). Until a person is born again, he is ruled by the spirit of Satan and remains within the kingdom of the devil (Eph 2:2). Nevertheless, the devil and his kingdom of death and Hades cannot stand against the church's assault as it proclaims to people the liberating gospel that Jesus is the Son of God who has brought God's kingdom (Matt 16:16–19).

Jesus Christ demonstrated his power over Satan and demons through his earthly ministry, but on the cross he won the ultimate victory. At the cross, even while we were bound to death and ruled by Satan, Jesus paid the debt that was ours. God now delivers us into life through faith (Col 2:12–14). At the cross, Christ took away the power of the demonic authorities and disgraced them publicly, having won the victory over them on our behalf (Col 2:15; Eph 1:21–22), as permanently demonstrated in his resurrection (1 Tim 3:16).

Although decisively defeated, Satan continues his work through deception, "prowling around like a roaring lion" (1 Pet 5:8) and disguising himself as "an angel of light" (2 Cor 11:14). Even now, Satan is trying his hardest to keep people from hearing and receiving the Word of God (Matt 13:19). Moreover, Satan schemes to keep Christians from living victoriously in Christ, but God equips us to withstand demonic assaults (Eph 6:11–17), and we are called to resist the devil and stand firm in the faith (1 Pet 5:9).

What will happen to them?

Although Satan and his demons have been decisively conquered by Jesus Christ, they will still do all they possibly can to persecute the church and to conquer the world, even into the last day. The book of Revelation prophesies a vivid series of apocalyptic battles that will result in the overthrow of the dragon and his imprisonment in the abyss for a thousand years (Rev 20:1–3). At the end of the millennium, Satan will be let loose for a short time to deceive the nations again, but he will be fully and completely defeated (Rev

20:7–9). His end is presented verbally as an accomplished fact: "The devil who deceived them was thrown into the lake of fire and sulfur where the beast and the false prophet are, and they will be tormented day and night forever and ever" (Rev 20:10). The hurtful deception of humanity that began in Genesis with a denial of the word of God will end with the eternal punishment of that false demonic trinity led by Satan. And the One who has accomplished that victory over Satan and his demons is Jesus Christ.

WHAT IS A HUMAN?

John Stonestreet

America's founders explained their rebellion against the British crown by appealing to a particular view of the human: "We hold these truths to be self-evident, that all men are created equal, that they are endowed by their Creator with certain unalienable rights; that among these are Life, Liberty, and the pursuit of Happiness" (*Declaration of Independence*).

Today there is little agreement about what human rights, dignity, and equality entail, and few remember just how tedious these concepts have proven to be. Throughout most of history, some lives were considered dispensable, and oppression was justified by aspirations to power, claims of ethnic or familial superiority, and economic disparities.

Humans come from different cultures, genders, and ethnicities. We do not possess the same abilities. These obvious differences make the answers to the important questions about life anything but self-evident.

Do all humans have value, or just some?

Are we distinct from the animals?

Is dignity shared by every member of the human race, or is it dependent on gender, ethnicity, or abilities?

Is our humanity fixed, or is it culturally determined?

As important as determining how people should behave is settling on what people are. Different visions about what it means to be human compete in the marketplace of ideas. These notions, when lived out in the real world, have serious consequences for individuals, communities, nations, and entire cultures.

Humanity and Other Worldviews

Non-Christian worldviews fail to ground the concepts of human dignity, value, and universal rights. *Naturalistic* worldviews such as atheism, Marxism, and secularism deny anything that is spiritual or metaphysical. Because all that is has resulted from natural, mindless physical processes, spiritual beliefs are fantasies that, like all human behaviors, result from chemical processes occurring in the brain.

In this view of reality, no Creator exists to endow special status to humans. Therefore, there is nothing *intrinsic* about humans that establishes their equality, dignity, or value. Instead, for naturalistic worldviews, there are only *extrinsic* realities, like appearance and abilities, to distinguish us from other humans, or even from "other animals."

Transcendental worldviews—such as Hinduism, certain forms of Buddhism, and New Age—understand all living things to be part of the impersonal spiritual oneness that is ultimate reality. Many of these religions hold to reincarnation, in which to be human is to be merely an expression of life trapped in the cycle of birth and rebirth along the journey to losing individual existence and rejoining the universal oneness to which we all ultimately belong. Humans, according to transcendental worldviews, are "divine" but ultimately not distinct from—and certainly no more valuable than—any other living thing.

Postmodernists deny that humans are able to know who we are. According to this view, everyone is trapped by perspectives shaped by culture. Categories that describe human nature, behavior, or roles—such as male, female, intelligent, leader, upper class, impoverished, antisocial, married, productive, etc.—are socially determined. In its more pessimistic forms, postmodernism despairs that humans can ever find meaning and purpose. In its less pessimistic forms, postmodernism ends in relativism, in which no individual or culture is allowed to judge any other.

Islam understands God to be so remote and far removed from anything in the universe that he cannot share his attributes. In Islam, humans only relate to God in service. Because God has not given of himself in creating humans, human dignity depends on obedience. Thus, the follower of God and the nonfollower do not share equal rights or value.

Humanity and a Christian Worldview

The Old and New Testaments, however, present an entirely different vision of what it means to be human. First, the creation of humans is the pinnacle of the biblical creation narrative. Of all the things God made, only humans bear his image. Many atheist thinkers, like Friedrich Nietzsche, recognized that only the biblical vision of *imago Dei* (the image of God) grounds universal human dignity, value, and rights.

Biblical scholars offer three different but complementary views of the *imago Dei*. The *functional* view suggests that humans resemble God in what we are able to do. Like God, humans create, reason, love, and imagine. This theory describes what results from the *imago Dei* more than it does what the *imago Dei* is. For example, someone unable to reason or create due to injury or disability still bears God's image.

The *relational* view emphasizes the Trinitarian nature of God as the key to understanding humanity. The Bible describes the eternal community that exists between the Father, Son, and Holy Spirit. Unlike in Islam, where the idea of God as Trinity is considered idolatrous blasphemy, God doesn't merely *do* relationships. He is, by nature, a relationship.

The *representative* view clarifies the unique role God bestowed on humans in the world. They are to rule over all he made, filling and subduing the earth, effectively continuing the creative work from which God rested (Gen 1:26–31). That God, *the* Sovereign, made humans sovereign over his world is unique to Christianity.

Unlike most other religious and cultural frameworks of the ancient world, the biblical creation story describes both male and female as representatives of God. Before we meet Eve, the first woman, the Bible is explicit that the status of image bearer applies to both genders (Gen 1:27), and it is a role not shared with the animal kingdom. Still, the Genesis account does not present male and female as identical. They are complementary. Alone, man is unable to accomplish his God-given task of filling and subduing the earth (Gen 2:18). With woman, God provides a helper for man uniquely suitable and distinct from man (Gen 2:20–24).

The significance of the *imago Dei* is underscored by how the Bible describes the fall of humanity. Not only are humans separated from God and one another by sin, but the entire creation is in "the bondage to decay" (Rom 8:21). Thorns, pain, frustration, and death infect the cosmos because of Adam's disobedience.

Finally and ultimately, human dignity is secured by the incarnation. That God became man in the person of Jesus Christ, C. S. Lewis wrote in *Miracles,* "was the central event in the history of the earth—the very thing that the whole story has been about."

Humanity Redeemed

Among the earliest and most persistent heresies condemned by the church is Gnosticism, which teaches that anything physical, including the human body, is evil. When mixed with Christianity, Gnosticism proclaimed that God could not have taken on human flesh without being corrupted. In response the church upheld that Jesus Christ was both fully God and fully man. Jesus physically rose from the dead, Paul proclaimed, or else our faith is "worthless" (1 Cor 15:17).

If Jesus was not corrupted by taking on the flesh of humanity, then our humanity can be made new. The NT authors describe the effect of Christ's work with "re" words: *redeem, restore, reconcile,* and *renew.* "Re" words imply the reversal of the corruption of sin. In Christ, the dignity, value, and rights given to humanity by God are restored, not lost. As Thomas Howard wrote,

> The Incarnation takes all that properly belongs to our humanity and delivers it back to us, redeemed. . . . All the dancing and feasting and processing and singing and building and sculpting and baking and merrymaking that belong to us, and that were stolen away into the service of false gods, are returned to us in the Gospel (*Evangelical Is Not Enough,* 36–37).

CHIEF PURPOSE OF HUMANITY

Jeremy A. Evans

The perennial question in philosophy is this: what is the meaning of human life? Another way to express the question is this: what is the end or purpose for which God created the world and the humans who inhabit it? Is there any objective meaning to life, or is every investment a matter of personal preference with no deeper meaning to be found?

God the Creator

It is important to recognize that God did not create humans to satisfy anything that was lacking in him. As Acts 17:24–25 says, "The God who made the world and everything in it—he is Lord of heaven and earth—does not live in shrines made by hands. Neither is he served by human hands, as though he needed anything, since he himself gives everyone life and breath and all things."

Orthodox Christianity affirms that God is triune, eternally enjoying fellowship between the Father, Son, and Spirit. Though God did not create anything to satisfy a deficiency within himself, we glean from the doctrine of the Trinity that just as God is inherently relational, so we are made as beings to live in community with one another, and ultimately to enjoy fellowship and unity with God and every facet of his creation. We see this relational aspect of creation in Scripture, for the Lord God said, "It is not good for the man to be alone. I will make a helper corresponding to him" (Gen 2:18). Accordingly, God fashions the woman from the rib of Adam and presents her as a suitable helper to him (Gen 2:23). Most importantly, God created us to walk and have fellowship with him (Gen 3:8).

Foundation for Meaning from the Existence of God

A theistic framework provides a rational account for the existence of an objectively meaningful and subjectively satisfying foundation for meaning in our lives. In his article "Religion Gives Meaning to Life," Louis Pojman notes that if theism is true and there is a benevolent supreme being governing the universe, then other things result.

1. Theism offers a satisfying explanation of the origins and sustenance of the universe.

Humans are not the product of chance or an impersonal big bang, nor are we merely a blind collocation of particles in motion. Rather, we are endowed with godlike properties that make us unique in creation but also accountable as to how we exercise dominion over and relate to other parts of it (Gen 1:26). As divine image bearers we are rational, emotional, and volitional.

That being said, we are more than rational creatures; we are also created for love. Jesus teaches that we are to love the Lord our God with all of our hearts, souls, strength, and minds and to love our neighbors as ourselves (Luke 10:27). By cooperating with God in his creation plan, we fulfill the purpose for which he created us and find satisfaction and meaning in life. We cooperate by knowing the gifts God has given us and by using them in such a way that God receives the praise (Matt 5:16; 1 Cor 13:1–13; Eph 4:7–16). Since each individual is endowed with spiritual gifts, his personal meaning is found in using these gifts for Christ and his kingdom. Moreover since God interacts in history, and history is directed toward the union of Christ and his church, each investment of these spiritual gifts is bound up in a larger story—one that spills over into the afterlife.

2. Theism can explain how the universe is suffused in goodness and that God will win out over all the evil we see in the world.

Scripture affirms that God is perfectly good (1 Chr 16:34; Pss 100:5; 136:1; 145:9). God looked on his creation and proclaimed it good (Gen 1:31). Unfortunately, Adam and Eve did not honor the end for which they were created. Instead of choosing fellowship and communion with God, they sought their own destiny independent from him. Thus begins the story of broken relationships and suffering that results from evil. Jesus, however, takes the broken world and recreates it, restoring what was lost in Adam's rebellion (2 Cor 5:17). Ultimately evil and death are defeated at the resurrection (1 Cor 15), and in the end God makes a new heaven and new earth (Rev 22:1–5).

3. God loves and cares for us, and as a result of his love we have a deeper motive for morally good actions, including acts of self-sacrifice.

4. Theists have an answer to the question, why be moral?

As noted above, God is the source of all that is good. But what is more, the existence of God best explains why we have moral duties. A duty is an obligation we have to perform or a certain action we must refrain from performing. For example, we have a duty to fulfill the Great Commission and the great commandments. We have a duty not to envy, gossip, malign, slander, or hate. Duties come from persons in authority, and there is no higher moral authority than God himself.

God provides a rich account of where our moral actions find both their value and our obligations. Moral decision making is significant for one's life. As John Cottingham explains,

> Without an overarching structure that confers meaning on life, and without a normative pattern or model to which the meaningful life must conform, then a meaningful life reduces to little more than an engaged life in which the agent is systematically committed to certain projects he makes his own, irrespective of their moral status. Accordingly, Fulfillment and meaning pursued in ways that involve deceiving or hurting others, or making use of them as mere instrumental fodder for one's own success, closing one's heart and mind to the voice of one's fellow creatures—these are modes of activity that make one less human. To put the matter somewhat grandly, a meaningful life will be oriented as far as possible toward truth and beauty and goodness, or at least by striving toward those ideals (*On the Meaning of Life*, 26-27).

5. All persons are of equal worth.

Since every person is crafted in the image of God, each is intrinsically valuable—and not simply valuable as a means to an end. God loves each person, for all are created in him and for him. Paul affirms the equal worth of persons, for Christ died as a sacrifice for all persons (Gal 3:28).

6. Life after death also guarantees that there will be no unaccounted-for injustices.

As the teacher concludes Ecclesiastes, "Fear God and keep his commands, because this is for all humanity. For God will bring every act to judgment, including every hidden thing, whether good or evil" (12:13–14).

In essence, the chief purpose of humanity is to claim every endeavor and institution in life for Christ. But what is more, when justice is brought to bear and all relationships are made whole, then God's original plan for all creation will be realized—each aspect of the good creation is at peace (*shalom*; Gen 1:26–27); that is, there is *shalom* in all of creation, all relationships, and all stewardship.

FALL AND REDEMPTION

ANTHONY L. CHUTE

The fall of humanity refers to the first act of human disobedience, enacted by Adam and Eve and recorded in Genesis 3. Prior to their rebellion our first parents had unbroken fellowship with God, unparalleled intimacy with each other, and undisturbed enjoyment in their Edenic environment. There has never been a time such as theirs when humans exercised biblical dominion over creation, complemented one another so completely, and joyously lived every moment under the rule of God. But there will be.

The Bible envisions a day when these broken relationships will be forever restored. God's people will inherit a new earth that bears abundant food apart from the sweat of their brows and without the threat of thorns (Rev 22:3). They will never feel pain or cause others to experience hurt of any kind as their tears are eternally wiped away (21:4). Death will no longer haunt the living. Gentle lambs will rest side by side with formerly carnivorous wolves (Isa 11:6). Best of all, God will dwell with his people (Rev 22:3). Nothing unclean will be allowed to enter the new creation. There will be no trees that lure or serpents that trick. Worship, not worry, will characterize the family of God in a world without end.

The Fall and Sin

The Christian worldview is premised on these two realities: currently God's good world is spoiled by human sin (fall), but sinful humans are made fit to enjoy God forever through placing faith in Jesus Christ (redemption).

Critics of the Christian worldview tend to dismiss the idea of the fall by minimizing the reality of human sinfulness. They likewise set aside the doctrine of redemption by maximizing their expectations of human progress. Sin is thus reduced to social constructs and self-help becomes the means of salvation. In one sense the denial of sin is another manifestation of sin. Just as Adam and Eve tried to hide their wrongs from the God who sees all things (Gen 3:8), humans habitually maintain their innocence in spite of the biblical claim to the contrary (Rom 3:23).

There is another reason why people reject the biblical teaching about the fall. It is because the world continues to work—sort of. After the fall, Adam and Eve's oldest son proved remarkably adept at navigating through life even though he was guilty of murdering his own brother (Gen 4:8). Cain married a woman and loved his son (Gen 4:17). The curse of the ground notwithstanding, Cain became a farmer and then a city builder (4:3,17). Cain's descendants were known for their creative prowess, including advancements in shepherding livestock, playing musical instruments, and developing sturdy weaponry (4:20–22). Put simply, even fallen people in a fallen world manage to contribute to human progress, by the grace of God.

On the other hand, even morally upright people manage to confirm the human predicament. Noah is such a man who, in the midst of a moral sewer, managed to find favor in God's eyes (Gen 6:8). His craftsmanship is demonstrated through his ability to build an ark that withstood the most destructive storm ever. His attention to detail spared not only his life but also that of his family and the entire animal kingdom (6:14–22). Nevertheless, in spite of God's grace toward him, Noah later became drunk and passed out naked in his tent (9:20–21). When he awoke, he cursed generations yet to be born (9:24). This is hardly the behavior one would expect from the man through whom God rescued the world, but Noah's life confirms that "there is no one righteous, not even one" (Rom 3:10).

The doctrine of the fall asserts that while most of us are not as bad as we could be, none of us is as good as we should be either. Humans retain the image of God, which accounts for any semblance of goodness and enables progress (Gen 1:26–27; 9:6). Nevertheless, life is not as it should be in this fallen world.

Theologians have differed over the means by which Adam's sin has been passed down to every person, but the reality of death provides sufficient confirmation that no one is exempt (Rom 5:12). Though Charles Manson and Billy Graham took completely different paths with their lives, both are subject to the death sentence—as are you and me. The Bible thus describes our common plight: we are "dead" in our "trespasses and sins," and we are "by nature children under wrath" (Eph 2:1,3).

Redemption as Reversal

Redemption is the reversal of the fall. In part, this reversal means that those who were spiritually dead are made alive (Eph 2:4), and those who were children of wrath are now children of God (1 John 3:1).

Though the Bible recognizes that fallen people may make positive contributions to the world as a whole, it is also clear that no one can contribute anything positive to their own redemption (Rom 3:23–28). The only person qualified to undo the effects of the fall is Jesus Christ who, as the eternal Son of God incarnate through the Virgin Mary, was exempted from inheriting Adam's sin. This is not to say that he was not tempted as he lived in a fallen world and as he experienced genuine struggles that all humans face (Heb 2:14–18). He was tempted as we are but never sinned (2 Cor 5:21; Heb 4:15; 1 Pet 2:22). Thus, he alone is the One who can make sinful humans fit to worship a holy God (Acts 4:12). Even the death of Jesus was not the result of any sin he committed but was, rather, the most gracious act of love ever displayed: he took upon himself the sins of the world so that all who believe in him will be saved (Rom 5:6–11).

The doctrine of redemption extends even beyond the matter of individual salvation. During his lifetime, Jesus provided abundant proof of his ability to completely restore a fallen world. He demonstrated his lordship over heaven when he calmed the storms on the sea (Mark 4:35–41); he demonstrated his lordship over hell when he exorcised demons from a troubled man (5:1–20); he demonstrated his lordship over life when he healed a woman of her incurable disease (5:24–34); and he demonstrated his lordship over death when he raised a young girl from the dead (5:35–43). With these and countless other miracles (John 20:30–31; 21:25), Jesus provided ample reason for us to conclude that this troubled world is not our home. He himself will, however, make all things new (Rev 21:5).

The final book of the Bible is therefore a fitting end to the story of the fall with its triumphant declaration of full redemption:

> Then he showed me the river of the water of life, clear as crystal, flowing from the throne of God and of the Lamb down the middle of the city's main street. The tree of life was on each side of the river, bearing twelve kinds of fruit, producing its fruit every month. The leaves of the tree are for healing the nations, and there will no longer be any curse. The throne of God and of the Lamb will be in the city, and his servants will worship him. They will see his face, and his name will be on their foreheads. Night will be no more; people will not need the light of a lamp or the light of the sun, because the Lord God will give them light, and they will reign forever and ever (Rev 22:1–5).

Fall and Redemption in the Christian Worldview

The Christian worldview thus includes both fall and redemption. To exclude the former is to deny the reality of sin; to exclude the latter is to deny the ultimate reality of Christ's work.

Living in a fallen world means that Christians will experience trials and tribulations, and they will continue to struggle with their own temptations and sin. We are forgiven, but God is not finished with us yet (Phil 1:6). Consequently, longing for a better world, even a perfect world, is not a form of escapism. Rather, it is the Christian's rightful anticipation of a promise made by the One who justly pronounced a curse on this world (Gen 3; Rom 8:20–22) and then lovingly took that curse upon himself in order to redeem people for his glory.

Jesus Christ and the Pattern of Christian Truth

WORLDVIEW THINKING, THE CHRISTIAN INTELLECTUAL TRADITION, AND THE PATTERN OF CHRISTIAN TRUTH

David S. Dockery

The Christian intellectual tradition serves as a valuable resource for Christ followers, helping them understand the way that Christians through the years have read the Bible, formulated doctrine, provided education, and engaged the culture. The apostle Paul, writing to the church at Thessalonica, urged the followers of Jesus Christ to "stand firm and hold to the traditions that you were taught" (2 Thess 2:15). Similarly, the apostle exhorted Timothy, his apostolic legate, to "hold on to the pattern of sound teaching" (2 Tim 1:13). The history of Christianity is best understood as a chain of memory.

The Christian Intellectual Tradition

Wherever the Christian faith has been found, there has been a close association with the written Word of God, with books, education, and learning. Studying and interpreting the Bible became natural for members of the early Christian community; it inherited the practice from late Judaism. The Christian intellectual tradition has its roots in the interpretation of Holy Scripture. From the church's earliest days, Christians inherited the approaches to biblical interpretation found in the writings of both intertestamental Judaism and the contemporary Greco-Roman world. From this dual heritage, there is an observable continuity with the hermeneutical methods of the rabbis and Philo as well as the followers of Plato and Aristotle. Yet, a discontinuity is also clearly evident as early Christianity established its own uniqueness by separating itself from Judaism and the surrounding Greco-Roman religions.

Since the earliest days of Christian history, Christians have drawn on the Bible in various ways. The rich heritage has shaped the Christian tradition in both individual and corporate practices. In order to recover this valuable resource for our contemporary context, we must seek to learn from interpreters of Scripture, from theologians, and from educators, as well as from other Christian leaders. We can learn to think deeply about the things of God from representatives of this tradition who have gone before us and on whose shoulders we now stand. Justin Martyr and Irenaeus were probably among the first in postapostolic times to articulate the importance of thinking in Christian categories. In Alexandria in the third century, both Clement and Origen instructed their converts not only in doctrine but also in science, literature, and philosophy. Augustine in the fifth century, in *On Christian Doctrine*, penned the thought that every true and good Christian should understand that wherever we find truth, it is the Lord's.

Similar patterns may be found throughout history, for wherever the gospel has been received, educational entities and Christian literacy have generally followed. This legacy can be traced not only though Bernard of Clairvaux and Thomas Aquinas but also Erasmus, Luther, Calvin, and Melanchthon. We learn much from post-Reformation philosophers, scientists, theologians, and literary scholars like Pascal, Kepler, Edwards, Washington, Lewis, Sayers, and numerous others. This pattern of Christian truth lies at the heart of the Christian intellectual tradition; it is a pattern that is both shaped and informed by our confession of the Christian faith. As we learn from the tradition, we will see our faith strengthened and will experience a renewal of our orthodox commitments to the divine nature and authority of God's written Word, to the deity and humanity of Jesus Christ, to a heartfelt confession regarding the holy Trinity, to the uniqueness of the gospel message and the enabling work of God's Holy Spirit, to salvation by grace through faith, to the global church, to the hope of the coming kingdom, and to the sacredness of life and family.

Thoughtful Christians will work to develop a model of dynamic orthodoxy in conversation with Nicaea, Chalcedon, Augustine, Bernard, Luther, Calvin, Wesley, the Pietists, and the influential global Christian leaders of the twenty-first century in order to reclaim and build upon the great Christian intellectual tradition. The great tradition of Christian thinking not only helps to shape our biblical and theological understanding but also provides a vast resource for philosophy, art, music, literature, drama, architecture, law, political and social thought, and other forms of cultural and academic engagement. Interestingly, Christian reflection and devotional practices were influenced by the work of this significant heritage. It is our hope that as we wrestle with the many challenges facing Christ followers in our day, the great tradition of Christian thinking will provide valuable resources and examples to encourage our faith and shape significant ecclesiastical, educational, and cultural pursuits—even as we grow in our appreciation for and commitment to thinking Christianly for the glory of God.

The Pattern of Christian Truth

The gospel, the Christian faith, becomes the interpretive framework with which to make sense of all other knowledge and experience. This interpretive framework, which guides the Christian in worldview thinking—in thinking Christianly—is shaped by primary Christian doctrines, what H. E. W. Turner has referred to as "the pattern of Christian truth," those key doctrines believed consistently and in consensus by Christians throughout the centuries, which have informed and shaped the best of the Christian intellectual tradition. We now turn our attention to these important doctrines that significantly inform all aspects of Christian thinking.

1. Creation: The Work of the Creator God

Christian thinking recognizes two broad dimensions of reality: God, the Creator, and the world, his creation. Scripture teaches that God, without the use of any preexisting material, brought into being everything that is. Both the opening verse of the Bible and the initial sentence of the Apostles' Creed confess God as Creator. The doctrine of creation contains truth of utmost importance: everything that is was created by God. The world, which was created by him, has been made for the good of men and women, who have been created in God's image (Gen 1:26–28).

This world is distinct from its Creator, the Triune God. The significance of the Trinitarian understanding of creation recognizes that it is not just any god who created the world; it is the Triune God who is Father, Son, and Holy Spirit. The great thinkers of the early church wrote numerous commentaries on the creation story of Genesis 1–3, more so than any other part of the Bible, because they understood that it contradicted the fundamental beliefs of their inherited pagan culture and challenged them to replace it with something that was true to reality.

2. Humanity and the Fall

Men and women are the highest form of God's creation. The primary reason for stressing the importance of humans in God's plan for creation, over against the rest of God's creation, relates to the distinctive description regarding humanity in God's image (Gen 1:26–27). Because they are created in the image of God, men and women have dignity, rationality, morality, spirituality, and personality.

Even though men and women are created in God's image, the entrance of sin into the world has resulted in negative influences on God's creation, especially humans. As a result of sin, they are separated from God, having fallen short of his glory (Rom 3:23). Nevertheless, the image of God, even though tainted, tarnished, and marred by sin, has not been lost (Gen 9:6; Jas 3:9). The role of exercising stewardship over the earth (Gen 1:28) has been drastically disturbed by the effects of sin on humans. The ability to live in right relationship with God, with others, with nature, and with our own selves has now been corrupted.

The impact of sin is significant when reflecting on the matters of our relationship to God. Because of the entrance of sin into the world and our inheritance of Adam's sinful nature (Rom 5:12–19), we are by nature hostile to God and estranged from him (Rom 8:7; Eph 2:1–3). We thus have wills that do not obey, eyes that do not see, and ears that do not hear because spiritually we are dead to our Creator. Because of sin, all dimensions of humans, including our thinking, have been distorted. The effects of sin, brokenness, and depravity, involve our total, willful rejection of the will and glory of God.

3. Salvation in Christ

Because of sin, all in this world are estranged from God, but the biblical answer for that problem is that Jesus Christ has regained what was lost in Adam (Rom 5:12–21). The grace of God has provided our restoration and brought about a right relationship with God, with one another, with nature, and with ourselves. Grace declares that salvation is not the culmination of humanity's quest for God but that it resides in the initiative of God toward men and women (Eph 1:4–7). Grace comes to us while we are still in our sins and brings spiritual transformation based on the accomplished cross-work of Jesus Christ. Grace is, as B. B. Warfield observed, God's "free sovereign favor to the ill-deserving." God does not graciously accept us because he sees our change for the better, as if conversion were the basis for receiving God's grace. Instead the Bible pictures God's coming into our lives and taking us just as we are because he is abundantly merciful (Eph 2:1–10).

As a result of God's grace, believers experience salvation from sin, which involves conversion to God. All of salvation is of God, yet we respond in faith and commitment. The Bible expresses these truths in various pictures, underscoring throughout that God is the author and finisher of our salvation (Heb 12:2). These various themes of regeneration, justification, adoption, and forgiveness are presented as the new sphere of union with Christ for all who have placed their faith in him (John 15; Rom 6:1–11; Eph 1:3–14). Our union with Christ presents us in a new position before God. Experientially, the union of believers with Christ is one of the most beautiful and tender concepts expressed in Scripture.

We recognize that this gift of salvation rests in what Jesus Christ has done for fallen people. Christ's life and death exemplified the love of God and exerted an influence for good by providing a model of servanthood and sacrifice. More importantly, Christ's death provided for sinners a sinless substitutionary sacrifice that satisfies divine justice, an incomprehensibly valuable redemption delivering sinners from estrangement to full fellowship and inheritance in the household of God.

We trustingly confess and affirm that Jesus Christ as the God-Man has fully revealed God to men and women. Having lived a sinless life, Christ died in our place for our sins. He now sits exalted at God's right hand, a position of honor and exaltation, exercising his rule and dominion. Those who have placed their trust in Jesus Christ for salvation gladly acknowledge Jesus as Lord; he is our Prophet, Priest, and King, who has completely revealed God, reconciled humankind with God, and who sits enthroned as Ruler of God's kingdom and head of his church. In him, we place our trust and hope, offering our thanksgiving for the salvation he has provided for us.

4. The Holy Spirit: Renewal and Community

With the coming of the Holy Spirit at Pentecost (Acts 2), there was a universalizing of the ministry and mission of Jesus. Jesus was God's final Word to humanity, and the Spirit's role was not to bring some new revelation of his own but to bear witness to Jesus and to interpret and explicate the full implications of God's final Word. The Spirit came in order to enable and unite believers in an unparalleled manner. The ultimate purpose of the Spirit was to bring life and renewal to Christ followers, drawing them together into the new community, the church of Jesus Christ, and to empower this community for mission, which was the spreading of good news and exalting the name of Christ. Life in the Spirit energizes and enables the new community of faith.

The basis for life in the Spirit must never be forgotten. Through the death and resurrection of Jesus Christ, the Spirit applies justification, regeneration, sanctification, and ultimate glorification to the lives of believers. Life in the Spirit is living out, by the Spirit's empowerment, what believers are because of Christ, exalting him in the expansion of the church's worship, ministry and mission, which includes conversion, evangelism, fellowship, renewal, and holiness.

5. Eschatology: God's Rule and Reign

God's final rule and reign will bring victory when Christ returns to establish and consummate his kingdom. Regardless of the diligent and industrious attempts by men and women to bring about righteousness and peace to earth, true peace and righteousness will take place only when Jesus Christ comes again. The agelong quest of the nations can only be fulfilled by the work of Christ. Sincere believers differ over their understanding of the nature and chronology of Christ's return as well as their expectations for the kingdom itself. Yet all orthodox Christians believe that following Christ's return, the dead will be raised, both the righteous and the wicked, leading to judgment and then to the eternal state.

The eternal climax of redemptive history is seen in the description of the new Jerusalem (Rev 21–22). The general image of a future Jerusalem symbolizes the fulfillment of many of God's promises to his people (Isa 2:1–5; 49:14–18; 52; 54; 60–62; 65:17–25; Jer 31:38–40; Mic 4:1–4; Zech 14). As is true of Christ's return and other features of his rule and reign, the trustworthiness of Scripture underscores our confidence that these prophecies are indeed true. The picture of the new Jerusalem emphasizes that the people of God will be a universal community of redeemed individuals living together in love.

For all eternity the redeemed of the Lord will worship the triune God supremely without impurity. We will enjoy fellowship with him without conflict. We will serve the living God forever. Worldview Christians, with eagerness and expectancy, hope for that day.

THE INCARNATION OF JESUS CHRIST

Daniel L. Akin

The incarnation of the Son of God is at the heart of the Christian faith. "The Word became flesh and dwelt among us" in the person of Jesus Christ (John 1:14). Christ's first coming is essential for the reconciliation of God and humanity and for Jesus's ongoing mediation on our behalf.

While there is an element of mystery surrounding the incarnation—the person of Jesus Christ the God-man—there are some foundational nonnegotiables that we affirm to be true to biblical revelation and that honor the witness of the church throughout her history.

Six Nonnegotiables of the Doctrine of the Incarnation

1. *First, we hold to the true incarnation of the Logos,* the Word (John 1:1,14,18), the Second Person of the Godhead. The Son of God, having been sent by the Father, truly assumed the whole of human nature. In this event, the Second Person of the Trinity invaded time and space, embracing humanity to himself. Therefore, any form of docetic theology—claiming that Christ only appeared to be human— must firmly be rejected (1 John 4:2–3).

The humanity of Jesus is like that of Adam and Eve prior to the fall: it is a sinless humanity (2 Cor 5:21; Heb 4:15). The human nature that the Son took to himself was not tainted by sin. The most genuine expression of humanity—what it means to be human—is manifested in Jesus Christ.

2. There is a necessary distinction between the two natures of Jesus Christ and his person. He is a single person who possesses both divine and human natures. A "nature" assumes the powers and qualities that constitute a being, while a "person" is the self-conscious, self-asserting, and acting subject. This distinction is embedded in Scripture, particularly in the NT (see Phil 2:5–8), and it was codified in the five great Christological councils (the First Council of Nicaea in AD 325, the First Council of Constantinople in AD 381, the First Council of Ephesus in AD 431, the Council of Chalcedon in AD 451, and the Second Council of Constantinople in AD 553). This human nature, possessing its full integrity, is united to the divine nature, possessing its full integrity, both wedded in the one person, Jesus Christ. The result is a theoanthropic person—one who is both fully divine and truly human.

3. The God-Man was made incarnate through the virgin birth—the means by which God chose to accomplish Christ's coming (Isa 7:14; Matt 1:18–25; Luke 1:26–38). The result is that Jesus Christ is not a double being, a compound being, or some kind of hybrid. He is the one person, our Lord Jesus Christ, complete in his deity and perfect in his humanity.

Several observations suggest a connection between the virgin birth and Jesus's sinless life.

- Jesus is the only virgin-conceived person and the only sinless human.
- The activity of the Holy Spirit in the process of conception is key.
- The virgin conception "helps us understand how Christ can stand outside the guilt of Adam" (Macleod, *The Person of Christ*, 41).
- A sinless humanity is scarcely conceivable, if not impossible, without divine intervention.

4. In the incarnation there is no qualification or diminution of either Christ's deity or his humanity. Each nature retains its own integrity and genuineness. Whatever constitutes God as God, the Son is this

in all its fullness (Col 2:9–10). Further, whatever constitutes man as man, Jesus of Nazareth is this in all its fullness. Sin is not needed for humans to be human. It is in Jesus that we see humanity perfectly expressed as God intended. Whereas fallen and sinful humanity lives on a subhuman plane, this is not true of Jesus.

5. There is a genuine hypostatic union in which the divine nature and the human nature come together and are present in the one person, Jesus Christ. This union is real, supernatural, personal, inseparable, and permanent (see 1 Tim 2:5). There is today in heaven a God-man who is "at the right hand of the Majesty on high" (Heb 1:3) and who "always lives to intercede for [us]" (Heb 7:25). The divine and human have been united truly in the one Lord Jesus Christ.

6. The whole of Christ's work is to be attributed to his whole person and not to one or the other nature exclusively. It is required that Christ be both God and man. As man, he identifies with humanity, enabling him to die in our place. As God, he is not an innocent third party; rather, through him God was "reconciling the world to himself" (2 Cor 5:19). Only a God-man is able to reconcile humans to God. Jesus Christ is that God-man, the Second Person of the triune God, who took to himself a human nature for this work of redemption.

Conclusion

The doctrine of the "two natures" is essential to any expression of biblical and historical Christology. Thus, to jettison the doctrine of the incarnation is to radically redefine Christianity. Jesus is coequal, coeternal, coexistent, and consubstantial (of the same substance) with the Father (John 1:1). Truly, in Christ God made his dwelling among us. Deity and humanity are perfectly and permanently joined together in Christ, with the fullness of his work attributed to his whole person. Any attempt to separate his natures or to ascribe certain actions or words to one nature or the other is wrongheaded and must be refuted. This truth is a foundational pillar on which the Christian faith rests.

RESURRECTION AND THE CHRISTIAN WORLDVIEW

Josh D. Chatraw

Through the resurrection we encounter God's promise of personal, holistic salvation, a promise that includes a bodily existence redeemed in nature and eternal in scope. It is an alluring doctrine that stands in contrast to a common, reoccurring view of eternal life: a depersonalized and disembodied soul. Yet despite its centrality to the rapid rise of Christianity and of later theological reflection, the claim of Jesus's resurrection was a surprising development in its historical context.

History

The future resurrection of all those redeemed by Christ is rooted in the claim that Jesus himself was crucified and raised from the dead. This belief was unlikely to gain headway in the first-century Greco-Roman world, as it sat outside the culture's prevailing plausibility structures. On the one hand, for pagan philosophers—who held to a dualistic view of the world, prizing the nonmaterial and denigrating the physical—the resurrection of a dead corpse was unacceptable. Their hope was to escape the body, not to see it redeemed. On the other hand, the Jews who affirmed a bodily resurrection (not all did), looked forward to a corporate resurrection of all the faithful at the end of the present world order. By no means were they expecting the resurrection of a single person after which the present world would continue (see Wright, *The Resurrection of the Son of God*).

First-century Jews, no less Gentiles, were not looking for a dead Messiah to rise again. This explains why in the canonical Gospels, even Jesus's disciples were confused when he informed them of his coming death and resurrection. Jesus's resurrection was surprising and certainly not something a Jew would have conjured up in hopes of convincing a skeptical first-century world. It was a challenging claim, and the early disciples knew they could not escape its public and outlandish nature. As N. T. Wright emphasizes,

> "Resurrection" was not a private event. It involved human bodies. There would have to be an empty tomb somewhere. A Jewish revolutionary whose leader had been executed by the authorities, and managed to escape arrest himself, had two options: give up the revolution or find another leader. . . . Claiming that the original leader was alive again was simply not an option. Unless, of course, he was (Wright, *Who Was Jesus?*, 63).

In the early tradition, evident in the canonical Gospels and throughout the New Testament (e.g., 1 Cor. 15:1–9), eyewitness testimony serves as the impetus for the proclamation of resurrection. This public confession that "he is risen" has echoed down through history and to the nations, changing not only history itself but also transforming lives and communities throughout the world.

Christology

It is difficult to understand first-century people's early devotion to and worship of Jesus if their behavior is separated from a sincere belief that Jesus had risen from the grave. Devout first-century Jews were staunch monotheists. While they believed in a host of heavenly beings (e.g., angels), they only worshipped one God, the Creator and Ruler of the universe (Bauckham, *Jesus and the God of Israel*, 1–59). Any change in this central belief, then, would seemingly have had to come through a long, gradual shift. Instead, however, soon after Jesus's death, this group of conservative Jews began to "define and reverence Jesus with reference to the one God" (Hurtado, *Lord Jesus Christ*, 151).

This rapid shift took place for several reasons. Firsthand experiences with Jesus, reflections on his teachings, and careful rereading of the Hebrew Scriptures played an important role. But their rereading of the Scriptures, reevaluation of Jesus's teachings, and—most importantly—their worship of Jesus are difficult to accept without the presence of a dramatic, paradigm-shifting event—Jesus's resurrection.

Creation, New Creation, and Salvation

Within the biblical story line, Jesus's resurrection points both backward to creation and forward to the coming new creation (O'Donovan, *Resurrection and Moral Order*, 56–57). Regarding the former, the resurrection of the whole person reaffirms the original goodness of God's whole creation. Regarding the latter, while sin has parasitically distorted God's good creation, Jesus's resurrection reasserts God's commitment to his created order. Christianity, then, is not bent on escaping the physical world but delighting and finding purpose in God's creation.

In the narratives of Jesus's resurrection, we see a mysterious picture of continuity and discontinuity between our world and the new creation to come. The disciples can touch his resurrected body and see the holes in his side. Jesus eats food and interacts as a fully embodied human. Yet Jesus also walks through doors, and at times the disciples have trouble recognizing their teacher.

While not downplaying individual salvation, Paul emphasizes the cosmic salvation that was secured by Jesus's resurrection. What results is a sort of dual emphasis, as seen in Romans 8, where Paul reasons that "if the Spirit of him who raised Jesus from the dead lives in you, then he who raised Christ from the dead will also bring your mortal bodies to life through his Spirit who lives in you" (Rom 8:11). He then adds a cosmic dimension of this future salvation, explaining how "the whole creation has been groaning together with labor pains until now. And not only that, but we ourselves who have the Spirit as the firstfruits —we also groan within ourselves, eagerly waiting for adoption, the redemption of our bodies" (Rom 8:22–23).

This picture, appropriately applied, gives the Christian reason to care about the physical world (body, culture, and environment) while looking forward to a glorified state beyond our present realities, recognizing that Jesus's resurrection secured a redeemed and transformed new creation.

The Existential: Meaning and Hope

The resurrection speaks powerfully into universal experiences. Death, for instance, is the universal shadow that hangs over all of life, its inescapable finality underlying every moment. There is no going back to our childhoods. No hearing the voice of the loved ones we've buried. Each new moment secures the loss of the one that came before. In this sense, death is the present. But death is also the future—our inevitable fate. And a frightening one at that, for we fear being cut off from all we love. Neither the hope of an impersonal existence nor the assurance that death is not followed by divine judgment—only a "nothingness," or an eternal sleep—can provide the solace we seek. The end of love, relationships, and meaning is what makes death so excruciatingly unbearable, even absurd. People today cope by trying to avoid its reality altogether, but imperfectly so—thoughts of death are undeniably difficult to rid from the human psyche.

But with the resurrection death loses its conclusive sting. The resurrection promises that our loves in this world—that is, the things we love in right relation to God—are not simply meaningful; rather, they will exist forever. In Christ, God has reversed what seems irreversible (John 11:25–26; 1 Cor 15:12–28). As the French philosopher Luc Ferry explains, our greatest desire as human beings is "to be understood, to be loved, not to be alone, not to be separated from our loved ones—in short, not to die and not to have them die on us" (*A Brief History of Thought*, 4). Christianity's response to this universal human desire to elude death is that in Christ death is not only not the end of life, love, and community but a door that opens to a deeper experience of all these things. In this life the Spirit offers a foretaste of this coming hope, but the consummation of this joy awaits the world to come.

THE GOSPEL AND THE FORMATION OF A CHRISTIAN WORLDVIEW

Robert B. Sloan

The gospel of the crucified and risen Jesus (see 1 Cor 15:1–11) is the core message regarding the climactic events central to a Christian worldview. To understand the Christian worldview, we must start with the word *worldview* itself.

A worldview is a way, a perspective, an outlook on the world, on all there is. While worldviews can certainly be described, analyzed, and compared to other worldviews—and thus debated—usually a worldview consists of the set of assumptions that govern how we view and understand all of reality. We don't ordinarily question our worldviews unless we feel ultimate issues need to be analyzed and debated. A worldview is the lens, the frame of reference, or, to change the metaphor, the scaffolding on which we build our living, our actions, our thinking, and our experiences. Thus, a worldview should not be limited merely to "seeing" or looking. It is our way of knowing and understanding, accomplished as we live and experience all that there is.

A biblical, Christian worldview begins with the assumption of the one true Creator God, who involves himself in history and seeks relationship with his creatures. It does not assume a deist god who is merely there and certainly not a pantheistic god whose existence is mingled in with all that there is. The God of Scripture is the God who creates, who makes all things good, who is intimately involved with his creation, and who is faithful in all his interactions with it. From a biblical perspective, there can be no argument as to whether or not God does the "miraculous" because the whole of creation is his world; he is involved in it; and his presence in the world occurs both by routine and by things wondrous and strange. The Scriptures refer to God as having covenants not only with his human creatures but also with the creation itself (cp. Gen 8:20–22; 9:8–17).

Most worldviews, whether secular or religious, have stories and narratives as part of their basic structure. In the case of a Christian worldview, the stories that lie at the heart of our perspective are essentially the narratives of what God has done in history. The God of Scripture is active in the world he made; thus, history witnesses to his presence both in creation and in his actions, particularly as these are revealed in the Bible. Thus, Scripture not only provides a worldview for those who accept its testimony, but it also reflects the worldview of its authors. Put another way, the writers of Scripture are themselves informed by the great truths that they teach—so that the biblical worldview provides a lens through which their writing should be understood—while they also establish the worldview that informs Christian theology.

The story of the Bible begins with the God who creates. But the narrative quickly moves to a crisis known as the fall. The rebellion of Adam and Eve provides the second fixed point in the narrative. The fall is the backdrop for the rest of the biblical story, in which God acts to redeem humanity and to restore the entire creation—to make a new heaven and a new earth. So, according to a biblical worldview, there is one Creator God who is involved in his creation. He acts to restore the world.

From the vantage point of creation and the fall, we then see the patterns of God's actions in history to redeem and rescue as they unfold in Scripture. This has implications for a Christian understanding of history. A Christian worldview assumes that history does not inevitably decline. There is always the prospect of God's divine action, which at any moment may set a new course for history. God works through circumstances both good and evil (cp. Rom 9:14–17) to move history along to accomplish his faithful purposes.

We can be somewhat specific regarding God's movements in history to redeem, since he has unfolded a strategy whereby he chose a particular people, Israel, and through this nation he has acted to bring the whole world back to himself. God's choosing of Israel underlies the stories of Abraham, Isaac, and Jacob, through to Joseph and the enslavement of God's people in Egypt. Israel's exodus from Egypt through God's dramatic plagues upon the former led his chosen people to Canaan. But Israel's story has multiple twists because, in the end, Israel herself was not faithful to God. Israel was sent into exile, but her prophets, who warned of her impending judgment, also reiterated God's promises that one day he would reign as King (cp. Isa 35:3–6; 40:3–5,9–10; 52:7–10; 60:1–2; Ezek 43:1–7; Zech 8:2–3; 14:1–17) and restore his people. Israel would be brought back from exile, and a Son of the great King David (Isa 9:6–7; 11:1–11; Jer 33:14–18), who would rule in the place of God, would be seated on a throne. He would not only rule Israel, but eventually all nations would pay him homage and worship the one Creator God.

But once again, the larger biblical narrative takes a surprising turn. The long-awaited King not only suffered for his people, Israel, in an act of propitiation and sacrifice that concluded their exile and redeemed them from sin. He also fulfilled Israel's unfinished work to be a light to the Gentiles and to bring the nations back to God. The death and resurrection of Jesus Christ are the climactic moments in the larger biblical story.

Now the people of God are organized around Jesus—the true Israel of God, and the second Adam—and must preach the gospel, the message of the crucified and resurrected Jesus, to the ends of the earth. As the gospel of Jesus is preached in all the world, the final vindication of Jesus will come, and the glorious day of resurrection and restoration will occur (Matt 24:14). Then, the restoration of heaven and earth will take place (Rev 21:1–5; cp. Isa 65:17; 66:22), and a final separation of all the peoples and nations of the earth will happen (Matt 25:31–46; 2 Thess 1:5–10; Rev 20:1–15). Those who embrace the one true God through Jesus will be raised to a glorious life, while those who have rejected God's Son are banished into outer darkness. Then God will be "all in all" (1 Cor 15:28).

This outline of the biblical narrative constitutes the lens through which Christians understand the world. Worldviews may be described, analyzed, and debated. But every worldview that claims to be Christian and biblical must start with the one true Creator God, who made man and woman in his image and who, despite the rebellion of his creatures and the consequent cursing of creation, longs to redeem his people—an action that he has accomplished through the coming of Jesus, the long-awaited Son of David. Christ fulfills the work of Israel, drawing the nations back to God through his obedient death, resurrection, enthronement at the right hand of God, and final appearance as King of kings and Lord of lords.

THE ETERNAL STATE

Russell D. Moore

The reigning worldview of contemporary secularism—rooted in Darwinian naturalism—assumes that death is itself natural and that it is a final end. The biblical perspective is startlingly different, revealing that death is an unnatural enemy, a predator stalking a human race meant to live forever. In the crucified and resurrected Jesus of Nazareth, death is undone and the cosmos redeemed.

The biblical story tells us that God imposed the curse of death as a result of the insurrection of the primal human pair, Adam and Eve (Gen 3:8). God had instructed Adam not to partake of "the tree of the knowledge of good and evil" (Gen 2:17), so when Adam and Eve rejected this prohibition and ate, God exiled them from his presence. He placed a fiery sword at the entrance of the garden precisely so that the sinful human race would no longer have access to the tree of life and thus be consigned forever to their devil-imaging, walking death (Gen 3:22–24).

After the fall, the entire universe revolted at its created kings and queens, no longer obediently heeding the reign of humanity. Disease, natural disaster, animal attack, and the like seem normal to us now; such is the only reality we've known, but the Bible says this reign of death is not natural, and it is not permanent. What seems to be normal is not actually how things are supposed to be.

Some religions have asserted that humans are reincarnated in a cycle of lives. Some have taught that the final goal of human existence is a personality-nullifying absorption into the cosmos itself. Others have envisioned a shadowy, otherworldly existence beyond the grave. Atheistic systems see human consciousness ending, like that of an animal, with the cessation of bodily life. The gospel of Jesus Christ, however, teaches that every human will end up in one of two possible eternal states: that of blessing or that of curse (Matt 13:41–43).

Hell

The Bible speaks of hell as a reality of indescribable torment. This place was not created initially for humanity but instead, as Jesus puts it, for the devil and his angels (Matt 25:41). Those who choose the headship of Satan as their god and who share in his nature will join the devil in his inheritance. The Bible says that this is the fate of all of us if we are left to ourselves (Eph 2:1–3). It is not possible for us to earn salvation through good works (Gal 2:16).

The Bible uses various images to convey the horror of hell. In his Patmos vision, John sees it as a "lake of fire" (Rev 20:14). Jesus called hell a place of "outer darkness" filled with "weeping and gnashing of teeth" (Matt 8:12). He also compared it to a Middle Eastern trash heap, a place where there is no end to the torment of the damned, for "their worm does not die, and the fire is not quenched" (Mark 9:48).

Those outside of Christ find themselves in punishment immediately upon death, as pictured in Jesus's account of the rich man and Lazarus (Luke 16:19–31). This intermediate state of torment, awful as it is, is not the final accounting, however. At the end of the age, the damned are resurrected and face trial before the great white throne of Christ himself (Rev 20:11–15). The sinner will give an account for every idle word, thought, and deed, as well as his or her response to Jesus himself (e.g., Matt 12:36). Sinners are then sentenced to the judgment they have already pronounced on themselves—exile from the presence of God and into the lake of fire. This eternal curse means suffering that is corporeal as well as spiritual, emotional, and psychological. Hell is not something that humans create for themselves on this earth. Hell is the reality of God's justice and wrath, and it reflects the dignity of the human: each person must be held accountable for decisions made.

Heaven

The distinction between those who inherit damnation and those who, as the Bible puts it, "inherit the earth," is found in obedience to the will of

God, summed up in loving the Lord and loving neighbor (Mark 12:28–31). Nevertheless, the depravity of humanity is such that every human, with the exception of Jesus, is found guilty as a lawbreaker, and is thus deserving of hell (Rom 3:10–18). Unlike the rest of us, Jesus of Nazareth lived a life of obedience to the law of God. He did this for our sake and died under the curse of the law for our sins so that the punishment that was due to us fell on him instead, securing salvation for all who place their faith in him. At his resurrection and ascension, Jesus was crowned the rightful King of the universe. Those who approach God, hidden in Jesus by faith, are already judged righteous; thus, their sentence to hell is cancelled, and God's justice is reconciled to his mercy. Those in Christ also now share in his life, in his resurrection, and in his inheritance.

Immediately after death, believers find themselves in the presence of God, a present reality known by Christians as "heaven" (see Jesus's words to the repentant thief on the cross in Luke 23:43 and Paul's comments about his desires in Phil 1:23). This disembodied existence of blessedness is not, however, the eternal state of those in Christ. God did not send Christ into the world to condemn the world, but to save it (John 3:17). The final state of redeemed humanity is life in a renewed cosmos, free from the curse and under the reign of Christ and his joint-heirs (Rev 21).

The New Earth

At the resurrection from the dead, believers join Jesus in his resurrection life—including the restoration of their bodies. This doctrine was doubted by the Sadducees in Jesus's era, and he refuted their stance in a memorable encounter (Mark 12:18–27). At the end times heaven and earth are joined in a new earth that is transfigured by the presence and glory of God in Christ. This eternal reality is not merely a restoration of Eden but a glorious civilization with a city in which the glory of the nations redeemed are brought into it. This presumably means that every aspect of culture will be present there. We reasonably may imagine this means music, painting, literature, architecture, commerce, agriculture, and any other worthy aspect of human endeavor will be practiced there and freed from sin, made holy in undiluted service to God.

While the Bible keeps much of the future from us, presumably because our minds at this point could not comprehend it, we know that the eternal state of those in Christ is one that includes work and labor (though freed from the frustration of the curse), personal relationships, worship, and ruling and reigning with Christ. The Bible uses the imagery of a wedding feast to signify the feasting and celebrating of the age to come (Rev 19:6–9).

In this everlasting age, God's covenants will be seen to have come to a climax in the identity and mission of Christ Jesus, and his reign will be all encompassing. The kingdoms of this world, as the apostle John was shown in the Revelation vision, will become the kingdom of our Lord and of his Christ, and he shall reign forevermore (Rev 11:15).

Philosophy and Ethics

FAITH AND REASON

Michael D. Beaty

There are points of tension in the Scriptures concerning the relation of faith and reason. Paul reminds us that Christ sent him to proclaim the gospel, but not by relying on worldly wisdom. Indeed, Paul insists that the wisdom of the wise will be destroyed and that nothing will come of their cleverness. Instead, those saved are saved by the "foolishness" of the gospel (1 Cor 1:17–24).

But Paul also suggests that, in their wickedness, people are stifling the truth even as knowledge of God lies plain before their eyes. Since the world began, God's invisible attributes, power, and deity have been accessible to human reason through the things God has made (Rom 1:19–20). Additionally, Paul uses a series of arguments to support the resurrection of the dead (1 Cor 15:12–20).

What follows is an exploration of this tension; it offers one Christian account of faith and reason.

What is reason and what is faith?
In its broadest sense, the term *reason* means "those natural human powers that enable access to a variety of truths." Such powers include sense perception, intuition of necessary truths, making inferences, deciding what to do, memory, and testimony. More narrowly, *reason* refers to reliable methods of inquiry about the world. Paradigmatic examples include the practices of the natural sciences. Even more narrowly, *reason* refers to forms of infer-

ence used to appropriately support one statement on the basis of other statements.

Christians generally agree that faith is the proper and primary response to God (Father, Son, and Holy Spirit). For a Christian, faith involves trusting Christ with one's whole life (Prov 3:5; John 20:31; Heb 12:2). Such trust requires embracing as true the testimony of the Scriptures and the church. Trusting in this way means accepting as true and binding certain understandings of what the Scriptures teach (2 Tim 3:14–17; 2 Thess 2:15).

Taken together, full-orbed Christian faith thus has three aspects: affective (assurance, confidence—1 John 5:14; Heb 10:22; 11:1–40), cognitive (knowledge or belief—Gen 15:6; Heb 11:3), and volitional (trust, obedience—Gen 12:1–4). Faith is both a state (e.g., assent or belief) and an activity (e.g., worship).

How do faith and reason relate?

What is the relationship between faith and reason? Historically, three kinds of answers have been given.

1. The Conflict Model

The conflict model contends that faith and reason are irreconcilably opposed to each other. Oxford biologist Richard Dawkins, who insists that faith and reason are enemies, provides a contemporary example. He endorses science as the paradigm of reason, contending that the claims essential to Christianity are unreasonable given the standards of science.

Have Christians endorsed the conflict model? The second-century church father Tertullian famously asked, "What indeed does Athens have to do with Jerusalem? What concord is there between the Academy and the Church? What between heretics and Christians. . . . With our faith, we desire no further belief. For this is our palmary faith, that there is nothing which we ought to believe besides."

If Tertullian is suggesting that faith is genuine only if one knowingly embraces a statement that is against or contrary to the deliverances of mere reason, then he endorses a conflict model.

2. The Independence Model

The independence model denies that faith and reason are necessarily antagonistic ventures. Instead, faith and reason are conceived as fundamentally independent. Evolutionary biologist Stephen Gould contended that science and faith occupy different, nonoverlapping magisterium (teaching authority). Science attends to facts and theories about the natural world (the what and how). Religion is about morality, the meaning and purpose of human life (the why). So, science and religion, reason and faith, are independent domains.

The earlier quote by Tertullian may be understood as emphasizing the independence of faith and reason, if Tertullian is suggesting that faith is merely indifferent to the deliverances of mere reason, that faith is about our response to what God has done for the sake of our salvation.

In his book *Credo*, Karl Barth, the twentieth-century theologian, writes about the relation of dogmatics and philosophy. His claim "that Dogmatics runs counter to every philosophy" seems to underscore a fundamental opposition between faith and reason. But he elaborates that "no philosophy can deliver the key to us. . . . The question of the 'proper' language of theology is ultimately to be answered only with prayer and the life of faith." Barth may be suggesting that reason and faith are independent from, but not necessarily in opposition to, one another.

3. The Harmony Model

For some, the domains of faith and learning overlap much more than the independence model endorses. The harmony model holds that faith and reason have mutual aims and that the methods of each can interact with, and support, the other. Geneticist and director of the National Institutes of Health, Francis Collins, insists that there is no essential conflict between faith as expressed in Christianity and reason as exemplified in the physical or social sciences. Both have similar aims: discovering the truth about how things actually are and responding properly to what is true.

Thomas Aquinas insists that faith and learning relate, ideally, in harmony. He argues that grace, which enables faith, doesn't destroy but rather completes nature (including reason). He holds that reason can demonstrate the preambles of the faith (that God exists, God is one, God is necessary), but by faith we know the articles of faith (Trinity, incarnation, resurrection). The latter are above or beyond reason but not contrary to it. Reason can help us understand the articles of faith and also help defeat objections to faith. In short, faith and reason work together to give us the full truth about God, the world, and ourselves.

How should Christians think?

What should Christians think about the nature of faith and reason? First, both faith and reason are God's gifts. Christians should receive them graciously and use them well.

Second, reason enables one to make many true judgments about the nature of things in the world, other persons, and self. Faith, likewise, gives humans access to many profoundly significant truths. Since both reason and faith are means of accessing truth, they share a cognitive end.

Faith, however, provides access to some truths that reason alone cannot access. These include that God is Triune, Jesus Christ is God incarnate, Jesus died and was resurrected, and Jesus's death and resurrection are the means of our salvation. Additionally, faith's access to such truths comes through willingness to accept God's testimony, especially through the Scriptures and the church's witness. Central to orthodox Christian conviction is that faith offers access to truths otherwise unavailable to reason.

The difference here between faith and reason is material, not formal. Reason also provides humans access to truths the Christian faith does not. For example, ordinarily, it is reason—not God's revelation—that helps humans know, for example, that chewing or smoking tobacco is harmful to one's health.

Moreover, reason is like faith in that reliance on the testimony of others is one of the ways reason functions to help humans acquire truth. For example, that a financial adviser is a reliable source of truth about stock market fluctuations means that her judgment that one should sell rather than buy a certain company's shares provides one a good reason to sell. Selling, however, is an act of faith (in a sense analogous to that of faith in God) in the trustworthiness of one's financial adviser, albeit a reasonable one.

Christians and the Harmony Model

How should a Christian think about the three models of the relation of faith and reason? Christians should embrace the harmony model because the goal of both faith and reason is grasping the truth. When reason functions well, we are able to access the truth about a wide range of things.

Faith operates to allow another means of access to truths, some of which may also be accessible to reason, in its normal operations, while others are not.

Still, we are fallible, finite, and fallen creatures. Our knowledge has limits. Even for things within the grasp of our reasoning powers, we make mistakes because our powers are not developed or deployed properly. Additionally, we are sinful creatures, having distorted passions and a misshapen will. Not surprisingly, then, faith and reason may sometimes appear to either be opposed or simply independent ventures. In practice, when conflict or independence models are advocated, it is because some distorted or defective version of either faith or reason is being employed. But faith and reason, rightly understood, are unified both by being gifts of, and having their ultimate source in, God. So, in principle there is no essential conflict between them.

Still, the independence and conflict models point to something important. The Christian faith demands that our fundamental posture toward God be utter reliance on him and not merely an assent to a set of propositions. Reason impedes faith when it is taken to be a rival to one's ultimate and unconditional reliance on God, as revealed in Christ.

GREEK PHILOSOPHY AND ITS INFLUENCE ON CHRISTIAN THEOLOGY

Douglas V. Henry

Twenty-four centuries after he lived in Athens, Plato's legacy looms large, for as A. N. Whitehead famously quipped, Western thought is "a series of footnotes to Plato." Given Plato's repute, his influence within Christian theology is not surprising. Indeed, Christians have long grappled with Platonism, generally finding it useful for biblically grounded theology. C. S. Lewis validates Plato's theological worth in *The Last Battle* when Professor Digory Kirke exclaims, "It's all in Plato, all in Plato: bless me, what do they teach them in these schools?"

Early Christian Views

Whether the Bible's authors knew Plato's dialogues or Platonist philosophers is debatable. We know, however, that the NT's authors lived in an age shaped by Platonic philosophy. We also know that the early church fathers studied and wrote about Platonism. Their interpretation of Scripture emerged in light of Greek philosophy, especially Platonism.

Tertullian (AD 160–220) questioned Platonism's value. He cited Colossians 2:8:

> Be careful that no one takes you captive through philosophy and empty deceit based on human tradition, based on the elements of the world, rather than Christ." He recalled Paul's missionary

encounter with the Athenian philosophers, and posed some memorable questions: "What indeed has Athens to do with Jerusalem? What concord is there between the Academy and the Church? What between heretics and Christians? . . . Away with all attempts to produce a mottled Christianity of Stoic, Platonic, and dialectic composition! . . . With our faith, we desire no further belief.

On a fideistic understanding of Tertullian, faith in Christ and philosophical reflection are irrelevant or even opposed. Fideism—from the Latin word *fides*, meaning "faith"—views faith and reason as separate, perhaps even contradictory endeavors.

Context matters, however, for rightly interpreting Paul's teaching and Tertullian's instruction. In the church's first centuries, various philosophies might easily have co-opted Christianity for their own purposes. Paul and Tertullian demonstrate appropriate concern for the preeminence of Christ and caution against heresy. Yet they do not reject philosophy. They confidently reason, address complex ideas, and adopt concepts coined by philosophers, even while unstintingly putting Christ first. By testing Greek philosophy "according to Christ," they show how faithful Christians can discern truth and refute error.

Many church fathers accordingly used Platonism to aid biblical understanding, including Justin Martyr (AD 100–165), Clement of Alexandria (AD 150–215), Origin (AD 182–254), Basil of Caesarea (AD 330–379), Gregory of Nyssa (AD 335–394), and Augustine of Hippo (AD 354–430). Justin Martyr wrote, "Whatever things were rightly said . . . are the property of us Christians. For next to God, we worship and love the Word . . . [and] all the writers were able to see realities darkly through the sowing of the implanted word that was in them." Clement speculated that philosophy was God's gift, "a schoolmaster to bring the Hellenic mind—as the law, the Hebrews—to Christ." Philosophy was "a preparation . . . for him who is perfected in Christ." Augustine praised God for a providential encounter with "some books of the Platonists," whereby he discerned Christianity's intellectually fulfilling possibilities. He invoked a biblical metaphor: "I fixed my mind upon the gold which you willed that your people should bring with them from Egypt: for it was yours, wherever it was." God let the Israelites plunder Egyptian gold in their exodus for the promised land. Similarly, God invites us to exploit Plato's philosophical "gold" in our pilgrimage.

Christian Uses of Platonism

Platonism provides rich resources for expressing biblical instruction about (1) God's being, (2) the nature of evil, and (3) humanity's highest hopes.

The Bible teaches of God's perfection (Matt 5:48), eternality (Deut 33:27), and unfathomable wisdom, power, and goodness (Job 38–42). Yet Scripture does not explain how the divine attributes relate to one another. Platonism can help. Plato developed a philosophy—metaphysics, epistemology, and ethics—in which perfect being, knowledge, and goodness are inextricably interconnected. Platonism thereby offers philosophical categories that enrich biblical understanding and undergird Christian doctrine.

For example, Platonists perceive that perfection entails eternality, for what is perfect is necessarily changeless (since changing the perfect would mar it), and what never changes is necessarily eternal (since it cannot cease to be unless it changes). What is perfect and eternal also outshines everything in truth, beauty, and goodness (since otherwise it would lack perfection). Plato could not conceive that something so described could be an impersonal force or property of matter. He envisioned it rather as a Being—a suprapersonal, superrational Mind, the "Maker and Father" of all, who desires that "all things should be good." Plato's conception of God, in short, binds together major biblical teachings about God's nature, making sense of the inseparable unity of perfectly divine being and perfectly divine essence.

The same philosophical framework clarifies the nature of evil. Because ultimate being—God himself—is identical with perfect goodness, anything lacking goodness also in some way lacks being. Evil is a privation not only of goodness, but of existence. A good thing's corruption mars its being. Evil is therefore always lesser than, weaker than, good. Where evil seems to prevail, it succeeds only in a parasitic parody of good. The theological upshot is crucial. Through both biblical faith and philosophical reason, we can speak confidently about evil's limits. Wickedness shall not abide and evil will not stand (Ps 1), for God's superabundant being and goodness ensure what Augustine confessed: "evil utterly is not." C. S. Lewis offers a fine literary illustration. In *The Great Divorce*, his fabulous "dream" of heaven and hell, he encounters "Bright People" possessed of a grace-filled goodness that gives them a readily apparent solidity, a "weight of glory." He also meets "Ghosts," whose insubstantial presence reflects their manifold sins. Sin has deprived them of being. Evil has literally unmade them.

Platonism proves helpful in a final area. We know the Father's loving adoption brings hope of eternal life through Christ (John 3:16; 1 Pet 1:3), and we wait in the Spirit to gather in God's light (Rev 22:5). Plato helps little with the substance of our highest hopes. Nevertheless, he offers an alluring account of the form of our heavenly sight of God. Our hearts' desire finds rest atop a metaphorical "ladder of love," which we ascend to behold divine Beauty itself. Tracing the lineaments of Plato's dramatization of human longing, theologians write of contemplative wonder at the sight of God, whereby we see God in effortless, endlessly delightful, intellectual vision. And in what theologians call *theosis,* our adoration of God transforms us, making us more like God as our participation in the divine life grows. Loving ascent, contemplative wonder, intellectual vision, participatory understanding, mimetic transformation—such theologically rich conceptions of heavenly life are indebted to Platonism. Plato has aided Augustine, Bonaventure, Aquinas, Dante, Milton, Bunyan, Tolkien, and Lewis in writing of our hoped-for sight of God.

Platonism's Shortcomings

Lucy Beckett says Plato's acknowledgment "of the unity in God of truth, goodness and beauty, fitfully intelligible but not yet visible in the Word made flesh, [is] unique in the pre-Christian world." From the church's early life to now, Platonic concepts and arguments have enriched biblical theology. Key elements of our doctrine of God, evil's limits, and Christian beatitudes are indebted to Platonism. Yet Plato was not a Christian, and his dialogues are not in the Bible.

Two major shortcomings arise. First, Plato denigrates the material world and the body instead of honoring God's good creation. Plato thus embraces a body-soul dualism, privileges the soul over the body, and does not countenance bodily resurrection. Second, Plato cannot fathom the self-emptying love of the incarnate Son of God. It is not only that he lived before Jesus. That God could become a man is altogether beyond Plato's imagination. Because he lacks Trinitarian theology and devalues matter, the idea of the Word become flesh (John 1:14) could not occur to him.

Recently so-called open theists have questioned traditional doctrines supposedly distorted by Platonism. God's simplicity (the unity of his existence and essence), aseity (absolute independence and self-existence), and omniscience are allegedly defective doctrines supported by Platonism but not the Bible. However, we should be wary of abandoning centuries-old

Christian teaching. Church fathers, medieval scholastics, reformation leaders, and modern theologians formulated doctrine "according to Christ," realizing that Platonism offers subordinate assistance. Again, Beckett says it well: "It is not the case that Plato's philosophy makes sense of the revelation of God in Christ, but that the revelation of God in Christ, the Incarnation and Resurrection that healed Plato's soul-body dualism, makes sense of Plato's philosophy, the sense that Plato himself could not make."

SOURCES FOR ETHICS

Kenneth T. Magnuson

When we consider sources for ethics, we may distinguish first between an ontological aspect (the source of ethics itself) and an epistemological aspect (the source of knowledge of ethics), each of which has implications for ethical authority.

The Ontological Aspect

The ontological question has to do with the nature of morality.

One common view is that of moral relativism, which understands morality to be subjective and created by humans (to enable a civil society and avoid anarchy or tyranny, to establish and protect individual rights, and so on), though proponents sometimes present their views as objective and authoritative. Furthermore, even though morality is considered to be subjective, it is derived in part by reflection on the world, so that human reason engages something that exerts itself as objective.

In contrast to subjective perspectives, Christian ethics holds that morality is objective and revealed by God. The ultimate source of ethics is God, who created the universe with moral order—determined by his character, purposes, and will—and graciously reveals to humans the reality of that order and how to live according to that reality. This perspective is one of moral realism.

The Sources of Ethical Knowledge

Christians affirm that the Bible is the primary source of knowledge for ethics, but there is a range of secondary sources, including reason, tradition, and experience. A key question concerns how these sources are coordinated or related. Some consider the appeal to *sola Scriptura* as a denial of other sources. A better understanding, however, is that other sources have validity, but must be tested by and subordinated to Scripture as the primary source (the "norming norm"). It would be naïve to ignore or deny other sources, for they are inescapable and will influence or determine moral judgments whether acknowledged or not. More importantly, Scripture affirms them, even if it qualifies them.

Tradition, understood here as the practices and teachings of the church, shapes us and our understanding of God and of Scripture. We must not affirm tradition uncritically, for sometimes it develops in ways that stand in opposition to God's commandments in Scripture (Matt 15:3). Yet the problem is not tradition itself, but unfaithful traditions. Jesus embraced the prophetic tradition that faithfully transmitted what was revealed by God, and Scripture instructs believers to pass on what we have received (Deut 6:1–9; Matt 28:18–20; Jude 3). The test of tradition is its fidelity to Scripture.

Reason is also necessary to understand and apply the truth of God's Word and to convey it to others (Acts 17:17; 1 Pet 3:15). But the Bible warns that fallen human reason suppresses the truth so that human minds are darkened and foolish (Rom 1:18,21), unable to discern the things of the Spirit (1 Cor 2:14). Yet, God's will is accessible to Spirit-filled reason (Rom 12:1–2; Col 1:9–10). Thus, the mind must be renewed by God's Spirit, and human reason must submit to and be tested by Scripture.

Natural Law

A word on natural law is appropriate here. Natural law is reason based and affirms that a moral order is revealed in creation. Creation stands alongside Scripture as a witness to God's goodness and glory (Ps 19), and it reveals something of God's divine nature and power so that humans are held accountable (Rom 1:18–20). Natural law asserts that morality is objective and accessible to all, for human reason is able to discern proper conduct in accordance with nature. It appeals to some Christians because it is consistent with a biblical perspective without requiring an appeal to revelation.

Nevertheless, its usefulness is limited. Paul's argument from nature in Romans 1 is not an appeal to the effectiveness of natural law. On the contrary, it highlights the depth of human sin and rebellion, which has corrupted human desires and our ability to reason. Apart from God's grace manifested in the gospel, humans are in a hopeless situation. Natural law is not for that reason useless, but it depends on and must be coordinated with revelation.

The Experiential Aspect

Experience is another source of knowledge, though it is viewed with great suspicion by many, and for good reason: humans are often self-deceived, and personal experience lacks moral accountability. Thus, appeals to it as a source of authority are dubious.

On the other hand, it would be a curious view of ethics to insist on its truth against all experience. Rather, we are invited to "taste and see that the LORD is good" (Ps 34:8); the faithful are able to confirm by their experience that God's Word is true and that his will is good (Rom 5:5; 12:2). Further, conscience is related to experience, and it may "accuse or even excuse" us (Rom 2:15), though it may be seared and untrustworthy (1 Tim 4:1). Thus, conscience and experience must be tested by the Word of God.

Conclusion

In sum, tradition, reason, and experience can inform our ethics in a proper way, but they are often distorted by sin and so are not fully trustworthy. These sources should be recognized as important but secondary, to be tested by Scripture within the community of believers. The Bible itself is the only fully reliable source for understanding the nature and substance of ethics; thus, the Bible should not be made to conform to other sources. Rather, those sources must conform to its authority and teaching.

The task at hand is not to develop the content of Christian ethics, but we may specify briefly how the Bible functions as its primary source:

- The whole of the Bible serves as a source for Christian ethics (2 Tim 3:16–17), and not only its direct moral exhortation.
- The Bible defines the "moral field" for ethics, including God as Creator (and his character, purposes, and will), humans and the world in which we live, and the relationships between them. Specifically, the Bible presents a metanarrative that is essential for ethics,

including the belief that the world was created to be good and was infused with moral order, yet it is disordered because of human sin, and yet again it is reordered by God, who by his steadfast love seeks to redeem and reconcile sinful humans and establish justice and peace. God gives a hope for a future that surpasses even the original goodness of creation. This metanarrative provides a worldview, a lens that sharpens our vision so we can interpret and understand the world more clearly. This is important for ethics because our worldview (what we think about God, the world, and humans, etc.) shapes our ethics; it is contrasted with alternative worldviews and ethics.

- The Bible is also a source of moral exhortation, which operates within the larger framework described, and is focused on doing God's will. Ultimately, moral responsibility is not to a command or moral principle, but to a personal God, though no sharp line is drawn between the two since God reveals his will and character through his commands. We may delight in the commands of a gracious God, which light the path of life and keep us from destruction (Deut 30:11–20; Ps 119). Properly understood, the law is structured by love (Matt 22:37–40). Further, Jesus reveals that true morality and righteousness involve the whole self, not merely external conformity to the law (Matt 5–7). In addition, Jesus declares to his disciples that after his return to the Father, the Spirit will come and guide them into all truth (John 16:13). Indeed, within the community of believers, the Spirit brings to bear the truth of Scripture and knowledge of God's will and gives believers the power to obey (Rom 12:1–2; Col 1:9–10).

In a text with great ethical significance, because it describes action within a larger vision of the world, Paul prays that new believers

> may be filled with the knowledge of his will in all wisdom and spiritual understanding, so that you may walk worthy of the Lord, fully pleasing to him: bearing fruit in every good work and growing in the knowledge of God, being strengthened with all power, according to his glorious might, so that you may have great endurance and patience, joyfully giving thanks to the Father, who has enabled you to share in the saints' inheritance in the light. He has rescued

us from the domain of darkness and transferred us into the kingdom of the Son he loves. In him we have redemption, the forgiveness of sins. (Col 1:9–14)

CHRISTIANITY AND MORAL RELATIVISM

Preben Vang

The notion that some actions can be objectively "good" while other things are objectively "evil" seems almost laughable these days. I asked a class of fifty freshman college students—90 percent of whom came from "strong evangelical homes and churches"—how they would define "morally good." How would they discern good from evil? One student's answer, that "it depends on what you like," became the basis for a conversation that lasted the class period. None of those students—not one—disagreed deeply with the first student's statement. They argued that Christians (they themselves) should follow the Bible's guidelines, but they had concluded that this very criterion just proved the first student's point that truth and goodness are relative to what one believes or feels is right.

That the common rationalistic argument of many apologists ("God" is necessary for any conversation about absolute good or evil) has failed to give a unified understanding of morality goes without mention. Disparate convictions and arguments, even among evangelicals, reveal such only too clearly. The best evidence for this may be the simple observation that when the Bible does not speak directly to an issue (and often even when it does), the default behavior of those who claim to follow its teaching is to mirror their surrounding communities. Propositional statements about right and wrong, then, fail to convince—regardless of claims to the opposite.

To this generation of postmoderns (and many moderns of earlier generations) there seems to be something inherently unsatisfactory in the claim that since relativists are caught in their own argument ("everything is relative" is nullified by itself being an absolute statement), there must be an absolute morality that is defined by a necessary higher being—God. So, is there another way to consider this? Would a narrative, rather than a propositional approach, offer a more useful avenue? It appears so.

A Narrative Approach to Morality

A narrative approach to the question of morality yields a natural way to contemporize the content of "God's morality" to issues, settings, and dilemmas of contemporary cultures that are now more mixed and diverse than ever. It enables a Christian testimony in settings that are otherwise hostile to traditional Christian language. A narrative approach to morality allows Christians to engage conversations on the subject as truth seekers, rather than as truth dispensers.

For example, few Westerners outside the church frame the question of morality as an issue of sin. Starvation of multitudes, oppression of the poor and the powerless, enslavement and tyranny that denies basic human freedoms, injustices related to ethnicity, gender, and age, physical handicaps, and war provide the focus and frame the language of most moral questioning and conversation today. Even on the narrower level of "home and neighborhood," questions about violence and gun control, bullying and kindness, sex and immorality, divorce and family life are rarely considered—even by Christians—in a framework shaped by the language of sin and righteousness.

Christian Morality and Discipleship

Does this mean that Christians no longer can or should speak with moral certitude? Not at all. Jesus is still "the way, the truth, and the life" (John 14:6). As we learn from Jesus's declaration of purpose in Luke 4:18, and from the Beatitudes in Matthew 5:1–9, the stage for a discussion of Christian morality must be firmly anchored in language about imitation of Christ. The very nature of Christian morality is discipleship—not theoretical propositional statements. Put differently, Christ followers recognize that judgment is coming to those passing by the needy "on the other side" (Luke 10:31–33). As the parable of the good Samaritan reveals, Christian morality is not merely a truth to be claimed; it is a life to be lived.

Paul's approach to morality follows a similar pattern and is closely tied to his personal testimony. His own story becomes his strongest argument for the truthfulness of his message and convictions—revealed in a life other believers will do well to imitate (1 Cor 4:11–16; 11:1). Presenting morality claims in a narrative setting does not make them private; rather, it reveals that moral questions are interrelated and cannot be separated from a grand narrative. Attempting to tackle one moral question as though it did not relate to other moral questions will ultimately prove self-defeating.

Major movements in church history reveal the same pattern. The German reformer, Martin Luther, began what became the greatest reformation in the history of the church with this intensely personal statement: "Here I stand, I can do no other." Like Paul, his point was not to give a private statement—attempting to explain a moral conviction that was exclusive to him and maybe a few others who felt the same way. Rather, Luther recognized the truth of the Bible's grand narrative and concluded that his opponents had not.

The statements of Paul and Luther are powerful because they were not mere relative statements designed to express personal convictions that were true for them but might not be for others. They did not aim to give a modern plea for the supremacy of the individual's conscience. Rather, their words were intended to show that morality is inseparably connected to God's interaction with his creation. They offered an invitation to consider God's story (the biblical narrative) as the story that holds the greatest truth value, makes the most sense of reality, and delivers the grandest rationale for the whole human situation.

Christianity's Story and Moral Relativism Today

To our generation—a generation who considers its own individual stories and situations the most significant guide for morality—the NT language of imitation of Christ is an invitation to reconsider our story and to read it anew in light of the gospel story. It's an invitation to consider the biblical narrative for the evaluation of any question related to human life and morality. Moreover, it's an invitation to consider it the only story that gives a sufficient and comprehensive answer to the human situation.

Because God's story remains relentlessly relational, a narrative approach to morality offers the best critique of moral relativism. God's history with humanity reveals the benefits of Christ's work for the whole human situation. It views all questions through one narrative that is grounded in the story of creation and purpose, fall and redemption. And, as this narrative unfolds, it reveals the rising of a new horizon on which to evaluate yet unknown moral questions. Jesus's message that the kingdom of God is here already, though not fully, gives fresh light that helps us see the road forward. It offers secure footing and enables us to tackle new questions guided by the old truth.

For Christians who are concerned that the story is not sufficiently powerful as a guide for moral questions, Paul's farewell to the Ephesian elders (whose setting was as pluralistic as the most urban of modern cities) serves as a helpful reminder (Acts 20:32). Rather than arguing propositionally, Paul reminded his hearers how God's story had already given moral guidance to their situation (Acts 20:35). Then, full of confidence, he simply committed them "to God and to the word of his grace" (Acts 20:32).

A narrative approach to questions of morality requires keen awareness of God's grand story. It will prove an effective tool in combating moral relativism, which mostly seems to pick and choose from whatever appears to be the most convenient contemporary narrative.

Conclusion

Some argue that people's judgment is relative to something they hold to be true. Others argue that moral decision is anchored in what counts as evidence in various situations and for various people. There are, in other words, differing arguments for moral relativism. Engaging such a conversation from a propositional perspective proves inherently difficult.

Approaching issues of morality from a narrative perspective, however, opens fresh conversation and drives it to a pursuit of the best story—the best foundation and guide for moral decision making. It reveals the insufficiency of other smaller stories, and it empowers the church to be fruitful stewards of God's story. The church community is commissioned to translate his story into ways of living that connect with and transform the communities in which it is located. Doing so enables us to counter moral relativism because the story of Scripture is the truth about life.

ISSUES IN MEDICAL ETHICS

Joy Riley

Jesus said, "It is not those who are well who need a doctor, but those who are sick" (Matt 9:12). While Jesus's statement had to do with spiritual illness, it expresses a truism about the role of the medical profession. Though issues in the twenty-first century differ from those of the first, people who are ill still need a physician; treatments have a cost; and not all treatments are successful (Mark 5:25–26).

For centuries physicians have been influenced by the Hippocratic oath that forbade them to take actions that would cause abortion or the death of their patients, while also calling them to other standard behaviors and virtues. In recent decades, however, the oath has been repeatedly rewritten, and the physician-patient relationship has undergone transformation from a primarily covenantal to an essentially contractual one (William F. May, *The Physician's Covenant*). This has resulted in less trust in and greater demands on the medical community.

Christianity and Medical Care

How should Christian physicians respond to people who are ill or suffering, in the face of treatments that are often costly but not always successful?

First and foremost, the physician must recognize the *imago Dei*, the image of God, that each patient bears. Only when the medical professional understands another person as a fellow human can he offer appropriate treatment. The realization that all people, including physicians, are beloved creations of God establishes a vertical relationship that grounds all other relationships. The physician's equality with the patient establishes the proper horizontal plane of relationship. It is in this context of vertical and horizontal relationships that right actions can be taken (Nigel M. de S. Cameron, *The New Medicine*).

Second, physicians must be competent in their care of patients. While mere technique cannot a physician make, lack of competence is battery to some, and a disservice to all.

Third, a physician must be compassionate, but this term needs explanation. Compassion is not simply feeling sorry for someone or feeling what the sufferer is feeling. To exhibit compassion, one "suffers with" another. The compassionate physician, therefore, sees the suffering of the patient and identifies with it: to suffer is to experience at some level the finitude of this life—indeed, it is a common experience for all people (Daniel P. Sulmasy, *The Healer's Calling: A Spirituality for Physicians and Other Health Care Professionals*). Moreover, the Christian recognizes the reality of suffering that is shared with Christ, along with the comfort and redemption that comes from him (2 Cor 1:3–7; Heb 4:13–16).

Questions to Ask Regarding Difficult Issues

How, then, does the competent, compassionate physician, who recognizes the *imago Dei* in his patients, face the issues of abortion, euthanasia, physician-assisted suicide, stem cell therapies, or a myriad of other controversial issues related to the medical field? When patients are suffering from various maladies that seemingly could benefit from the well-placed suction or curette (abortion), the use of medications to end their pain (euthanasia or physician-assisted suicide), or the use of other humans as therapies (embryonic or fetal stem cells or parts), how does the physician show compassion? Is compassion simply giving someone—who images God and who is one's equal—what he or she desires? Is it always compassionate to relieve suffering?

Several tests may be applied in answering these questions. The physician should ask the following:

1. Am I recognizing the humanity of the person(s) involved?

Do I see the patient, or any individual involved in this situation, as fully human and as my moral peer? Does my definition of *human* depend on qualities expressed, the location of the person, or merely legal terms? These queries particularly apply to persons unborn, as well as to those considered incompetent by law or "nondecisional" by health care professionals.

2. Will my actions ensure that another human, of whatever age, unborn or living ex utero, does not come to harm?

Embryos used for research, including embryonic stem cell research, are inevitably destroyed.

3. If someone has already come to harm in order to produce that which I would need to use to help someone else, am I complicit in that harm?

This question is an appropriate one for the development of vaccines, as well as for any other process that uses embryonic or fetal cells.

4. Will taking an action maintain the horizontal position between the patient and myself as a physician, or would it elevate me to a vertical (and therefore, inappropriate) position in relationship to the patient?

Examples would include physician-assisted suicide or euthanasia.

5. Is the patient seen as someone made in the image of God or as a commodity to be bought or sold in this situation?

This is applicable to the use of sperm, eggs, embryos, or organ donors, as well as to surrogacy.

6. Am I devaluing or overvaluing the life of one person compared to another?

Such inappropriate valuation of human life occurs in abortion, embryonic stem cell research, and the selling of organs or other body parts.

7. Do I participate in protocols or activities that take precedence over rightly respecting human life?

Examples would be the use of embryonic stem cells in research or treatment; allowing patients to be evaluated as potential organ donors before being evaluated for treatment as patients themselves; failing to provide full disclosure for a proposed treatment; and financial affiliations with manufacturers or treatment facilities.

8. Am I treating others as a project or a means to an end, as opposed to ends in themselves?

Viewing others as a means to an end can occur at various times: seeking eggs, sperm, or womb donors (usually at a cost); forming in vitro embryos for research or treatment; prematurely declaring "dead" people whose organs could be used for transplantation.

9. Is a proposed action consistent with a stance of protecting life?

Abortion, the procurement of embryonic stem cells through the disruption and subsequent destruction of an embryo, physician-assisted suicide, and euthanasia all contravene the protection of living humans. Performing any of these actions is antithetical to a physician's training as a healer.

Conclusion

There are untold numbers of ways in which we, who are called to love the Lord our God with all our hearts, souls, and minds, and our neighbors as ourselves (Matt 22:37–40), can fail to do both. It is prudent to examine ourselves and to invite our Creator to examine our hearts, to see if there is any wicked way in us. He can lead us in the everlasting way (Ps 139:23–24).

World
Religions and
Competing
Worldviews

WHERE DID OTHER RELIGIONS COME FROM?

Winfried Corduan

The Bible never states how nonbiblical religions got their start. Genesis begins with the one true God. There certainly were people who lived in defiance of him (e.g., Cain and Lamech in Gen 4), but there is no account therein of people making substitutes for God. We know that Abraham's family had worshipped other gods in Ur (Josh 24:2), but when Abraham met Melchizedek (Gen 14:20), he turned out to be a priest of El Elyon, "God Most High," an expression that in this case clearly refers to Abraham's God (Dan 4:2,34; Num 24:16; Ps 78:35). We finally see mention of idols as they are brought up by Jacob's entourage (Gen 31:19; 35:4), but by then owning such objects is already an established pagan custom.

We see a major eruption of idolatry in Exodus 32—and it concerns the people of Israel themselves and the golden calf. The Bible assumes the nations worshipped false gods, but they are only mentioned when they directly affect the Hebrews. Scripture's concern is to trace the history of God's covenant people, and it does not immediately pay attention to other nations that do not worship him. Similarly, when we learn more about Canaanite religion, it is not in the context of condemnation of Baal worship per se (though it is certainly implied) but as a prohibition for God's people to worship him alone (Num 25:1–5). So there is no biblical narration of the historical origin of idolatry.

The Bible does make it clear that the reason for false religion was for people to seek independence from God or, more bluntly, to be their own gods. This attitude characterized the fall (Gen 3), when the serpent claimed that Adam and Eve could become like God and they were lured by the idea. The apostle Paul elaborates on this theme in Romans 1. He states that humans could know that there was a transcendent Creator who should receive their worship and gratitude. Yet they worshipped the creation instead. They applauded one another's genius, committed acts contrary to nature, and recruited others to join them.

This suggests a puzzle: if people wanted to rid themselves of God, why did they start to worship other gods and spirits? We will attempt to solve this puzzle in four steps.

1. First, one cannot excise from human nature our need to worship.

This fact was brought out clearly in the late nineteenth and early twentieth centuries during debates on the evolution of religion. Many scholars reasoned that the earliest religious beliefs must have been "primitive," consisting of the recognition of a magic force pervading the world or the veneration of ancestor ghosts. These scholars sought to prove their thesis by pointing to modern tribal cultures having little material sophistication, who practiced appeasement of spirits and magic rituals; they assumed their religion was akin to that of earliest humankind.

These scholars, however, did not differentiate among those cultures that accurately reflect the earliest cultures and those that had clearly diverged from a previous pattern. Subsequently, scholars such as Andrew Lang and Wilhelm Schmidt demonstrated that those cultures that were closest to original human culture actually held to monotheism along with a high standard of morality.

2. We live in a world that was created by God, and its very nature leads us to recognize the reality of the one who made it.

Many people come to this conclusion simply by an intuition based on the grandeur of the universe, its beauty and complexity, from the smallest level of subatomic particles to the largest realm of galaxies. These reflections can also be expressed rationally by means of the classic arguments for God's existence, that unless there is a God, this universe could not exist.

3. Some prominent atheists have conceded that they sometimes feel a need for a divine being in their lives.

For example, in the area of morality, we may have to choose between satisfying our own interests and doing what is right. Even people who do not believe in God as the Author of moral standards will usually still attempt to act morally. And so they are confronted with the fact that at times they have rationalized themselves into breaking the rules. In moments of clarity they may recognize that they have acted immorally or sinfully, and their wrong-doings affect other people as well as their own identities, consciences, and souls. Aware of their shortcomings and knowing that as humans they are unable to undo them, they must seek a superior being to forgive what they have done.

Anyone who goes through life with his eyes open recognizes that it is impossible to steer the ship of one's own life. A person may claim that God is unnecessary, but it is a different thing to maintain that stance when one's own child is sick, his crops fail, his marriage crumbles, or his life is in danger. In such times one realizes that he is not truly in control, so he takes recourse to spiritual powers.

4. But to which powers will one turn?

A person could pray to God, but he appears remote and not as someone with whom one can negotiate toward a desired outcome. On the other hand, in an animistic or polytheistic context, the powers are often weak and subject to manipulation; they come with the false promise that if one meets certain conditions, the desired solution will occur. So, even if the outcome should be negative, the person who turns to these powers feels he is some-how in control since the lack of success was his fault.

The monotheism of the earliest humans required a high level of behavior, but with little ritual attached to it. People made offerings as thanks and acts of devotion to God, but God did not need to be fed or persuaded to be good, and carrying out these simple ceremonies lay entirely in the hands of householders and patriarchs.

But as soon as people shifted away from worshipping the one true God toward gods with less knowledge and power, religion could become a profitable business. There arose experts, such as shamans or priests, on how to negotiate properly with the spiritual world. They claimed exclusive rights to the rituals, which they carried out mechanically, and bound people to their religion with fear.

Summary

While the Bible does not give us the history of false religion, it makes clear that the motivation for it was the quest for human autonomy. Nevertheless, the story of the Bible does offer all people reconciliation to the true God through the gift of his Son, Jesus Christ. Through Christ, true worship of God is made possible for all people, regardless of their spiritual history.

JUDAISM

Elijah M. Brown

"Listen, Israel: The LORD our God, the LORD is one. Love the LORD your God with all your heart, with all your soul, and with all your strength. These words that I am giving you today are to be in your heart. Repeat them to your children" (Deut 6:4–7).

These vibrant words continue to be recited by observant Jews as the central component of their daily morning and evening prayers. Known as the Shema, it is the dominant expression of the fundamental axioms of Judaism: (1) absolute monotheism, (2) unwavering and holistic love for God, and (3) steadfast commitment to the teachings of Scripture as rightly interpreted and applied.

History of Judaism

Repeated six times in just the book of Genesis, God entered into a special covenant relationship with Abraham and his Hebrew descendants with a promise of blessing should they remain faithful (Gen 12:1–3; 18:18–19; 22:17–18; 26:2–5; 28:13–15; 35:9–12). The Torah, meaning "teaching" or "law" and known in the OT as the Pentateuch, relays the Jewish understanding of creation, the election of Abraham and his family, the salvific redemption of the exodus, and the promulgation of the initial laws that form the foundation for faith. The *Nevi'im* (Prophets) and *Ketuvim* (Writings), subsequent sections in the Tanak, the Jewish acronym referencing the totality of the OT, offer an expanded understanding of faith as well as a theological reflection on the extent to which Jews historically embodied that faith.

Traces of modern Judaism are perhaps first located in the actions of Ezraa. As theologically interpreted by multiple prophets, repeated failures in monotheistic belief, corporate societal injustice, and individual unrighteousness resulted in seventy years of Babylonian exile beginning in 597 BC (Isa 28–30; 39–40; Jer 2–6; 25; Lam 1–2; Hab 1–2). When the Jews returned home to start a multigenerational process of painstaking restoration, a key architect was Ezraa. He is remembered today as the "Father of Judaism." This moniker stems from Ezraa's reestablishment of corporate ritual purity, Torah obedience, and protected ethnic homogenization maintained through marital endogamy, a practice that has helped the Jews remain a unique people group even in the midst of frequent dispersion (Ezra 8:15–10:17; Neh 8–10).

Additional developments following the years of Ezraa include a religious shift from temple, priestly, and sacrificial focus to lay-rabbinical leadership and prayer and faithful study of the Torah. This corresponded with the slow emergence of synagogues, "houses of assembly" for prayer and study, and the office of Pharisee and Sadducee. Perhaps most significantly was an intensification of theology anticipating a salvific Messiah who would fully restore the Jewish nation in the vein of King David that endures even today as an expectant but unfulfilled hope. For many Jews, a crucified and resurrected Jesus remains an anathema.

When Roman forces destroyed the Jerusalem temple in AD 70, allegiance to the divinely revealed law strengthened and transitioned. Rabbis began teaching that at Mount Sinai, God handed down a two-part revelation. The first was the installation of 613 laws codified in the Torah and divided into 248 positive commandments and 365 negative ones. Moses was also gifted with a second revelation: the Talmud. The Talmud is an "oral Torah" comprised of two major sections, the Mishnah and Gemara, imparted first by Moses, preserved by prophets, and sealed by qualified rabbis around AD 500. With sixty-three tractates, the Talmud is a central text of contemporary Judaism and channels the static, written laws of the Torah into an official interpretation of dynamic application to daily living that allows flexibility and ongoing adaptability of Jewish practice.

The razing of the temple further reinforced a migratory Diaspora of Jews living as minorities within other lands. Throughout medieval Europe, Jewish life ebbed and flowed often in newly emerging ghettos, special Jewish quarters frequently surrounded by walls with gates that closed at night. While this allowed the flourishing of a distinct ethnicity, religion, languages, and cultural customs within foreign lands, it foreshadowed darker measures. By the twentieth century, in many important respects, Eastern Europe, with its distinctive Yiddish dialect intermingling German and Hebrew, was the heart of Jewish civilization. Tragically, this time also corresponded to a mounting anti-Semitism.

By the middle of the twentieth century, two major developments were significantly altering contemporary Judaism. First was the emergence of Reform, Orthodox, and Conservative Judaic groups. Reform Judaism, among other changes, rescinded dietary laws, prayer shawls, and head coverings in an attempt to conform tradition to modern realities by emphasizing ethics over ritual. Orthodox Judaism, on the other hand, has continued a strict traditional belief in the binding character of the Torah and Jewish laws and resists efforts to amend or otherwise conform. Conservative Judaism has sought a delicate middle ground, balancing traditional adherence with cautious openness and adaptation.

The horrors of the Holocaust and the genocidal elimination of six million Jews was the second major development of the twentieth century. It considerably bolstered Zionism, a modern political movement to secure a permanent Jewish homeland in Palestine. Though initially contentious, Zionism was essential to the creation of the state of Israel in 1948, a process continuing to shape and divide the Middle East today.

Judaism Today

Though Reform, Orthodox, and Conservative Judaism have different approaches and emphases, Jews tend to agree that individuals are born with two intrinsic drives: *yetzer hatov*, the inclination to do good, and *yetzer hara*, the inclination to do evil. The latter inevitably results in sin, *averah*. *Yetzer hatov* leads individuals to obey the commandments of the Torah as interpreted by the Talmud and applied by the Halakhah, a Jewish legal tradition intended to govern every aspect of an individual's life and that of the community. In other words, when rightly interpreted, the *mitzvoth* (commandments) are not static but dynamic principles holistically applying to religious elements such as prayer and worship as well as to so-called secular areas such as male circumcision on the eighth day, Bar and Bat Mitzvahs celebrating adulthood, marriage, death and burial, the treatment of others, and food and its preparation. Halakhah is a lifestyle expecting external obedience leading to internal change.

To summarize, humanity needs to experience internal transformation, a process beginning with personal repentance completed by God who is

Creator and ultimate Redeemer, and maintained when individuals faithfully choose to obey the Torah *mitzvoth* as rightly interpreted by the Talmud and applied to daily life by the Halakhah or "the way of walking." Importantly, Reform, Conservative, and Orthodox Judaism expect different degrees of adherence and conformity to the Halakhah lifestyle. Individuals born into Judaism, which is a matrilineal religion, strive to live a life of obedience and worship of God. They are grateful for being born onto the path of salvation while non-Jews are welcomed to the faith through a process of conversion.

Key festivals and holy days as well as communal worship strengthen and reinforce adherence. The Sabbath (Shabbat) is the key weekly celebration beginning on Friday at sundown and ending at sundown on Saturday. Observant Jews use Friday evenings as occasion for communal services at local synagogues and spend the remainder of the Shabbat in rest. Other key celebrations include Rosh Hashanah (Jewish New Year, usually in September), Yom Kippur (a solemn day of repentance as the Day of Atonement), Sukkot (the Festival of Shelters, a celebratory autumn harvest festival), Hanukkah (an eight-day celebration known as the Festival of Lights), Passover (a spring festival focusing on new life with a highly symbolic familial meal called the Seder), and the Festival of Weeks (seven weeks after Passover commemorating the giving of the Torah).

At the heart of Judaism is the monotheistic worship of God. Prayer is most properly completed when offered in community and according to the appropriate prayer book, though individual, private, and spontaneous prayers are also encouraged. Prayer is further enhanced when complemented with a yarmulke (a head cap), tallit (a prayer shawl), and tefillin (a small black box containing the words of the Torah and attached to the forehead or arm by leather bands).

Worldwide, the number of messianic Jews remains small. According to Operation World, less than 2.5 percent of modern Israel is Christian. Given ongoing anti-Semitism and historical hostility, healthy interfaith dialogue and relationship building remains essential. Especially relevant, however, is the critical need to support Christian believers living within Israel—particularly those of Arab descent, who are often marginalized and caught in the crossfire of Arab-Israeli conflicts.

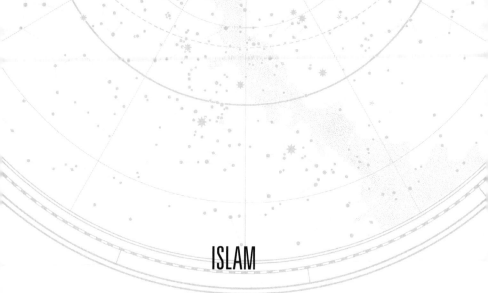

ISLAM

Michael H. Edens

Islamic culture is diverse. The unifying factors of this global people group are their common Islamic beliefs and the use of Arabic as the language of prayer. In this article, we will explore three important questions and Islamic answers.

Three Questions

1. Who is God?

Muslims believe the Creator God is a simple, indivisible Spirit who is far above relating to his creation. He has decreed and revealed Islam to be the religion of humanity.

There are problems with both parts of this belief, however. When a Muslim talks about God, his or her concept is different from God as presented by Jesus Christ and the Bible. Allah or "the God" is the only word used to translate the Bible's word for God in Arabic Bibles. Muslims will quickly point out that God has no one with him and that he is beyond having a Son.

In addition to their rejection of the incarnation of Jesus and God's entering into his own creation, they reject the biblical presentation of God who is simultaneously Father, Son, and Holy Spirit. This is regarded as polytheism, or more accurately, Tri-theism. Rather, Islam presents God as the transcendent, remote observer who is sovereign over all things, while the Bible portrays God as transcendent, sovereign, and intimate. These are significant differences related to who God is.

According to Muslims, God planned for humanity to worship through Islam from the beginning. They believe that even today all babies are born with an inclination toward Islam. The essential meaning of *Muslim* is "one who is submitted to God," and Christians agree that God wants all to submit to him. Nevertheless, we disagree on the plan for submission. The Bible teaches that God laid out a way back to himself before creation. In Islam, God simply forgives sin and lays out a plan for a worshipping community and a life of submission. For Muslims, knowing what God wants people to do is the whole purpose and content of God's revelation, the Qur'an. In the Bible, revelation presents the sovereign God choosing, before creation, to adopt sons and daughters through receiving his own personal self-sacrifice as the slain Lamb. The Bible is the story of God revealing himself to his creation.

2. What is humanity's problem?

Muslims believe that while people sin, these are actions against themselves and not against God. God can simply and mercifully absolve whom he pleases of sin. Sin is not seen as rebellion against him but as a mistake in a person's thoughts, attitudes, or actions.

In Islam, humanity is not damaged by Adam's sin to the extent that people cannot please God in this world. God will judge all human actions and will mercifully grant entrance into paradise to the faithful. Because the Muslim community externally reinforces correct Islamic behavior, many outsiders see the religion as teaching "works based" salvation. This, however, is incorrect. Entering paradise (salvation) is something based solely on God's decision. While he weighs all aspects of life, no action or attitude can assure a Muslim of entry into paradise except for dying in the cause of Islam. This lack of assurance causes most Muslims to think of God with abject fear that he would capriciously reject them. For this reason, Muhammad requested that Muslims pray for him because he did not know if God would allow him into paradise.

3. How does God communicate his solution with humanity?

The simple answer is through revelation (*wahy*) in which God's message was delivered to messengers (e.g., Moses, David, Jesus, and Muhammad) as well as hundreds of prophets. Islam teaches that each of the biblical messengers recognized and predicted the ministry of Muhammad. They point to two passages where they claim this happened but was masked by Christians and Jews. First, God promises the people of Israel a successor to Moses (Deut 18:15–22). The prophet is to be like Moses in that he is raised up from among the family of Israel. Muslims assume, incorrectly, that Muhammad's descent from Ishmael would qualify him for this role. Second, Jesus promises a Comforter to his disciples (John 14:16–17; 16:5–11). Muslims claim that there is a scribal error in this passage and that Muhammad was the promised one spoken of by Jesus. The problem with this interpretation is the context. Jesus offered an immediate and constant presence to guide his disciples as he was about to leave them by way of his death and resurrection. Muhammad's birth 600 years later would be no comfort to them at all.

The Worldview of Islam

The worldview of Islam is constructed differently from that of Christianity and of the West in general. A major element in the formation of a worldview is the way cultures make moral decisions. Western culture in general forms moral decisions based on innocence or guilt; Islamic cultures are based in honor or shame. Both types of cultures form moral values, but the basis for considering an action as "the right thing to do" is different. Generally, in the West, to say "it's the right thing to do" means that if you do this, people will see you as blameless and innocent. The parallel in Islamic cultures means that the action will bring honor to your clan—the extended family, nation, or the Islamic community—and will avoid shame. These principles inform and guide Muslims in developing cultural norms, values, and worldview. In short, Islam and Islamic culture are as complex as Christianity and as diverse as Western culture.

As for the place of reason in worldview formation, all Muslims limit the power of rational thought to build their religious communities and culture. This is why qur'anic statements that conflict with historical facts are not a problem for Muslims. In Islam, history is dwarfed in the presence of the Qur'an. This unquestioning attitude has spread to much qur'anic interpretation. Traditional explanations of truth have become very authoritative.

The content of Islamic revelation consists solely of God's decrees and desires. God's character and nature—other than the fact that he is a solitary Spirit—is not the subject of revelation. Furthermore, Islamic inspiration and transmission of the divine message differs from Christian revelation in several ways.

First, the concept of the Word of God is different for Muslims. Whereas the Bible is God's Word revealed to various persons he inspired throughout history, the Qur'an is understood to be the exact copy of a book of divine speech that is recorded in a permanent form, residing with God. The Arabic Qur'an was delivered to Muhammad by the angel Gabriel in a piecemeal fashion. The Qur'an essentially exists only in Arabic. All translations of the Qur'an are merely aids to understanding it.

Second, the content is different. The Bible seeks to reveal God and enable a relationship with him. The Qur'an seeks to reveal that God is one and that identifying someone as his associate is blasphemy. The Qur'an presents God's decrees to create a community that worships him accurately. The third element an Islamic-revealed book contains is witness to the preceding and succeeding messengers and books of revelation.

Finally, the Qur'an precludes the possibility of God becoming flesh and revealing himself personally. Thus, the speech of God is revealed by the angel Gabriel. But in Jesus Christ, God presents himself clearly by providing redemption through the cross and empty tomb.

HINDUISM

Elijah M. Brown

Hinduism is a religion with approximately 820 million adherents, constituting roughly 13.5 percent of the world's total population. All but 6 percent of Hindus live within India, a country with more than one billion people. India has twenty-two constitutionally recognized languages and is home to the cultural contributions of 2,234 unique people groups. India is truly a beautiful and diverse kaleidoscope.

History of Hinduism

The history of Hinduism falls into four successive eras. The first era, the Vedic Period, lasted from 1500 to 1000 BC. That roughly covers the time of the biblical exodus through the prophetic ministry of Samuel and the anointing of King Saul. In this period a migrant group known as the Aryans, or "noble ones," absorbed an older Indus Valley civilization and spoke Sanskrit, which remains the liturgical language of Hinduism. Hindus believe ancient seers and prophets heard and orally transmitted timeless truths during this Vedic Period. These eternal incantations were recognized as *shruti*, or divinely revealed teachings; they were codified into the authoritative Vedas. The oldest and most important is the Rig-Veda, which contains more than a thousand hymns and forms the sacred body of belief and practice for all Hindus. The remaining three collections (the Samaveda, Yajur Veda, and Atharvaveda) are used by priests and other specialists during worship rituals.

Further development of the scriptural canon occurred during Classical Hinduism (ca 1000–400 BC), the second great historical era. To the conclusion of each Veda was added an Upanishad containing philosophical and dialogical speculation about the relationship between the soul and eternal reality and the process of soul liberation. Brahmanas were also attached to each Veda as ritual commentaries offering further instruction about the use of the Vedas in worship. The Hindu scripture is thus an anthology comprised of four Vedas (hymns and incantations) with corresponding and supplemental Upanishads (philosophical and theological reflections) and Brahmanas (ritual instructions).

The Epic Era (400 BC to AD 400) was the third great historical period. Notable developments from that time include (1) the advent of yoga with various practices seeking inward withdrawal and release from the outer world, (2) the establishment of proper order within society based on karma and caste, and (3) the emergence of multiple epics which are popular and sometimes mythological stories meant to convey religious meaning. One well-known example is the Mahabharata epic; it contains the famous passage Bhagavad Gita, "Song of the Lord," and teaches soul liberation in the form of bhakti or total devotion and self-surrender to one god. (This represents a loose approximation of monotheism in practice, though not in theology.)

Continuing and Contemporary Transformation forms a fourth historical era. Since AD 400, Hinduism has undergone numerous developments. Partly as a response to the growth of British colonialism and Christian missionary activity within India, the nineteenth century sparked a major renewal of Hinduism that resulted in far greater systemization in terms of theology, religious practice, and worldview. The twentieth century witnessed meaningful popularization of Hinduism within Euro-American contexts largely because of immigration, the historical importance of Mahatma Gandhi, and an amorphous spirituality propagated by some Western gurus.

Key Beliefs of Hinduism

Similar to other Eastern faiths and in contrast to a more linear view of history found in areas influenced by the Abrahamic religions, Hindus believe the universe undergoes cyclical processes of creation and destruction that lead to innumerable universes. In this view, the current age, Kali Yuga, began around 3000 BC and is destined for destruction and replacement after 432,000 years.

The supreme reality beyond this cyclical process of never-ending birth and death is Brahman. To know and be absorbed into Brahman, which is eternal, transcendent, and without limitation, is the ultimate goal of Hinduism.

Brahman is sometimes described as netti, *netti* meaning "neither this, neither that" to indicate the inherent impossibility of either human language or any singular divine manifestation to express the full totality of the actual reality of Brahman. Hinduism can therefore be described as monotheistic polytheism. There is one supreme reality (monotheistic) revealed through multiple gods and divine manifestations (polytheism) in order to convey the various characteristics and nuances of this one reality. Though there are more than 3,000 gods within the Hindu corpus, each god is properly understood as a limited manifestation of Brahman. Several of the most important gods include Vishnu, the preserver of the cosmos; Shiva, the divine dancer of creation and destruction; Durga or Devi, the protector from evil; Ganesha, the elephant-headed god presiding over obstacles; Lakshmi, the goddess of prosperity and good fortune; and Krishna, an avatar or human incarnation of Vishnu who established order in a time of chaos.

Hinduism and Christianity

Given theological emphases and narratives attached to each god, the pantheon can seem vague, confusing, and overlapping to the uninitiated. This amalgamation emerges from a Hindu concentration on eternal truths residing outside of time rather than on concrete historicity. This is a significant divergence from Christianity's claim in 1 John 1:1–4 that Jesus was not simply a spiritual manifestation but lived in a verified historical context as a full human who was heard, seen, observed, and physically touched. While Hinduism teaches that Brahman can only be known indirectly and in a nonpersonal manner, Christianity categorically confesses Jesus as the full and complete incarnation of God (John 1:1–18; 1 Cor 8:5–6; Col 1:15–20) with whom there can be a personal relationship (John 3:16; Rom 10:9–10; 1 John 4:9–10).

Furthermore, Christianity has a rather high view of the physical body, declaring in 1 Cor 6:19–20 that one's "body is a temple of the Holy Spirit" meant to "glorify God." Hinduism, on the other hand, understands the physical body as part of the bondage from which liberation is demanded. Each individual is comprised of an atman, or eternal soul, placed within the receptacle of a physical body that can be human, animal, or plant depending on the soul's accrued karma. Karma is a neutral mechanism based on the actions one performed in previous lives. Inappropriate actions result in "hot" karma adversely affecting the future of each atman, while appropriate actions cause "cool" karma that ensures higher birth. The hope is to gain enough "cool" karma over many lifetimes in order to be born into a high enough state that gaining the liberating knowledge of Brahman is possible.

Thus, the main problem for Hinduism is not "hot" karma or sin per se, but ignorance—and in particular ignorance of Brahman as the one and supreme reality in which everything is in fact already encompassed. Liberation, called moksha, is attained through the absolute elimination of all desire, total inward withdrawal, and a deep experiential realization, or knowledge, that one's true self is already part of Brahman. Such knowledge can be gained through meditation that uses the sacred sound of Om, bodily renunciation and restraint, yoga and inward reflection, living according to the right dictates of one's caste, celebrating key festivals such as Diwali and Holi, participating in ritual worship at Hindu temples, engaging in personal and daily worship to an image of a god, and absolute love and self-surrender to a singular god (*bhakti*) in order to gain the knowledge of that particular aspect of Brahman. The path of salvation is therefore open to all individuals. But in reality, liberation from the painful and ongoing cycle of birth and death can only be achieved over many lifetimes and only by a few individuals at any particular historical moment.

The Hindu worldview can thus be summarized: the divinely revealed timeless truths of scripture (*shruti*) teach that knowledge of Brahman (the one supreme reality) brings liberation (*moksha*) for the individual, eternal soul (*atman*) from the painful cycle of samsara (a continuous and cyclical process of birth and death based on karma).

Against this Hindu worldview, Christianity offers a gospel of immediate salvation through a grace-filled personal relationship with Jesus, the unique fullness of God, and a salvation that does not deny the goodness of God's physical creation but promises its ultimate redemption (Rom 8:18–25).

Given that less than 7 percent of India claims Christianity, multifaith dialogue remains essential—as does prayer for bold, humble, and protected public witness (Eph 6:19–20) in the midst of sporadic but regular Christian persecution emerging out of the close connection between Hinduism and Indian nationalism. According to Operation World, of the 639 worldwide unreached and unengaged people groups having a population of at least ten thousand, almost 75 percent are located within India.

MONISM, PANTHEISM, AND PANENTHEISM

Paul Copan

In 1983 actress Shirley MacLaine, a proponent of New Age spirituality, wrote this in her book titled *Out on a Limb*: "The tragedy of the human race was that we had forgotten that we were each Divine. You are everything. Everything you want to know is inside of you. You are the universe" (p. 347). This viewpoint is known as pantheism—the worldview claiming that all or everything (*pan*) is God (*theos*)—and God is everything. They are identical.

Pantheism and Monism

We should differentiate pantheism from monism ("one-ism"). Certain Hindus hold to monism—as do Zen Buddhists and philosophical and religious schools in other traditions.

For example, certain Hindu scriptures known as *The Upanishads* affirm that the soul (*atman*) is really God (*Brahman*). Importantly, Brahman isn't some personal Creator, as theistic religions claim. Rather, Brahman is pure consciousness. Just imagine emptying your mind of all content and distinction. Let's say it's completely blank—that you make no distinctions between yourself and, for instance, the Empire State Building and that your thinking is without any impressions, moral judgments, emotions, or logical reasoning. That is the featureless, quality-less Brahman. This version of Hinduism (*Advaita Vedanta*) affirms that pure consciousness is the only reality there is; everything else—including a physical world—is an illusion. The Hindu philosopher Shakara, who died in AD 820, held this view.

Let's imagine that monism is symbolized by a circle with nothing in it—a oneness without differentiation. By contrast, think of a circle with little clearly defined circles or squares within it—oneness with differentiation. This symbolizes pantheism: differences exist within "God." This view was held by the Hindu philosopher Ramanuja, who died in AD 1137.

Assessing Monism

How do we begin to assess these viewpoints? Let's consider monism first. This view is deeply problematic because it tells us to deny what seems so obvious to us—that a world of tables, chairs, trees, and stones exists outside our minds—and to accept what seems utterly contrary to our everyday experience. After all, we each have to deal with traffic jams, grumpy people, and finding a restroom—all experiences that assume a distinct reality outside of our minds. So why deny what seems so undeniable? Why embrace a worldview that seems so counterintuitive?

Consider these questions, too: Don't monists read and write books? Aren't they trying to persuade other minds to believe what they do? And what gave rise to the illusion in the first place if all reality is undifferentiated oneness? And isn't the illusory belief in differences itself real? What are we to make of the psychotic, whose problem is being out of touch with the real world outside of his mind? Or what about AIDS, pollution, or crime? Surely these aren't just an illusion? It would be irresponsible and immoral not to do anything about them by claiming they don't exist. When pondered critically, monism seems more like an escapism that avoids the world's difficult problems. It just makes better sense to affirm the reality of a world outside the mind since there is no good reason to deny it.

Furthermore, monism must ultimately deny real differences between good and evil: were Adolf Hitler's concentration camps and Joseph Stalin's labor camps just an illusion, and is there no difference between these horrific tyrants and Mother Teresa? Monism also must reject logical thinking, which makes distinctions between logical error or fallacies and sound reasoning. One sixth-century Zen Buddhist poem is very telling: "If you want to get to the plain truth / Be not concerned with right and wrong. / The conflict between right and wrong / Is the sickness of the mind" (*Hsin-hsin Ming* by Seng-ts'an, quoted in *The Way of Zen* by Alan Watts). These considerations expose some of the deep problems of monism.

Assessing Pantheism

What about pantheism, to which Shirley MacLaine subscribes? While pantheism is right to emphasize real differences that exist, it suffers from the fact that evil really exists in the world. Pantheism, therefore, must acknowledge that evil is somehow part of "God."

But a further problem then emerges: if evil is part of God, why try to change anything about it since we can't truly improve on God, can we? And from a practical point of view, this would lead to fatalism—that there's nothing we ought to do to change things since everything is part of God and we just need to accept this.

Panentheism

Pantheism differs from panentheism ("all in God"), in which the world and God exist in an eternal interdependent relationship. This view is sometimes called "process theology." (Noted process theologians include Alfred North Whitehead, Charles Hartshorne, and John Cobb.) Some panentheists will compare God's relationship to the world as the soul's relationship to the body. God doesn't exist without the world, and the world doesn't exist without God. Rather than being sovereign over the world, God attempts to influence or direct the world. And unlike the biblical view of God who is faithful and unchanging in his nature, process theology emphasizes an ever-changing, ever-improving god. In panentheism, God does not create a universe out of nothing: the universe is eternal along with God.

Some philosophers of science adopting panentheism (Arthur Peacocke, Ian Barbour, Philip Clayton) have marginally attached themselves to biblical themes and doctrines. Yet they deny the fundamental importance of creation out of nothing. And many thinkers adopting this type of model of God's relationship to the world reject a God who is "sovereign" and who "rules over" creation. Why? Because this model of God can lead to oppressing others and to destroying creation.

Assessing Panentheism

Think of the topic this way: if everything is changing—including God, as well as individual human persons—how can a person possess moral responsibility? After all, since "I" am not the same person "I" was twenty or thirty years ago, "I" can't be held responsible for anything "I" did back then.

But this idea of constant flux (much like Buddhism's doctrine of impermanence) is itself flawed. After all, the claim that everything is perpetually changing is itself a permanent, unchangeable doctrine. Also, change presupposes sameness since something is moving from one state to another (like a leaf's color changing from green to red in the fall).

Moreover, panentheism not only rejects the biblical doctrine of creation out of nothing (cp. Gen 1:1); it flies in the face of contemporary science, which indicates that matter, energy, space, and time came into existence with a big bang—in striking support of Genesis 1:1. In other words, if the universe began to exist, then God and the world could not be interdependent. Unlike the everlasting God, the universe is not eternal (Ps 102:25–26); rather, it is winding down after having been wound up in a sense, according to the second law of thermodynamics. No, the world is not God's body.

Further, panentheism diminishes God's transcendence (his distinction from the world) at the expense of God's immanence (his nearness to his creation). Panentheism presents God as a needy, dependent entity rather than the self-sufficient, all-powerful God of Scripture (Ps 50:12). The Bible affirms that God is both transcendent and immanent, and he needs nothing outside himself.

Finally, panentheism fails to take seriously a biblical understanding of the triune God, who is inherently relational and self-giving. Because God is relational by nature (as Father, Son, and Spirit—the "divine family"), he creates with relationship in mind. God engages with humans on the stage of history; he suffers with humans and even endures great suffering on the cross. The biblical God is not detached; rather, he gets his hands dirty, faces injustice and evil, and overcomes them by dying naked on the cross in weakness but rising from the dead in power.

Philosophy and the Trinity

In large part, the history of philosophy has been an attempt to make sense of the relationship between "the one" and "the many." The pre-Socratic philosopher Parmenides argued for one unchanging reality (no plurality). By contrast, another pre-Socratic, Heraclitus, said that you can't step into the same river twice; everything is in flux, always changing. On the side of Parmenides, monism and pantheism express the one without the many—unity at the expense of significant distinction. In panentheism, we have continual flux in the world and in God, and there is nothing fixed and enduring that unites all of these changes—the many without the one.

By contrast, the Christian doctrine of the Trinity affirms both the many and the one—a robust unity and plurality: God is three persons sharing the same nature in one being. In God, we have an explanation for the universe—a coherent unity amid diversity. This impacts everyday life as well. For example, the Christian can also affirm the place of the community (the body of Christ) and the significance of the individual (e.g., the Christian's spiritual gifts within that body) so that neither swallows up the other. Biblical theism brings together what pantheism, monism, and panentheism cannot.

AGNOSTICISM AND SECULARISM

Robert M. Bowman Jr.

The term *agnosticism* derives from the Greek word *gnosis*, meaning "knowledge," with the prefix *a–* meaning "not" and the suffix *–ism* meaning "belief." In a generic sense, agnosticism can mean the belief that one does not or cannot know something, whatever that might be (e.g., someone may be "agnostic" about whether humans will ever travel to other planets).

Its original and most common usage, however, is specifically in reference to the belief that humans cannot know whether God exists. T. H. Huxley (1825–1895) coined the term in 1869 to denote his own belief that questions about the reality of nonempirical concepts such as God's existence or life after death were "insoluble," beyond the capacity of human minds to know. David Hume (1711–1776) had argued that it was never rational to believe that a miracle had occurred, regardless of the apparent evidence for it. Immanuel Kant (1724–1804) had argued that all of the philosophical proofs for God's existence failed. With the rise of evolutionary theory, for which Huxley was a noted advocate, arguments for God's existence from nature also seemed to have been overturned. The result was that in the second half of the nineteenth century, many people felt that there were no good reasons to accept religion or belief in God.

So-called soft or weak agnostics are unsure as to whether God exists, but they do not think the question is necessarily beyond investigation. So-called hard or strong agnostics like Huxley, on the other hand, are convinced that such questions are in principle unanswerable; they believe the nature of the problem is such that no one can know whether God exists.

Agnosticism and Atheism

The boundary between agnosticism and atheism is a fuzzy one. Agnostics have often denied being atheists while stating in one way or another that they disbelieve in God.

For example, Robert Ingersoll (1833–1899), in an 1896 lecture entitled "Why I Am an Agnostic," explained that while he did not know if there was a God, he believed there was "no supernatural power that can answer prayer—no power that worship can persuade or change—no power that cares for man." The belief that there is no supernatural power that can answer prayer would seem to qualify as a type of atheism.

On the other side, atheists often define *atheism* not as the dogmatic assertion of God's nonexistence but as the lack of belief that God exists— it's a lack of belief, however, they try to justify rationally. In his book *The God Delusion*, atheist Richard Dawkins proposed a continuum between strong theism (belief that God certainly exists) and strong atheism (belief that God certainly does not exist), with agnosticism in the midrange of the continuum. Dawkins considered himself to be very close to strong atheism with only modest reservation. He said, "I cannot know for certain but I think God is very improbable, and I live my life on the assumption that he is not there" (73). Dawkins's statement here is actually fairly representative of most people who identify themselves as agnostics: they disavow certainty as to God's nonexistence, but they feel confident in living their lives on the assumption that he is not there.

Agnosticism and Christianity

The Bible presents a two-pronged response to disbelief in God, whether cast as agnosticism or atheism. First, Scripture teaches that God has made himself known through the natural world. People who reject God "suppress the truth," because since the creation of the world "his invisible attributes, that is, his eternal power and divine nature, have been clearly seen . . . being understood through what he has made. As a result, people are without excuse" (Rom 1:18,20; see also Neh 9:6; Ps 19:1–6; Acts 17:24–28). Recent advances in science furnish abundant evidence in support of the Bible's teaching on this point. It is now beyond reasonable doubt that the universe had a beginning, and the evidence is mounting that life was initiated on earth by a supremely intelligent Creator.

Second, God has acted to reveal himself even more directly in order to restore humans to a relationship with him. He did so by speaking to various individuals such as Abraham and Moses, by miraculously freeing the Israelites from their bondage in Egypt, and by demonstrating his sovereign rule in Israel's history (Gen 12:1–3; 17:1–5; Exod 3; Deut 4:32–39; Neh 9:7–15; Isa 43:10–13). God has supremely revealed himself in Jesus Christ, who is God the Son incarnate (John 1:1–18). The Bible itself is a collection of writings inspired by God the Holy Spirit, who spoke through human authors (2 Tim 3:15–17; 2 Pet 1:20–21). This same Spirit illuminates people's minds to accept God's revelation of the good news of Jesus Christ (1 Cor 2:10–16).

Agnosticism and Secularism

Secularism as a worldview attempts to state positively what can be believed once one has concluded that life should be lived on the assumption that God is not there. The English word *secular* (from the Lat *saeculum*, meaning "age," "world") means anything pertaining to regular, earthly, mundane life (work, marriage, family, politics), as distinguished from religious or sacred matters (church, prayer, theology, Scripture). In this classic sense, there is nothing wrong or controversial about something being called secular.

Secularism, however, is a belief that all of human life and society should be secular. George Holyoake (1817–1906), who coined the term in 1851, defined it to mean "giving the precedence to the duties of this life, over those which pertain to another world" (*Christianity and Secularism*). Secularism focuses on the material world, seeks knowledge through science alone, and separates morality from religion.

In the twentieth century, secularism came to be known by the term *secular humanism*: this designation is understood as a positive, life-affirming worldview that inculcates such values as tolerance, respect, and kindness without any religious or spiritual foundation. Groups of influential secularists issued statements advocating their worldview in a work entitled *Humanist Manifesto I* (1933) and *Humanist Manifesto II* (1973). Secular humanists include both self-described agnostics and atheists.

Secularism and Secularization

Secularism is closely associated in the modern world with secularization, so much so that the two terms are often used synonymously or interchangeably. To be precise, secularism is a belief or worldview whereas secularization is a corresponding movement or social process. Specifically, *seculariza-*

tion is the process of removing religious, theological, or spiritual elements or influences from various aspects of society. The "separation of church and state" is an example of secularization.

The older, more moderate secularization removed ecclesiastical control or authority from government, as in the United States Constitution's Bill of Rights prohibiting the imposition of a religious test by the government on any candidate or official. The newer, more radical secularization is an overt campaign to bar religious expression or influence in government, politics, or civic matters—as in efforts to remove references to the Ten Commandments from government properties or to prohibit schoolteachers from expressing religious opinions in state-funded classrooms.

Moderate secularization was driven by the belief that religious institutional control of government, as when states recognized specific Christian denominations as the official state religion, interfered with the free expression and practice of religion in public life by those with different religious beliefs. Radical secularization, on the other hand, is driven by the belief that religious beliefs and values should have no influence in public life and so should be marginalized and limited wherever and as much as possible. This radical secularization, then, presupposes secularism as a worldview; it assumes that religious or spiritual beliefs and values are of no practical significance or benefit to society.

Secularism and Christianity

Secularism presupposes that God either does not exist or is irrelevant to human life, assumptions countered by the Bible's teaching noted above that God has made himself known in many ways. Scripture is clear that every aspect of life is to be seen in the light of the Creator. Followers of Jesus seek God's kingdom above all else (Matt 6:33). Their whole lives are geared toward loving God and other people (Mark 12:28–31). Far from irrelevant to society, a biblical worldview is the foundation of an enlightened view of relationships between men and women and of social matters of class and ethnicity (Gal 3:28).

Agnosticism and secularism are in the end unrealistic ways of viewing the world. The biblical worldview, according to which God exists, humans are fallen in sin, and God is at work to restore our relationship with him (Ps 14), is the only sound foundation for life.

THE NEW ATHEISM

R. Albert Mohler Jr.

The New Atheism is now an established feature of the intellectual landscape of our age. Thinkers such as Richard Dawkins, Daniel Dennett, Sam Harris, and the late Christopher Hitchens are among the figures most regularly featured on the front tables of America's bookstores and on the front pages of our newspapers.

Atheism is not a new concept. Even the OT speaks of the one who tells himself in his heart, "There's no God" (Ps 14:1). Atheism, however, became an organized and publicly recognized worldview in the wake of the Enlightenment. It has maintained a foothold in Western culture ever since.

Prior to the development of the theory of evolution, there was no way for an atheist to settle on any clear argument for why the cosmos exists or why life forms appeared. Charles Darwin changed all that. The development of Darwinian evolution offered atheism an invaluable intellectual tool—an alternate account of beginnings. Richard Dawkins, perhaps the world's best-known evolutionary scientist, argues that the explanation offered by a frustrated atheist before Darwin "would have left one feeling pretty unsatisfied" (*The Blind Watchmaker*, 6).

Darwin's theory of natural selection and the larger dogma of evolution emerged in the nineteenth century as the first coherent alternative to the Bible's doctrine of creation. This revolution in human thinking is well summarized by Dawkins, who conceded that an atheist prior to Darwin would have to offer an explanation of the cosmos and the existence of life that would look something like this: "All I know is that God isn't a good explanation, so we must wait and hope that somebody comes up with a better one."

In a single sentence, Dawkins gets to the heart of the matter: "Darwin made it possible to be an intellectually fulfilled atheist."

Nevertheless, atheists have typically represented only a small (if vocal) minority of Americans. Surveys estimate that atheists represent less than 3 percent of the population, although those "unaffiliated" with any religion is nearly 20 percent. As a worldview, atheism is overrepresented among the intellectual elites, and atheists have largely—though not exclusively—talked to their own.

Until now. The New Atheists have emerged as potent public voices. They write best-selling books, appear on major college and university campuses, and extend their voices through institutional and cultural influence.

The New Atheism is not just a reassertion of atheism. It is a movement that represents a far greater public challenge to Christianity than that posed by the atheistic movements of previous times. Adherents see science as on their side, arguing that scientific knowledge in general, and evolutionary theory in particular, is our only true knowledge. They argue that belief in God is organized ignorance, that theistic beliefs lead to violence, and that atheism is liberation. They are shocked and appalled that Americans refuse to follow the predictions of the secularization theorists, who had assured the elites that belief in God would be dissolved by the acids of modernity. They have added new (and important) arguments to the atheistic arsenal.

Dawkins, for example, not only believes that Darwinism made it possible to be an intellectually fulfilled atheist, but he also argues that religious belief is actually dangerous and devoid of credibility. Thus, he argues not only that Darwinism made it possible for an atheist to be intellectually fulfilled but that the theory of evolution undermines belief in God. In other words, Dawkins asserts that Darwinism makes it impossible to be an intellectually fulfilled Christian.

Daniel Dennett, another of the "Four Horsemen" of the New Atheism, has argued that Darwin's theory of evolution is a "universal acid" that will burn away all claims of the existence of God. His confidence in Darwinism is total. Dennett is honest enough to recognize that if evolutionary theory is true, it must eventually offer an account of *everything* related to the question of life. Thus, evolution will have to explain every aspect of life, from how a species appeared to why a mother loves her child.

As we might expect, the theory of evolution is used to explain that there must have been a time when belief in God was necessary in order for humans to have adequate confidence to reproduce. Clearly, Dennett believes we should now have adequate confidence to do so without belief in God.

Sam Harris, also a scientist by training, pushes the argument even further than Dawkins and Dennett. Harris has argued that belief in God is such a danger to human civilization that religious liberty should be denied in order that science might reign supreme as the intellectual foundation of human society. The last of the "Four Horsemen," author Christopher Hitchens used his considerable wit to ridicule belief in God, which he, like Dawkins and Harris, considered downright dangerous to humanity.

The dogma of Darwinism is among the first principles of the worldview offered by the New Atheists. Darwin replaces the Bible as the great explainer of the existence of life in all of its forms. The New Atheists are not merely dependent on science for their worldview; their worldview amounts to *scientism*—the belief that modern naturalistic science is the great unifying answer to the most basic questions of human life.

As Richard Dawkins has argued, they feel that disbelief in evolution should be considered intellectually disrespectable and as reprehensible as denial of the Holocaust. Thus, their strategy is to use the theory of evolution as a central weapon in today's context of intellectual combat.

The New Atheists write from positions of privilege, and they know how to package their ideas. Books by Richard Dawkins and Christopher Hitchens have spent weeks and months on the best-seller list published by *The New York Times*. They know that the most important audience is the young, and they are in a position to reach young people with their arguments.

The New Atheism has exploited an opening presented by significant and seismic changes in prevailing patterns of thought. We must acknowledge that most educated persons living in Western societies now inhabit a cultural space in which the conditions of belief have been radically changed. Whereas it was once impossible not to believe in God and later possible not to believe, for millions of people today, the default position is that it is impossible to believe.

In terms of our own Christian evangelistic and apologetic mandate, it is helpful to acknowledge that only a minority of those we seek to reach with the gospel truly and self-consciously identify with atheism in any form. Nevertheless, the rise of the New Atheism presents a seductive alternative for those inclined to identify more publicly and self-consciously with organized nonbelief. The far greater challenge for most of us, then, is to communicate the gospel to persons whose minds are more indirectly shaped by these changed conditions of belief.

The church must respond to the challenge of the New Atheism with the full measure of conviction and not with mere curiosity. We must remember that the church has faced a constellation of theological challenges throughout its history. Then, as now, our task is to articulate, communicate, and defend the Christian faith with intellectual integrity and evangelistic urgency. We should not assume that this task will be easy, and we must also refuse to withdraw from public debate and private conversation in light of this challenge.

In the final analysis, the New Atheism presents the Christian church with a great moment of clarification. The New Atheists do, in the end, understand what they are rejecting, as Paul's teaching in Romans 8:18–22 makes plain. Further, when Sam Harris defines true religion as that "where participants' avowed belief in a supernatural agent or agents whose approval is to be sought" is met, he understands what many mired in confusion do not. The only god who matters is a supernatural God—a personal God—who will judge. In the end, the existence of the supernatural, self-existent, and self-revealing God is the only starting point for Christian theology. God possesses all of the perfections revealed in Scripture, or there is no coherent theology presented in the Bible.

The New Atheists are certainly right about one very important thing— it's atheism or biblical theism. There is nothing in between.

POLYTHEISM IN BIBLICAL TIMES

Kenneth A. Mathews

Polytheism is the belief in or worship of many deities. Polytheism as a system reigned in the ancient world. One celebrated exception to polytheism was the revolution of Pharaoh Akhenaten in the fourteenth century; he elevated Aten (the sun disk) while outlawing the worship of other gods. Nevertheless, this was not a true expression of monotheism and also was short-lived.

Why Polytheism?

Why did the peoples of the nations almost universally, except for the Israelites, accept the idea of polytheism? First, the concept of many deities may be traceable to the original idea of monotheism (the existence of only one god). That all the deities ultimately had an origin in a primeval force or god suggests an original idea of monotheism. The deities themselves were born, so to speak. This concept may have had sociological as well as philosophical motives. The gods functioned as go-betweens, bridging the gap between the community and the Creator source. These intermediary deities provided a vital connection with the original primeval material.

Second, and more importantly, polytheism resulted from a spiritually corrupt mind. The apostle Paul explained: "For though they [the nations] knew God, they did not glorify him as God or show gratitude. Instead, their thinking became worthless, and their senseless hearts were darkened" (Rom 1:21).

Features of Polytheism

There were many features of polytheism held in common across the spectrum of ancient religions.

1. Polytheism was closely connected with what today is understood as the "natural world."

The material entities of the universe were filled with the power of the deities, that is, the supernatural. The ancients, however, did not differentiate between the natural world, which is governed by the cause and effect of natural forces, and the supernatural world, which is the sphere of the gods. Deities and "natural" beings (e.g., sun) and forces (e.g., wind) were interdependent. In the viewpoint of polytheism, for example, there was a link between the function of the sun and the existence of the sun deity. For the universe to provide a habitat for life and for the afterlife, the corresponding deities to each facet of nature must be functioning.

2. Since the gods were supreme in power, humans feared them and sought ways to engender favorable treatment. Ritual worship, especially incantations and sympathetic magic, were essential patterns of worship.

Specialization accompanied ritual worship, giving rise to temples, priests, and formulaic rites of sacrifice. Hymns of praise and confessions of offense also characterized human efforts to manipulate the activities of the deities.

3. The deities were sexual, male and female deities.

This facet reflected the human makeup of two genders and mirrored the human means of producing and sustaining life. Sexual relations between the deities were necessary for the world to continue its natural cycles of existence: life and death, rain and drought, and fecundity and infertility. Sexual union between deities was also a common explanation for the origin of lesser gods. The sexual character of pagan gods was mirrored in human worship by cultic prostitution and deviant sexual practices.

4. Polytheism assumed a community of gods that was hierarchical.

At the highest level were the cosmic deities who exercised universal rule and who determined the fate of the lesser gods and of humans. One deity ruled over the pantheon, such as the Greek god Zeus who was over the twelve gods of Olympus. Polytheism included intermediary deities who were connected with specific activities (e.g., storm gods) or environmental spheres (e.g., sea gods) or were patron deities (of the state). The idea of a pantheon, in fact, imitated the social institutions of family and state. Family religion consisted of worshipping local deities close to the common person as part of family and ancestral heritage (e.g., household gods, cp. teraphim, Gen 31:19). State religion, however, was at the national level and involved the patron deity of the royal house, such as Babylon's chief deity, Marduk. State religion was typically syncretistic, but ultimately a single deity received foremost attention. Patron deities were therefore associated with specific people groups and territorial lands. The concept of a pantheon also permitted the addition of new deities when nations entered into treaty or a nation defeated a rival.

5. Although the gods were inextricably tied to the natural order, they also impacted the direction of history.

Nations attributed their victories to the national god. The Moabite Stone, for example, gives credit to the god Chemosh for Moab's victory over Israel's king Ahab (ninth century BC). Nevertheless, the nations primarily viewed history as a cyclical pattern. History did not have an ultimate goal; there was no overarching plan for the development of history.

6. The personalities of the gods were anthropomorphic; they paralleled the character of humans.

The gods routinely exhibited the same range of activities and emotions, such as procreation, daily activities, love, and anger. Patron deities supported the welfare of the people if the people fulfilled their responsibilities to the gods, including veneration and cultic performance. Worship involved prayers of praise and of confession so as to achieve favor and produce a stable, predictable relationship between a god and an individual or society. Commonly, the gods behaved capriciously, keeping their adherents uncertain of their favor. Divine anger was appeased through cultic rites. Babylonian and Egyptian literature, for example, contemplated the source of evil and injustice but they offered no resolution to the problems. There was no certainty that moral equity would win out in the end. The gods were selfish by nature, creating humans solely to serve their own interests. Humans built cities to the glory of the gods and provided animal sacrifices to feed them.

7. Accompanying polytheism were myths (stories) regarding the gods.

Myths were not essentially intended to entertain. Rather, the concept of myth explained present reality; it gave a timeless picture of human society's institutions. The pantheon had a ruling god, king of the gods, and this supreme deity enjoyed a stately palace or temple and the loyalty of the lesser deities. This ideological template justified the hierarchy and hegemony of the state.

8. Polytheism universally involved images (idols) of the gods that were made of various materials like wood, clay, or metal.

Images were not the same as the gods; rather, they were inhabited by the gods. Images were alive in that sense, and they linked the human worshiper and the god (cp. Isaiah's parody on image making, 44:9–20). The Jews were accused of being atheists because they did not have an image in their temple. Christians, too, were accused of atheism because they did not worship Roman gods and bow to the imperial cult (for the Christian view of idols, see 1 Cor 8:4; 10:19–21).

SPIRITUALISM

Felix Theonugraha and Zachs Gaiya

Spiritualism is the belief that an individual can exert control on one's world through worship of spirits. Spiritualism believes the world consists of two interconnected realms: the spiritual realm and the material realm. Events in the material realm can be explained through a system of good and evil spirits at work. Spirits, ancestors, ghosts, witches, and other supernatural beings are believed to interfere with and interact with human life. Thus, they must be appeased or coerced in exchange for prosperity and a good life.

At its core, spiritualism is a human attempt to understand the misfortunes of life and to exert a semblance of authority over life. It seeks to effectively answer these questions: What is the meaning of life on earth, and how can death be explained? How can one attain a good life? How does one explain accidents and calamities? How does one plan for the future in the midst of many unknowns? How does a community of people maintain a moral order and deal with violations of community ethics?

Scripture clearly forbids human attempts at divination through the spirit world. Necromancy, defined as attempts to predict the future through contact with the dead, is forbidden in the OT (Lev 2:5–8; 19:31) and is considered detestable (Deut 18:9–14). King Saul, frustrated because the Lord did not answer his prayers, went to a medium and asked her to bring up a ghost in order for Saul to learn about his future. This act was noted as an example of his disobedience to God (1 Chr 10:13).

Spiritualism Today

In today's Majority World context, spiritualism has been syncretized with various world religions. In many Southeast Asian countries, spiritualism is interwoven with formal religions as a result of the interaction between indigenous beliefs and established systems of religion. In Indonesia, spirit houses can often be found outside a home or a store to appease the local spirits. In Cambodia, the spirit houses hold offerings given to the *neak ta*, or the spirits of the deceased village founders. The people of Laos revere the *nak* spirit, a serpent-like creature who is seen as the protector of the nation. Two practices—ancestor veneration and witchcraft—deserve a closer look.

Ancestor veneration has been historically understood by Western missionaries as worship of ancestral spirits and, therefore, forbidden. But it is important for Christians to comprehend the worldview of those who venerate ancestors in order to develop a proper response to it.

African and Asian religious beliefs recognize only one Supreme Being and several mediatory spirits. Unlike the Supreme Being, the mediatory spirits—such as ancestors—only have derived power. Although they are dead, they are considered "living-dead." They are perceived to be present and active as mediators for members of their family and clans. As Kwame Bediako noted, there is a strong sense of mutual obligations, affection, and respect between the "living dead" and the "living living."

An ancestor is one who has lived a virtuous and long life in the community. Such a pristine life cannot wish evil even after one has died. Therefore, ancestors are perceived to bestow blessings like good harvest, protection, fertility, and success in the present life. Because they lived a virtuous aged life and will continue with their good works in death, they are considered worthy of veneration (not worship). Furthermore, some ancestors are "glorified" and thus "serve" families outside of their own family and clan.

Another worldview issue commonly associated with Africa involves belief in witches and witchcraft accusation. These matters are pervasive and complex. The word *witch,* for instance, can have positive or negative usage. In the Hausa language, *Maye* could mean exceptional ability. Nonetheless, the popular understanding of a witch is one who is oriented toward evil. Witches are malevolent cannibals.

In the religious consciousness of an average African, nothing simply happens. People want to know who, and not simply what, caused death, sickness, barrenness, lack of promotion, or poverty. Just who or what is behind all perceived misfortune? The need to name an agency becomes imminent. Unfortunately, the vulnerable and weak in society usually become the victims of witchcraft accusation. Perceptions regarding who a witch is and what that witch can do need to be transformed by a God-centered view of reality.

Spiritualism and Christianity

Engaging spiritualism from a Christian worldview means engaging questions of ultimate reality. Developing a theology of the spirit world is critical for our engagement both in the Western world and in the Majority World, if we are to engage converts from other religions or those people whose cultural practices revolve around the worship of spirits. Harold Netland, an authority in the field of religious pluralism, cautions against seeing spiritualism as a sign that a culture is premodern or primitive in spite of the fact that it's often considered a folk religion since forms of spiritualism can also be observed in modern culture alongside formal religions.

Missiological anthropologist Paul Hiebert observes that many Western missionaries often deny the existence of the spirit world, thus causing new converts to revert to their old beliefs or to return to diviners who give them familiar answers for their present problems. Hiebert suggests that a key to developing a theology of the spirit world is to correct the flaw of "the excluded middle" in Western Christian thought. Western science has primarily focused on the immanent empirical world of human existence (that which can be confirmed by our senses), while Western Christian thought on the spirit world has primarily focused on the transcendent theistic world (heaven, hell, and eternity). Western missionaries, therefore, have traditionally not had robust understandings of the "middle world," a world for which other religions and other cultures have developed complex systems which include beings like spirits, trolls, pixies, gnomes, and fairies that cannot be observed by our senses but are thought to occupy the human world nevertheless. Thus, historically, when Western missionaries encounter various forms of spirit worship, the tendency is to dismiss the reality of these spirits.

Following Paul's example set at the Areopagus (Acts 17), Christians ought to respond to claims of spiritualism by affirming a God-centered view of reality rather than simply dismissing the presence of the spirit world. God created the world (Gen 1:1; John 1:3; Rev 4:11), and he continues to act in it through his providence, presence, and power (Job 37:6–13; Ps 135:6; Col 1:17; Heb 1:3). The Triune God is in active and direct relationship with humans, through his Son Jesus Christ and the Holy Spirit, who lives in us. Jesus Christ is supreme over all of creation, and "everything was created by him, in heaven and on earth, the visible and the invisible" (Col 1:16). Our relationship with God is mediated through Christ—not through any other created beings. Individuals are therefore accountable for their own actions. As a result, our focus must be on God, on his divinely ordained principles for his creation, on our submission and obedience to him, and on our faith in his plan for our lives. We should not focus on how we might control our futures by manipulating God into doing our bidding. Instead, we worship God the Creator. Our trust must be in the Lord (Ps 37:3; Prov 3:5; Isa 26:4).

POSTMODERNISM

Justin Carswell

As Jesus stood before Pilate and claimed to be the true witness of God for salvation, Pilate's response was this question: "What is truth?" (John 18:38). That question summarizes the condition called postmodernism.

What is postmodernism?

Postmodernism is a term used to describe a host of suspicions about what has been taken for granted in ethics, religion, science, technology, and many other fields of study. Postmodernism questions the nature of what is real, the human ability to know truth, the ability of language to convey right meaning beyond just what the reader or hearer understands, the limits of science, the existence of human consciousness, and especially the promise of the ever-increasing progress of freedom, prosperity, justice, and truth.

As a cultural condition, the contours of postmodernism reach beyond philosophy proper and have broad influence in other academic disciplines like literature, art, architecture, and theology, as well as the general cultural consciousness. This, in fact, is perhaps its most influential aspect. Postmodernism is often expressed by slogans such as, "That is true for you but not for me," "So many people disagree, so truth is relative," and "No culture's values are better than another's."

Postmodernism Versus the Enlightenment

The force of postmodernism is its suspicion and doubt of the so-called certainties of the modern period (roughly the intellectual ideas and the climate they have created since 1750). The Enlightenment philosophers, whose ideas gave birth to the modern period, believed that truth and certainty were attainable by using human reason alone rather than also accepting outside authorities such as Scripture or the received teachings of the Catholic Church. These philosophers described knowledge as a quest for certainty. Accordingly, any claim to knowledge that could not connect to the foundations of logic, or that could not possibly be doubted, or that was not immediately evident to the senses was considered at best opinion and at worst pseudo-knowledge.

This narrow definition of what could be known encouraged hostility toward faith and exalted science and technology as a path to a better future for humanity. However, after the employment of science and technology to kill millions of people as a result of the totalizing worldviews of Marxism and Nazism, questions about modernity's claims of progress came to the forefront in philosophy. Specifically, postmodern thinkers questioned the concept of truth within the modern worldview that had produced these totalizing worldviews. They demonstrated that the condition for knowledge advocated by modern thinkers could not account for itself, let alone a host of things we do and can, in fact, know. Thus, for them, truth was overthrown.

The Postmodern Critique of Certainty

Postmodern thinkers encourage suspicion and doubt about absolute truth claims. Jean François Lyotard states, "All that has been received, if only yesterday, must be suspected" (1984) because those, for example, who appeal to "science" and "reason" to prove that their worldview is correct are also committed to presuppositions or prior commitments that cannot arise from science or reason. He writes, "The recourse to narrative is inevitable, at least to the extent that the language game of science desires its statements to be true but does not have the resources to legitimate their truth on its own" (Lyotard, 1984). In other words, science is founded on ideas that are not the result of science but rather come before it, making science possible.

In their rejection of the narrow certainty of modernism, some postmodern thinkers pressed the suspicion of knowledge claims to the point that they doubted any claims to knowledge, assuming them to be potential power grabs or just the perspective of a particular person from a particular cultural and historical context. There is no universal truth, they assert, no universally accessible human rationality for all people at all times. The result of that critique is a pervasive doubt in our culture regarding universal or total claims to knowledge. In particular, postmodernists critique autonomous reason, universal truth claims, access to one's own inner consciousness, and all attempts to tell a universal history.

Christianity and Postmodernism

Biblical Christianity affirms some of the concerns raised by the postmodernists, such as the importance of story in human existence, or their critiques of modernity (as in the case of the unfounded exaltation of science above other ways of knowing truth). But Christianity rejects the fundamental story of postmodernism because it results in a profound skepticism toward truth, meaning, and morality.

The biblical story reveals God's existence, his creative will, and his active presence in the world as Father, Son, and Holy Spirit (Gen 1–2; John 1:1–18; Acts 2:1–13). The active will and creative presence of God is graciously and lovingly demonstrated in the accounts of Jesus's incarnation, life, death, resurrection, and ascension. For example, Jesus says of himself, "If you continue in my word, you really are my disciples. You will know the truth, and the truth will set you free" (John 8:31–32). To fully understand what Jesus means requires an engagement with the entire biblical story: creation, fall, redemption, and restoration. The Scriptures claim to tell the story of humanity from beginning to ultimate redemption.

Paul, reflecting on the results of Jesus's life, death, and resurrection for his ministry, masterfully summarizes the significance of God at work in Jesus Christ: "In Christ, God was reconciling the world to himself, not counting their trespasses against them, and he has committed the message of reconciliation to us. . . . He made the one who did not know sin to be sin for us, so that in him we might become the righteousness of God" (2 Cor 5:19,21). In this passage lies the universal truth that the biblical story tells. God has graciously revealed the truth: the world in which we live is under the curse of sin because of humanity's choice to disobey God. Still, God has lovingly and graciously chosen to redeem those who put their faith in Jesus Christ, the Lord, whom God raised from the dead (Rom 10:9).

Within the Christian worldview, then, is a rejection of many of the suspicions of postmodernism. For example, that God is the Creator implies that things in this world have real existence. That humanity can know itself as well as the created world by which they are surrounded implies that knowledge is possible. That humans are accountable for their actions implies that at least a handful of moral universals are true for all people at all time.

THE NEW AGE MOVEMENT

Taylor B. Worley

I'm spiritual but not religious."

"I believe in the power of positive thinking."

"I follow my heart."

Claims like these reflect the popular influence of New Age spirituality. New Age movement(s) (hereafter "NAM" or "NAMs") represent an eclectic blend of elements from ancient paganism, astrology, the occult, Eastern religions, and some Judeo-Christian themes aimed at self-actualization through personal healing practices like yoga, meditation, crystal therapy, and spirit channeling.

The NAM grew out of the countercultural shifts of the 1970s and the pop psychology of more recent self-help fads. Celebrity advocates include Deepak Chopra, Eckhart Tolle, and even Oprah Winfrey. The self-spirituality of NAMs holds a pluralistic view of religious authority and emphasizes what religions from various places and cultures seemingly share rather than their important distinctives. What is most valued, however, are ancient or secret truths. NAMs rely on the arcane, the esoteric, or hidden wisdom, a habit that closely resembles the Greco-Roman gnosticism that was fervently critiqued in the NT.

But those associated with NAMs are nothing if not hopeful and optimistic, embracing a profoundly utopian vision for the so-called Age of Aquarius, a time characterized by international peace, ecological sensitivity, and social enlightenment. Thus, NAMs anticipate that things will begin getting better as more people come together and seek mutual harmony with nature and one another. Unfortunately, these hopes are a thin parody of the biblical hope of Christ's eschatological kingdom—the "age to come" described in the NT Gospels.

Basic Tenets of the New Age Movement

Due to their pluralistic orientation, NAMs are inherently difficult to study as a coherent worldview. Nevertheless, they adhere to the basic tenets of pantheism. Pantheism comes from two Greek words, *pan* meaning "all" and *theos* meaning "god." Pantheism equates God with nature and everything in it. God is the universe and the universe is God.

Thus, NAMs differ from Christianity on several important points.

1. Denying reality. NAMs seek to transcend this world and contact a separate level of existence beyond the visible world. This is either an age to come, another dimension of this universe, or a parallel universe.

2. Escaping reality. NAMs seek to access a higher plane of existence by connecting with an eternal spirit or universal consciousness that transcends space and time, thereby escaping the illusion of physical death.

3. New morality. Since the New Age is void of evil, all actions are good, and codes of morality are no longer relevant. This moral relativism erodes an objective account of truth, and individuals are invited to create their own truth.

4. Cyclical history. Time becomes a gradual process of trial and error that repeats itself until humanity graduates to a higher form of consciousness

Christianity and the New Age Movement

The Christian worldview rejects the NAM on each point:

1. Reality is God's creation, and therefore deserves our attention and care (Gen 1–2; Num 35:33; Ps 24:1).

2. Humanity has not been rejected by the world but instead has rejected God's order for this world. In choosing to rebel against the Creator's design, all humanity has fallen from the grace of God. Salvation from this fallen state depends on God's initiative in Jesus Christ to save the world (Rom 8:22–24; Eph 1:3–14; Gal 3:11).

3. Truth is found in God's revelation of himself to humanity and is absolute and eternal (Ps 86:11; John 14:6; 17:17; 2 Tim 3:16). Morality thus flows from this unchanging Word (Matt 5:17–19; Col 3:1–17; Jas 3:13; 1 John 3:18).

4. Finally, history is ultimately meaningful because of God's involvement in the world; namely, his act of creation, the act of initiating redemption by Christ's work on the cross, and the promise of a complete restoration for creation on Christ's return (1 John 3:16; 2 Pet 3:1–6; Rev 21:5).

Although contemporary Christians should be as suspicious of the NAM as the early church was about gnosticism, NAMs illustrate some important aspects of our postmodern age that can help Christians better understand the culture in which they live. In particular, NAMs seek to recover a spiritual element that is absent in a world dominated by scientific naturalism and disdain for the supernatural. NAMs also recognize that meeting spiritual needs belongs to basic human flourishing.

Further, NAMs maintain hope in a comprehensive or holistic peace between God, humans, and nature. Indeed, everything is spiritual by God's design, but how we experience it is a result of his gracious gifts and not human effort or manipulation.

NAMs fundamentally err in their account of human agency (i.e., what an individual can accomplish on his or her own) for the spiritual life. More often than not, spiritual power is sought to extend personal experience or knowledge and is not used in service to the one true God (as with Gen 3:5; Rom 1:21–23).

NAMs elevate humanity to a divine status, and individuals thus become masters of their own spiritual destinies. Nothing could be further from the biblical account of spiritual renewal offered by God the Father, accomplished by Christ the Son, and applied by the Holy Spirit.

The NAM denies God's sovereignty over our lives, inflates human participation beyond the parameters of Scripture, and ultimately substitutes an impersonal world spirit for the Holy Spirit. The Bible makes clear that God is sovereign over the human soul, and unless he acts in grace toward humanity, no change results (Isa 46:10; Rom 9:19–24; Eph 3:14–21). In light of God's sovereignty, humans are responsible for responding to his grace, and human participation in the work of individual spiritual renewal is always in cooperation with God's grace (Rom 10:9–10; Phil 2:12–13; 1 John 2:3–6). For the NAM divinity is subjectless and impersonal. According to Chuck Colson, it is more akin to electricity than deity. Scripture attests, however, to the supremacy and power of the Holy Spirit as the One who convicts the world of its sin, reveals the truth of the gospel, and leads us in following God's Word (John 14:15–27; 16:5–15; Rom 7:4–6; Eph 1:13–14).

While some adherents of the NAM may be well intentioned in their hopes, New Age spirituality cannot ultimately be reconciled to the Christian worldview or the life of a biblical disciple. In light of that inescapable truth, we should seize each opportunity to share the biblical gospel of Jesus Christ. He did not call us to escape this world but instead stepped into our shoes, paid the price for our sin, and is even now working through the church to bring about the redemption and restoration of the world. In his *Miracles*, C. S. Lewis warns that pantheism is Christianity's most formidable and most perennial threat. It is the worldview alternative that humans naturally want to believe; we foolishly hope that by our own efforts we might save ourselves. For this reason, NAMs must be consistently resisted and carefully refuted.

THE (RELIGIOUS) PROBLEM WITH POLITICAL CONSERVATISM AND PROGRESSIVISM

Bruce Riley Ashford

Politics in the United States has, for some time, assumed a binary structure. On one side stand the Republicans, many of whom hold to some form of social conservatism. On the other side stand the Democrats, many of whom hold to some form of social progressivism. But what many Americans fail to see is that conservatism and progressivism are similar in several respects. In their pure forms, both ascribe ultimacy to something other than God. Both lack transcendent norms of their own. And thus, both can lead to a variety of social, cultural, and political ills.

Political Conservatism and Progressivism as Ideologies

Conservatism

Ideological conservatism tends to view a particular cultural heritage as normative and by extension views social revolutions as the greatest political evil, fearing that macro-level social changes will have unintended negative consequences. Instead of reforming social ills through massive reform agendas or revolutions, they seek to reform by reaching back into the best of their past history and cultural heritage.

Conservatives are open to social reform, of course, because the only way to bring back that elusive golden age is to reform the present one. Political scientist David Koyzis describes the conservative impulse:

> If reforms are to be attempted, then they must be small in scale, incremental in pace and firmly grounded in past experience. The conservative prefers to see people attempt to alleviate poverty in their own neighborhoods than to try to eliminate it throughout the entire nation. Because of its local nature, the former is a much more realistic and manageable effort than the latter and is thus more likely to meet with success (*Political Visions & Illusions*, p. 77).

Thus, conservatives want any reforms to be implemented in a careful and deliberate manner.

[In the United States, the word *conservative* is used in a narrower and broader sense. This article is addressing conservatism in its narrower sense as a specific political ideology. However, *conservative* can also be used in a broader sense to mean "somebody whose political views tend to fall on the right side of the American political spectrum." In that sense, I consider myself a conservative as I have written in an article entitled, "How Can a Faithful Evangelical Be a Political Conservative?"]

Progressivism

Ideological progressivism is in some ways the antithesis of conservatism, in that it looks to the future instead of the past, ascribing ultimacy to social reform. While conservatism looks back over its shoulder to a golden age of the past, progressivism tries to peer over the next hill to a golden age of the future. And it is often, though not exclusively, driven by government initiatives. In our American context, progressivism pairs with democratic socialism and whatever is left of liberalism to serve as the heartbeat of the Democratic Party.

Progressivism tends to define itself in contrast to conservatism. For progressives, social conservatism is the primary evil from which society needs to be rescued. To put it simply: progressives are suspicious of the past and optimistic about the future. Positively, progressives rightly recognize certain evils in a given social order. There are always sins of our past that we should avoid repeating and sins of our present that we must eradicate. But progressives too easily conflate those societal ills with the social order itself. They, like the conservatives, throw the baby out with the dirty bathwater.

Conservatives are wrong to react reflexively and negatively against change. Progressives are wrong to react reflexively and negatively against traditional values. Neither conservation nor progress is the core problem. The core problem is idolatry and its twisting and distorting effect on politics. Every nation in history has proven a lush environment for idols, and every modern political ideology suffers the ill effects of idolatry.

The Problems with Idolatrous Conservatism

Inconsistency

A significant problem with both conservatism and progressivism is that, unlike socialism (on the left) or nationalism (on the right), conservatism and progressivism are time-bound ideologies and as such are always on the move. They are not abstract ideologies but contextual responses.

This may embarrass many conservatives, who consider conservative principles immovable and universal. They are not. What counts as conservatism in one country will have very little to do with "conservatism" in another country. While conservatives in the United States might be trying to conserve the economic and political policies of Ronald Reagan, conservatives in another country might be trying to revitalize the authoritarian structures of a previous era. What a society aims to conserve can vary wildly depending on the nation and its history. Pure conservatism, as David Koyzis notes, is an ideological parasite that feeds off other ideologies. It has no identifiable doctrinal position of its own (*Political Visions & Illusions*, p. 72).

Even within a single nation, conservatives have a hard time making strategic alliance with one another. What exactly are we aiming to conserve? Our constitutional order? Wealth? Race? Judeo-Christian morality? Americans are seeing this right now in our country. Some conservatives are more primarily motivated by a free market agenda, others by maintaining "white America," and yet others by Judeo-Christian moral issues. These competing groups make good tactical allies because they all oppose progressivism and also because they often have a common desire to conserve their own power and privilege. But they should not be assumed to be ideologically identical.

Lack of Transcendence

Conservatives, despite their high opinion of the past, cannot merely accept all of it uncritically. So when conservatives criticize their own tradition, as they must, they are forced to rummage around for some norms that transcend history (e.g., opposing slavery). Pure conservatives, therefore, often find themselves in tactical alliance with Christians, even if they cannot stomach a long-term strategic alliance with them. In other words, ideological conservatism can tolerate or even embrace Christianity but only as a means to an end.

But being a "means" to someone else's "end" is tricky business. Faithful Christians in the United States might be surprised to learn that many of the powerful conservatives in the United States view evangelicals as useful idiots. Christians may fancy that political conservatives stand with them ideologically and strategically, when in fact many conservatives would reject many of the deeply held convictions of Christians. The alliance is more temporary and tactical, perhaps, than it is long-term or strategic. In upcoming years, as historic Christianity looks more and more strange to American society, Christians may no longer be viewed as *useful* idiots. We may be seen merely as *idiots.*

The Problems with Idolatrous Progressivism

Inconsistency

Progressivism, like conservatism, lacks consistency. It is always on the move, lacking a doctrinal creed that other ideologies—such as socialism and libertarianism—have. What counts as progressive in one nation may have nothing to do with progressivism in another nation. For instance, progressives in the United States are currently pushing for the expansion of federal regulation into nearly every sector of society. But progressives in China are doing the opposite, pushing for smaller government.

Lack of Transcendence

Like conservatism, progressivism lacks transcendence. When progressives criticize a traditional social order, they have to rummage around to find some principle or preference they can elevate to the level of a transcendent standard. But whereas conservatives have the entirety of history from which to borrow their ideas, progressives are at a disadvantage. Their god is the future, but the future is a bit more hazy. Thus they are forced to borrow their standards from another ideology, sometimes almost arbitrarily, to suit their particular agenda.

In the United States, progressives often pair with liberalism in pushing for social reform that frees individuals from regnant social and moral norms. In order for individuals to have maximum autonomy, especially sexual autonomy, progressives seek to redefine what it means to be human, what it means to be a man or a woman, and what it means to be moral.

In relation to humanity, many secular progressives want to redefine what it means to be a human person. Human beings, they argue, are not created in the image and likeness of God (to be created in God's image would make us accountable to God, after all). Human beings are, instead, advanced animals who differ from animals only in their consciousness and functionality.

In relation to gender, many progressives want to redefine the human person along the lines of ancient Gnosticism (though they hardly ever make this connection overtly). They want to separate a person's identity from his or her body. In this view, the true "self" is independent of the body to the extent that a man who doesn't feel like a man can mutilate his body (through gender-reassignment surgery) in order to make it more physiologically similar to a woman. We are not men or women by birth, the argument goes, but by choice, and advanced technology is allowing us to become who we truly are.

In relation to morality, many progressives want us to suspend judgment about good and evil. As J. Budziszewski notes, progressivism promotes a type of tolerance that requires us to avoid having strong convictions—except, ironically, for the convictions progressives deem good or acceptable (*Revenge of Conscience*, pp. 93–95). When and where progressivism overturns traditional morality, it attempts to absolve itself from responsibility for decisions: "I am not pro-abortion; I am pro-choice." "I am not killing a baby. I am removing the products of conception." In order to overturn social and moral norms, progressives generally push for the government to replace family and religion as the primary agent of moral instruction and formation.

This progressive overturning of the moral order has caused numerous problems in American society. By overturning traditional teaching about human dignity, we have turned the safest place in our society—the womb—into the most dangerous. As public data indicates, we have killed nearly 60 million babies in the last half century. By attempting to overturn nature, we have turned gender—an aspect of God's creational design and one of society's bedrock realities—into an artificial construct devoid of stability or meaning.

As R. R. Reno recently argued, this dismantling of traditional norms and rules is surely one of the reasons for society's disorientation in general, and destructive behaviors in specific ("Deadly Progressivism," online at *First Things*). It is no surprise that in a society as disoriented as ours, suicide and drug-related deaths are on the rise. We no longer have certainty about the most basic facts of life.

Conclusion

Christians must evaluate our cultural heritage to determine what we think is worth conserving and what needs to be rejected so that we can progress beyond it. And, as I argue in *Letters to an American Christian*, this sort of evaluation must be made primarily by viewing the world through the lens of the Christian worldview rather than the political narrative of some cable news network. In other words, standing alone, conservatism and progressivism are both errant and even idolatrous.

[Portions of this article are indebted to David Koyzis's fine critique of conservatism in *Political Visions & Illusions: A Survey & Christian Critique of Contemporary Ideologies* (Grand Rapids: IVP, 2003).]

THE (RELIGIOUS) PROBLEM WITH POLITICAL LIBERALISM

Bruce Riley Ashford

In the lead-up to the 2018 midterm elections, it became clear that a progressive version of political liberalism is one of several behemoth political visions shaping and expressing the will of many Americans. But, as I've argued previously about socialism and will argue in the next article about nationalism, modern political ideologies tend to be idolatrous and should be exposed for what they are—flawed human systems of political salvation that cannot deliver on their promises. But what is meant by *liberalism*?

The word *liberal* is used in significantly different ways in the United States today. Some Americans might use the word positively, signifying that a particular person or policy is open-minded or tolerant. Other Americans use the word negatively, signifying a person who doesn't value America's cultural heritage. For yet others, the word conjures up sometimes vague but always grand notions of equality and freedom.

But for today's purposes, we'll use the word in a broader and more historic sense. In this sense, liberalism refers to a constitutional and representative political arrangement that emphasizes liberty and personal freedom. In this sense, both of America's major political parties and many of their elected representatives have been shaped in profound ways by liberalism.

The Rise and Development of Liberalism in the West
In *Political Visions and Illusions*, political scientist David Koyzis gives a brief history of the rise and development of Western liberalism (pp. 53–60), revealing the ways individual autonomy (freedom from external authori-

ties and norms) is the core belief of the liberal creed. Liberals believe that humans should be free to direct their own lives. From this belief stems a corollary belief: individuals have the right to own property and to make their own choices. There is only one inherent limit on these choices—the rights of other individuals. But provided a person's choices do not directly interfere with the rights of another, the liberal ideology gives carte blanche.

Thus, liberalism emphasizes the individual over the sociopolitical community. Indeed, liberals tend to reduce the community to little more than an aggregate of autonomous individuals. Liberals argue that in a hypothetical "state of nature" (an imaginary state of affairs in which there are only individuals and not governments) individuals are free. The downside of this freedom, however, is that individuals do not have sufficient protection from various dangers, and so they enter into a contract with one another, voluntarily, to form a governed society. Thus, even the best government is a sort of necessary evil, in that it plays the minimal but necessary role of protecting individuals from threats to their personhood and property.

Koyzis goes on to note the way this creed has taken shape in the West. At first, the state existed to protect people and their property. Before long, however, Western liberals were asking to be protected not only from powerful threats to their personhood and property but also to other less obvious "threats," such as a lack of sufficient resources. Instead of wanting the government to clear the space so they could pursue life, liberty, and happiness, people wanted the government to step into that space in order to provide those interests (p. 59). And why not? When "I want" lies at the center of the ideology, it becomes natural to look to a power as large as the state to make up for what I cannot provide for myself.

Finally, liberals expect the government in its present state to accommodate their personal desires and to accommodate them in a religiously and morally neutral manner. More to the point, they expect the government never to cast moral judgments on their desires. Thus, when their poor judgment or immoral choices cause negative consequences, the liberal populace expects the government to ameliorate those consequences (e.g. "Have you had five babies out of wedlock? The government will take care of those babies. But even better, it will encourage you to kill them in the womb beforehand.")

The Idolatry in Ideological Liberalism

Political liberalism finds itself in a real dilemma: on one hand, it has deified individual autonomy and free choice; on the other hand, it naturally inclines to pull the levers of government to assist when that autonomy doesn't work out well. Thus, under liberalism, government intervention increases even though this runs contrary to liberalism's original aim. How, then, should we evaluate liberalism?

We should be grateful for liberalism's emphasis on human rights, liberty, and equality and should be especially grateful for those emphases that influenced America's Founding Fathers, who hammered out a working political arrangement for our nation. Yet, the problem is that liberalism misidentifies society's "root evil" as a heteronomous authority (any type of authority that does not issue from within the autonomous individual). Errantly, it places its hopes in ideologically liberal political parties that promise to maximize the individual's autonomy and minimize any external authorities. Because of its excessive allegiance to individual autonomy, it cannot in the end make sense of the individual's need for community. In its worst forms, it forthrightly wishes to abolish God so that individuals can finally create themselves and belong to themselves.

The negative consequences of political liberalism are many, but foremost among them are the ironic loss of freedom because of government expansion and the loss of human flourishing because of the sidelining of moral law. Ideological liberalism buys the lie that state-sponsored undermining of moral law will lead to greater fulfillment for society. But it learns, as did Adam and Eve, that what seems pleasing to the eye only leads to disappointment and death. If we saw it for what it truly was, none of us would desire independence from God.

In Western nations, political liberalism has led to swollen governments that suffocate society. Western liberal governments have evolved to become, in Koyzis's words, "choice enhancement" and "desire fulfillment" providers (p. 61). But this is a pricey venture. In this situation, the state constantly raises taxes so it can redistribute according to its own preferences, fulfilling desires and enhancing choices (e.g., government-funded abortion). It must become involved in image management, helping various actors or sectors of society achieve the social or institutional status they desire (e.g., judicial legislation of same-sex marriage). It oversteps its bounds by extending federal oversight into cultural spheres where it has no jurisdiction, such as family and church (e.g., government intrusion into the family's right to raise and educate their own children).

The latest iteration of liberalism—provider of choice enhancement and desire fulfillment—is especially opposed to a transcendent moral framework. Thus, it is willing to overthrow any moral underpinning that threatens the god of individual autonomy. It encourages its citizens to suspend moral judgment and dispense with religious and moral convictions—except, of course, those judgments and convictions that are currently favored by the liberals of that era.

Such an emphasis on individual desires and choices degrades civic life in ways too myriad to mention. This culture of rampant individualism influences American public life to the point that it becomes institutionalized in the political realm. Thus institutionalized, it reinforces autonomous individualism in every realm of society and culture. Social philosopher Elaine Storkey puts it well when she writes:

> The culture of individualism is vast . . . and goes far beyond the political realm. It is bolstered, for example, by a daily reinforcement of themes such as success, happiness, reward, personality, choice, independence, and self-discovery. The result is a philosophy of life that sees relationships as externally constructed, and centered around fulfillment, happiness, or some self-constructed goal or ideal to which the dynamics of relationships become subject. Personal achievement, psychic rewards, self-esteem, popularity, and self-presentation are highly valued, while humility, vulnerability, modesty, and patience score less well. . . . *The overall impact on relational living has been that relationships, formerly characterized by truth, increasingly are assumed to be impermanent. The normative structures of trust, mutuality, love, and faithfulness have been replaced by ones where negotiation, reward, litigation, and power dealing are seen as normal* ("Sphere Sovereignty," pp. 198–99).

Ideological liberalism, we have argued, enthrones the self, demonizes external authority, and therefore functions as a false religion that cannot deliver the salvation it promises. As J. Budziszewski so aptly put it, political liberalism is "a bundle of acute moral [and, it should be added, religious] errors, with political consequences that grow more and more alarming as these errors are taken closer and closer to their logical conclusions" (*Revenge of Conscience*, p. 89).

Therefore, even while we can and should affirm the good intentions and insights found in the liberal project, we should reject its tendency to deify the self and demonize external authority. And (as Koyzis does in the last several chapters of *Political Visions and Illusions* and as I have tried to do in *One Nation under God* and *Letters to an American Christian*), we should work together to construct a nonideological alternative that values liberty but recognizes that true freedom is found within a transcendent moral framework.

[This article is indebted to David Koyzis's fine critique of liberalism in *Political Visions & Illusions: A Survey & Christian Critique of Contemporary Ideologies* (Grand Rapids: IVP, 2003).]

THE (RELIGIOUS) PROBLEM WITH LIBERTARIANISM

Bruce Riley Ashford

The last twenty years in American life have seen the rise of libertarianism as a force to be reckoned with in American politics, especially within the Republican Party. Libertarianism is a view that places an extraordinary emphasis on liberty—as it defines liberty—and orders society in a particular manner in order to achieve that liberty.

Libertarian Ideology

Libertarianism includes a range of theories and attitudes wanting to roll back collectivism and authoritarianism in modern Western society. Some libertarians (e.g., Robert Nozick) are principled and primarily concerned with inalienable rights to life, liberty, property, and the pursuit of happiness. Other libertarians (e.g., Ludwig von Mises) are utilitarian and primarily concerned with the benefits of the free market. Some libertarians (e.g., Nozick, Ayn Rand) are "minarchists" who argue for a minimal state that involves itself only in police protection, enforcement of contracts, and national defense. Other libertarians (e.g., Murray Rothbard) are "anarchists" who view all government as illegitimate and would prefer to outsource police protection to private protection agencies.

American libertarians are generally "conservative" in the sense that they wish to conserve vital aspects in the American tradition, such as liberty, rights, and equality. But they are not "conservative" in that they resist all legal and political attempts to impose social or moral norms on society. Political authority and power, they argue, should not be employed to enforce or upgrade society's morality or way of life.

Although there are many varieties of libertarian ideology, a family resemblance can be discerned, a resemblance which can be found in libertarianism's elevation of individual liberty to the status of "supreme political good." Thus, Karl Hess writes:

> Libertarianism is the view that each man is the absolute owner of his life, to use and dispose of as he sees fit; that all social actions should be voluntary; and respect for every other man's similar and equal ownership of life and, by extension, property and fruits of that life, is the ethical basis of a humane and open society. In this view, the only function of law or government is to provide the sort of self-defense against violence that an individual, if he were powerful enough, would provide for himself ("The Death of Politics," in *Mostly on the Edge*).

This one principle—individual liberty as the supreme political good—is the common factor that unites minarchists and anarchists, principled libertarians and utilitarians, as well as other divided factions within the libertarian community.

The Idol in the Ideology

Liberty as the Supreme Political Good

As David Koyzis argues in *Political Visions & Illusions*, modern political ideologies have idolatrous tendencies. Libertarianism is no exception as it tends to make liberty and personal choice an end to itself rather than a means to a better end. Some libertarians are not guilty, but as a general rule a libertarian's clinching argument is to point out that a given policy proposal or law interferes with an individual's right to choose.

This approach wrongly elevates liberty above a higher political good, namely, the common good that comes from human flourishing and virtue. Christian citizens should encourage our elected officials not to tolerate certain vices, even if legislation against those vices curtails individual choice. Why should we legalize opioids when doing so causes great harm not only to drug addicts but also to families and communities? Why should the government not outlaw prostitution, knowing that it degrades women, spreads disease, and destroys families?

Thus, although Christians should make common cause with libertarians in fighting for individual liberties, we should refrain from elevating liberty to the status of supreme political good. Liberty should be anchored in an objective moral order and normed by that order.

Human Beings as Autonomous and Rational Choosers

All libertarians place a high value on the individual's freedom to choose, and many libertarians claim that every human person owns himself or herself. As Paul Kurtz put it, the human being is "the master of his own fate, responsible for his own career and destiny" ("Libertarianism" in *Freedom and Virtue*, p. 146). The alternative to self-ownership, many libertarians argue, is slavery. Thus, all forms of rule are necessarily enslaving the persons who are being ruled.

Consider libertarian Murray Rothbard's argument that the government cannot coerce parents to care for their children. While the government can and should make laws against parents murdering or mutilating their child, Rothbard argues, it should not make or enforce laws that coerce the parent to feed or care for the child properly because to do so would be government overreach (*Ethics of Liberty*, p. 100).

But Scripture posits the goodness of heteronomous authority in many instances, including especially the parent's responsibility and authority over the child. Of course parents should care for their children; and, yes, the government should punish a parent who deliberately starves his child. Without parents norming their children, and a nation's laws appropriately norming its people, the worst in humanity not only goes unchecked but is encouraged to flourish.

Furthermore, Scripture teaches us that the essence of human being does not lie in autonomous choice. Human beings are not only rational agents but affective beings. We are driven not only by intellect but also by love and affection. Thus, when a government refuses to legislate certain moral standards and principles, it encourages its people to place their affections on the worst and most harmful objects.

The Government as Minimal or Illegitimate

All libertarians are suspicious of government. Some libertarians allow government a limited role in police protection (criminal law), contract enforcement (civil law), and national defense. Other libertarians, such as Rothbard, view the government has no right to rule. Governments, by definition, initiate coercion and thus are incompatible with libertarianism.

Neither approach gets it right, though the minarchists are much closer to the truth than the anarchists. The truth that minarchists uphold is that God's best intention for the created world is for each sphere of culture (e.g., family, church, state, art, science, business) to mind its own business, to tend and cultivate its own area of the world. And when the government unnecessarily interferes with the other spheres, it violates its own calling.

However, as Christian political theorist Abraham Kuyper argued, there are at least three situations in which the government can and should intervene in the business of another sphere of culture (*Lectures on Calvinism*, p. 97). The government can step in to protect the weak from the strong in a given sphere (e.g., child abuse). It can intervene to resolve conflicts between two different spheres (e.g., a middle school challenges a strip club's bid to open its business next door). It can step in to provide services that are needed for all of the spheres (e.g., road system).

Indeed, we should recognize the government as God-ordained institution whose goal is to achieve justice for the individuals and communities under its purview (Rom 13:1–7). And justice, in the biblical view, involves not only the individual good but also the common good. Thus, the government should provide its citizens with a properly "normed" liberty rather than with unfettered freedom, and when our elected officials and judges enact appropriate norms, we should thank them for doing so.

The Economy as Complex and Unmanageable

Many libertarians, such as Ludwig von Mises and Friedrich von Haye, are utilitarian economists who focus their attention on rolling back government intervention in the markets. They are concerned to extol the aggregate benefits a free market bestows upon citizens and the aggregate costs of state intervention in the markets. State intervention is costly for many reasons, foremost of which is that no economic or political leader, or group of leaders, is able to predict the consequences of their intervention in the market, and usually interventions reap unforeseen and negative consequences.

Other libertarians make principled arguments against government intervention in the economy, saying that taxation is an act of violence, a sort of legalized robbery of individual citizens. For some libertarians, the government should not even tax citizens in order to provide police protection, contract enforcement, or national security.

My view is that economic libertarians are right to recognize the irreducible complexity of the markets and the finitude and fallenness of the financial managers and political leaders who want to try their hands at guiding the market. But while we should support a free market, and we should be aware of the unintended negative consequences that can stem from intervention, we should not support a totalizing market. In other words, we should work to provide correctives to a market that is not serving virtue and the common good. In a best-case scenario, citizens, institutions, and associations will use their buying power to steer the market toward virtue and away from vice. In a worst-case scenario, immoral market actors are so powerful that the government needs to intervene.

My view is that property rights are not absolute. The government is operating appropriately within its own sphere when it taxes its people to provide for services such as police protection, contract enforcement, and national security (Matt 22:15–22; Rom 13:1–7). It seems right that the government should provide other public services for the common good, such as public roads and parks. Finally, it is just and right for the government to interfere in other spheres in certain limited instances (e.g., to break up monopolies or to provide welfare for persons who are needy through no fault of their own), as long as the government views itself as a temporary curator who will step back out as soon as the problem is fixed.

Justice as Clear-Cut Protection of Personhood and Property

At the heart of libertarianism is the fundamentally good desire to protect people from violence against their person or property. But unfortunately, many libertarians think that this sort of protection sums up the state's responsibility toward its citizens. Philip Vander Elst's criticism of libertarians is worth quoting in full:

> The Libertarian rule that personal liberty should only be limited by the obligation on all individuals to respect the equal rights of others, not only ignores the fact that there are other moral values with which a compromise may need to be struck; it also makes the mistake of

thinking that there is an absolutely clear and rigid distinction between actions which affect only ourselves, and actions which affect other people. Hence the Libertarian belief that "victimless crimes" like "sexual deviancy" and drug addiction should not be restricted or punished by law. The truth, however, is that most of our actions have some impact on other people. (*Libertarianism,* pp. 20–21).

Indeed, individual liberty should not be set over and against the common good. The common good enables human flourishing, and the subversion of the common good hurts individuals in many complex and even subtle ways.

The Unintended Negative Consequences of Idolizing Liberty
As David Koyzis, Jordan Ballor, Yuval Levin, and others have argued, consistent libertarianism has the unintended and ironic consequence of suppressing liberty. As Ballor argues, "A core principle for many libertarians, the view that there is nothing between the individual and the state, has arguably done more to permit, if not promote, tyranny, and to undermine true liberty, than pragmatic reliance on state power in pursuit of a particular social agenda" ("Avoiding Confusionism").

It makes sense that any ideology that isolates the individual and suspends him beneath the government—no matter how minimal the government initially is—will undermine the very institutions and associations that cultivate morality in individuals and provide a bulwark against state intrusion. Additionally, as Van der Elst has argued, it encourages moral relativism, which allows powerful political actors to justify more easily the misuse of power, which in turn can easily lead to statism.

Conclusion
Libertarians have made impressive gains in recent years, electing significant politicians to office, establishing think tanks and publications, and winning allegiance from an increasing number of American citizens. We should be grateful for the libertarian emphasis on liberty, dignity, equality, and nonviolence, and for the way libertarian ideology serves as an articulate counterweight to totalizing pretentions of socialism and secular progressivism. Yet, when it is untethered from a more fully biblical framework of thought, "liberty" becomes an idol, unintentionally subverting the common good, undermining society's mediating institutions, thus ironically strengthening the hand of the state and suppressing liberty.

THE (RELIGIOUS) PROBLEM WITH NATIONALISM

Bruce Riley Ashford

When we examine the rise and development of political ideologies in the United States, we will find that each system of thought essentially creates an idol from key concepts within that ideology. For instance, liberalism makes an idol out of "individual autonomy," while socialism absolutizes "material equality." In this article, we will examine the idolatrous nature of political nationalism. Before delving into political nationalism, however, we must first define *nation*.

Defining nation is more difficult than an American might typically assume. The experts don't even agree. Various unifying features are trotted out as the key to identifying a true nation—language, culture, race, homeland, or constitutional order. None of these criteria, however, serve universally to make sense of all nations. Thus, for the sake of this article, we define a nation as "any group of people who claim to be a nation (and have some plausible claim to do so), and who both include and exclude people by their own standards."

This type of definition allows for various "nations" that are not officially a part of the United Nations General Assembly. Westerners may find this difficult to grasp. But many nations transcend the boundaries of contemporary nation-states. The Kurds, for example—scattered across Iraq, Iran, Turkey, and Syria—consider themselves one nation rather than Iraqi, Iranian, and so forth. And in our own country, many of the Native American tribes, such as the Cherokee Indians, identify primarily with their Native American tribe rather than their United States affiliation. So modern nation-states, such as the United States, are not the only "nations."

Nationalism, on the other hand, is easier to define. David Koyzis, for instance, offers a theological definition of *nationalism* as "a political arrangement in which the people deify the nation, viewing their nation as the Savior that will protect them from the evil of being ruled by those who are different from them" (*Political Visions & Illusions*, pp. 103–8). Sometimes this rhetoric of salvation is overt, as was the case in Nazi Germany and Soviet Russia. At other times it manifests in more subtle ways. But regardless of how subtle the rhetoric, ideological nationalism should be recognized as idolatrous.

Varieties of Nationalism in the West

In the modern West political nationalism centers on modern nation-states. Nationalists view their nation-state as more than merely the aggregate of its citizens. Usually, the nation is seen as superior to other nation-states in its ability to exemplify some transcendent value. For Americans this value is usually freedom. Because our nation possesses the highest virtue, the argument goes, our nation must therefore be God's "favorite." This sort of thinking goes beyond *patriotism* (which can be healthy and good) in its elevation of the nation-state to a status reserved for God alone.

Our state-based form of nationalism is relatively novel, at least historically speaking. Tribal-based nationalism predominated in earlier eras in Western history and still does in many parts of the globe today. For these nations allegiance is given first to a particular ethnic group. This people group shares a common ethnicity, language, culture, and religion and generally sees its way of life as superior to other ways of life. They may or may not place much pride in their style of government (as in the state-based variety), but the end result of tribal nationalism is similar: our tribe is better than your tribe.

The Nazis were a hybrid of state and tribal nationalism, with their *volk* (i.e., folk) ideology. Undeniably centered in a particular nation-state, the Weimar Republic or German Reich, the Nazis' privileged "German race" included not only the German people but also the Scandinavians, the English, and the Dutch. Nazi nationalism was especially pernicious because it made the Nazi community itself the source of value. All manner of evil became possible as a means toward their end of promoting the perfect Germanic race at the expense of other peoples and races.

Varieties of Nationalism in America

As fallen beings, we might find it easy to spot the idolatry in Nazi Germany's nationalism, given that the nation under consideration is not our own. We pick the speck out of another nation's eye while ignoring the log in our own. If we're going to be honest, therefore, we need to identify and speak out against distinctively American varieties of political nationalism. Of the various types of American nationalism, this article will discuss two: white nationalism and God-and-country nationalism.

White Nationalism

As I argue in *Letters to an American Christian*, one especially odious variety is white nationalism. White nationalists tend to argue that ethnic groupings are the most natural unit of culture, that whites are the most basic unity of American culture, and that white culture possesses certain traits that are uniquely exemplary. They focus on the uniqueness of white culture, call upon whites to preserve it by transmitting it to future generations, and seek a governing structure that will protect the national culture so they can be handed down to future generations. Many white nationalists want to get rid of the Constitution and its Amendments in order to constitutionalize a double standard of justice, one that carves out a special place for whites and for white culture.

White nationalism is un-American and, more significantly, unchristian. As an American Christian, I want local, state, and national governments to exercise power with an eye toward justice for all people within our borders and not merely for people of a particular ethnic, socioeconomic, or religious grouping. "The danger of the ethnic variety of nationalism lies," Koyzis writes, "in the pursuit of a double standard of justice. When ethnic nationalists come to power in a given state, they privilege the members of the titular ethnic group over those of other ethnic groups" (*Political Visions & Illusions*, p. 115). Evangelicals should thus reject any attempt to value one ethnic group over another.

Racism and racial injustice manifest themselves both in individuals and institutions. In individuals, it manifests itself as personal prejudice toward persons of a different ethnic heritage. In institutions, it manifests itself when social and cultural institutions give preference to one race over another. Of all people, evangelical Christians should understand the reality of both types of racism. Scripture emphasizes that sin is committed by individuals (e.g. Gen 3) but that individual sins coalesce on the macro level to warp and corrupts society and culture (e.g., Gen 4–11). We should fight racism tooth and nail, in all its forms, not only from the voting booth but also in our churches and coffee shops and on our social media accounts.

God and Country Nationalism

Another variety of American nationalism can be found in "God and country" circles. Now, there is nothing wrong with loving God and one's country. I love God and, at the same time, am deeply and profoundly grateful that I am an American citizen. I even coauthored a book entitled *One Nation under God: A Christian Hope for American Politics*. But an unhealthy type of "God and country" patriotism views the United States as a chosen nation in the same way that Israel is described as a chosen nation in the Bible. Even as great a president as Ronald Reagan misappropriated the phrase "City on a Hill" (which the Puritans and other Christians rightly applied to the church) by applying it to the United States.

Similarly, political candidates and commentators often misappropriate the promise God made to his people in 2 Chronicles 7:14. In this verse, God says to Solomon if "my people, who bear my name, humble themselves, pray and seek my face, and turn from their evil ways, then I will hear from heaven, forgive their sin, and heal their land." After quoting this verse, many politicians apply it to the United States rather than to God's people.

Now, 2 Chronicle 7:14 contains a universal truth. God will, in fact, respond mercifully to all who turn to him with repentance and humility. But those quoting it often go beyond this modest application by believing the United States is a chosen people on the same level as biblical Israel. But to do so is to err. The people of God, those "called by [his] name," are those who gather around the throne of Christ—not those who salute the Red, White, and Blue. And once we lend our identity as "people of God" to the nation-state, we relinquish our unique and indispensable role as salt and light in the world.

These sorts of theological mistakes often lead to even greater political mischief. For example, if we view the United States as a chosen nation on the level of biblical Israel, it's all the more easy to assume "divine backing" for whatever political programs or foreign policy agendas that a particular "God and country" proponent favors. In other words, it gives one nation-state a higher ontological and moral status than all other nation-states, thereby making it easier to justify various injustices or evils as the means toward the end of propping up "God's" nation.

Conclusion

We Americans are a patriotic people. None of what is said here should make us ashamed to look on our country with affection, devotion, and even a measure of pride. Still, we must prevent our natural and admirable patriotism from becoming an idolatrous type of nationalism. To effectively counter nationalism, we need not love our own nation less; we need only love, honor, and obey God more.

The United States is, as our Pledge of Allegiance puts it, "one nation, under God." As Richard John Neuhaus noted, calling ourselves "one nation, under God" is not a statement of patriotic *pride* but of patriotic humility ("Seeking a Better Way," online at *First Things*). Our nation stands under the watchful eye of God, and we will be held accountable for whether we ascribe ultimacy to Christ or to our nation. "One nation, under God" is also a statement of hope and aspiration. For all of our failings as a country, we still have the opportunity to shape politics through the lens of the gospel.

[This article is indebted to David Koyzis' critique of nationalism in *Political Visions & Illusions: A Survey & Christian Critique of Contemporary Ideologies* (Grand Rapids: IVP, 2003).]

THE (RELIGIOUS) PROBLEM WITH SOCIALISM

Bruce Riley Ashford

Socialism has served as a polarizing phenomenon globally and is emerging to the forefront of our political divide in the United States. It caught the nation's attention during the 2016 election cycle when Bernie Sanders ran for president openly as a "Democratic socialist." Not only was the race close, but many experts think Sanders would have won the Democratic nomination if the Clinton family had not manipulated matters behind the scenes.

But Sanders's views should be recognized as Socialism Lite®, given that he calls himself a "socialist *capitalist*," a notion which most socialists would consider a contradiction in terms. The more serious socialists in the United States are identified with an activist group called Democratic Socialists of America (DSA). The DSA should not be ignored by American citizens because of its stated intention to get rid of capitalism (for being "oppressive") and abolish the Senate (because it is "unrepresentative"), along with its membership having increased sevenfold since 2015.

Neither should socialist ideology be ignored. But what is *socialism*? And why should we resist its emergence as an economic and political force in the United States?

Many Varieties of Socialism

There are, in fact, a number of varieties of socialism. Each variety emphasizes material equality and communal property ownership, but each does so in its own way.

Most varieties of socialism are macro-level varieties that want nation-wide revolutions, although there are versions that promote their socialism on the local or personal levels. Some varieties preach sudden, and even violent, overthrow of capitalism, while others seek a gradual and peaceful approach to undermining capitalism. Some versions, like Sanders's, don't wish to do away with capitalism at all. Some varieties claim to be based on social science and scientific approaches to history, while other varieties are more cultic in nature.

In the midst of this diversity, the unifying factors are always material equality and communal property ownership. Although these factors are economic, their realization is directly tied to political agendas.

We will focus on the most famous and widespread version of social-ism—Marxism. Marxist socialism has exercised an enormous influence over some of the world's superpowers and over hundreds of millions of people. Perhaps more so than the other political ideologies, Marxist socialism man-ifests itself more obviously as an all-encompassing worldview. But like every other political ideology, when given the ultimate allegiance it demands, it is exposed for the false religion it is.

Marxist Socialism

Karl Marx (1818–1883) believed that economic factors were the most determinative factors in any society. He argued that world history can be summarized by a series of economic struggles, as people came to grips with economic realities and treated one another well (or poorly) based on those realities. In his famous essay, *The Communist Manifesto*, written with Friedrich Engels, Marx wrote, "The history of all hitherto existing society is the history of class struggles, [contests between] freeman and slave, patri-cian and plebeian, lord and serf, guild-master and journeyman, in a word, oppressor and oppressed" (in *Karl Marx: Selected Writings*, pp. 158–59). Marx believed that humanity had evolved in stages economically—from hunter-gatherer societies, to slave-based societies, to medieval feudalism, to modern capitalism. And in his mind, capitalism needed to evolve into socialism.

Marx criticized capitalism by arguing that it undermined national identities and cultural distinctives because it encouraged people to clamor for wealth rather than honoring those traditional identities and distinctives. Most importantly, he argued that capitalism dehumanized humans by alien-ating them from their labor. In his view, capitalist economies valued money and wealth acquisition more than they valued their workers. Capitalism, he argued, tended to treat workers as mere business expenses rather than as human beings. With wealth as the unquestioned center of capitalism, Marx felt that people became faceless machines to be manipulated, replaced, or eliminated.

In response to the evils of capitalism, Marx believed workers of the world should (and would) eventually overthrow capitalism. Capitalism was a doomed system, on the cusp of collapse—a collapse that Marx intended to hasten. When that happened, Marx foresaw workers abolishing private property and eventually abolishing the state itself.

Socialism, however, was only a temporary stage for Marx on the way to an even better economic system—communism. Marx envisioned a day when his socialism (with state ownership of property) would be replaced by communism (in which the state would no longer exist). As history reminds us, Marx's wishes were never fulfilled. In fact, the opposite tragically occurred: Marxist socialism, in every instance, has created bigger and more intrusive governments than ever before. Much like liberalism, what began as an attempt to minimize state power led inherently to an expansion of state power.

Marxist Socialism as False Religion

It bears mentioning, especially in our capitalistic context, that Marxist socialism is not entirely bad. No idolatrous ideology is or even (by definition) can be. Any and every ideology latches on to a good aspect of God's creation but wrongly elevates it to the status of deity and twists it toward wrong ends. An ideology composed solely of evil would not exist because evil is only and ever a derivation of good. Satan cannot create; he can only distort and disfigure.

In the case of Marxist socialism, the good was Marx's commendable desire to do away with poverty. He not only saw but deeply felt the devastation poverty brings. He understood intuitively that poverty casts a long shadow not merely in a lack of physical resources but in the psychology and culture of those mired in it. Marx and his wife, Jenny, struggled with poverty themselves in the 1850s, a time in which they saw three of their six children die. Even those who disagree with Marx's project should recognize that his theoretical work was rooted in personal compassion and a desire for humanity to flourish.

However, Marxist socialism, with most other versions of socialism, is not an appropriate alternative to the excesses of capitalism. Beginning with the commendable desire for material equality and communal ownership of property, socialism goes too far, extending communal ownership beyond its normative limits. In other words, it transforms material equality into a deity.

Thus, this otherwise anodyne goal becomes a beast whose tentacles reach past the public square into every sphere of life, including the arts and sciences, business and entrepreneurship, education and scholarship, and even home and family life. Socialism offers a critique of society that becomes inherently totalizing (including every sphere of culture) and radical (seeking to reconstruct from the roots up).

Marxism, like the world religions, provides a comprehensive way of viewing the world, of interpreting various social and cultural phenomena. It identifies one aspect of society, economically based class struggle, and demonizes it as the overriding evil corrupting life in this world. And if class struggle is the devil, Marxism is god, the only viable route to "salvation."

What makes Marxism particularly persistent is its full-bodied eschatology. As David Koyzis notes, most non-Marxist forms of socialism never provided a clear enough view of the societal end goal. They merely encouraged society to work hard to achieve a socialist state. But Marx promised that socialism would win the day. In his mind, socialism was better than competing economic theories or religions because history was on its side.

David Koyzis writes:

> This then is the primary appeal of the Marxian vision: much as Scripture teaches the ultimate victory of Jesus Christ over his enemies and the reign of the righteous over the new earth in the kingdom of God, so also does Marxism promise an eschatological consummation of human history (*Political Visions & Illusions*, 172).

Additionally, as Koyzis notes, Marx provides a type of ecclesiology. For Marx, a person's primary community is economic class (not family, church, nation, or state). In his plan, the "redeemed community" would be one in which such class divisions have been erased. As a false religion, Marxism's salvation comes from within history, is ushered in by socialist humanity, and will eventuate in a redeemed community. Or so it was hoped.

Negative Consequences of Marxist Socialism

The Marxist project has been shown to be bankrupt by its own benchmark—the course of history. Marxist socialism did not win the day because Marxism is an idolatrous ideology. It elevated one aspect of creational life over all others, and even over God himself. Thus it is no surprise that it also subverts human flourishing.

One of the clearest examples of Marxism's dead ends is its desire to abolish private property. Owning property is closely tied to freedom and liberty—which is why property ownership arises so often in political theory. And when, as in Marxism, the government takes public ownership of most property, it reduces our liberty and freedom as citizens. Your property is no longer yours; the rules for that property, then, are dictated from without.

Another example is Marxist socialism's disastrous effect on the economy. The economy cannot be centrally planned, as Marxists have attempted to do, in an effective manner. The economist Ludwig von Mises is well known for demonstrating that (1) economic calculation is necessary for economic activity, (2) pricing is necessary for economic calculation, and (3) a free market is necessary for pricing. The Soviet version of Marxist socialism provides a tragic illustration of the deleterious effects of a centrally planned economy.

Prices were determined not by supply and demand but artificially by the government. Officials in the capital determined everything from the price of milk in Moscow, to the price of tractors in the farms outside of Kazan, to the price of heart surgeries in the hospitals of Leningrad. The result was that certain major incentives toward creativity and excellence in one's work disappeared.

With no financial reward for innovation or hard work, innovation and hard work were scarce. After all, if heart surgeons get paid the same as street sweepers, then the men and women who have the potential to make breakthrough discoveries in heart surgery might never have the motivation to go through many years of medical school or to work the 60–70 hours per week that world-renowned heart surgeons work. The overall effect is that the culture stays flat or declines rather than progressing and making breakthroughs. The larger the economy, the more devastating the decline.

A final criticism, and a serious one, is that socialist forms of government are inevitably more coercive than democratic capitalist forms. Like other ideologies, socialism worships a jealous god. The idol of economic equality eventually demands that anybody or anything that gets in its way should be sacrificed on the altar. The Soviet experiment is illustrative, though it is by no means the only example, as the Communist Party increasingly used systematic terror to try to usher in the Communist utopia by force. Systematic terror was not only possible but easy because socialism had already put nearly all power in the government's hands. It is no accident that most versions of twentieth-century socialism were authoritarian or totalitarian.

Conclusion

An increasing number of Americans today find some version of socialism attractive. A new Gallup poll reveals that 57 percent of Democrats are favorable toward socialism ("Democrats More Positive about Socialism Than Capitalism"). The socialist vision for material equality is grand—even utopian. Yet, untethered from a biblical framework, "equality" becomes an idol and a weapon in the hands of an increasingly strong and oppressive state.

Indeed, no idol can bear the weight of our eschatological hopes and dreams. Thus, if we wish to see members of every social sector, ethnic heritage, and economic class flourish together in a roughly equal manner, it will not be through the implementation of socialist ideology. It will only come when something greater—Someone greater—is on the throne. And in the meantime, before Christ returns, we will need to work through other more realistic means to seek the common good and flourishing of our nation.

(A version of this essay was first published on the website of the Ethics & Religious Liberty Commission. It is indebted to David Koyzis's critique of socialism in *Political Visions & Illusions: A Survey & Christian Critique of Contemporary Ideologies* [Grand Rapids: IVP, 2003].)

Christian Worldview and Cultural Engagement

THE BIBLE AND CREATION CARE

Glenn R. Kreider

The biblical story begins with God and his creative work. God spoke the universe into existence. He separated light from darkness, day from night, water under the expanse from water above it, and water from land. Then he caused vegetation to grow on the dry ground. He filled the waters with fish, the sky with flying creatures, and the earth with a variety of living things, each created according to its kind. He blessed the creatures he had made and commanded them to fill their domain (Gen 1:22). Then, as the pinnacle of his creative work, he made humanity (male and female) in his image and likeness and commanded them to fill the earth and rule over all the creatures he had made and blessed (Gen 1:26–28). Rather than caring for it himself, God entrusted the care of his creation to humans. He placed the man and woman "in the garden of Eden to work it and watch over it" (Gen 2:15). It was a world of order, harmony, and blessing for all created things.

But then order was turned to chaos, harmony to turmoil, blessing to curse, and life to death. Creation's caretakers chose to believe the serpent, a creature, rather than God; they ate the fruit from the one tree from which God had forbidden them to eat (Gen 3:1–6). God cursed the ground as his judgment on these rebels. He removed them from the garden and promised them that death would be their end. Nevertheless, he did not rescind the command to rule over the earth and to care for the creation. Instead, he said that their creation care would be more difficult; their work would now be characterized as "painful labor . . . until [they returned] to the ground, since [they] were taken from it. For [they were] dust, and [they would] return to dust" (Gen 3:17–19).

As humanity multiplied on the earth, they became more corrupt and filled with wickedness (Gen 3:1–5). God was "deeply grieved" (Gen 6:6). He sent judgment on the earth in the form of a flood in order to "wipe mankind, whom [he] created, off the face of the earth, together with the animals, creatures that crawl, and birds of the sky" (Gen 6:7). But God delivered Noah and his family and representatives of every kind of living creature. When the flood waters receded and the inhabitants of the ark returned to the dry ground, God reiterated his purpose for humanity when he said to Noah and his family, "Be fruitful and multiply and fill the earth" (Gen 9:1). God made a covenant with all living creatures and the earth itself, in which he promised never again to destroy all life on the planet (Gen 9:11). This covenant had a sign, a rainbow, which God established as a reminder of the everlasting covenant between him and "all the living creatures on earth" (Gen 9:16). The everlasting covenant presupposes an everlasting earth, cared for by those created in God's image and likeness.

In the incarnation, in Jesus of Nazareth, the eternal Son of God entered creation. The Creator took on flesh and resided in the world he had made (John 1:14). In so doing, he revealed God to the world and became its Savior (John 1:14–18,29). Christ's work of redemption is not merely good news for humans. The salvific plan of God is cosmic in scope.

The apostle Paul explains that creation has been longing for its redemption since the day it was cursed. Human creation care cannot remove the curse. That can only be done by the Creator, and he has promised to do so in the restoration of all things, in the redemption of all creation: "Creation eagerly waits with anticipation . . . in the hope that the creation itself will also be set free from the bondage to decay into the glorious freedom of God's children" (Rom 8:19–21). Creation's redemption is tied to humanity's redemption. Creation groans as it looks forward to its liberation. God's love for the world means that the world will be redeemed by the work of the Savior (John 3:16).

In his letter to the Colossians, Paul asserts that Jesus Christ is "the image of the invisible God" (Col 1:15), the One who created "everything" (Col 1:16), and the One who came "to have first place in everything" through his resurrection from the dead (Col 1:18). Paul concludes: "For God was pleased to have all his fullness dwell in him, and through him to reconcile everything to himself, whether things on earth or things in heaven, by making peace through his blood, shed on the cross" (Col 1:19–20). In the God-man, the Creator entered creation in order to redeem creation. As the head of his body, the church, Christ cares for his creation through his followers (Col 1:18).

The biblical story concludes with the promise of a new creation. In his vision of the completion of the work of redemption, John sees a new heaven and a new earth coming down to the earth from heaven. He also hears a voice from the throne of God:

> Look, God's dwelling is with humanity, and he will live with them. They will be his peoples, and God himself will be with them and will be their God. He will wipe away every tear from their eyes. Death will be no more; grief, crying, and pain will be no more, because the previous things have passed away (Rev 21:3–4).

When redemption is completed, the curse and all its effects will be removed, the earth will be made new, and the Creator will make the creation his home forever (cp. Isa 65:17–25). Then, forever, humans will serve God by caring for the world he made.

Humanity has been given the responsibility to serve God by caring for his creation, the place in which God will make his home eternally. Creation care is a stewardship given to us. It is a biblical mandate that predates the fall and has never been repealed. The fall makes our care more difficult, but it does not remove our responsibility. One indication of the seriousness of this responsibility is seen in the declaration of the Judge that those who destroy the earth will be judged. In Revelation 11:18, according to the song of the 24 elders, in the day of God's wrath, "the time has come for the dead to be judged and to give the reward to your servants the prophets, to the saints, and to those who fear your name, both small and great, and the time has come to destroy those who destroy the earth." Destruction of the planet is not merely accomplished by active and willful rebellion. Passivity, too, is failure to care for the earth and is tantamount to destroying it.

Several practical implications follow. (1) Creation care is a gospel concern, for it is a life issue. Healthy human and animal life depends on a good environment that includes clean air and water and one in which disease and decay are controlled. (2) In James 1:27, the apostle describes "pure and undefiled religion" as looking "after orphans and widows in their distress" and keeping "oneself unstained from the world." Later, he characterizes a faith that does not provide clothes and daily food for the needy as "dead" faith (Jas 2:15–17). Surely, providing clean air and water is as important as providing food and clothes. (3) Since no one knows when the end will come (Matt 24:36–44), caring for the creation benefits all inhabitants of the planet. Extending lifetimes and improving life's quality is good stewardship.

THE APOCALYPTIC AND THE ENVIRONMENT

Glenn R. Kreider

Widely quoted is this quip, often attributed to J. Vernon McGee: "You don't polish the brass on a sinking ship." This statement succinctly summarizes the view that since in the final judgment the earth will be consumed by fire, to support conservation and environmental causes is to oppose the will of God. According to this view, Christians should devote their attention to preaching the gospel and avoid working to care for the creation.

D. L. Moody famously said,

> I have felt like working three times as hard ever since I came to understand that my Lord was coming back again. I look on this world as a wrecked vessel. God has given me a life-boat, and said to me, "Moody, save all you can." God will come in judgment and burn up this world, but the children of God don't belong to this world; they are in it, but not of it, like a ship in the water. The world is getting darker and darker; its ruin is coming nearer and nearer. If you have any friends on this wreck unsaved, you had better lose no time in getting them off. (*New Sermons, Addresses, and Prayers*, 535)

Several key convictions characterize this apocalyptic worldview, for which its advocates believe they have biblical support. First, the world is declining, going from bad to worse (cp. 2 Tim 3:1–5). Second, this age ends with destruction by fire (2 Pet 3:7,12). When that judgment comes, the earth will be annihilated and replaced by "a new earth" (Rev 21:1). Third, the gospel is the promise of escape from the world, either through death or by deliverance from the earth before final judgment is unleashed on it (John 14:1–4). Finally, to care for this world would be to pour one's efforts into a lost cause, into caring for a world that will soon pass away. It would be much better to spend limited time and resources storing up treasures in heaven (Matt 6:19–21).

Will God destroy the world?

But are such antienvironmental attitudes really biblical? When God sent judgment on the earth in the flood (Gen 6–8), he destroyed all living creatures except those who were in the ark with Noah—and the aquatic life that survived the onslaught in the waters. When the flood receded, Noah and the rest of the inhabitants of the ark resettled the earth. Then God made a covenant with all living things in which he promised never again to destroy all life with a flood: "I establish my covenant with you that never again will every creature be wiped out by floodwaters; there will never again be a flood to destroy the earth" (Gen 9:11). Those who believe in a coming apocalyptic conflagration understand this as a promise that God will never again destroy the earth in a flood but believe he will destroy it—completely—by fire.

Yet, when he continues, God describes the rainbow as "the sign of the covenant I am making between me and you and every living creature with you, a covenant for all future generations. . . . I will remember my covenant between me and you and all the living creatures: water will never again become a flood to destroy every living creature" (Gen 9:12,15). This everlasting covenant implies that God has promised the earth that she will endure, that the earth will not be destroyed totally in the future. Further, since the flood did not annihilate the earth—for after the flood the earth remained—the fire of the eschatological judgment need not consume the earth entirely.

The apostle Peter responds to scoffers who reject the promise of the Lord's return, rebuking them for their willful ignorance of the doctrine of creation and the judgment in the flood:

> By the word of God the heavens came into being long ago and the earth was brought about from water and through water. Through these the world of that time perished when it was flooded. By the same word, the present heavens and earth are stored up for fire, being kept for the day of judgment and destruction of the ungodly (2 Pet 3:5–7).

Since the earth itself did not perish in the flood, the comparison might be that the future judgment by fire will destroy wicked people and the effects of the curse, not the earth itself. Peter is comparing the destruction of the earth in the flood to the destruction of ungodly men in the final judgment. In both cases, the earth is the locus of the judgment, not its focus. The wicked inhabitants of the earth are destroyed, not the whole planet itself.

Peter uses apocalyptic language to describe this day of judgment: "The heavens will pass away with a loud noise, the elements will burn and be dissolved, and the earth and the works on it will be disclosed" (2 Pet 3:10). But rather than destroying the earth, the fire will be purifying and revelatory. It results in the works of humans being disclosed or made visible, not in the annihilation of the planet. Later, he says that "the heavens will be dissolved with fire and the elements will melt with heat" (3:12). The fire of judgment will be destructive, but that does not mean the earth will be annihilated.

The New Earth

When the apostle John sees the heavenly city come down to earth at the end of the age, he exclaims that "the first heaven and the first earth had passed away" (Rev 21:1). This might mean that the earth will cease to exist and will be replaced by another. But, as Richard Bauckham explains, the terms "first" and "new" indicate the "qualitatively quite different life of the eternal age to come. The discontinuity is parallel, on a cosmic scale, to the discontinuity, in the case of human persons, between this moral life and the eschatologically new life of resurrection" (*The Theology of the Book of Revelation*, 49).

In short, in the same way there is continuity between the human body that is buried in the ground and the body that is raised in the day of resurrection, there will be continuity between the first earth and the redeemed or recreated one. When Thomas saw the risen Lord, he recognized him (John 20:27–29); there was continuity between the body that died and the one that was raised. And so believers look forward to the resurrection of their bodies (1 Cor 15:51–57).

Hope for Creation

Finally, it is difficult to reconcile annihilation of the earth with Paul's personification of creation's hope. He writes, "Creation eagerly waits with anticipation . . . in the hope that the creation itself will also be set free from the bondage to decay into the glorious freedom of God's children" (Rom 8:19–21). Annihilation could hardly be expressed as the hope of liberation. In short, the re-creation of heaven and earth fits this language better than annihilation, and it fits better with the pattern of God's redemptive work. When God redeems, he does not destroy but regenerates and re-creates.

But even if the earth will be annihilated, that still does not mean Christians should oppose environmental and conservationist efforts. Preaching the gospel is not antithetical to care of the creation. In the first place, stewardship of creation is a divine mandate that was not revoked (Gen 1:26–28; 2:5,7). In the second, since no one knows when the Lord will return (Matt 24:36–41), it makes sense to act in the knowledge that providing clean water and air preserves and extends human life. And third, since no one knows when his life will end, everyone has a vested interest in caring for the environment. In a similar way that exercise is profitable for the body, saving for retirement is wise, and caring for our earthly possessions is good stewardship, caring for the environment is wise.

ANIMAL RIGHTS

Erik Clary

Few social issues of our day have become as celebrated as so-called animal rights. Chiefly the concern of philosophers only a few decades ago, the movement now boasts a sizable following of A-list celebrities and generally youthful converts eager to proclaim the purported evils of meat eating, hide wearing, hunting, and laboratory animal research. The core contention is not that animals used for these purposes ought to be treated compassionately but rather that they should not be used at all. Animal liberation is a moral imperative for animal rights activists.

The Basis for Animal Liberation

Animal liberationists view the dividing line between humans and animals as arbitrary and unjust. In their way of thinking, to bear a right or an interest worthy of protection one must have "moral standing," and they assert that any species that has the capacity to suffer or experience pain ("sentience") qualifies. Many animals (not just humans) appear sentient, so with respect to moral status, animal liberationists proclaim a radical equality wherein, as prominent activist Ingrid Newkirk has stated, "a rat is a pig is a dog is a boy" (quoted by Katie McCabe in "Who Will Live, Who Will Die?" *Washingtonian*, August 1, 1986, p. 115).

The Value of Animals

At the heart of animal rights lies a kernel of truth. Animals are due moral consideration—not because they are sentient but because they are creatures of

211

God and he cares for them. Created by him and for him (Col 1:16), they belong to him (Ps 24:1), and he rejoices in them (Ps 104:31). He pronounced them good and blessed them apart from humans (Gen 1:21–22,25); thus, they have value beyond what may be attributed to their utility for human ends. Such value is further seen by God's preservation of every kind of wildlife during the flood (Gen 7:14–16) and in his concern for the "many animals" of Nineveh (Jonah 4:11).

That God cares about animals is also evident in his provision for their needs. The psalmist declares, "All eyes look to you, and you give them their food at the proper time. You open your hand and satisfy the desire of every living thing" (Ps 145:15–16). For the herbivore, God "causes grass to grow" (Ps 104:14), and to the lion he delivers the prey (Ps 104:21). To the bird he gives the tree for shelter and as a stage from which to sing (Ps 104:12,16–17), and to the sea creature Leviathan, he provides an environment suited to its playful disposition (Ps 104:26). God knows the needs of his creatures, and he provides accordingly.

As God values animals and concerns himself with their well-being, he demands that we do the same. Scripture thus declares, "The righteous cares about his animal's health, but even the merciful acts of the wicked are cruel" (Prov 12:10). Tending to the needs of animals only when it aligns with self-interest misses the mark. Instead, care that is morally praiseworthy reflects genuine compassion for the beast, and here again God provides the example for "his compassion rests on all he has made" (Ps 145:9). Obligations extend not just to animals we call our own, so God commands that livestock belonging to friend or foe be treated mercifully (Exod 23:4–5; Deut 22:1–4). The ox in the ditch is to be rescued and stray animals taken in and cared for until they can be returned to their owner. In these situations, obligations exist even when human interests are not at stake. Wild animals are due our concern, and Scripture mandates that the feral hen brooding a clutch be left alone (Deut 22:6–7) and that fields, vineyards, and groves be regularly fallowed in provision for the beasts that roam (Exod 23:11).

Animals and Human Worth

While affirming the moral value of animals, the Bible provides no support for the claim of their equality with humans. Indeed, it refutes that notion. Like the animals, we have been fashioned from the earth and infused with the breath of life (Gen 1:30; 2:7), but we alone have been made in the image of

God (Gen 1:26–27) and are rendered creatures of his special concern. Jesus testified to our favored status: "Aren't five sparrows sold for two pennies? Yet not one of them is forgotten in God's sight. Indeed, the hairs of your head are all counted. Don't be afraid; you are worth more than many sparrows" (Luke 12:6–7). By God's accounting, animal life has value, but human life is of greater worth; thus, God demands that it be treated with an elevated measure of respect.

In Scripture, the differential in respect due animal and human life is readily apparent. For example, the passerby encountering the wild hen is permitted to take her chicks but kidnapping a child is a capital offense (Exod 21:16). Similarly, we may with God's blessing kill and consume animals posing no threat to human life (Gen 9:3; Rom 14:2–3), but on account of our image-bearing status, the shedding of innocent human blood is strongly condemned (Gen 9:6; Exod 21:12). Thus, Cain sins greatly in killing Abel (Gen 4:10) and David also in ordering the death of Uriah (2 Sam 11:15–27), but Jesus commits no transgression in directing a great catch of fish or in preparing from the netted bounty breakfast for his disciples (John 21:1–13). In God's moral order, human life is in a category of its own.

Humans' Dominion as a Blessing

In affirming the unique moral status of humans, Scripture offers to balance animal rights ideology. The biblical proclamation of human headship over creation is a matter of divine purpose and blessing. "God blessed [Adam and Eve], and God said to them, 'Be fruitful, multiply, fill the earth, and subdue it. Rule the fish of the sea, the birds of the sky, and every creature that crawls on the earth'" (Gen 1:28). Frequently, proponents of animal rights read into this dominion mandate a license for animal abuse, as if to subdue (*kabash*) and rule (*radah*) can only mean that humans are called to function as merciless tyrants. This is a misrepresentation of the biblical teaching. The dominion mandate was established before humanity's fall into sin and after God had already indicated his intention for the animals to flourish (Gen 1:22). In other words, our function as vice-regents over creation comes part and parcel with God's plan to bless all creation.

Under human stewardship the creation is intended to flourish, yet because of the curse wrought by sin, its present condition is one of futility and corruption (Gen 3; Rom 8:20–21). The mandate to rule remains after the fall, but it is not immune to the perverting effects of sin and with the

Noahic covenant its provisions were expanded by God to include eating meat (Gen 9:3–4). Dominion can indeed manifest as cruelty in this present age, but as Scripture presents it, the solution lies not in the abdication of human authority, as animal liberationists propose, but in our redemption through Christ. "The creation eagerly waits with anticipation for God's sons to be revealed" in the sure hope that it will be "set free from the bondage to decay [and corruption] into the glorious freedom of God's children" (Rom 8:19–21).

Judged in light of Scripture, the ideological commitments underlying the animal rights movement can be a false morality. Its ethic is a product of a secular philosophy that looks no further than nature for the ground of moral value. True goodness and justice find their source not in the creation but in the Creator in whom "there is absolutely no darkness" (1 John 1:5). "All his ways are just" (Deut 32:4). God has made humans creatures of special worth. He has assigned us the responsibility to care for his creation and the privilege to employ its resources. In that context we bear a duty toward animals and their welfare.

A BIBLICAL ASSESSMENT OF ABORTION

Steve W. Lemke

Abortion has been one of the most controversial issues in American culture over the last 50 years. What guidance does the Bible give us about the topic? Although it might seem surprising that an ancient document would address such a contemporary problem, the Bible in fact offers a number of clear teachings that address abortion from several perspectives.

Who creates life?

Life comes from God. God created humans in his image; therefore, persons are treasured above all creation (Gen 1:26–27; 9:6). God is involved directly and personally in our creation. "The Lord is God," Ps 100:3 teaches. "He made us, and we are his—his people, the sheep of his pasture." Psalm 139:13–14 declares, "It was you [God] who created my inward parts; you knit me together in my mother's womb. I will praise you because I have been remarkably and wondrously made." Elsewhere the Creator is described as literally breathing into humans the breath of life: "Then the LORD God formed the man out of the dust from the ground and breathed the breath of life into his nostrils, and the man became a living being" (Gen 2:7). "The Spirit of God has made me," Job affirms, "and the breath of the Almighty gives me life" (Job 33:4). Because God the Life Giver has granted life (Job 10:12), who are we to be life takers?

Is human life sacred?

The Bible stands strongly for the protection of human life and cries out against the taking of it. Scripture affirms the sanctity of life in numerous places, including Gen 2:7; Pss 127:3; 139:13–16a; and Jer 1:4–5. Human life began when God shaped Adam in his own image and breathed into him. "He created them [meaning humankind] male and female" (Gen 1:27). Being made in the image of God, in fact, gives human life its sacredness. The image of God is present when a new life starts in the womb.

The Bible places a strict prohibition against taking human life. The sixth commandment prohibits murder (Exod 20:13). Likewise, after the great flood, God reaffirmed the sacredness of human life and instituted the death penalty for those who take it; this was done to underscore the value of human life (Gen 9:5–6). To take a life at any point following conception is to kill one whom God has made in his own image (Gen 1:27; 9:6).

The OT law identifies punishments for actions that cause even an accidental miscarriage or premature birth (Exod 21:22–25). One particular law concerns two men whose fighting leads to a woman being hit accidentally, causing her child to be born early. Whether miscarriage or premature delivery is in view, the inadvertent action is considered a sin to be punished by law. If even an accidental injury were fatal for either the mother or the child, the perpetrator could be liable and executed; this is a harsher penalty than any other form of involuntary manslaughter receives in the OT law. The concern for the health of the mother in Exodus 21 may provide an allowance for the life of the mother to be taken into consideration in exceptional cases in which both the mother's and child's lives are at risk.

Is the unborn child a person?

The Bible is clear that life and personhood begin before birth. Unborn infants are shaped by God, known personally by him, and reflect the image of God. Moreover, God has a plan for their lives. Many Scriptures affirm that even as unborn children, we humans are shaped by God. Job 31:15 asks, "Did not the one who made me in the womb also make them? Did not the same God form us both in the womb?" In Psalm 22:9, the psalmist says, "[God,] you . . . brought me out of the womb, making me secure at my mother's breast." And Ps 139:14–16 declares, "Your works are wondrous, and I know this very well. My bones were not hidden from you when I was made in secret. . . . Your eyes saw me when I was formless."

Several biblical words are used to describe the mother's womb as the location of the unborn child, supporting the affirmation that life begins in the uterus. Two roughly synonymous Hebrew words are translated "womb" in the OT: *rachem* (Gen 20:18; 49:25; Num 12:12; Jer 20:17–18; Job 10:18; 20:18; 38:8; Isa 46:3; Hos 9:14) and *beten* (Job 3:10; 31:18; Ps 22:9; 71:6; 139:13; Isa 49:1; Jer 1:5). The NT also uses two broadly synonymous Greek words—*koilia* (Luke 1:15,41,44) and *metra* (Luke 1:15; 2:23)—to describe the womb as the baby's location before birth. Elizabeth's experience of feeling John kick when Mary was visiting her made it evident that the baby was alive and even socially interactive in the womb (Luke 1:15,41,44).

The language of Psalm 139 provides a rich resource for a biblical view of unborn children. The Hebrew word *golem*, used only in verse 16 in the Bible, is sometimes translated as "formless" or "unformed substance" (NASB); nevertheless, it can accurately be translated as "embryo" or "fetus." The Bible thus affirms that a developing child within the mother's womb is a human who has essentially the same potential as would a born child at any other stage of development.

The author of Psalm 139 refers to himself as an unborn child multiple times, using the personal pronouns "me" and "I." Scripture thus clearly affirms that unborn children have personhood even in utero. Personhood does not change in any fundamental way between conception and birth. Personal identity has an unbroken continuity from the joining of sperm and egg through senior adulthood. The soul that is in the womb originated by the gift of God. That same soul exists outside the womb after birth.

Psalm 139 also speaks of God's having an intimate knowledge of the unborn child. Note also the psalmist's recognition that God has a plan for his life. "All my days," he says, "were written in your book and planned before a single one of them began" (Ps 139:16). Remarkably, Luke even describes John the Baptist as having the Holy Spirit within him while still in his mother's womb (Luke 1:15b). The affirmation that God has a calling in mind for individual lives, even when those lives are in embryonic or fetal stage, is taught in other Scriptures as well. In Isaiah 49:1, the prophet says, "The LORD called me before I was born. He named me while I was in my mother's womb." In Jeremiah 1:5, God told Jeremiah, "I chose you before I formed you in the womb; I set you apart before you were born. I appointed you a prophet to the nations." The apostle Paul shares a similar revelation about his own beginnings in Galatians 1:15–17: "When God, who from my mother's womb set me apart and called me by his grace, was pleased to reveal his Son in me, so that I could preach him among the Gentiles . . . I went." The NT makes no clear distinction between the personhood of born or unborn children.

Conclusion

To summarize, the Bible regards unborn infants as fully human individuals who, even in their earliest stages of development, have the potential to achieve that which persons in adulthood might. Though life is a constant process of adjustments, the full person and unique soul formed in the womb remain the same person and soul throughout life. Unborn children have the God-given right to life and should be accorded all the rights normally granted to humans. Christians do well to stand for and protect the lives of the unborn.

THE CHRISTIAN WORLDVIEW AND THE OVERCOMING OF EVIL

Mary Jo Sharp

Jesus acknowledges that the world has a problem. When John writes that memorable phrase, "Jesus wept" (John 11:35), he provides a powerful glimpse of the God who created the universe as "very good" (Gen 1:31), experiencing in the flesh the evil of this world that is under the curse of sin. And even though Jesus was about to demonstrate his divine authority by raising Lazarus from the dead, his reaction to the evil of death is one of utter sorrow.

The Teacher wrote that he looked out into the world at everything "under the sun"—that is, everything apart from God—and he saw such great evil, oppression, and suffering that he concluded it would be better never to have existed at all if this life is all a person could expect to live (Eccl 3:16–4:3). He clearly observed the problem of evil—that this world is a place in which people and circumstances have gone terribly wrong. In it justice and righteousness are noticeably lacking.

Not all worldviews, however, entail a belief in real good and real evil. According to some beliefs, such as eastern pantheistic monism (found in Buddhism and Hinduism), good and evil are illusions. Atheistic materialism holds that there is no absolute standard of good and evil, since there is nothing at work in the universe besides natural, physical processes, which are amoral, or neutral. "Good" and "evil" may be illusory projections of an ignorant mind, but they are not grounded in any objective reality.

In the Christian worldview, God's essential nature is good (Ps 119:68; Luke 18:19), and his inherent goodness provides the standard for what we understand to be "good." Anything that lacks God's goodness is "evil." We know what is good and evil because God created us with the capacity to know it. If a person doubts God's goodness due to the observation of evil's presence in the world, then he must establish how he can even comprehend what is "good" and "evil." The skeptic's frustration with evil implies that he believes in the absolute concepts of good and evil. Yet, since his worldview cannot provide philosophical grounding for them, he denies these concepts. But such denial is inconsistent with our experience of evil in this life.

Real Evil and a Real Problem

According to atheistic materialism, everything in the universe is dancing to the tune of its DNA, as Richard Dawkins suggests. The singer sings, the artist creates, the murderer murders, and the rapist rapes. Nothing is "good" or "evil" in this view: everything is just the way it is because each person is biologically determined to do whatever his or her genes tells them to do. According to Nancy Pearcey and Randy Thornhill of the University of New Mexico and Craig Palmer of the University of Colorado, then, one can "advance the startling thesis that rape is not a pathology but an evolutionary adaptation—a strategy for maximizing reproductive success." Rape is "a natural, biological phenomenon that is a product of the human evolutionary heritage," just like "the leopard's spots and the giraffe's elongated neck" (Nancy R. Pearcey, *Darwin's Dirty Secret*, http://www.leaderu.com/orgs/arn/pearcey/np_world-rape0300.htm). Although atheists generally deny that there is an absolute moral law, deep down most will agree that rape and murder are truly wrong.

So atheists are aware of the existence of evil, but this creates more of a problem for them than for the Christian. If we are purely the result of DNA, there is no immortal soul, and death is the end of our existence, then all of our human sensibilities and attempts to relieve the suffering of the world are useless and absurd. As William Lane Craig states, "If life ends at the grave, then it makes no difference whether one has lived as a Stalin or as a saint. Since one's destiny is ultimately unrelated to one's behavior, you may as well just live as you please" (*Reasonable Faith*, 60–61). The fact that many atheists pursue meaningful and altruistic lives illustrates the impossibility of living consistently within such a worldview.

Jesus, on the other hand, understands that evil is a real problem that cannot be ignored or denied. Death is not just the dance of our DNA. Death is the enemy (1 Cor 15:26). Jesus teaches that evil affects all of us through death (Luke 13:1–5). And it is Jesus's confrontation of evil provides a real solution offering hope to mankind.

Real Hope

Hope acknowledges that there is a problem in the world, but at the same time hope confidently holds out for something better to come. The uniqueness of the Christian worldview resides in the hope provided through the resurrection of Jesus Christ. "Death is the ultimate weapon of the tyrant; resurrection does not make a covenant with death, it overthrows it" (Wright, *The Resurrection of the Son of God* , 730).

Suffering, pain, and ultimately death are not part of the way things should be; rather, they are the consequences of evil (Rom 6:23). The resurrection is a clear defeat of these consequences. Peter explains in Acts 2:24, that "God raised [Jesus Christ] up, ending the pains of death, because it was not possible for him to be held by death." Paul declares the impotence of death's sting and its shattered victory (1 Cor 15:55–57).

Jesus gives us hope because by his resurrection he overthrows death and demonstrates that God's good creation will be restored (1 Cor 15:20–22,42–44). Things will be as they should be. Our painful comprehension of evil and our hopeful longing for goodness are neither vain nor illusory. They are evidence that we are created by a good and mighty God. No other worldview can compete with what Christianity has to offer: a grounding of real evil, a definitive defeat of that evil, and real hope for mankind through the actual restoration of goodness, as seen in the resurrection.

EQUALITY OF THE RACES AND RACIAL RECONCILIATION

Robert Smith Jr.

In civil rights activist James Weldon Johnson's musical rendition, "Lift Every Voice and Sing," he spoke about the tear-watered, blood-stained journey toward racial equality (*Worship and Rejoice*, 729). Today talk of *race*, a word referring to ethnic distinctions associated with culture and skin color, is a treacherous matter. But in the beginning, God created all peoples out of one blood to dwell on the face of the earth (Acts 17:26), and in the Bible we see his intentions for humanity: "A vast multitude from every nation, tribe, people, and language, which no one could number, [was] standing before the throne and before the Lamb. They were clothed in white robes with palm branches in their hands" (Rev 7:9). All humans are descended from Adam and Eve (cp. Gen 3:20), and Jesus died so that *all* who would accept him by faith could spend eternity in his presence.

Yet in spite of these biblical realties, the enslavement of peoples from Africa survived the two great religious movements in American history—the first and second Great Awakenings. Western Christianity, in fact, still struggles with conscienceless power and powerless conscience as Christians sit around their Communion tables and worship in segregated church contexts. In adopting racist attitudes and remaining in separate camps as it were, humanity, who was made in the image of God and after God's likeness (Gen 1:26) has not only attempted to make God in its own image (that is, prone to categorize by appearances) but has also tried to detheologize the divine DNA within mankind.

The establishment of racial hierarchy has led to apartheid, anti-Semitism, and rampant racism. History records educational exclusion and societal separation, resulting in bloodstained streets. The sacrificial blood of Christ shed at Calvary, however, was offered to cleanse humanity from sin, thus enabling us to move even beyond racial reconciliation to Christo-conciliation—fulfilling the prayer of Jesus in Gethsemane. He wanted his followers to "be one" (John 17:11). "As you, Father, are in me and I am in you, may they also be in us," he said (John 17:21).

Christo-conciliation, then, is better than mere racial reconciliation. Because of the death of the Son of God, Jesus Christ, Christians from all backgrounds are not just members of one biological family; we are one spiritual family, coheirs with Christ. South African Archbishop Desmond Tutu places strong emphasis on forgiveness with regard to this matter: "Forgiving means abandoning your right to pay back the perpetrator in his own coin" (*No Future without Forgiveness*, 219). African theologian Allan Aubrey Boesak contends that forgiveness is "taking the sting out of memory" (*Radical Reconciliation*, 138).

Christ-Centered Reconciliation

If we are to move beyond superficial conversation and onward to true healing with regard to this topic, we must consider three points. First, the evangelical church too often seems more influenced by sociology than by Scripture. Second, the evangelical church must take seriously the oneness of the human race. Third, that the gospel was intended for everyone is clearly understood, but the evangelical church tends to handle the gospel differently as it addresses different people groups. That needs to change.

In Dr. James Earl Massey's autobiography, *Aspects of My Pilgrimage*, he recounts being a delegate to the World Congress on Evangelism in 1966 in Berlin, Germany. The delegates represented nations from the farthest corners of the world. At that time, the Congress on evangelism was the largest ecumenical and evangelical gathering of the church since Pentecost in AD 33. The theme of the Congress was "One Race, One Gospel, One Task." But Dr. Massey and other African American delegates detected that there was an obvious omission in the dialogue—the topic of race. Dr. Carl F. H. Henry confessed to the African American delegates that the aspect of race, which was a part of the theme, had been taken for granted. He proceeded to apologize for this omission and asked the African American delegates to prepare a summary statement on "One Race."

Evangelicals must not merely assume the equality of the people groups; this truth must be embraced and proclaimed. Evangelicals must think seriously about the topic, drawing on Acts 17:26, and pointing toward the eschatological reality of the beloved community made up of different tribes and nations and tongues and peoples. We all descend from one couple, and as Christians, we have been washed in the blood of Jesus Christ.

Dr. William Holmes Borders, an African American pastor of the Wheat Street Baptist Church in Atlanta, Georgia, once told this story:

> [A Negro] had been denied an education, political and economic opportunity, and was forced to beg for food. He rang the front doorbell of a southern mansion and the owner of the house answered. "I'm hungry," the Negro said. "Go around to the back door," he was told. Food was prepared, and the owner of the house brought it to the Negro. "First we will bless the food," the white man said. "Now you repeat after me, Our Father . . ." The Negro said, "Your Father . . ." "Why do you insist upon saying, 'Your Father,' when I keep telling you to say, "'Our Father'?" the white man asked. The Negro beggar replied, "Well, boss, if I say, 'Our Father,' that would make you and me brothers, and I'm 'fraid the Lord wouldn't like it, you makin' your brother come to the back porch to get a piece of bread." (English, *Handyman of the Lord*, 33–34)

Conclusion

The apostle Paul reminds us that all persons have come into being out of one blood. That one blood makes each individual equal within the human race. The blood of Christ shed for the forgiveness of the sins of humanity, however, makes believing humanity brothers and sisters. May we move forward to embrace the divine design.

* * * * *

Lyrics to the song "Lift Every Voice and Sing" can be found at http://www. pbs.org/black-culture/explore/black-authors-spoken-word-poetry/lift-every-voice-and-sing/.

THE BIBLE AND CIVIL RIGHTS

Kevin Smith

The Bible was central to the thought, rhetoric, and development of the civil rights movement. This was influenced by the essential role of black churches and preachers in the organization of the movement. Not only was the movement characterized by meetings in churches and the singing of Negro spirituals; it was also marked by biblical themes and language. Although many non-Christians participated in and supported the aims of the civil rights movement, the underlying truth claims about the nature of all humanity, regardless of ethnicity, were grounded in the Scriptures.

The central intellectual strain behind the movement focused on the issue of the equality of all humans, since they were "created . . . in the image of God" (Gen 1:27), no matter the color of their skin. Throughout the black freedom struggle in American history, the biblical teachings on creation and human dignity were foundational to the arguments being put forth both by scholars and by everyday people. Even those who were illiterate knew from the rhetoric of the movement that God had created all people from one man (Acts 17:26). This distinguishes the civil rights movement from other revolutions that may have been rooted in political, economic, philosophical, or other ideas. This unique biblical foundation provided a basis for the invocation of the God revealed in the Bible to be a participant in the movement—just as he had empowered the exodus.

In his famous "Letter from Birmingham Jail" written April 16, 1963, Dr. Martin Luther King Jr. used biblical examples as a defense when he was accused of being an interloper and an extremist for participating in demonstrations, sit-ins, and boycotts. When justifying his presence in Birmingham, Dr. King noted that he was invited by local organizers, as well as noting the example of OT prophets leaving their villages to proclaim "thus saith the Lord" wherever God would send them. Additionally, he applauded the apostle Paul's travels in response to the call for help from the believers in Macedonia.

Grounding the movement morally in the Bible, King said, "A just law is a manmade code that squares with the moral law or the law of God." Therefore, the movement was able to attack laws that supported segregation and discrimination as laws that were ungodly, unjust, and against the clear teaching of Scripture. Certainly, America's founding documents—the Declaration of Independence and the U.S. Constitution—were an important part of the discourse, but the moral motivation and spiritual energy of the movement were grounded in the Bible. King even identified segregation as "sin" and called its proponents "sinful." He grounded his understanding of civil disobedience in the biblical example of Shadrach, Meshach, and Abednego, who refused to bow to the laws of Nebuchadnezzar because of their loyalty to a higher law—God's law. This was a vital part of his argument against passive or indifferent clergy, who sometimes grounded their opposition to King's actions in the rhetoric of "law and order." Many of the preachers involved in the movement would cite OT prophets, especially Hosea and Amos, when "prophesying" against corrupt officials—especially sheriffs and other law enforcement officers that would attack protestors and demonstrators.

In a provocative section of his letter, King responds to charges that his activities will bring about negative consequences—conflict, possibly violent, between demonstrators and local law enforcement. The Baptist preacher chastised his critics by likening them to those that would say the teachings, actions, and devotions of Jesus the Christ "precipitated the evil act of crucifixion." This thinking was flawed and unethical in King's mind. In contrast to the violence that was brought to bear on protestors, King noted that the nonviolent approach of the civil rights movement was grounded in "the Negro church" and its biblical understanding of loving one's neighbor and praying for one's enemies.

Some of the clergy that refused to support King's efforts suggested the church should not get involved in "secular" affairs. Additionally, they retorted that the church's business was the saving of souls, not political concerns. The letter responds that such a neglect of social concerns is not

logical, ethical, or bibl
Christian ethics, saying, fact, King finds it a strange understanding of
to a completely otherworl watched many churches commit themselves
distinction between body a igion which makes a strange, un-Biblical
between the sacred and the secular."

Finally, the Bible and its s ng story are on display in an extended
passage where King cites biblical aders and figures from church history in
defense against the assertion tha was an extremist.

> Though I was initially d inted at being categorized as an ex-
> tremist, as I continued to nk about the matter I gradually gained
> a measure of satisfaction fro he label. Was not Jesus an extremist
> for love: "Love you enemies, ss them that curse you, do good to
> them that hate you, and pray fo em which despitefully use you,
> and persecute you." Was not Amo n extremist for justice: "Let
> justice roll down like waters and rig ousness like an everflowing
> stream." Was not Paul an extremist fo he Christian gospel: "I
> bear in my body the marks of the Lord us." Was not Martin
> Luther an extremist: "Here I stand; I cann do otherwise, so help
> me God." And John Bunyan: "I will stay in il until the end of my
> days before I make a butchery of my conscien." And Abraham
> Lincoln: "This nation cannot survive half slave a d half free." And
> Thomas Jefferson: "We hold these truths to be sel vident, that all
> men are created equal . . ." So the question is not w ether we will
> be extremists, but what kind of extremists we will be. Will we be
> extremists for hate or for love? Will we be extremists for the preser-
> vation of injustice or for the extension of justice? In that dramatic
> scene on Calvary's hill three men were crucified. We must never
> forget that all three were crucified for the same crime—the crime of
> extremism. Two were extremists for immorality, and thus fell below
> their environment. The other, Jesus Christ, was an extremist for
> love, truth, and goodness, and thereby rose above his environment.
> Perhaps the South, the nation, and the world are in dire need of
> creative extremists.

Martin Luther King Jr. served many roles in the civil rights movement:
he was its face, an ethicist, a theologian, an organizer, and a public relations
agent. In all of these roles, his thinking and rhetoric were shaped and influenced by the Bible. Thus, so was the larger movement.

THE BIBLE AND SLAVERY

Craig Mitchell

As one reads the OT and the NT, slavery is clearly part and parcel of the whole ancient economic system. Throughout the ancient Near East (and everywhere else for that matter), slavery was a common solution to many problems. Bible readers are often confused with how we can reconcile such an evil as slavery with the Christian worldview. To do so, we have to take a number of things into account.

The first thing that we as Bible believers must recognize is that we live in a fallen sin-sick world. With the fall of man, many things came into existence that should not be. Murder, rape, warfare, and crime are just a few of many things that are distortions of the social order God desires. Slavery must first be understood as a corruption or distortion of the social order that results from the fall. The Bible does not endorse slavery; it merely realizes it as a state of affairs with which believers must contend.

Throughout the OT we find that the term *ebed*, meaning "slave" or "servant," is used more than 800 times. In more than a fifth of those instances it designates a household servant. Unfortunately, we also find that the number of slaves is often listed with animals to demonstrate the wealth of a patriarch. Throughout the ancient world, slaves were considered as part of a household, and as such, those people lost their own individual identities. They could be beaten, bought, sold, and inherited—even within ancient Israel.

Though the OT record makes clear that slavery was practiced within ancient Israel, the Hebrews practiced slavery in a way that differed from the practices of surrounding cultures. While other nations viewed slaves as nothing more than tools to be used, the Hebrews never lost sight of the fact that slaves are humans made in the image of God. As such, men retain a certain dignity that was not to be violated. Consequently, we find all kinds of laws in the Pentateuch (Genesis through Deuteronomy) regarding how slaves can and cannot be treated. In fact, in ancient Israel slaves even had the rights of citizens. All of this is because the Hebrews were constantly reminded that God brought them out of the land of slavery (Exod 20:2). One way the Hebrews differed in their approach to slavery was the Sabbath release after six years. Slavery was not intended to be a perpetual state of affairs for the enslaved unless they chose to stay.

In the NT, the most common word for slave is *doulos* (Gk), which is used 124 times. Aristotle argued that all things seek to achieve autonomy and self-sufficiency. Hence, slavery is the worst of all situations for the Greek citizen. The *doulos* may have some degree of autonomy but not self-sufficiency. In the ancient Greek world, it was sometimes better to be a slave and part of a household than to be free and separate from a household. At the time of the NT, 50 percent or more of humans served in some type of slavery. Slavery was often cruel, and there was little regard for human life. The *Patri Protempis* (Law of the Father) gave the *paterfamilias* (father, head of the household) power over punishments and rewards, as well as the life and death of slaves.

In the NT, slavery was neither condemned nor affirmed. In 1 Corinthians 7:20–23 the apostle Paul tells his readers that if they are slaves, they should not seek to be free. He emphasizes in Galatians that we are all equal in Jesus Christ. In Ephesians 6:5–10 and Colossians 3:22–25 he reminds masters not to be oppressive. In these sections of Scripture, Paul also reminds slaves to be obedient, aiming to please Christ rather than men.

The concept of slavery in the American context often complicates the issue because of the way that the Bible was used to justify slavery and its abuses in times past. Slavery in the United States was as cruel as it was in the ancient world. While some slave owners recognized the need of salvation for their slaves, others did not. The major difference between slavery in the United States and slavery in the ancient world is that in America people were enslaved solely based on of their ethnicity. This made for a more sinful institution.

A BIBLICAL VIEW OF MARRIAGE

Alan B. Terwilleger

God loves marriage. The Bible, after all, begins with a marriage as lonely Adam receives his bride, Eve, and celebrates with the world's first love song (Gen 2:22–25). The Bible ends with a marriage as Jesus, the Lamb of God, receives his bride, the church, at the great marriage supper of the Lamb (Rev 19:7). And Jesus, anticipating that final marriage supper, performed his first miracle at a wedding celebration (John 2:1–11).

The Bible presents marriage as the sacred, foundational institution designed by God for human flourishing, the well-being of children, and the advancement of his kingdom.

Marriage is a gift to all humanity. Roger Scruton puts it this way:

> In all observed societies some form of marriage exists, as the means whereby the work of one generation is dedicated to the well-being of the next. Marriage does not merely protect and nurture children; it is the shield against sexual jealousy and a unique form of social and economic cooperation, with a mutually supportive division of roles that more than doubles the effectiveness of each partner in their shared bid for security. (*The Meaning of Marriage*, p. 6)

While culture today exerts a significant influence on our attitudes and behavior surrounding marriage, Christians should desire to know what God thinks about this most sacred of institutions that he designed and loves. If God left us no instructions about marriage, we could go about it according to our personal or societal whims. But he hasn't left us uninformed. His revelation in Scripture guides us to his design for marriage, and through embracing it we will see his human creatures flourish.

People need companionship.

After God created the heavens and the earth and all that lives therein, he created man in his own image to rule and manage his creation. He did not create us all the same, but "he created them male and female" (Gen 1:27). In the process of creation, God repeatedly declared his creation good (Gen 1:4,10,12,18,21,25,31). But there was one exception. God stated that it was not good for man to be alone, to exist as a solitary being (Gen 2:18). Without human companionship, creation was incomplete. If man was alone, there could be no procreation and, more importantly, no possibility for man to experience the kind of intimate relationship that exists within the Godhead. And so God created woman to complement the man and thus complete the good design he had for humanity.

In his delight with Eve, Adam calls her "bone of my bone and flesh of my flesh; this one will be called 'woman,' for she was taken from man" (Gen 2:23). In the next verse we read, "This is why a man leaves his father and mother and bonds with his wife, and they become one flesh" (v. 24).

As seventeenth-century Bible commentator Matthew Henry wrote, "Eve was not taken from Adam's head that she should rule over him, nor from his feet, to be trampled under foot, but she was taken from his side that she might be his equal, from under his arm that she might be protected by him, near his heart, that he might cherish and love her."

In this way men and women provide companionship for each other in laboring together interdependently in God's kingdom work and in having children and nurturing families to populate God's creation.

One Man and One Woman

At creation God established marriage as the union of one man and one woman. Since then, our fallen state has created all kinds of distortions in God's design for marriage, including the moral confusion of our day. But God clearly demonstrates his design for one man and one woman to come together in this sacred union.

It is critical to understand that while God made man and woman as equals, he also created them to be different from one another. Men and women are not interchangeable; they are complementary. In marriage they become one flesh (Gen 2:24), one functioning unit, especially in pro-creation. H. C. Leupold explains that becoming one flesh "involves the complete identification of one personality with the other in community of interests and pursuits, a union consummated in intercourse" (*Exposition of Genesis*, vol. 1, 137).

In our culture it is vital to remind ourselves that in addition to the joy of husband and wife, sexual intercourse is designed for procreation. Marriage, sex, and children go together. The family, which is central to God's design for his kingdom, is made possible through the procreative act that brings together one man and one woman and defines the one-flesh unity of marriage. "Reproductive technologies" aside, only a man and a woman, complementing one another, can create another human person.

Marriage is a covenantal relationship.

Just as God and his bride, the church, are bound together by the new covenant of Christ crucified (Luke 22:19–20; Heb 9:15; 12:22–24), so husband and wife are bound together by the covenant of marriage (Mal 2:14).

While some talk about marriage as a contract, marriage is not a contract. It is a covenant. Contracts are agreements of "consideration given for consideration received." They are 50–50 arrangements in which one partner puts something in expecting to get something out. And contracts are over once they are fulfilled or when both parties agree to break them. Covenants, then, are radically different. In covenants, both parties are expected to give 100 percent, offering consideration even when none is received in return. Covenants are established by solemn vows invoking the name of God. And covenants are never fulfilled, can never change, and there is no point short of death at which the account can be closed. Those bound together by the covenant of marriage in the name of God through solemn vows witnessed by family and friends are sealed with God's divine blessing in a permanent relationship. "Therefore," as Jesus said, "what God has joined together, let no one separate" (Mark 10:9).

Since marriage is a lifelong commitment, the Christian's goal should not be just to have a "good" marriage, but to have a godly one. And while our fallen nature does not provide for marital bliss all the time, we must remember that where sin abounds, grace abounds (Rom 5:20) and where grace abounds, so does the potential for lifelong, loving marriage. While the Bible acknowledges the concession of divorce under certain circumstances, this falls short of God's ideal for marriage (Matt 19:1–9; 1 Cor 7:10–16).

Death to Self

A wedding day marks an end of a single man and a single woman who have been working on their own. Once the vows are said and the marriage sealed, the two become one. As Peter J. Leithart puts it,

> The wedding day is only the beginning of death. A man and a woman who go through a ceremony and then live as they have always lived have not really understood what marriage requires. Death at a wedding is a call to continual dying. At their wedding, a man and woman die to singleness, to the old relation with parents, to old habits and plans, and that death has to be worked out throughout the course of the marriage. ("When Marriage Is Dying," *Touchstone Magazine*)

Witness to the World

In their complementarity, married couples represent to the world the beauty and mystery of the love relationship God has with his people. Beginning in the OT, God referred to his people as his bride, bound to him by covenant (Isa 54:5–8; Ezek 16:8; Hos 2:19–20). He calls Israel's breaking of the covenant "adultery" and "prostitution" (Ezek 23; Hos 2:2–13). At the same time, he promises a day will come when "as a groom rejoices over his bride, so your God will rejoice over [Israel]" (Isa 62:5).

That same promise carries over into the NT. Paul concludes his instructions about Christian marriage with this statement: "This mystery is profound, but I am talking about Christ and the church" (Eph 5:32). Christian marriages demonstrate the love of God to a world in need of that love, and every wedding day anticipates the day Jesus will return to glorify and honor his bride, the church, and be with her forever (Rev 19:7–9; 21:2,9).

IS GENDER A CHOICE?

Stanton L. Jones

Sex and gender are commonly differentiated, with sex referring to the biological components of maleness and femaleness, and gender referring to their psychological and cultural components.

More precisely, the biological components of sex resolve into four facets:

1. chromosomes, with the prototypical male having one X and one Y chromosome and the female having two X chromosomes;
2. gonads and the hormones they produce, with males having testes and females ovaries;
3. sexual anatomy, with male external structures including the penis and scrotum and internal structures including vas deferens and prostate, while females externally have a clitoris and labia and internal structures including the vagina, uterus, and fallopian tubes;
4. secondary sex characteristics, including for males denser, coarser body and facial hair, larger stature and greater muscle mass, while females manifest enlarged breasts, wider hips, less body hair, and less muscle mass.

The psychological/cultural complements of gender resolve into at least three separate facets:

1. gender identity, the subjective sense of being a man or woman;

2. sexual orientation, with the prototypical male experiencing only erotic attraction to females and the female to males; and
3. gender role, the person's adoption of cultural expectations for maleness/masculinity or femaleness/femininity.

Given the complexity of the seven factors and their development, it is remarkable that so many adults align consistently on all seven factors, thus experiencing a somewhat uncomplicated sense of being a woman or a man. But some individuals deviate from the norms in one or more of the seven areas, as the following examples illustrate:

1. Some individuals inherit extra chromosomes (e.g., XXY and XYY, conditions with attendant complications).
2. Some persons experience incomplete gonadal development, and others develop gonads of mixed testicular and ovarian tissues (e.g., true hermaphroditism).
3. Malfunctioning gonads or a hormonally abnormal uterine environment may result in problematic anatomical development (e.g., Androgen Insensitivity Syndrome; micropenis; ambiguous genitalia [such as enlarged clitoris and labia that are mistaken upon birth as a penis and scrotum] that are sometimes called Intersex conditions); further, environmental events may create problems (e.g., a botched circumcision that amputates a penis).
4. Hormonal problems can result in minimized or exaggerated secondary sex characteristics.
5. Certain individuals report emphatic gender identification in contrast with their biological sex (transgenderism).
6. Three to 5 percent of the population report consistent, stable erotic attraction (orientation) toward persons of the same sex or to both sexes in varying degrees; others report stable attractions in other directions (e.g., pedophiles).
7. Some individuals are drawn to gender-atypical roles; further, cultures vary widely in their prescribed gender roles, including their clarity and rigidity.

Scientific evidence exists for some biological contribution to the three gender variables and for some psychosocial contribution to the four biological aspects of sex, though we are uncertain how determinative these contributions are or how they interact with human choice.

Is sex or gender a choice?

Christians begin by recognizing that God is the Creator and we are not, that humans are of two sexes by creational intent ("he created them male and female," Gen 1:27), and that our sexuality is intended as a gift to be first received with gratitude and humility and then to be formed responsibly by our parents and our choices. God exists eternally in Trinitarian community, and in his divine image we exist as embodied women and men in community and charged under the authority of our Lord with the proper stewardship of these gifts of sex and gender. Given that our sin blinds us at times to understanding what is good, we affirm with gratitude God's moral guidance of this stewardship.

Our sexuality is a gift given for purposes beyond our individual existence: maleness and femaleness typically set the foundation for marriage, a covenantal union of one man and one woman that includes full sexual intimacy often resulting in the procreation of children and the extension of multigenerational families. Sexuality is a gift with relational and community entailments; the husband and wife are gifts to each other.

Christians do not insist that every biological or psychological given is God's eternal will. Because of sin, neither humanity nor the world around us is as God intended. We are disordered. Thus, we cannot take our experience as God's intent. Where cruelty or immorality is a cultural norm (e.g., the practice of female genital mutilation in certain African and Islamic cultures, or the Hindu practice of *settee*, the burning to death of a widow at the cremation of her husband's body), we seek to produce cultural change.

Further, we recognize our finite limitations in interpreting God's special revelation. For example, in the realm of gender roles, reasonable Christians recognize that there is room for responsible choice; many would support the young woman who wants to study business leadership or the young father who chooses homemaking in support of his wife's career given her higher earning power. Neither choice, however, denies the unique callings of men and women.

There is legitimacy to seeking to correct disorders in the realm of physical sexual characteristics as well. As we would support surgical correction of a child's cleft palette, so we would support reattachment of a severed penis, surgical breast reduction for a woman whose heavy breasts contribute to muscular and spinal pain, or testosterone-enhancing treatments for a chromosomally and anatomically male teenager with delayed puberty and development of male secondary sex characteristics.

But more radical options are now possible. The question of whether sex or gender is a choice is challenging today because our technological prowess allows us to intervene medically or psychologically in ways once impossible. Such options present us with dilemmas. What of cases like the homosexual transsexual who, though born biologically female, undergoes sexual reassignment surgery to remove her ovaries and construct an artificial penis, takes testosterone, and develops male secondary sex characteristics, reports psychological identification as a man, adopts culturally masculine roles, yet desires sex with other men? In this case, six of the seven dimensions of sex/gender have been deviated from the presumptive norm with only the chromosomes unchanged. What do we make of her/his argument that "LGBT identity is congruent with how I have always felt and how God has made me"?

Biblical Christians in humble and full submission to Christ will accept the gift of their sexuality along with biblical norms for expression of that sexuality. But we live in a secular culture that rejects the Creator and his creational intent. This, in turn, leads to the rejection of any norms governing behavior and of the idea that departures from these norms constitute disorders in any objective sense. In the area of sexuality, we have seen steady shifts in the official mental health diagnostic criteria defining what constitute sexual disorders. Many behavioral or arousal patterns that were once regarded as "deviant" have been normalized; this includes nonheterosexual orientation and "fetishes."

Even more fundamentally, a materialistic worldview that assumes that chance alone determines life outcomes robs us of any deep sense of meaning or the good. With only a vague aspiration of genetic propagation and evolutionary progress as a guide, brute assertion of human will against cruel chance may be all that is left. This can lead to a broad societal embrace of something like the original temptation placed before Adam and Eve at the time of the fall, that through exercising one's choice in violation of norms, "you will be like God, knowing good and evil" (Gen 3:5).

We are living at a time when some fit the apostle Paul's harsh description in Romans 1 of persons who exchange "the glory of the immortal God for images resembling mortal man" (1:23) with the result that "they did not think it worthwhile to acknowledge God" (1:28). As a possible example of such a prioritization of human will, the American Psychological

Association's (www.apa.org) 2009 report on *Appropriate Therapeutic Response to Sexual Orientation* contrasted two perspectives: (1) a Christian religious understanding of personal identity grounded in external and transcendent norms, against (2) LGBT affirmation: psychological approaches of "living with a sense of wholeness in one's experiential self . . . [a] perspective [that] gives priority to the unfolding of developmental processes, including self-awareness and personal identity" (p. 26). The Christian stance of personal submission to God's will indeed contrast with an insistence that personal identity is best established by achieving congruence first with "one's experiential self."

Christians recognize that as a result of our disorder and that of our world due to humanity's choice to sin, we experience discord in many ways: between physical sex and the sexual prototypes, between facets of our sex and gender, between our personal inclinations and cultural standards, between biblical norms and our personal inclinations (or cultural standards), and others. Resolution of such discord may take many forms, requiring us as humble stewards to make complex choices. There are times to intervene medically or psychologically to correct disorders, following Christ's model as Healer. There are times to violate prevailing gender roles at God's calling; for instance, we have positive precedents in biblical stories of women who were prophetesses, judges, or who participated in acts of war.

More troubling are cases like transsexualism in which one's gender identity is discordant with the clear testimony of biological sex. Many today reject viewing this condition as a disorder in favor of celebrating it as part of human diversity. But in the Christian perspective incorporating God's creational intent, such conditions must be seen as disorders. Indeed, all human life is disordered because of sin. Our overarching call is to pursue conformity of our lives (body and soul) to God's revealed will (1 Tim 4:1–5) and to seek his sovereign healing of our brokenness in confidence of our ultimate healing in eternity.

While it can prove difficult to discern the proper response in complex cases, the simple prioritization of the experiential self and a facile manipulation of biological sex must be rejected even as we seek compassionate responses to persons suffering with an objective disorder. We must resist the illusion that the ultimate determination of sex and gender is ours to make autonomously. There are many choices to be made about how we live out our sexuality in godliness. But in the deepest sense, our choices that shape sex and gender should first reflect humble submission to God's choices for us.

RESPONSES TO TRANSHUMANISM

M. Todd Bates

Most of us at one time or another have wished to be a little taller, thinner, or healthier. Most of us have desired to be a little more intelligent, more self-controlled, perhaps even a little more virtuous. These desires seem universal, but now, with the advancements in modern technology, a movement called transhumanism wants to make these enhancements and many others available to all.

Generously defined, *transhumanism* is "a loosely defined movement that has developed gradually over the past two decades. It promotes an interdisciplinary approach to understanding and evaluating the opportunities for enhancing the human condition and the human organism opened up by the advancement of technology" (Nick Bostrom, "Transhumanist Values").

More ominously described, "Transhumanists view human nature as a work in progress, a half-baked beginning that we can learn to remold in desirable ways. Current humanity need not be the endpoint of evolution" (ibid.). While the second description is worded more blatantly, the ideas that make it ominous are present in the first definition.

Two further terms help give perspective to transhumanism—the *transhuman* and the *posthuman*. A transhuman refers to an intermediary form between the human and the posthuman. A posthuman is a possible future being whose capacities exceed those of present humans to the extent that it is no longer clearly human by current standards. Thus, a transhumanist supports transhumanism's effort toward the posthuman by way of the transhuman.

In practice, many elements of transhumanism are consistent with a biblical view of human nature and the human condition. Pronounced efforts to relieve human suffering and foster virtues that sustain human flourishing motivate transhumanist labors. Indeed, there is such significant overlap with the gospel and the transhumanist narrative that a prominent transhumanist website responds to why so many call it the "new religion." In an uncanny way, transhumanism tells a story of redemption: it has a view of the human predicament and why "salvation" is needed. It has a view of the nature of salvation and of what that salvation consists. It even has a vision of the future that could be called eschatological hope.

From a biblical perspective, however, transhumanism is rooted in key assumptions about human nature, the human condition, and the nature of reality that are antithetical to a biblical understanding of each. So, despite the superficial similarities, transhumanism represents a different gospel.

The Beliefs of Transhumanists

The transhumanist movement, according to Nick Bostrom, a transhumanist philosopher from the University of Oxford, has roots in secular humanist thinking but extends beyond it. Secular humanism chooses to begin with several beliefs about the nature of reality and knowledge, beliefs that are shared equally by transhumanists. The first few statements of the secular *Humanist Manifesto I, II,* and now *III* pronounce these beliefs.

First, there is a fundamental denial of God. Humanism is a progressive philosophy of life that, without supernaturalism, affirms our ability and responsibility to lead ethical lives of personal fulfillment that aspire to the greater good of humanity (*III*).

Second, human life arises from a naturalistic evolutionary process. Humanism believes that man is a part of nature and that he has emerged as the result of a continuous process (*I*). Holding an organic view of life, humanists find that the traditional dualism of mind and body must be rejected (*I*).

Third, consistent with its denial of supernaturalism, knowledge about and from God is denied and only naturalistic knowledge is available. Knowledge of the world is derived by observation, experimentation, and rational analysis. Humanists find that science is the best method for determining this knowledge as well as for solving problems and developing beneficial technologies (*III*).

These so-called beneficial technologies are those through which transhumanism extends beyond secular humanism.

According to Humanity Plus, an international transhumanist organization, transhumanists "are not limited to traditional humanistic methods, such as education and cultural development. We can also use technological means that will eventually enable us to move beyond what some would think of as human." This organization boasts more than 6,000 members from more than a hundred countries, with many affiliated organizations.

Transhumanism Versus the Gospel

The "move beyond human" idea is where the movement's superficial similarities with the gospel appear. A key term used in transhumanist writing is *enhancement*. In the opening definition it is in reference to the use of emergent technologies to enhance the human condition. This includes such things as vaccinations and using technology to eradicate deadly diseases and unnecessary human suffering.

Bringing healing to those in pain, aid to those in need, and care for the aged are certainly consistent with the gospel. Many transhumanists even appeal to the words and work of Jesus as support for their efforts, claiming that Jesus did not simply accept sickness and death as "the Father's will," but sought to alleviate suffering. Indeed, Jesus exerted great effort in healing as a sign of his ministry. When questioned by John the Baptist's disciples (Matt 11:2–6), Jesus directly pointed to this part of his ministry as verification of his identity.

The transhumanist appeal to Jesus fails, however, when two things are considered. When the words and work of Jesus are kept in context, it becomes clear that Jesus's healing signified that God's kingdom had come and the power of sin had been broken. The healing and restoring were not ends—restoring life for life's sake—but means that signified that God in human form had come to redeem the world from sin.

While a biblical understanding of the brokenness of the human condition is shared with transhumanists, what causes that human predicament, and how redemption occurs, are drastically different. Because the brokenness of the human body is a result of sin's effects on the world, simply "enhancing" the body will never truly heal the human condition (Luke 5:31–32 and Mark 7:23).

A second related consideration is the nature of Jesus's healing and the distinction between restoration and alteration. When Jesus heals the blind, he restores sight. While technology has created the possibility of restoring sight to the blind by way of small cameras and "neural prostheses," bearing witness to the wonder of human ingenuity, technology used to "upgrade" natural sight to long-range zoom or night vision is alteration rather than restoration. Thus, the move toward the posthuman is made.

Here the presuppositions of transhumanism become evident. If there is no God and humans are a work in progress, then man's current limitations are a predicament and are in no way linked to sin. Implicit in this belief is that all current biological limitations are humanity's problem. These limitations are both physical and intellectual, so if the human organism can be enhanced, then overcoming current limitations is inherently good and is a step toward "redemption." Technology becomes the savior and "techno-sapiens" are born.

Consider this comment by transhumanist philosopher Max More:

> The transhumans or posthumans we may become as individuals or as a species may quite possibly share our current DNA, but implants, regenerative medicine, medical nanotechnology, neural-computer interfaces, and other technologies and cultural practices are likely to gradually render our chromosomes almost vestigial components of our individual and species identity ("H+: True Transhumanism," 137).

Biblically understood, the life of Jesus gives a glimpse of the truly human life. In our fallen condition we might be called merely human. The truly human life did not see biological limitations as something to be overcome. When Jesus was thirsty, he drank; when hungry, he ate; when tired, he slept. None of these are portrayed as inherently problematic—something to be overcome—but as a source of delight in God the Father's provision. Jesus's resurrection likewise gives perspective to our current life. Jesus was resurrected to new life. This was not simply an enhanced version of his previous human life; rather, it consisted of a glorious resurrection body that will never again face death.

Another question worth considering is how the transhumanist knows that humanity could be so much more than it currently is. Interestingly, Bostrom suggests, "[T]he limitations of the human mode of being are so pervasive and familiar that we often fail to notice them, and to question them requires manifesting an almost childlike naiveté." If current limitations are so pervasive, how would it occur to us to question them? Here, it seems, is a tacit recognition that humans were created in God's image and that we were made for eternity (Gen 1:27; Eccl 3:11). Because of sin, all of creation, human nature particularly, is in an unnatural state. Implicit in the transhumanist life view is the recognition of this and the impulse to fight against it is right. The problem, however, is that the remedy suggested is the precise move that brought about our unnatural state. It was, and always will be wrong to extend the hand for fruit that promises to make us like God.

Proper hope, then, is not in technologically enhanced "ageless bodies and indefinite life spans," but rather our final resurrection. Our resurrection bodies will be like Christ's—glorious and no longer subject to death or decay. While the transhumanist hopes for such a reality in this life, prior to death, our hope is for the next life, when death is finally overcome. It is then that "this corruptible body [will] be clothed with incorruptibility . . . thanks be to God, who gives us the victory through our Lord Jesus Christ" (1 Cor 15:53,57).

THE MIND-BODY PROBLEM

Jennifer A. Marshall

Self-consciousness is a blessing of being human and an aspect in which the burden of sin may be felt acutely. The capacity to reflect on one's own existence and actions and to make rational choices based on such reflection distinguishes humans from other living creatures. In this way, human beings have the privilege of bearing a unique likeness to the Creator and enjoying communication and friendship with him.

Yet where harmony originally existed in God's good creation, the effects of sin have produced tension, shaking human self-perception. For example, the error of materialism reduces the mind and soul to physical existence. On the other hand, some worldviews identify the self entirely with the spiritual aspect of human nature and see it as alien to or conflicting with the body. At the level of individual experience, such body-self dualism can lead to doubts about the objective reality, integrity, and goodness of one's bodily identity. Interpersonally, it can lead to denying the dignity of all humans at all stages of life.

Both personally and relationally, the temptation is to treat the body as a means to the end of self-gratification, ignoring its status as an integral part of human nature and denying the moral implications of choices about bodily actions. Such views are at odds with the biblical account of the nature of the human as a union of body and soul, created in the image of God and designed to represent his glory.

The Good of Creation and the Image of God

The created, material world is a result of God's good design, intended to display his glory (Pss 8:1–4; 19:1). Sin has marred that goodness and distorted that reflection, and no part of creation has escaped the curse of the fall. But this does not destroy the reality of God's design. Nor should humans ignore God's purposes in creation or treat the physical world with moral ambivalence. This is especially true when it comes to the physical aspects of human nature itself.

To be human, the Bible teaches, is to be made in the image of God (Gen 1:26–28; 5:1–2; 9:6). Distinctive aspects of this representation of the glory of God are illuminated in the details about God's creation of Adam and Eve (Gen 1:26–28; 2:7,21–22). Genesis 1:26 presents God's deliberation about his intention in creating the human race: "Then God said, 'Let us make man in our image, according to our likeness.'" No other part of the creation account discloses this divine reasoning and intention, and in the forming of no creature other than humans is analogous rational deliberation found. Previously in the creation account, God had simply commanded the earth to bring forth living plants and animals. When he makes Adam, by contrast, God takes earthly matter, fashions it into human form and breathes life into it: "Then the LORD God formed the man out of the dust from the ground and breathed the breath of life into his nostrils, and the man became a living being" (Gen 2:7).

The spiritual nature and rationality of humans reflect attributes of God in ways that other creatures do not, but the image of God is not limited to these or any particular part or capacity of a person. The totality of what humans were created to be represents God in body, soul, intellect, will, and all faculties and capacities. The body, like the soul, is essential to human nature (Job 10:8–12; Isa 64:8). That the body is an integral aspect of the image of God is confirmed in the creation account of God's forming humanity of matter and spirit, the incarnation of Christ (whom to see is to see the Father, according to John 14:9), and the promise of a bodily resurrection after death (1 Cor 15:44–45,49).

Once again, no part of any person remains untouched by the effects of sin. But neither can sin obliterate the image of God (Gen 9:6). Redemption reaches far as the curse is found and restores believers in the image of God (Eph 4:24; Col 3:10).

Scripture repeatedly conveys that God's design of humans in general and each human life in particular is deliberate and full of care. Psalms 8 and

139 especially highlight this, as these excerpts from Psalm 139:13–16 illustrate: "For it was you who created my inward parts; you knit me together in my mother's womb. . . . My bones were not hidden from you when I was made in secret. . . . Your eyes saw me when I was formless; all my days were written in your book and planned before a single one of them began."

Implications

God's purposeful creation of humans in his image as a union of body and soul has many implications. Because human existence entails both body and soul, the organic unity, the whole person, makes all human choices and takes all human actions. God's design of this reality shapes norms for self-perception and personal conduct, as well as interpersonal relations and social ethics.

One important aspect of imaging God is the charge to exercise leadership and stewardship of creation according to God's purposes, reflecting his authority over all the earth (Gen 1:27). This includes the responsibility to make choices with one's own body in keeping with God's design and to submit all of one's existence to the lordship of Christ (1 Cor 6:19–20).

To be made in the image of God means that each person is created male or female (Gen 1:28; 2:20–22; 5:1–2). Sex is a created biological reality, not a construct of human socialization. The suggestion that gender identity exists as a category different from or even at odds with biological sex assumes an opposition between body and self that is contrary to what Scripture teaches about God's design of humans. An individual bodily reality, including being created male or female, is one of the most particularized forms of God's good provision for each person. The experience of this gift may be troubled by sin, but God's design is not the source of such grief, and his redemption offers the hope of overcoming it.

These truths about the nature of persons also have implications for how we treat others. For example, some perspectives in ethical debates suggest that human dignity depends on the presence of particular attributes, such as a certain level of rationality or functionality. Such arguments have been used to justify abortion in the case of severe abnormalities in unborn children or assisted suicide for those whose mental or physical incapacities have become exceptionally burdensome. But to determine a person's right to life on such variable characteristics of human existence is arbitrary. Rather than the presence of a spectrum of particular attributes, the definitive fact of human nature created in the image of God is the biblical basis of human dignity.

Only after crowning creation with humanity, does God declare all he has made "very good" (Gen 1:31). Humans have unique dignity as the image of God in body and soul and unique responsibility to bring him glory in every thought, word, and deed.

CHRISTIAN WORLDVIEW AND SAME-SEX MARRIAGE

Andrew T. Walker

Same-sex marriage presents a great cultural challenge to the Christian worldview. As it becomes increasingly normalized throughout Western culture, Christians will face a great temptation to grow indifferent toward biblical teaching on marriage, to fear culture's disapproval of Christian teaching about it, or to reluctantly accept same-sex marriage as a reality of civil life. But because the Bible's teaching on marriage is connected to the gospel and to God's vision for human flourishing, Christians committed to the authority of the Bible must reject these temptations and remain committed to the biblical teaching that defines marriage as a union of two opposite-sexed persons.

Marriage and Gender in the Bible

Marriage is a gendered institution in the Bible. The early chapters of Genesis offer a blueprint for God's design for marriage. Being made male and female, Adam and Eve are sexually differentiated but made for each other. Because God has knit their distinction down to the deepest levels of their being, a male husband and a female wife are designed for each other emotionally, physically, and even anatomically. The complementarity of Adam and Eve is what makes their marriage union achievable and procreation possible (Gen 1:27–28; 2:24). Genesis paints a picture of marriage that is complementary (that is, relating between the two sexes), exclusive between two opposite-sexed persons, and meant to be permanent for the duration of their lives.

The most basic element of marriage, however, is the physical difference that exists between men and women, which manifests itself in sexual union. Together man and woman possess a design oriented toward procreation, but each requires the other in order to realize or fulfill reproduction. Marriage is a comprehensive union, as authors Robert P. George, Ryan T. Anderson, and Sherif Girgis note in *What Is Marriage?*: "Marriage is ordered to family life because the act by which spouses make love also makes new life; one and the same act both seals a marriage and brings forth children. That is why marriage alone is the loving union of mind and body fulfilled by the procreation—and rearing—of whole new humans" (33).

This pattern set forth in Genesis is a pattern Jesus Christ reaffirms as authoritative in the NT (Matt 19:4–6). The Bible always bundles these aspects of marriage together. Without complementarity and all that follows from it, it is difficult to explain why an institution like marriage would exist at all and why marriage ought to be both permanent and exclusive between only two persons. Marriage is what the Bible says it is, or else marriage does not exist. Christians have disagreed on many things throughout history, but they have always been united around basic truths that the Bible makes clear, and the biblical definition of marriage as between one man and one woman is one matter on which Christians have spoken clearly and uniformly heretofore.

The Impossibility of Same-Sex Marriage

The biblical picture of marriage presented above is why same-sex marriage is not only a violation of God's moral law governing sexual relations between men and women (Rom 1:18–32; 1 Cor 6:9–11) but also why same-sex marriage cannot ever truly exist. Governments may create a legal entity that two persons of the same sex consider a marriage; but government does not have the authority to redefine God's moral law. According to the Bible, marriage can never exist between two persons of the same sex because marriage is designed exclusively for two persons of the opposite sex. This is an unpopular teaching in the eyes of the world, but faithfulness to Scripture demands our obedience on all matters—even those that are controversial.

The Implications of Revisionist Definitions of Marriage

Same-sex marriage is a bad path for society. It puts into principle troubling patterns that can hinder human flourishing. First, children need moms and dads. Same-sex marriage denies this truth altogether by insisting that there is no difference between mothers and fathers. Our consciences know this is false. Each of us recognizes that a mother's love and a father's love are different and yet necessary and vital for children. In reality, there is no such thing as "parenting"; there is only mothering and fathering. Therefore, it is in the best interest of government and society to promote the ideal place for children to be raised: in a married household with a mom and dad.

Redefining marriage hands immense power to the state, essentially allowing it to redefine the family. By cutting off biological connection to the definition of marriage and family life, natural foundations and natural rights that follow from family life are called into question. This is a dangerous precedent.

Redefining marriage does not simply expand who can marry; it fundamentally alters what marriage is and what the foundation of a stable social order consists of. Marriage is not something the state creates; rather, the state recognizes marriage as something that exists prior to the state, and thus the state acknowledges it has no control over it.

Same-sex marriage is based on incoherent premises that lead to the further erosion of marriage. By denying the truth that marriage is based on the physical differences of men and women, same-sex marriage is based on the premise that what makes marriage achievable is the emotional union and physical attraction that exists between two persons, regardless of sexual difference. But this is not a solid foundation. Indeed, same-sex marriage is a historical anomaly not found anywhere throughout human history. Why is this? Because all societies have understood that the basis of society hinges on the union of man and woman joined together in marriage. Were it not for the procreative potential between men and women, the institution of marriage would have little reason to exist in the first place. Society has no need for an institution like marriage if marriage is simply about licensing physical attraction between two persons who exchange legal benefits.

A Christian Response to Same-Sex Marriage

So, what is marriage? Marriage is the union of a man and a woman who come together as husband and wife to be father and mother to any children their union produces. Notice that the progression of roles in this definition relies centrally on the truth that men and women are distinct. Marriage is based on the anthropological truth that men and women are different, the biological fact that reproduction requires one man and one woman, and the sociological reality that children need moms and dads. Based on the definition above, same-sex marriage fundamentally rejects and thwarts these central truths about marriage.

The most consequential concern surrounding same-sex marriage is the message we who hold a Christian worldview send to our neighbors. The Bible condemns sexual relations between persons of the same sex. While some revisionists depict the Bible as condemning only certain forms of homosexual practice seen in ancient times, these flawed arguments overlook the Bible's broad and sweeping condemnation of homosexuality. Homosexuality violates the physical boundaries God placed between men and women. In the NT, homosexuality is listed as an offense that provokes God's wrath and denies entry into the kingdom of God to those who choose indulging in it over submission to Christ (1 Cor 6:9–11). Therefore, if Christians are to love their neighbors, they can never support an institution based on sexual activities and disordered desires prohibited in Scripture. First Corinthians 13:6 declares, "Love finds no joy in unrighteousness but rejoices in the truth." We must tell the truth about marriage to our neighbors, work to uphold it in our laws, and seek to share it with all of society. Christians can never accommodate or accept same-sex marriage.

It is common to hear proponents of the issue saying something like this to those of us holding biblical convictions: "Same-sex marriage doesn't harm you, so why should you care?" This is demonstrably false. Same-sex marriage harms society by casting uncertainty onto marriage's role as the basic unit of society. It harms children by denying them their right to a mom and dad, and it evokes great challenges for religious liberty. Moreover, it harms individuals by putting them on a path that rejects God's design for marriage and sexual morality. While these truths are understandably challenging to uphold in a time like ours, God has given his people a wonderful opportunity to learn afresh his vision for marriage. It is meant not only to bring about flourishing to society. Marriage is, ultimately, a picture of the gospel itself (Eph 5:22–33; Rev 19:6–9).

PURPOSE AND PARAMETERS OF SEXUAL RELATIONS

Christopher Yuan

In a world of infinite shades of gray, ambiguity is elevated as a virtue, and sexual freedom has become the religion of our land. Now, with mere consent as the standard for sexual morality, intercourse is seen by some to be as essential as food and water. Herein lies the deception of today's secular worldview: your sexual desires define you, determine you, and should always delight you. When seen in light of Scripture, however, it becomes clear that the idolatry of sexuality is on a collision course with the gospel.

Before we bemoan the hedonism of modern Western culture, let's not forget that sexual immorality was commonplace in the ancient world. Israel and the early church introduced a new worldview with a unique approach to sexual expression that most likely seemed ridiculous to their pagan neighbors. The ancient Israelites and first-century Christians placed a strong emphasis on sexual purity (sex within marriage) while stressing the existential consequences of sexual immorality (sex outside of marriage). This distinctive paradigm for sexual ethics (which unabashedly celebrates the beauty and virtue of sexual intimacy between a husband and a wife) is grounded in Scripture. Sexual relations in marriage is good (Gen 1:31; 2:24). Sex is God's idea. He created it and blessed it. God created sex as a special and exclusive gift, something to be enjoyed between husband and wife. The Hebrew writers often use euphemisms for sex, and "know" is one of those substituted words (Gen 4:1; CSB translates the word as "was intimate with"). "Know" is an appropriate word because, through sex, you know another intimately.

In a sexually liberated world, more sex outside of marriage—premarital and extramarital—doesn't celebrate this most intimate act, but devalues it. When it is shared with anyone, even with strangers, sex becomes just common and is no longer good. Sexual relations in marriage consummates the two becoming one flesh (Gen 2:24). The biblical concept of one flesh points back to the beginning when God made Eve from one of Adam's ribs (Gen 2:21–22) and brought her to him. Adam rejoiced and proclaimed, "This one, at last, is bone of my bone and flesh of my flesh" (Gen 2:23). This "one-flesh union" elevates marriage from simply being a convenient coupling of two people physically attracted to one another into an onto-logical reality that transcends the material and emotional. God's intent for sexual relations is to be the physical, emotional, and spiritual oneness that only a husband and a wife should share. Sexual relations in marriage helps fulfills the creation mandate (Gen 1:28). Any good Jewish boy or girl attending Hebrew school would know the first commandment (*mitzvah*) of the Torah found in Genesis 1:28, "God blessed them, and God said to them, 'Be fruitful, multiply, fill the earth, and subdue it.'" The context of this commandment is a divine blessing.

This connection between blessing and offspring can be seen later in the book of Genesis with the establishment of God's covenant with Abraham. In Genesis 12:2, God called Abram to leave the country of his fathers. God promised him, saying, "I will make you into a great nation, I will bless you, I will make your name great, and you will be a blessing." This blessing included offspring in such abundance to be considered a nation, as numer-ous as the stars in the sky (Gen 15:5)! The psalmist writes, "Sons are indeed a heritage from the LORD, offspring, a reward. Like arrows in the hand of a warrior are the sons born in one's youth. Happy is the man who has filled his quiver with them" (Ps 127:3–5). And Proverbs 17:6 states, "Grandchil-dren are the crown of the elderly, and the pride of children is their fathers."

Sexual relations in marriage is a sign of the marriage covenant. The Hebrew word for covenant, *berit*, occurs 287 times in the Jewish Bible. These God-initiated covenants were often marked with signs, which served to make tangible the intangible reality of a covenant. In Genesis 9, God made a covenant with Noah, his offspring, and all of creation, and the sign of the covenant was the rainbow (vv. 11,13). One of the signs of the covenant with Abraham was that God gave him a new name. "Your name will no longer be Abram; your name will be Abraham" (Gen 17:5). In addition, God's covenant to give Abraham many offspring and much land

(Gen 15:18) was marked by the sign of circumcision. "You must circumcise the flesh of your foreskin to serve as a sign of the covenant between me and you" (Gen 17:11). The prophet Malachi calls marriage a covenant: "Because even though the LORD has been a witness between you and the wife of your youth, you have acted treacherously against her. She was your marriage partner and your wife by covenant" (Mal 2:14). And in Genesis 2:24, the "one flesh" metaphor is covenantal language. "This is why a man leaves his father and mother and bonds with his wife, and they become one flesh." Adam gave a name to Eve as he entered into covenant with her (Gen 2:23). This adds to the significance of a wife taking on her husband's name as they enter into this new covenant in modern times. And this "one flesh" union of sexual relations in marriage can also be understood as a sign of the marriage covenant.

Sexual relations should not be understood as the prize received after a wedding. Rather, it is the physical sign of the marriage covenant. Each time a husband and a wife engage in sex, it reconfirms the covenant made before God and brothers and sisters in Christ, and it serves as a reminder of that beautiful covenant. Sexual relations in marriage is other-centered. Sexual pleasure is one of the most powerful forces on earth, and the incentivizing nature of it easily turns sex into something self-centered. Pleasure can become an idol, promising more than it can deliver. However, God's Word reminds us that the focus and attention of sexual intimacy must be outward toward our beloved spouse in the context of marriage.

As much as the ancient and modern worlds equate sex with self-gratification, the apostle Paul brought some important clarity. In 1 Corinthians, Paul reminds married couples that love for your spouse is the correct focus. "A husband should fulfill his marital duty to his wife, and likewise a wife to her husband. A wife does not have the right over her own body, but her husband does. In the same way, a husband does not have the right over his own body, but his wife does" (7:3–4). Then in Ephesians 5:28–29, Paul makes another similar statement, "In the same way, husbands are to love their wives as their own bodies. He who loves his wife loves himself. For no one ever hates his own flesh but provides and cares for it, just as Christ does for the church." Not only does the wife have authority over her husband's body and the husband over his wife's body, but also, they must love each other as their own bodies.

The world has it all wrong. Sex is not about ourselves. It is for our spouses. It's not about self-gratification but rather spouse-gratification. This doesn't mean you should resist personal pleasure, nor does it mean that finding pleasure in sexual intimacy with your spouse is wrong. But self-gratification is a natural outcome requiring no effort or choice, while pleasing your spouse requires decision, intentionality, and effort.

Sexual relations in marriage means surrendering self-determination and pursuing mutual affection, respect, and loyalty. Love "is not self-seeking" (1 Cor 13:5). Thus, reframing sex in this way affirms the concept of faithfulness in marriage between one man and one woman because it is not possible to belong wholly to more than one person. Adultery is completely out of the question, for my body is not my own to give. Thus, if sexual relations are for marriage only, then God calls us to two specific paths. If you are single, then be sexual abstinent. If you are biblically married, then be faithful to your spouse of the opposite sex. We call this holy sexuality: chastity in singleness and faithfulness in marriage.

ELDERLY CARE

Daniel Darling

Most Christians are appalled by and work against the kinds of laws that make it easier to take the lives of the elderly. Most recoil in horror at news stories that report on corruption and abuse at nursing homes. But the real scandal might be the way God's people subtly contribute to a culture of discard and death for those considered past their prime.

Honor your father and mother.

Scripture is clear on the Christian responsibility for the elderly. "Honor your father and your mother" is an ethic woven throughout the Bible; it's a command given (Exod 20:12) and repeated (Eph 6:2) as a commandment from God in the old covenant and a responsibility of God's people in the new covenant (Eph 6:2). We moderns often read this as an admonition to be polite to mom at Thanksgiving, but it means so much more than merely contributing to good vibes around the holidays.

The call to honor parents implies that children will not only respect those who brought them into this world but will be responsible for their care in this life. Both the ancient Near Eastern culture of Exodus and the first-century culture of Ephesians devalued the elderly. Unlike Western societies, which fund safety nets like social security and Medicare, there were few provisions for aging populations within those cultures.

Early church fathers took the command as a mandate for younger children to financially provide for their parents. Origen, Ambrose, and Jerome are just a few who used these texts to encourage the people of God toward intentional care of elderly populations.

The Dignity of the Elderly

Our views on the elderly should be shaped by the uniquely Christian concept of human dignity. The Bible teaches that every human life possesses value, not because of utility but because each life bears the image of the Creator. Sin has corrupted the human condition, bringing death and disease, corruption and confusion. It has also turned humans against one another. One of the ways we strike out at our Creator is when we consider his image bearers disposable enough to ignore or discard. Societies that reject Christian witness are often marked by their cruelty to elderly populations.

Jesus's life, death, and resurrection reversed the curse of sin and offer the promise of full bodily restorations for his people when he returns to fully consummate his kingdom. Those who follow Jesus embody this gospel news by caring for the most vulnerable, including those who advance in age and can no longer care for themselves. We should also follow an example from Jesus's earthly life: when nearing death, he instructed his best friend John to provide for the physical well-being of his mother Mary. Jesus, even while bearing our sin on the cross, still took time to honor his mother.

The Gospel and Elder Care

A Christian's attitude toward the elderly is a good indicator of just how much he or she believes the gospel. We care for our infirm parents not because they parented us well but because they are image bearers deserving dignity. We respect rather than dismiss our elders because we recognize the good fruit of God's sanctifying work in giving them wisdom beyond our years. We resist the culture's worship of youth and sex appeal because we as Christ followers find our value not in our appearance but in our status as sons and daughters of the King.

When we marginalize older generations, either by overt neglect or by subtle disrespect, we communicate to the world a different gospel from the upside-down kingdom of Christ. When we worship at the altar of relevance, we are, like the rich man in Jesus's parable in Luke 16, living as though we believe this life is all there is instead of believing the truth that Jesus will renew us, body and soul, in the final resurrection. When our churches prioritize the young at the expense of the old, we are living out an altogether different ethic than the intergenerational ideal of Titus 2.

A twofold responsibility for the church is thus implied. First, we should advocate for the dignity of the elderly in society. Today, in many Western societies, there are powerfully active movements to marginalize the elderly as a burden on society. We should use our voices and our votes to stand against inhumane government policies, utilitarian marketplace economics, and predatory financial practices.

Second, we should teach and model for the next generation of Christians what it means to respect and honor parents and older generations. Our church communities should be oases of dignity, embodying the true religion of caring for "orphans and widows in their distress" (Jas 1:27). In a cut-throat world that values people for their sex appeal and short-lived youthfulness, may the church resound with the countercultural message that all human life has dignity endowed by a Creator who visited sinners when they were least desirable (Rom 5:8).

A BIBLICAL VIEW OF WORK

Gregory B. Forster

Work is central to human life. Between work in the home, on the job, in schools, and in neighborhoods, the overwhelming majority of our waking hours is taken up by it. How we work and how we view work are major factors determining the shape of our whole lives. And a culture's understanding of work is one of its most important defining elements, as important to its identity and functioning as its understanding of sexuality, justice, or worship.

When the Holy Spirit changes the way we work, he changes the way we live—all day, every day. This is why throughout history a biblical view of work has been central to Christian spiritual and cultural revival. From Gregory the Great and the scholars of the High Middle Ages to Martin Luther and John Calvin to the Wesleyan movement and twentieth-century heroes like Martin Luther King Jr., it's always the same story: if you look at Christian reformers who had a huge impact on our lives, you always find they had a lot to say about work.

Work presents one of the most central and far-reaching contrasts between the Bible's teaching and the way human cultures naturally tend to think. In the ancient world, a common element among pagan religions was the teaching that the gods don't work; they made people to work so they wouldn't have to. Work is mere toil and drudgery in this view, a curse. In the modern world, as the influence of Christianity on our worldview has receded, we increasingly view work either in similar terms—as a curse, mere toil, and drudgery—or else as an idol, an obsession, what we trust in to provide money, power, status, security, and self-expression.

We certainly do experience pain, frustration, and injustice in our work. Most people aren't going to pay attention to any view of work if it doesn't begin from our lived experience of suffering. Moreover, those who idolize work are right that human work is one of the world's most powerful forces: it can take a pile of sand, a puddle of oil, and a few other basic elements and transform them into a smartphone capable of recording video and beaming it around the world.

God as a Worker

The Bible makes a shocking and outrageous claim that transforms both the suffering of work and the power of work. It makes this claim boldly right on its first page (Gen 1:26–30; 2:15) and again on its last (Rev 21:24–26; 22:5). In the OT, this claim has a central place in the Ten Commandments (Exod 20:9), the Mosaic law (Lev 19:9–18; Deut 25:13–16), the Wisdom books (Prov 12:11–14; 16:3; 18:9; 22:29; 24:27; 31:1,13–31; Eccl 3:22; 5:6; 9:10), the prophetic witness against injustice to the poor (1 Sam 8:14; 1 Kgs 21:1–19; Isa 3:13–15; 5:8–10; 10:1–2; Hos 5:10; Mic 2:1–4,8–9), and much more. In the NT it has a central place in the parables (45 of the 52 parables draw on work and business as images of spiritual life). It also appears in the teachings of Jesus (Mark 10:42–45; John 13:1–20), the conflict between Jesus and his enemies (Matt 12:1–8; Mark 2:23–3:6; Luke 6:1–11; 13:10–17; 14:1–6; John 5:1–18; 7:23; 9:14–41), and the ethics of the letters (Eph 4:28; Col 3:23–24; 1 Thess 4:11; 2 Thess 3:10–12; 1 Tim 5:8; 2 Tim 2:6; 1 Pet 2:18–25).

The Bible claims that God is a Worker, and work is a primary reason he created humanity, because when we work rightly, we glorify God by loving him and neighbor. Because he is love, God works (Gen 2:2–3; John 5:17), and so do we. God also rests, appreciating the beauty of the divine work (Gen 1:31–2:3), and so do we. Through our work we exercise stewardship over the world God created. When we work faithfully as God's stewards, we manifest the glory of the holy love of God, and we make the world under our care manifest it as well.

Work as Stewardship

We serve God as stewards of his world individually, and also collectively, as we labor together in households and businesses and trade our work with one another through economic exchange. Thus we were made as an image of the holy love that is the triune God, unity in diversity and diversity in unity.

This claim is shocking and outrageous to our natural sensibilities because it transforms the suffering of work. We experience toil, frustration, and injustice in our work not because work is bad but because we are bad (Rom 3:23). Work is not a curse, but our work is one of the main places where we experience the curse on our sin that God, in his holy love, has ordained (Gen 3:17–19).

This is also a reason the Bible's shocking claim is necessary if we are to have any hope for joy, peace, and righteousness. If Jesus is in us through our faith in the gospel, we can take comfort that God is using our perseverance through the suffering of our work to transform us (cp. Jas 1:2–4; Rom 8:28). Worldly people working in worldly ways are shaping themselves, all day every day, into ever more worldly people. But we, as we make the difficult choice to keep on working faithfully, day in and day out, are shaped into Christlikeness by King Jesus.

The Power of Work

The Bible's claim about work is also shocking and outrageous to our natural sensibilities because it transforms the power of work. The enormous power of our work is indeed breathtaking; even God himself seems amazed at it (Gen 11:6). But this power was given to us to glorify the holy love of God by serving God and neighbor. When we trust in our work rather than in God for identity, security, and provision, we fall into a monstrous evil that will enslave us, turn us against one another, make us miserable, and bring us to ruin.

Doing our daily work with ethical integrity for the love of God and neighbor in Jesus is a high and difficult calling. Moreover, a special responsibility rests on business leaders to order work ethically, as an expression of voluntary stewardship and mutual love. Another responsibility falls on political leaders to protect this ordering of work. The complex challenge of extending the opportunity of gainful work to the poor and the oppressed also weighs on us.

But this too is a reason the Bible's shocking claim is necessary if we are to have any hope for joy, peace, and righteousness. Those who follow God's calling in their work discover a new kind of life. For them, glorifying God by loving God and neighbor as a citizen of God's kingdom is not a special activity they squeeze into a few hours a week or an add-on they are constantly straining to shoehorn into their daily routine. It is their daily routine. Our work, done in this way, is the main way we give God a return on his investment in us (Matt 25:14–30). It allows us to feed the hungry, clothe the naked, and visit the sick (Matt 25:31–46) These are among the good works we were saved to do (Eph 2:10), which force even the enemies of God to give him glory (Matt 5:16; 1 Pet 2:15).

This is not just one more biblical truth among thousands of others. It is a central pattern in the narrative of Scripture. It is one of the deep, defining elements of the biblical testimony. That only makes sense. Work takes up the overwhelming majority of our lives and is central to our understanding of who we are as individuals and as cultures. Why are we surprised that the Bible says God designed us with work at the center? Or that Holy Spirit transformation of our work has always been—and continues to be today— one of the most important paths to spiritual and cultural reformation?

PRAYER AND RECOVERY FROM ILLNESS

Joy Greene

Is anyone among you sick? He should call for the elders of the church, and they are to pray over him, anointing him with oil in the name of the Lord. The prayer of faith will save the sick person, and the Lord will raise him up; if he has committed sins, he will be forgiven. Therefore, confess your sins to one another and pray for one another, so that you may be healed. The prayer of a righteous person is very powerful in its effect (Jas 5:14–16).

Throughout God's Word, we find the words "pray" or "prayer" many times; in fact, more than 600 prayers are recorded in the Bible. God's Word tells us to "pray constantly" (1 Thess 5:17). Jesus told his disciples they should always pray "and not give up" (Luke 18:1). We often define prayer as the way we communicate with God, but when we take a closer look at the Scriptures, we find that the word has a much deeper meaning.

The Greek word most often used for prayer is *proseuche,* and it denotes an encounter with God through intimate relationship. It implies a person coming to God in an act of sacrificial surrender. Prayer, then, is not just asking God to give you what you desire. Prayer is one way we have communion with God. It draws us closer to God and brings us strength.

In Ephesians 6:18 we are told, "Pray at all times in the Spirit with every prayer and request, and stay alert with all perseverance and intercession for all the saints."

Traditionally, Christian prayer has been seen primarily as petitionary. When we pray, we come to God with a request. As followers of Christ, we believe there is value in petitioning God to intervene in our circumstances. We know from Scripture that nothing is impossible with God (Luke 1:37). We believe God listens to our prayers, and he is faithful to give us what we need (Matt 7:7; Luke 11:9). The psalms are rich with prayers and praise affirming that the ears of our mighty God are attentive to our cries for help (Pss 34:15,17; 116:1). We read countless stories in God's Word about healing and the power of prayer.

In the life of an effective Christian, then, prayer is essential. But why do our prayers sometimes fail to work? Why does God choose to heal one person while another person for whom we pray dies? Was something wrong with our prayers? Did we not pray the right way? People have pondered questions such as these for millennia.

As we lift up intercessory prayers for people who need healing, these questions arise: Does prayer make a difference in patient recovery? Is there concrete, scientific evidence that prayer is effective? If I pray for a friend and my friend gets well, did the healing happen because I prayed? Would her health have improved even if I had abstained from praying? Can we accurately answer these questions using scientific tools?

The effectiveness of prayer in patient recovery is gaining interest in the research community. In the last ten years, in fact, research focused on the effectiveness of prayer in recovery has nearly doubled. Most experts agree that prayer offers comfort and spiritual support to patients, but many are skeptical of the role of prayer in patient care. While some research has shown a positive association between improved health and prayer, other studies have shown a negative association. When we examine the scientific research, there is no reliable evidence to support the notion that people who receive intercessory prayer recover more than those who do not.

Researchers have conducted a variety of clinical trials seeking to prove or disprove the effectiveness of prayer. Attempting to accurately conduct a clinical trial involving the effects of prayer invites questions that are difficult to measure. Do the outcomes of prayer depend on the spiritual state of the person who is praying? Will prayer be more effective if a large number of people pray instead of an individual? It is impossible to measure all of the variables that are important in such research, including how to measure a person's faith or level of spirituality. Moreover, such research is clouded with contradictions, challenges, and assumptions that make researching prayer and recovery a "scientific and religious minefield" (Andrade and Radhakrishnan).

There is no scientific formula to prayer. Prayer exists around a personal relationship with Jesus Christ. Prayer is intimate. Prayer is supernatural. Scientific methods cannot measure the supernatural. There is no consistent scientific proof that prayer affects patient recovery, but that does not mean prayer is ineffective.

As Christians, we must be careful not to equate prayer with magic. God is not a magic genie who appears out of a golden lamp ready to grant our wishes. God's decision to grant some requests while refusing others does not prove or disprove his existence. It demonstrates that he is sovereign. His thoughts are not our thoughts; neither are his ways our ways. His thoughts and ways are higher than ours (Isa 55:8–9). He bends his listening ear to his people, but his will is far better than ours and his ways are perfect. Sometimes he chooses to grant our requests; sometimes he does not. We do not always know the will of God, but we know that God desires to do more in our lives than simply bring healing to our bodies when we are sick. He often uses our physical sufferings for a higher purpose. We can be certain that, as we pray, God hears our prayers, and he answers in accordance to his perfect will.

Our Savior, Jesus, was fully God and fully man. His purpose for entering this world was to save us. His death was a requirement in order for us to have salvation. The night before his crucifixion, Jesus prayed in the garden of Gethsemane: "My Father, if it is possible, let this cup pass from me. Yet not as I will, but as you will" (Matt 26:39). Jesus knew the sins of the world would be on him. This cup was much to bear. Jesus prayed that this cup might pass from him. It did not. God's perfect will was accomplished.

Government

A HISTORY OF CHRISTIANITY'S IMPACT ON GOVERNMENTS

Carl R. Trueman

The NT does not present an elaborate manifesto for the direct impact of Christianity on government. Christ indicates that the payment of taxes by his disciples is a legitimate imperative (Matt 22:15–22). Paul indicates that the civil magistrate is to be obeyed and respected as one established by God (Rom 13:1–7) and that the church is to pray for those in civil authority (1 Tim 2:2). Elsewhere, Paul is happy to appeal to his Roman citizenship as a means of obtaining legal privileges (Acts 25).

The Ancient Church

In the late first century, the earliest portion of the postapostolic period, the Roman government features not so much as something to be principally opposed by the church but as a source of martyrdom, as seen in the various letters of Ignatius, bishop of Antioch (ca AD 107). Then, in the second century, the Greek apologists spent much time arguing that Christians actually make the best citizens and should therefore be tolerated within the empire. In short, they did not present Christianity as an idiom of protest but as something that was compatible with living as obedient citizens and subjects of Rome.

Sporadic persecution of the church was supplanted by more pan-imperial campaigns in the third and the beginning of the fourth centuries. The requirement to pledge allegiance to the emperor and to sacrifice to him as to a god precipitated widespread Christian opposition and apostasy. Eventually, at the start of the fourth century, Emperor Constantine converted to Christianity, and a new era of church-state relations commenced.

Though often criticized, the world of Constantine and beyond brought many benefits to the church, including the end of formal persecution in the West. By the end of the fourth century, the rapprochement between church and state was such that Ambrose, having served as a regional governor, was called as bishop of Milan before he was even baptized. The skills needed to rule the church were apparently thought to be the same as those needed to run the empire. In addition, in the case of Priscillian, an ascetic teacher of the late fourth century, we have the first example of a heretic being prosecuted by the civil authority. Right doctrine had become a concern of state enforcement, not just church discipline.

The Middle Ages

The Middle Ages (ca 500–1500) saw major struggles between church and state in both the West and the East. In the East, Caesaropapism (the practice of combining church and state powers under the rulership of the governmental head) was not an official dogma. Nevertheless, it was the practical position for the Byzantine Church, as the emperor exerted the right to appoint patriarchs. This was also the practical position of the Russian Orthodox Church under the tsars.

In the West, the pope's crowning of Charlemagne as Holy Roman Emperor in AD 800 and then the various so-called investiture controversies of the eleventh and twelfth centuries helped define church and state relations in terms of an often uneasy standoff, with the church exhibiting military and political ambitions outside of the strictly ecclesiastical sphere.

The Reformation

Magisterial Reformers like Martin Luther, Huldrych Zwingli, John Calvin, and Thomas Cranmer worked in coordination with the civil magistrate to effect reform of the church. This took different localized forms: Zwingli and Calvin were reforming in cities with moderately representative governments; Luther worked under a medieval feudal system; Cranmer labored under a monarch. This somewhat shaped their respective attitudes to church and state. Luther generally counseled nonresistance, seeing church and state as operating in two different spheres with different tools. Zwingli saw church and state as closely identified, especially on matters of discipline. Calvin sought to free the church in terms of its ministry from state interference, although he was never able to achieve this quite as he wished in Geneva. Cranmer laid the foundations for an English church that was essentially Erastian in concept, with the head of state functioning as the supreme governor of the church. Thus, the church was essentially an arm of the state, a position sketched out in the writings of the medieval English theologian, John Wycliffe.

Radical groups were initially associated with the Magisterial Reformers but came to advocate models of reformation that pressed beyond that which the civil magistrate was prepared to tolerate. The results were the Peasants' Rebellion in Germany in 1525 and later the violent seizure of the city of Munster by radicals in 1534–1535. After the Munster siege ended in a bloodbath, Anabaptism, under the influence of Menno Simons, whose brother had perished in the siege, moved in a strongly pacifist and social separatist direction. It formed alternative, peaceful communities.

John Knox and Christopher Goodman radicalized the position of both Luther and Calvin and extended the right of rebellion to subjects if the head of state committed idolatry, specifically in the form of the promotion, tolerance, or practice of Roman Catholicism. This notion bore fruit in the seventeenth century in the covenanting political theology of Samuel Rutherford and others. It also provided the ideological conditions for the English Civil War.

The Modern Era

The last 200 years have seen a great diversity in the approaches of Christians to the church and to politics. In the Eastern Bloc during the Cold War, both Roman Catholicism and Eastern Orthodoxy provided idioms of protest against the avowedly atheist totalitarian regimes.

Some have argued on both the left and the right that the Bible calls for the church to be an agent of fundamental social transformation. Thus, in South America, Roman Catholic liberation theology involved a basic synthesis of Christian and Marxist themes. Protestant theonomists have looked more to premodern models of social organization and OT case law as having perennial biblical sanction; thus, they wish to establish Mosaic law and OT case laws as the laws of the land. (Some go so far as to say non-Christians should not vote or hold office.) In the United States, the Reagan era saw the appropriation of biblical rhetoric for political purposes in the dying years of the Cold War. This appears to have left a lasting legacy of a connection between conservative Christianity and conservative politics. This position has been intensified in recent decades by the partisan alignment on the issue of abortion and also by the increasing role played by the politics of sexual identity in public political discourse.

There are alternatives to the close identification of church and society that one finds in liberation theology, theonomy, and Christian America movements. A strand of Presbyterian thinking has emphasized the fundamentally spiritual nature of the church whereby on principle the church does not speak directly to the political issues of the day but is careful to allow for Christian freedom on such matters. The church simply preaches the Word as it culminates in Christ and administers sacraments and discipline. In recent years this has sharpened into what is known as Two Kingdom Theology, which sees its roots in the Reformation, especially in the thought of Martin Luther. This is in some ways akin to certain forms of Anabaptist thinking, which sees the church as an alternative community to the world and as fulfilling its task not by directly transforming political institutions but by modeling an alternative way of life.

THE BIBLE AND GOVERNMENT MODELS

Micah J. Watson

As with so many topics, a Christian understanding and evaluation of government begins with the book of Genesis. What is the purpose of government? What needs do governments meet, and how should they serve? Once we understand the biblical foundation for government, we will be able to assess any particular form of it.

The creation account reveals four foundational truths for any Christian understanding of politics and government. First, everything comes from the hand of Creator God, and this includes any sort of authority. The words "in the beginning God" are not only the words that open the Scriptures; they should ground all Christian thinking (Gen 1:1). This is particularly true for political thinking, as few vocations are as susceptible to the temptations of pride and idolatry as governance.

Second, men and women are created in God's image (Gen 1:27). God declares all of his creation to be good, but only humans bear the image of God and thus enjoy a particularly special relationship with him. This relationship between God and humankind sets us apart from the rest of creation with regard to our dignity and our responsibilities.

Third, the first problem described in Scripture is not that Adam and Eve disobeyed God but that it is not good for man to be alone (Gen 2:18). This tells us that God created humans not only to be in proper relationship with him but also with one another. We are created to walk with our Creator and with one another, and we see this truth reflected in the greatest commandment and the second greatest, which is like it (Matt 22:37–40).

Fourth, beginning with Adam and Eve's disobedience, humans have rebelled against God (Gen 3). The doctrine of the fall describes how our originally good nature, authored by God, has become corrupted by sin and selfish desires in such a way that our relationships are damaged beyond our power to repair (Rom 7:23; 3:23). We see our vertical relationship with God damaged in Adam and Eve's expulsion from the garden, and we see other tragic consequences of their rebellion in the horizontal fracturing of human brotherhood in Cain's slaying of Abel.

These four foundational truths describe the fundamental groundwork for human relations and politics. We are made by God and in his image; thus, we humans are sacred. We are called to live together in harmony, yet our rebellion makes relating to God and getting along well and consistently with one another impossible in our own power. God's solution to our brokenness is found in the work of Jesus Christ on the cross and through his resurrection from the dead, as prophesied in Genesis and attested to in the Gospels (Gen 3:15; John 3:16). We wait, along with all of creation, for the culmination of this work when the risen Messiah will return in glory (Rom 8:19–23).

Government's Temporary Role

Since this plan of salvation is God's ultimate solution, human government plays but a temporal role in restraining evil and promoting the good in the meantime. It exists between the sin of the first Adam and the return of the second Adam, Jesus Christ (Rom 5:12–21; 13:1–6). While Christians differ as to the proper role of government, most agree that the Scriptures portray government as a God-ordained institution, citing Jesus's Matthew 22:15–22 distinction between what belongs to Caesar (coins bearing Caesar's image) and what belongs to God (humans bearing God's image), and Paul's affirmation that governing authorities are instituted by God for our good (Rom 13:1–7). This idea is echoed by Peter in 1 Peter 2:13. Paul reveals a central purpose of government in his letter to Timothy, urging "that petitions, prayers, intercessions, and thanksgivings be made for everyone, for kings and all those who are in authority, so that we may lead a tranquil and quiet life in all godliness and dignity" (1 Tim 2:1–2). We pray for political authorities so that we may lead peaceful lives.

We are now in a position to apply the four foundational truths to our thinking about governmental models and politics generally.

First, if God really is first and foremost, as the opening line of Genesis attests, then any government that attempts to usurp God's place runs afoul of its purpose. Christians should be wary of any governing philosophy that denies God or sets itself up in his rightful place. We should pray for the governing authorities so that we may have peace, but if there is no peace and we are forced to choose, "we must obey God rather than people" (Acts 5:29).

Second, since people are made in God's image, each individual has intrinsic value. Governments are meant to protect people and promote their good. Governments exist for the sake of humans. They should not act as if citizens are expendable.

Third, as surely as God declared of Adam's lone state that "it is not good" (Gen 2:18), God has created humans to live together—not to exist as loners. We see this in God's plan for marriage and family as well as in his design of the church, his bride. We pray to "*our* Father in heaven," asking him to "give *us* today *our* daily bread" (Matt 6:9,11; emphasis added). One purpose of governments, then, is to protect society so that humans can flourish through their interactions in families, marriages, churches, clubs, and charities. Whether in principle or practice, a governing philosophy that unduly interferes with the various social spheres is a cause for concern.

Fourth, perhaps no Christian doctrine is more obvious to common-sense observation than the doctrine of the fall. Humans are selfish creatures, and we are often motivated to do the right thing more by the prospect of punishment than we are by what is intrinsically right. It follows that governments are to restrain human wickedness. Moreover, given that God's ultimate solution for human sin is Jesus's work on the cross, any political philosophy that denies the fall or purports to solve human evil once and for all is bound to fail. It's also likely to leave a trail of misery and suffering in its wake.

Christianity and Government Models

Given these benchmark principles from Scripture, how should Christians evaluate the various government models on offer? In the last 150 years or so, we have seen the rise and fall of several political approaches. These include communism, socialism, monarchy, constitutional democracy, fascism, and Islamic fundamentalism.

The first place we look for guidance on these issues is Scripture, yet here we encounter a difficulty, for, unlike the OT, the NT does not address the particulars of a governmental system. There we learn a great deal about how to relate to political authority, and we can know that God authorizes governments, but we do not find anything there that could serve as a political blueprint. Nevertheless, God in his wisdom has given us political ends to aim for, such as peace and justice, while leaving much of the means up to us (Lewis, *Mere Christianity*, 79).

This does not mean we cannot make informed judgments about governing models. Communism, for example, denies God's existence and original sin even as it purports to create a version of heaven on earth. Fascism elevates the state to a position of ultimate importance in society, usurping God's rightful place and subjecting the importance of individuals made in God's image to the needs of an all-important government. A fundamentalist Islamic regime rules out Christianity altogether and in practice has not treated people as intrinsically valuable. These approaches clearly violate the biblical principles articulated.

Assessing other models of government proves more complex. Strictly speaking, socialism is not a governing philosophy; rather, it advocates a collective economic arrangement for any given government. Monarchy has clear biblical roots but is also accompanied by significant dangers—as seen both in Western history and in the biblical record. Constitutional democracy is consistent with a biblical approach to politics, though as a political system its manifestation of the will of the people will only be as just and good as the people who give it its power. Representative democracy depends on the people, and people are fallen.

Recognizing biblical principles as they apply to politics and government does not offer all the conclusions we might want with regard to current political systems and controversies, but it is a start. God's Word gives us the means to evaluate the political world and governments large and small.

A BIBLICAL VIEW OF CRIME AND PUNISHMENT

Hunter Baker

Today we most often use the terms *jail* or *prison* to describe the places where criminals are sent once they are convicted of crimes, but the name *penitentiary* is also commonly used. One need not be a language scholar to discern the root of *penitentiary*, which is *penitent*. In its adjectival form, *penitent* is used to denote a strong sense of regret. Taken as a noun, a *penitent* is a person who seeks forgiveness from God. The founding of penitentiaries, beginning in the eighteenth century with John Howard in England, expressed the Christian hope that criminals could repent, find forgiveness from God and people, and return to the community as citizens who contribute to the common good.

The Bible's influence on approaches to crime and punishment preceded the rehabilitation movement of the eighteenth century. The Hebrew Scriptures (OT) tell us that God chose a people (the Hebrews) and set them apart from all other peoples by giving them regulations for running a just society.

Although it is sometimes argued that codes from Hammurabi or the Hittites provided inspiration for the laws set forth in the OT, Jewish scholars point to important distinctions which show the uniqueness and greater justice of the laws given by God. They argue that the Hammurabi code is more brutal and primitive than the laws of Israel. For example, the Hammurabic legislation required that a man's daughter be taken if he killed another man's daughter. The injustice in such a rule is evident as the punishment extends beyond the offender to an innocent person, the

277

perpetrator's daughter. The Hittite code, which was compensation based, also falls short of the standards expressed in the law as given by God in the OT. Even an offense as serious as murder could be bought off with enough cash, according to the Hittite approach. In contrast, Exodus 21:23–25, with its eye-for-an-eye reasoning, is more proportionate to the offense and is thus more just.

The Hebrew law codes reveal a great desire for true justice rather than a rush to judgment. One example is Deuteronomy's rule requiring two eye-witnesses to be in agreement in order to establish evidence of a crime (Deut 17:6; 19:15). This means no one shall be put to death without the evidence of more than one witness. It should be noted that the laws of the United States offer less protection than this. Similar to the instructions in Deuteronomy, Matthew 18:16 indicates that one should take witnesses along when attempting to resolve a dispute. Such advice demonstrates a concern with establishing truth in a reliable fashion, drawing on the perspectives of multiple persons. In both Testaments great care is taken to be certain of the truth of an offense, and emphasis is placed on the strong connection between the punishment, the offender, and the severity of the offense.

One thing that is striking about how the Bible approaches punishment of crime is that imprisonment is uncommon. Deuteronomy, Exodus, and other OT texts offer examples of compensatory payments, exile, corporal punishments, and death sentences but do not advocate sending large numbers of criminals to prison. The first and most obvious reason for the absence of prisons is that ancient agrarian societies did not have the resources to imprison and feed significant numbers of offenders. Aside from this logistical factor, one might also wonder whether the mass incarceration model we currently practice is wise. We tend to view biblical punishments such as lashing as barbaric, but is it really better to incarcerate an offender with those who might reinforce his bad behavior? Could it be that a policy of corporal punishment would prove more effective?

Three Schools of Thought
In contemporary thinking about crime and punishment, there are at least three major schools of thought regarding how to deal with lawbreaking. Theorists often speak and write in terms of retribution, utilitarianism, and rehabilitation.

Retribution

Retribution-based thinking is at odds with the more social-scientific thrust of much of today's thinking about punishment. It is seen as crude, vengeance based, and perhaps barbaric. Many of the punishments in the OT are perceived in this light. Nevertheless, others have argued convincingly that retributive approaches are anything but crude and cruel. Rather, the choice of retribution attributes dignity to both the victim and the offender. Retribution vindicates the rights of the victim because it recognizes that something important has been violated and punishment must follow the violation. At the same time, retribution assigns respect to the offender as well because punishing the offender indicates that God and society had real expectations for better decision making and behavior. In essence, people who transgress have not lived up to God's standard (or society's) and thus must be reminded that we respect them enough to punish the wrongdoing.

Utilitarian

Utilitarian theories of crime and punishment focus less on the rights of individuals and more on the scientific control of populations. For example, a utilitarian might say that we should come up with laws that reduce social friction between citizens rather than continuing to enforce laws that lead to conflict. The danger of the utilitarian approach is that it is mostly concerned with social regulation. For example, let us imagine that a series of murders have been committed. In the utilitarian view, it would be nearly as good to convince the public that the murderer has been caught and punished (even if that weren't true) as it would be to actually catch the villain. Perception would count nearly as much as reality. It might even be better to pin the crime on an innocent party, if it could be done convincingly, than to let the public go on thinking a murderer is on the loose.

Rehabilitation

As mentioned above, rehabilitation theories were originally motivated by Christian thinking about crime and punishment. The Christian view tended to support retribution-based consequences while adding a component of rehabilitation. Forgiveness does not necessarily wipe out the penalty, but it does pave the way for full acceptance back into the social body once punishment and rehabilitation are complete. During the twentieth century, however, thinking about rehabilitation went through a transformation, dropping the idea of a "penitent" person paying a debt and seeking forgiveness. Rehabilitation approaches came to view crime as a result of broad, structural social injustices that produce marginalized victims of the system who perpetuate injustices by engaging in social pathologies such as stealing. While there is some value to thinking about social systems in this way, the effect can be to undermine the moral dimension of crime and the recognition that the offender has personally done wrong against others and should repent of sin.

Not everyone has appreciated these developments. Anger at progressive penal policies has led to the creation of victim's rights movements. Among other things, these movements have sought to make society and the judicial system aware of the harm victims suffer when they perceive that the wrongs perpetrated against them have gone unpunished or inadequately punished.

Christians remain highly active in prison ministry today, though often with less official influence in the penal system than they once had. Prison Fellowship, founded by Charles Colson after his imprisonment following the Watergate scandal, has led the way in sharing the good news of redemption through Jesus Christ with prisoners. After many years of effective ministry to prisoners and their families, Prison Fellowship gained the ability to participate in some institutions by hosting special Christian cellblocks and offering seminary programs in others. Early evidence indicates that their ministry reduces recidivism among those released.

Whatever good government may achieve through attempts to address the social causes of crime—and we must not dismiss these—crime remains a manifestation of a spiritual problem that must be addressed. The true rehabilitator and vindicator of injustices is Jesus Christ, the Son of God, and we must point both victims and criminals to his gospel.

THE BASICS OF CIVIL LAW

Hunter Baker

The United States House of Representatives contains a number of interesting features. The bullet holes from an attack by Puerto Rican terrorists are an unusual example. More relevant to our subject are portraits of history's great lawgivers. Three in particular invite special attention: Moses the Israelite, Justinian the Byzantine emperor, and Sir William Blackstone—one of the greatest jurists in English history.

Moses the Israelite

Through Moses we received the most famous set of laws in the history of humanity—the Ten Commandments (Exod 20:1–17). According to the Hebrew Scriptures, God gave Moses the famed tablets of law on Mount Sinai. He then conveyed them to the Israelites and established the single most enduring depiction of the duties people owe to God (the four vertical commandments) and to one another (the six horizontal commandments).

In the horizontal prohibitions concerning disrespecting parents, lying, stealing, adultery, murder, and even coveting, we see the building blocks of modern law. For example, lying is an actionable offense in the forms of fraud, misrepresentation, and perjury. Parental rights still count for much as children do not enjoy full constitutional rights until they reach the age of majority. Theft and murder occupy a giant share of the criminal law. Even covetousness remains part of our codes. If an individual can be shown to have coveted, then it is possible to establish the *mens rea* or "guilty mind" necessary to prove the severe gravity of some civil or criminal offenses.

Of the horizontal commandments, adultery now receives least attention in modern law. Adultery has gone almost entirely out of the criminal law, though it remains relevant to divorce proceedings—even though it legally counts for less now in the era of no-fault statutes.

In recent years, a controversy regarding church and state separation has revolved around the posting of the Ten Commandments in public places. Judge Roy Moore in Alabama gained notoriety for mounting the commandments in his courtroom as a lesser judge and then bringing them into the Alabama Supreme Court after his election there. Though Judge Moore lost in that case, other monuments and postings of the commandments have survived challenge. For example, the commandments on the capitol grounds in Austin, Texas, remain in place. Courts have accepted the argument that the commandments represent an important source of law. Successful challenges have not suggested that the commandments are unimportant to modern law but rather that certain displays involved some improper purpose. Whether the modern state publicly embraces the Ten Commandments, their formative influence on the law—both in the West and, increasingly, worldwide—is difficult to question.

Justinian the Byzantine Ruler

Enter the second portrait. Justinian was a Christian ruler of the Byzantine Empire during the heart of the sixth century AD. He took up the project of systematizing and rationalizing the various laws and precedents that had sprouted during the long tenure of the Roman Empire. Interestingly, Justinian demonstrated fealty to God in the initiation of the project. He called for "the aid of God" in governing the empire "delivered to Us by His Celestial Majesty." The emperor further claimed that the protection of the state depended not upon arms but rather upon "the providence of the Holy Trinity." The *Corpus Juris Civilis* had its beginning in this way; the collection was far more explicit in its reliance on the Christian God than is the American Constitution.

Justinian's work demonstrated a view of law that fully embraced God as lawgiver. The *Corpus* refers to jurisprudence as the knowledge of things both human and divine. Civil law defines the arrangements that a nation makes for its people. The "law of nations" reflects what we all know through the exercise of our natural reason. This is natural law. In Christian societies natural law has been understood as a part of God's common grace, protecting the world from chaos and strife. Indeed, in John Locke's famed social contract, he did not think we needed government to give us a moral law since it already existed in the natural law. Rather, he felt government should enforce the dictates of natural law.

The *Corpus Juris Civilis* became the model for the civil law systems of continental Europe. The civil law that survived the Byzantine Empire also inspired the development of the canon law of the Roman Catholic Church. Together, the two types of law formed the basis of European legal thought.

Sir William Blackstone

The English model of common law is a different system that emerged in the Middle Ages. Whereas civil law systems are highly codified, common law systems rely much more on precedent interpreted by judges. The nations derived from England, such as the United States, also have common law systems. It has not been unusual for American judges to look to English cases to shape opinions. Despite differences in method (codification versus precedent), common law systems have also been significantly inspired by Christianity's ideas about natural law.

As for our third portrait, Sir William Blackstone was perhaps the greatest exponent of English common law. His commentaries sought to systematize precedents and ideas into a comprehensible whole. American law students today study some of his opinions and concepts. In his commentaries Blackstone wrote about natural law in terms of how it applied to creation and to creatures.

For example, God had imbued matter with certain properties as part of his law. He made the planets move along predictable paths. In the same way, God created natural laws to govern relations between humans in such a way as to bring about justice. By Blackstone's reasoning, we must obey these laws because of our dependence on God who has ordained them. Notably, Blackstone held the revealed divine law next to God's natural law and viewed it as authoritative. Human laws ought not be permitted to contradict either of these two sources.

Through Blackstone, it is easy to understand the concept of theonomy over against autonomy. *Theonomy* refers to adherence to God's law, whereas *autonomy* views the individual as a law unto himself. Blackstone's legal reasoning operated from a position of theonomy based on our apprehension of natural law.

But what was once commonplace has become the subject of significant dispute. Oliver Wendell Holmes Jr. famously attacked natural law, emphasizing that the law "is not some brooding omnipresence in the sky." He viewed the law as an instrument designed to reduce social friction and to achieve other desirable outcomes. Regrettably, this new and positivistic view of law has gained much ground during the last century, while natural law reasoning has fallen into disfavor. Nevertheless, the places where laws are made, such as in the U.S. Congress, provide ample reminders from whence we came and on what foundations we rest.

CHURCH AND STATE

Micah J. Watson

The phrase "church and state" generally refers to the ways Christian churches and other houses of worship relate to the governing political authorities in any given society. More specifically, "church and state" denotes the particular relationship between the two throughout the American religious and political tradition. This relationship is as important as it has been controversial, and Christians have been wrestling with the intersection of faith and politics for two millennia.

The relationship is important because both God's church and the state are ordained by God for particular purposes. The church universal is the bride of Christ, being made ready to meet the Bridegroom and comprised of all orthodox Christians, living out their faith in local churches (Rev 17:7–9). God's church is the new Israel, partaking in the new covenant under Christ and helping to fulfill our calling to live holy lives together (Heb 10:24–25). Christians also know that government is "God's servant for [our] good," wielding coercive force to "punish those who do what is evil" (Rom 13:4; 1 Pet 2:14). All is well when each institution does its job. The state restrains evil and promotes the good; the church worships God, raises the next generation, and meets the spiritual and physical needs of a lost world by sharing the gospel, feeding the hungry, and clothing the naked (Matt 25:31–46; 28:19–20).

Yet it is rarely the case that all is well. Political leaders often see religious authority as a threat to their own power, or they wish to usurp the appeal of religion for their own purposes. Even Israel's first king, Saul, confused the lines between God's purposes by attempting as king to perform a sacrifice God had reserved for his prophet Samuel (1 Sam 13).

Moreover, just as political leaders can abuse religion for political reasons, Christians have misused the reigns of coercive political power to enforce their particular religious beliefs and practices on others, including many fellow believers. Sadly, history is replete with the tragic and blood-stained consequences of political and ecclesial leaders violating the God-ordained purposes and boundaries of the church and the state.

Christian thinking about these matters falls into two broad categories. The first is how individual Christians should understand their identities as citizens of heaven (Phil 3:20) and citizens of their earthly polities (Acts 22:22–29). Scripture instructs us to obey, honor, and pray for our political leaders (Rom 13:1; 1 Tim 2:2), pay our taxes (Mark 12:13–17, Rom 13:7), and seek to "live at peace with everyone" (Rom 12:18). At the same time, our political loyalties are secondary. We are to "seek first the kingdom of God," and if the kingdom of man interferes, "we must obey God rather than people" (Matt 6:33; Acts 5:29).

If this first category focuses on individual duties for Christians, the second way of thinking concerns how churches and governments should interact from a macro perspective. That is, how might political institutions be arranged such that political leaders can best achieve government's purpose while at the same time allowing the church the freedom to fulfill its purposes?

In response to this question, the American experience with politics and religion is instructive. From the earliest colonies to the present time, the balance and potential tension between church and state has been a perennial concern. Some figures, like the early Baptist Roger Williams, were primarily worried about the state's propensity to interfere with the freedom of the church and the consciences of believers. Others, like Thomas Jefferson, were more concerned with the possibility of church leaders interfering in the political sphere by claiming exclusive privileges for particular denominations. On the one hand, the role of faith in public life was seen as both an incredible good to be protected, and on the other a potential powder keg of controversy and faction to be cause for concern.

The importance of religion is further evidenced by the privileged place it holds in the governing document of the United States, the Constitution. The first priority of the First Amendment is to protect religion and religious exercise from the federal government: "Congress shall make no law respecting an establishment of religion, or prohibiting the free exercise thereof."

This language has led to the development of the establishment clause and free exercise jurisprudence. The former is concerned with whether the government favors religion in some manner; the latter addresses whether the religious beliefs and practices of citizens have been unduly infringed by the government. While originally the First Amendment only applied to the federal government, a subsequent legal development called "incorporation" means that states and local governments are subject to the religious clauses as well. The enormous challenge facing Christians and other citizens is how to interpret these ideas in the founding documents and apply them to contemporary situations and conflicts.

Opinions on what the American founders meant by the religion clauses range from "strict separation" to "accommodation." Strict separationists follow Thomas Jefferson's language in his letter to a group of Danbury Baptists, in which he invokes a "wall of separation" between church and state. When it comes to the establishment clause, this view invests the government with a kind of watchdog role, such that the government will ensure that it will never appear to endorse religion. Strict separationists object to governmental support of religious schools, prayers at public events, and symbolic gestures like nativity scenes at city halls or "In God We Trust" on our coinage.

Accommodationists interpret the Constitution somewhat more broadly. The founders' primary intention, they feel, was to prevent the establishment of a national church and to provide space for religious groups to flourish free from the intolerance that marked many European church-state arrangements. The founders did not intend to erect a wall denying all cooperation between church and state but envisioned a benign cooperation that would still protect religious liberty. Accommodationists would object to the government's adopting a Presbyterian denomination as the official religion of the United States, but they would be more flexible about public prayers, the use of "In God We Trust," and similar matters.

Christians thinking about these matters should differentiate between historical debates about what the founders meant and normative debates about what would be the best state of affairs for church and state. It is far too easy to read back into history the views one presently holds and favors. The founders themselves disagreed about these matters, though it is clear that faith was understood as intrinsically valuable and deserving of protection and, in some instances, promotion.

Fortunately, a Christian worldview rests on much more than the accomplishments of man—as admirable as some of those accomplishments may have been. Christians should continue to draw from Scripture in working and thinking together about how God's particular mandates for his church and for the state intersect. Given the fall, Christian attempts to live out their identities as citizens of heaven and of earth will always fall short; nevertheless, such endeavors will contribute to their being "salt" and "light" until the true King returns and establishes his reign forever (Matt 5:13–14; Rev 21:1–6).

RELIGIOUS FREEDOM

Scott H. Moore

Religious freedom is a political principle that affirms the right for individuals and communities of faith to believe, worship, and live out their religion as they see fit.

The origins of religious freedom can be traced to the fourth century AD when the Roman emperor Constantine abolished those laws that proscribed Christian faith and practice, giving Christians the "freedom" to worship without fear of imprisonment or persecution. Religious freedom as a formal concept, however, only comes to fruition in the early modern period after the Protestant Reformation of the sixteenth century. John Locke's "Letter Concerning Toleration" (1689) is often recognized as a foundational document for the notion of religious freedom.

Religious freedom is affirmed in the Bill of Rights to the United States Constitution (1791), and the United Nations Universal Declaration of Human Rights (1948) asserts that religious freedom in all nations is necessary for justice. The most important Christian reflection on religious freedom is found in *Dignitatis Humanae*, the Second Vatican Council's Declaration on Religious Freedom (1965).

Despite this long substantial heritage, in today's religiously pluralistic world it is not uncommon to find religious believers of many faiths who face discrimination, persecution, or even death because of their belief and practice. Against such injustice, religious freedom allows one to practice one's religion without fear of coercion from political, cultural, or religious authorities.

While religious freedom is an important concept for modern political thought, no explicit defense or robust account of religious freedom can be found in either the OT or the NT. Moreover, religious freedom is not a doctrine of Christian theology that can be inferred explicitly from the teachings of Scripture, the tradition of the church, or the vast majority of its most prominent theologians and teachers.

The Bible does not set forth specific political principles for perpetuating religious pluralism. Quite to the contrary, in the OT the defeated Canaanites—adults, children, and livestock—are to be killed at God's command (Deut 20:16–18). Similarly, the people of Nineveh face utter destruction if they do not repent (Jonah 3). Nowhere in the Bible is true religious belief optional. The people of God and nonbelievers alike are called to repentance, faithfulness, and sanctification.

The Bible does consistently affirm the legitimacy (but not the infallibility) of conscience, and religious freedom can be understood as following from the principle of conscience. An acknowledgment of conscience is integral to a respect for human dignity, and at its best, religious freedom is the political principle that attempts to ensure that the nation state does not infringe on the exercise of conscience. Even so, religious freedom embraced as a political principle can be used for good or ill; it thus requires careful consideration by Christians.

In the modern religiously pluralistic world, for instance, religious believers face a variety of challenges. In recent non-Western history, certain atheist nation states have sought to abolish religious belief entirely, while others, particularly those practicing Islamic Sharia law, have outlawed rival religious traditions altogether. In Western countries as well, geographical regions with a dominant Christian tradition have sometimes made the practice of minority Christian traditions difficult (e.g., Protestantism in the American South or Catholicism in certain urban, immigrant neighborhoods of the American North). In all of these contexts, there is a need for the permissive sense of religious freedom that ensures that minority religious traditions are free to practice their various faiths.

If religious freedom in the permissive sense seeks to protect religious practice from the authority of the dominant culture or nation-state, religious freedom in the restrictive sense seeks to protect the nation-state from the demands of religious belief and practice. Implicitly this occurs when these are domesticated, trivialized, and relegated to the margins of "respectable" society, so that religion becomes inward and private rather than communal and public.

The restrictive sense occurs explicitly when litigation and public policy disallow individuals and communities from exercising their beliefs in the many and diverse areas of their public and private lives. From the outlawing of polygamy in the American West to the prosecution of businesses that refuse to recognize sexual orientation as a civil right, the reach of the restrictive sense of religious freedom is broad, deep, and complex. The dilemmas presented by the double-edged sword of religious freedom cannot ultimately be resolved by case law.

Some might suggest that the restrictive sense is not an authentic manifestation of religious freedom. On the contrary, the permissive and the restrictive sense necessarily require each other for political coherence. What one community sees as permissive another may find to be restrictive. Moreover, it is always the case that when religious believers follow the dictates of conscience rather than those ordained by the state, they place themselves in potential conflict with the state. Unfortunately, to appeal to the nation state to protect religious freedom means that this freedom itself is beholden to the entity from which it seeks protection. The state will only protect religious freedom so long as the state does not deem the religious practice as a challenge to its own hegemony.

Religious freedom cannot be entrusted to the modern nation-state. While the biblical record does not address the question of religious freedom directly, it is abundantly clear on the question of to whom the Christian must pledge allegiance: we must "give . . . to Caesar the things that are Caesar's, and to God the things that are God's" (Matt 22:21) and "we must obey God rather than people" (Acts 5:29).

Education

CHRISTIAN PERSPECTIVES ON CHILDREN'S EDUCATION

Timothy Paul Jones

To have a biblical worldview is to interpret every aspect of life within the framework of God's story. At the center of God's story stands this singular act: in Jesus Christ, God personally intersected human history and redeemed humanity. Yet this central act does not stand alone. It is bordered by God's good creation and humanity's fall into sin on the one hand and by the consummation of God's kingdom on the other. This story of creation, fall, redemption, and consummation is the story Christians have repeated to one another and to the world ever since Jesus ascended into the sky and sent his Spirit to dwell in his first followers. This age-old plotline should frame every aspect of our lives including how we treat and train children.

Gifts from God and Sinners in Need

In each movement of God's story line, children are neither burdens to be avoided nor byproducts of sin. Every child is a gift (Ps 127:3–5). Even before humanity's fall, God designed the raising of children to serve as a means for multiplying his glory (Gen 1:26–28). After the fall, men and women still exercise divinely ordered dominion over creation by raising children (1:26–28; 8:17; 9:1–7; Mark 10:5–9). What has changed in the aftermath of the fall is that children have become not only gifts to be nurtured but also sinners to be trained.

The training of little ones is a primary parental responsibility. Parents are responsible not only to provide for their children's needs but also to train them to reflect God's glory. This doesn't release the larger faith community from a responsibility for shaping children's souls. The Great Commission to "make disciples" was given to the whole people of God and includes every age group (Matt 28:19). Parents may partner with church ministries or enlist teachers to develop certain skills in their children, but parents bear final responsibility before God for how their children are trained for life.

In the OT, Moses commanded parents—particularly fathers—to train their children in God's ways (the pronouns translated "you" and "your" in Deut 6:6–7 are masculine singular in the original language). Moses expected children to ask their parents about their family's spiritual practices, and he prepared fathers to respond in ways that highlighted God's mighty works (Exod 12:25–28; Deut 6:20–25). These expectations persisted throughout Israel's songs and early history (Josh 4:6; Ps 78:1–7). This ancient heritage of songs, statutes, and ceremonies foreshadowed the coming of Jesus and explicitly recognized the primacy of parents in their children's training.

Paul reiterated this in the NT when he reminded fathers to nurture their children in the "training and instruction of the Lord" (Eph 6:4). Paul seems to have derived this phrase from Deuteronomy 11:2, where "discipline of the Lord" prefaced a description of how God disciplined his people to remind them of his covenant with them.

In other letters, Paul applied these same two terms—*training* and *instruction*—to patterns that characterized the disciple-making relationships of brothers and sisters in the faith. *Training* implied discipline and described one of the key results of training in the words of God (2 Tim 3:16). *Instruction* included warnings to avoid unwise behaviors and ungodly teachings (1 Cor 10:11; Titus 3:10). Such texts suggest that Paul was calling parents to do far more than manage their children's behaviors and provide for their needs. Paul expected parents to train their children to engage with their world in light of God's words and ways.

Children's training is worldview training. This training includes more than merely increasing children's biblical knowledge or involving them in a community of faith. Moses commanded the Israelites to teach their offspring to view all they did ("hand") and all they chose ("forehead"), as well as how they lived at home ("doorposts") and how they conducted business ("your city gates") within the all-encompassing framework of a God-centered worldview (Deut 6:8–9).

"Wisdom" in Proverbs was conveyed from parent to child and included not only knowledge about God but also practical skills for engaging with the world in light of God's truth. Skills in craftsmanship, leadership, and a broad range of other fields fell under the heading of wisdom, which begins with "the fear of the LORD" (Prov 1:7). Persons outside the believing community may possess these skills, but only the believer sees them as God intended: they are signposts pointing to the order and glory of God. There is no biblical warrant for separating the training of children into "secular" and "sacred" categories, with one handled by the world and the other superintended by parents. God is Lord over all of life.

Children's training includes formal and informal components. Moses commanded the Israelites to teach God's words to their children and to discuss these truths informally throughout each day (Deut 6:7–9). In Proverbs, the father passed on particular teachings to his son (Prov 4:2) and provided occasional instructions in response to specific situations (4:1). The biblical pattern is for parents to be involved in formal and informal training. The book of Proverbs mentions the mother's role five times (1:8; 4:3; 6:20; 31:1,26). According to biblical scholar Peter Gentry, this inclusion of the mother is unparalleled in the Wisdom literature of ancient Near Eastern nations. In Scripture the father possessed a particular responsibility to lead, but the father's responsibility did not negate or diminish the mother's supportive role in the nurture and admonition of children.

Every child is more than a child.

No amount of training can ever raise a child to the level of God's perfect righteousness. Even the best training may not result in a child's perseverance in the faith. Proverbs 22:6, the text that declares "even when he grows old he will not depart," is not a promise to parents but a proverb. It's a pithy observation about how life typically works.

Every order of creation, including our relationships with children, has been subjected to frustration due to the fall (Rom 8:20–22). The ultimate solution is not better training but a perfect substitute, and that's precisely what God provided in Jesus Christ. Through Christ, God bridged the gap between his perfection and humanity's imperfection (2 Cor 5:21). The death of Jesus brought about the possibility of redemption here and now; his resurrection guaranteed the consummation of God's kingdom in the future.

This introduces a radical new dimension to how we view children. To embrace God's redemption is to be adopted in Jesus Christ as God's heir; it means gaining a new identity that transcends every earthly status (Rom

8:15–17; Gal 3:28–29; 4:3–7; Eph 1:5; 2:13–22). United in Christ with other believers, the church becomes the believer's first family. Because the church is a family, in instances where one parent is absent or is an unbeliever, other believers may become that child's parents in the faith (2 Tim 1:2,5; 3:15). "Whoever does the will of my Father in heaven is my brother and sister and mother," Jesus said (Matt 12:50). Paul made much the same point when he directed Timothy to encourage "younger men as brothers" and "younger women as sisters" (1 Tim 5:1–2).

For followers of Jesus, this means that every child is far more than a child. Every child is a potential or actual brother or sister in Christ. The children who stand beside us in eternal glory will not stand beside us as our children or as our students. They will stand beside us as our brothers and sisters, "heirs of God and coheirs with Christ" (Rom 8:17; see also Gal 4:7; Heb 2:11; Jas 2:5; 1 Pet 3:7).

Every child is an eternal soul whose days will long outlast the rise and fall of earthly kingdoms. They and their children and their children's children will flit ever so briefly across this life before being swept away into eternity (Jas 4:14). If these children become our brothers and sisters in Christ, however, their days on this earth are preparatory for glory that will never end (Dan 12:3; 2 Cor 4:17–5:4; 2 Pet 1:10–11). That's why our primary purpose for the children we educate must not be anything as small and miserable as earthly success. Our loving purpose should be to leverage children's lives to advance God's kingdom.

THE BIBLE AND INTELLECTUAL PURSUIT

Christopher W. Morgan

Some presume Christianity is anti-intellectual. But does the Bible actually promote anti-intellectualism? On the contrary, the Bible promotes the life of the mind. Indeed, the Christian worldview values learning, and it grounds, fosters, and clarifies such intellectual pursuit.

Note, for example, how the nature of God does so. God's infinity clarifies that he alone possesses full knowledge—past, present, and future. God's graciousness initiates all learning as all knowledge of him, and life flows from his generous self-revelation. God's truthfulness shows that his self-disclosure communicates truth and does so coherently. God's personal nature means that knowledge is also relational, pointing us to a covenant relationship with him.

1. God's self-revelation reflects God and is likewise instructive about intellectual pursuit.
2. God's self-revelation is gracious: God freely initiates it and blesses through it.
3. It is truthful, faithfully representing who God is, what God does, and how God relates to humans.
4. It is a unity: though coming in a variety of forms (see below), God's communication about himself, humanity, and life coheres.
5. It is personal, as it communicates who God is and his ways.
6. It is propositional, disclosing truth about God, humanity, life, history, and salvation.

7. Since humans are the recipients of God's self-revelation, it is analogical, as God uses human contexts, cultures, and languages to communicate.
8. It is partial, since the infinite God can only reveal limited information to finite humans.
9. It is historical, as God communicates with humans in space and time.
10. It is progressive within Scripture, since God relates to multiple generations of humans and gradually expands his self-disclosure over time.

As such, God's self-revelation clarifies the educational pursuit: it is only possible through divine initiative, rests on the content and unity of revealed truth, has objective and subjective components, requires insight into human culture, cannot be exhaustive, is linked to all of life, and is a perennial process.

Further, God's gracious self-disclosure has been given in a variety of ways and in a variety of contexts, yet with striking unity.

- God has revealed himself to all people at all times in all places through creation, which witnesses to him as its Creator and Lord (Ps 19:1–6; Rom 1:18–32). He has also done so through creating humans in his image (addressed below) who have a conscience, the moral law written on the heart (Rom 2:12–16).
- God has also revealed himself to particular people at particular times and places, gradually and more clearly communicating himself and his covenant relations. He has displayed himself through historical actions (e.g., the exodus), through divine speech (e.g., the Ten Commandments), and through his covenant people, whose holiness, love, and justice are to reflect God's own character (Exod 19:5–6; Lev 19:1–18).
- God has revealed himself most fully in Jesus and his incarnation, sinless life, teaching, proclamation of the kingdom, miracles, crucifixion, resurrection, ascension, reign, and return (John 1:1–18; Heb 1:1–4).
- God has also revealed himself through the inspired prophetic-apostolic Holy Scriptures, which accurately record and interpret God's self-revelation. Even more, the Scriptures are called God's Word and are themselves a significant form of God's self-revelation (Pss

19:7–14; 119; Matt 5:17–20; John 10:35; 2 Tim 3:15–4:5; 1 Pet 1:22–25; 2 Pet 1:16–21; 3:15–16).

Because of this, proper human intellectual pursuit begins with the fear of the Lord (Prov 1:1–7) and requires the standpoint of creatures seeking to know the Creator and his world through dependence on his self-revelation.

Creation and the Intellectual Pursuit

Creation likewise grounds, fosters, and clarifies intellectual pursuit. The infinite, self-existent, sovereign, personal, holy, and good Lord powerfully speaks and creates a good cosmos, evidenced by the steady refrain, "God saw that [it] was good" (Gen 1:4,10,12,18,21,25). This goodness was accentuated on the sixth day: "It was very good indeed" (1:31).

God's generous provisions of light, land, vegetation, and animals are blessings given for humanity's benefit, as are the abilities to know God, work, marry, and procreate. In the first chapters of Genesis, God blesses man with the Sabbath, places him in the delightful garden of Eden, gives him a helper, and establishes only one prohibition—given not to stifle him but to promote his welfare. Thus, the good God created a good world for the good of humanity. Truth, goodness, beauty, and peace abound. As a result, it is fitting that humans seek to understand all of creation, all of life, in light of God's revelation.

Humanity and the Intellectual Pursuit

Humanity is also instructive with respect to intellectual pursuit. As creatures, humans naturally bear all of the marks of finitude. All human knowledge is therefore limited, reflective of the Creator-creature distinction.

Even more, humans are created in God's image to love God, reflect his character, and serve his mission. As such, knowledge is not merely a nice additive to pursue but relates to God's original and fundamental purposes for humanity—to love and serve God, others, and the creation (Gen 1:26–28). Such love and service require knowledge of God, self, culture, and creation. Humans are therefore created to learn and rightly pursue truth, goodness, beauty, and peace as noble ends in themselves and as ways of glorifying God by knowing, reflecting, and serving him.

Sin and the Intellectual Pursuit

Unfortunately, the reality of human sin distorts this intellectual pursuit. Humans rebelled against God, disrupting their relationship to him, themselves, others, and creation (Gen 3; Rom 5:12–21). Humans are now characterized both by the image of God and sin. They appropriately long for justice, peace, and beauty but tend to distort it or seek it for self-interest rather than for the glory of God and the good of others. Indeed, sin affects and infects the mind, affections, attitudes, will, actions, and even inactions.

Scripture explains this corruption in various ways, using metaphors such as spiritual death, darkness, hardness, bondage, and blindness (Mark 7:20–23; Rom 1:18–32; 3:9–20; 2 Cor 4:3–4; Eph 2:1–3; 4:17–19). As such, the human intellectual pursuit is too often marked by finitude, bias, and cultural myopia and driven by selfishness, pride, prestige, greed, and thirst for power.

Salvation and the Intellectual Pursuit

Thankfully, Christ is greater than sin and sheds light on the intellectual pursuit. Jesus is the Word, the fullest and clearest revelation of God (John 1:1–18; Heb 1:1–4). Jesus is the Light and the Truth in a world darkened by sin (Matt 5:13–16; John 1:4–18; 8:12; 14:6). Jesus is the Lord, the preeminent authority who deserves and demands allegiance and submission in all of life, including thinking (Phil 2:5–11). He is also a teacher who molds disciples and invests in them, teaching them about the kingdom of God and building a messianic community.

Further, Jesus proclaims that true worship is in spirit and in truth, urges people to search the Scriptures which testify of him, expects them to examine his miracles and teachings to gauge whether he is from God, links himself to the truth, corrects error, sends the Holy Spirit as One who will guide the disciples in the truth, relates eternal life to knowing God, and prays that God will make his people holy by the Word, which he characterizes as truth (Matt 5–7; John 1:15–18; 4:20–24; 5:19–47; 6:32–33; 7:18; 8:14–18; 14:6; 15:26; 16:13; 17:3,17).

The Church and the Intellectual Pursuit

Indeed, through his life, death, and resurrection, the Lord of truth redeems a people for himself. The church is marked by truth as she is shaped by the apostles' teaching, shares life together as a community of the Word, refutes error, and through union with Christ even displays the goodness of

God—particularly his oneness, holiness, love, and truth (Acts 2:41–47; Eph 2:4–10; 4:1–24).

The people of God worship him by yielding themselves to him as living, holy, and acceptable sacrifices, in part through being transformed by the renewing of their minds and the discernment of God's will (Rom 12:1–2; Eph 4:17–24). As such, the intellectual pursuit is not merely an individualistic endeavor but is integrated into the whole of life and pursued in community with the people of God under the authoritative Word of God. It requires humility, faith, dependence on grace, respect for others, patience, carefulness, and persistence.

Eternity and the Intellectual Pursuit

God's ultimate purposes for history are also instructive for the life of the mind. Jesus's return, triumph, and judgment declare his lordship, vindicate his people, and permanently establish cosmic justice and peace (2 Thess 1:5–10; Rev 20:10–15). The new heavens and the new earth will be characterized by God's personal presence, glory, holiness, unity, love, goodness, and truth. All falsehood is overthrown, and all who practice falsehood are banished (Rev 21–22). History is eschatological, linear, purposeful, for our good, and preeminently for God's glory (Rom 8:18–39; Eph 1:3–14); and learning is a worthy process that seeks to understand goodness, love, justice, and peace. It allows humans to serve one another and to glorify God.

Christians rightly value learning, reading, knowing, and teaching. Such pursuits glorify God and naturally grow out of the Christian worldview. Indeed, the nature of God, his self-revelation, creation, humanity as his image bearers, Jesus's saving work, the church, and eschatology call for and crystalize such education.

CHRISTIAN HIGHER EDUCATION

Barry H. Corey

The notion that colleges and universities can be deeply Christian in their mission is hardly a modern concept. Many of today's Christian institutions of higher learning were founded in the middle 1800s, while many European and North American schools were established centuries earlier and have deep roots in Christianity.

Over time, the leaders of many of these institutions untethered their decision making from the convictions of their forebears. As a result, these schools today do not resemble the Christian intent of their founders. Several reasons account for the drift away from Christ-centeredness and biblical authority. One is that over time faculty no longer were expected to teach from a perspective that all learning is connected to all truth—truth authored and ordered by God, truth that transcends all of life and all disciplines.

Knowledge and the God of Truth

Christians who see life from a biblical worldview understand learning differently. They do not believe scholarship and faith are incompatible. Rather than education disconnected from faith, Christian thinkers believe all knowledge falls within the realm of God's sovereignty and should be studied with that in mind. They believe all matters related to the arts and sciences—in fact, the entirety of life—were created by God as good and contain truth that ultimately points back to him.

In Colossians 1, Paul summarizes Christ's dominion over all of life. It's a passage often cited in advocating for the great Christian intellectual tradition. Notice the repetition of the phrase "all things" in verses 16 and 17, strengthening the biblical argument that a Trinitarian God is the Creator of all things, the object of all things, and the connector of all things. Of Jesus the Son the passage says:

> He is the image of the invisible God, the firstborn over all creation. For everything was created by him, in heaven and on earth, the visible and the invisible, whether thrones or dominions or rulers or authorities—all things have been created through him and for him. He is before all things, and by him all things hold together (1:15–17).

Integrative Teaching

Christian colleges and universities teach from the perspective that God is the Creator of all things and that God holds all things together. Teaching this way is often referred to as "integrative teaching." In the ideal Christian higher education setting, God's created and connecting truth ought to be evident throughout the entire curriculum and community. Christian higher education is not "Christian" because faculty members sign a faith statement or students are required to attend chapel. Christian higher education is "Christian" when the understanding throughout the institution is that the entirety of knowledge and wisdom comes from God and points toward God.

Being part of a Christian college or university, therefore, means students grapple with the truths within each academic discipline and among all academic disciplines by seeing them as under God's sovereignty. This is what the Dutch theologian Abraham Kuyper meant when he said, "There is not a square inch in the whole domain of our human existence over which Christ, who is Sovereign over all, does not cry, 'Mine!'" The same is argued by Christian scholars John Henry Newman, Arthur Holmes, Mark Noll, George Marsden, and others, who say that learning separated from faith is woefully incomplete.

This approach to learning is what characterizes Christian higher education, and it must stay as a distinguishing mark of an exemplary Christian university. In the world's marketplace of ideas, the person and work of Jesus

Christ and the implications of a biblical worldview currently hold little sway, yet they are vitally important to the Christian's assessments of and responses to dominant cultural ideologies. The role of Christian higher education is to preserve and advance the Christian intellectual tradition and to glorify God.

Christianity for All of Life

As Christian higher education enables Christians to think from the center of all knowledge—knowing that God is the Author of all truth—students begin asking new questions.

"How do faith and reason intersect in all of life and not run on separate tracks?"

"How should I live in a way that honors Christ and brings glory to God in the world of finance or law, medicine or politics, art or media?"

"What does it mean to think Christianly about the big questions of our times?"

"How does a biblical worldview influence the way I run my business or give away my money, nurture my family, or serve my community?"

Both the curricular programs in Christian higher education and cocurricular activities create a community in which students explore the answers to these and other worldview questions within a theological framework. Christian higher education is far more than sprinkling Christian flavorings on a college degree. Instead, it is an intellectually robust and academically holistic way of thinking.

To get there, scholars at the university need to be intentional about integrative thinking—the idea that academic disciplines are not disconnected from one another but are held together, since all truth is within the realm of God's ordered creation. An integrated faculty in Christian higher education allows professors to set aside time for discussing what God's revealed Word brings to bear on their respective disciplines and on the educational mission of the institution. This notion of integration brings together faculty from the social sciences, theology, the arts, the physical sciences, the humanities, business, education, and so forth, into a community with a shared approach to the connectedness of all things. If most of what is taught in the classrooms of a self-identified Christian college is indistinguishable from what is taught in non-Christian schools, then integration is evidently not a priority, and a full understanding of a Christian worldview is being shortchanged.

Education and Spiritual Formation

Since a Christian college or university provides a foundation for intellectual development, academic competence will accompany thought leadership in church and society. Much happens within the life of a university to cultivate this discipline of the mind and soul together. It is the idea Paul writes about to the church in Rome, explaining that spiritual transformation takes place "by the renewing of [the] mind" (Rom 12:2).

Colleges or universities that appoint faculty who are first-rate scholars, have a deep love for Christ, and are well-articulated integrators of scholarship and faith will impact generations of students. Such Christian thought leaders shape communities, congregations, and cultures for the advancement of Christ's kingdom.

Because God's Word bears witness to the truth of Christ at the core of all things, a Christ-centered university must be biblically grounded. The cornerstone of the evangelical movement from its starting point was an ineradicable belief in the authority of the Bible, alongside serious scholarship. Such commitment to the revealed Word of God is at the core of exemplary Christian universities. Being a Christian college or university means the Christian Scriptures—as originally intended and as understood through the ages—have a central role in all programs.

Christian Education as Worship

Christian higher education is an act of worship, built on the lordship of Christ over all things—including our lives. Scholarship separated from loving God is a type of idolatry. By seeing all of life and vocation as a holy calling, graduates of Christian higher education should be alive in a way that encourages others to see Christ's redemptive work and to receive God's grace.

Learning this way is not an act of self-enrichment. It is an act of worshiping Creator God. This is what Jesus meant when he called his followers to love the Lord with all their hearts, souls, strength, and minds (Matt 22:37; Luke 10:27). The purpose of theology is not mere intellectual exercise but doxology, an expression of praise to God. We study all of God's truths so that we may love God more.

LITERATURE AND A CHRISTIAN WORLDVIEW

Gene C. Fant

Wherever humans gather, they tell stories. Storytelling is a distinctly human activity found nowhere else in creation. Literature expresses in writing the shared experiences that people have lived or have imagined.

For millennia, literature, or more broadly narrative, has held an instructional role across cultures. Once literacy was attained, writers used it to explain what was valued in their cultures: What does it mean to be honorable? How do we relate to nature? How do we live under the specter of death? Who (or what) is God? What is love? One of the best ways to understand a culture's worldview, in fact, is to read its literature.

Literature is significantly more effective than other means of discourse precisely because it is affective: it evokes emotions that enhance our thoughts in order to create lasting insights. In this way, literature cultivates empathy, through which we can step into other people's shoes.

Stories and poems thus allow us to share others' experiences. We may become friends with the characters; we may laugh with them, cry for them, and even pattern our own lives after those we find in literature. Reading literature helps prevent the sense of isolation and even egocentrism that can easily slip into our lives.

The Bible as Literature

For Christians, the quintessential work of literature is the Bible itself, with its incredible range of history, poetry, and narratives. It contains the greatest masterworks of the ages—material that may be mined repeatedly for moral insights. Even secular thinkers and atheists often note that an understanding of the Bible's basic contents is necessary for any educated person.

The Bible employs many genres of literature in its communication of truth. Likewise, it uses many common literary techniques such as allegory, metaphor, hyperbole, and many others.

Appreciating Scripture as a literary triumph, however, in no way undercuts its unique status as the authoritative, written revelation of God to his creation. The Bible is not merely another human story; it is the inspired Word of God. While it displays the qualities we recognize in other written works, its unique status exalts it above all other stories, both thematically and theologically. Indeed, just as Christ is "the author and finisher of our faith" (Heb 12:2 KJV), God is the ultimate Author of the Bible. We rightly expect him to produce a work of exquisite perfection.

Moreover, understanding the literary qualities and techniques employed by the Scriptures is important to their interpretation. Without such tools, we may create weak or even false theological positions based on misreadings of the text. When Jesus said, "I am the gate for the sheep" (John 10:7), he employs a metaphor that helps us see his role as the ultimate gatekeeper to eternity. His is the name by which all must be saved. A slavish literality would actually shortchange the theological force of the declaration, which is foundational to understanding the exclusivity of Christ.

Literature and Christianity

In the West, most literary traditions are either rooted in the Judeo-Christian tradition or are deeply complementary to them through the heritage of the Greco-Roman world. Rare is the work prior to the twentieth century that is not in some way generated with a foundational understanding of humankind that underlies the Christian faith. More recent literature may claim to make such a break, but even when it reacts against orthodoxy, it still touches on many of its presuppositions.

Christian thinkers have always wrestled with the right way to handle literature where it reflects divergent worldviews. Since Cyprian and Tertullian, some critics have called non-Christian thought worthless to the faithful, a charge that was countered by Augustine in particular. Augustine believed that because God created truth, just as he created gold, we have the right to reclaim truth, in this case literary gold, from those who have mixed it with error.

The wise reader will read literature in one hand with the Bible in the other, panning for the metaphorical gold Augustine identified. In secular literature, we can see the foreshadowing of the truth that comes by the light of Christ. Such works struggle with brokenness, alienation, sin, and death—all of which culminate in a longing for something more, the kind of reconciliation that anticipates the Redeemer who will restore all things.

Literature and Christian Mission

Acts 7:22 tells us that "Moses was educated in all the wisdom of the Egyptians and was powerful in his speech and actions." Daniel likewise learned the literature of Babylon (Dan 1:17), which prepared him for his important calling. Believers are expected to prepare themselves to serve an unbelieving world, and understanding literature is foundational to being able to communicate with our culture or others. Just as Paul quoted from secular writers at the Areopagus (Acts 17), Christians are wise to develop the kind of cultural relevance that allows them to communicate the gospel in effective ways.

Someone who is undertaking a mission trip to another culture would be wise to read translations of the poetry and stories of that other culture; this act of cultural humility pays significant dividends not only in understanding the other people group's worldview but also in developing a genuine love for the people who love those stories. When traveling to India, for example, the wise Christian reads the *Ramayana*, their national epic, which contains many tales that can provide gospel bridges to transformational relationships.

Finally, literature provides an incredible opportunity for Western Christian thinkers to engage our own culture. As our society becomes increasingly postliterate, the stories we tell and share with others continue to have power to reach into their lives. History has shown that the intellectual culture of Christianity is both durable and effective in reflecting a Christian worldview. For example, while most of Europe now shows little commitment to Christian thought, a visit to almost any town in Europe will include a tour of the churches and cathedrals, whose stained-glass windows and architecture still provide witness to the faith that created them. In the same way, well-written literature persists for decades and even centuries. Works such as John Milton's *Paradise Lost* and the medieval dream-vision *The Pearl* continue to communicate Christian ideas long after their authors' deaths.

The Power of Good Literature

Good literature always finds a hearing because it owes its power to something transcendent to the drabness of everyday life. Literature that reflects the timeless truths of Christianity enjoys a matchless power—that of the faith communicated as the purest form of truth.

Advances in technology have allowed literature to find fresh platforms for exposure to new readers across the globe. While literature gives voice to the past, it also anticipates the future vision of Revelation 7:9, with "every nation, tribe, people, and language" giving praise to God. In this way, our present lives are enriched through the novels, stories, plays, and poems from around the world. Christian thinkers have a responsibility to include literature in the development of their own intellect and character, as they explore the worldviews that fill the globe and develop their own understanding of the Christian worldview.

A BIBLICAL VIEW OF PSYCHOLOGY AND PSYCHIATRY

Eric L. Johnson

Psychology, psychiatry, and psychotherapy have as their root stem the Greek word *psyché*, translated "soul" in English. *Psychology* (created by adding the Gk word *logos*, meaning "word" or "knowledge") refers to the "study of the soul." The words *psychiatry* (created by adding the Lat *iatreia*, meaning "healing") and *psychotherapy* (created by adding the Gk *therapeuō*, meaning "healing") both mean the "healing of the soul." Psychiatry, however, is practiced by medical doctors who specialize in the treatment of mental illness. Psychotherapy is practiced by doctoral-level trained psychologists who use cognitive, emotional, and relational techniques for the treatment of the broader category of psychological disorders. (In American culture, the word *counseling* is another category of "soul healing." It is often practiced by ministers as well as by masters-level-trained professionals.)

All three are widely considered modern disciplines. That is because they recently advanced greatly, beginning in the late 1800s and throughout the twentieth century, because of the dedicated application of natural science sensibilities and methods to the human sciences. Historians of these disciplines, however, know that their precursors can be found, in some form, as early as ancient times.

Philosophers in ancient Greece, such as Plato (429–347 BC) and Aristotle (382–322 BC), brilliantly analyzed the soul. A Roman physician named Galen (AD 129–200) attempted to describe the medical basis of mental illness. More importantly for Christians, the Scriptures are saturated with psychological and spiritual wisdom and provide a divine framework for the healing of the soul based on the person and work of Jesus Christ. The apostle Paul, in particular, was mindful of psychological topics related to Christian salvation (Roberts, 1995).

In comparison to contemporary psychology, biblical teaching was written in everyday language for average readers; it is not written in scientific genre. Nevertheless, the Bible provides believers with divinely inspired lenses through which they can rightly interpret the world, including human struggles. Thus, throughout the centuries many Christians wrote about Christian psychology and soul healing with a pastoral, monastic, or philosophical agenda; they were more or less influenced by previous thinkers such as Plato, Aristotle, and Galen, as well as early church figures like Augustine, Maximus the Confessor, Bernard of Clairvaux, and especially Thomas Aquinas. Relevant voices from the Middle Ages include Martin Luther, Blaise Pascal, and Søren Kierkegaard. Countless others arose in the modern era. By 1850, a substantial range of Christian psychological and soul-healing literature existed.

Nevertheless, concurrent with the application of natural science methods to the human sciences was a secular revolution (Smith, 2003) that resulted in the replacement of a Christian worldview with a secular one. Naturalism became the common basis of intellectual discourse and scientific and therapeutic practice in the West. As a result, by 1950 all major universities, particularly in America, had reinterpreted the human sciences, understanding them to be intrinsically secular, natural sciences. As a result, modern psychology, psychiatry, and psychotherapy are versions of science devoid of biblical, theological, and metaphysical considerations.

Such differences are unsurprising in light of Augustine's Two-Cities Framework (sometimes called the "doctrine of the antithesis"). Near the collapse of the Roman Empire, Augustine defended Christianity by arguing that the human race is composed fundamentally of two communities: the City of Man, into which all humans are born, and the City of God, into which one has to be born again by placing faith in Christ (John 3:3). The City of Man, Augustine wrote, is composed of those who love self and despise God, whereas the City of God is composed of those who love God and despise self, only because they have been regenerated by God's grace in Christ (Titus 3:5). When modern psychology was in its infancy, Abraham Kuyper (1898) applied the Two-Cities Framework to the human sciences. He concluded that they will necessarily reflect the influences of the Two Cities, with one kind of psychology based on naturalism and the other kind based on spiritual regeneration, thus leading to two markedly different versions of the human sciences.

A Christian approach to the human sciences will differ from modern versions in these ways:

1. God is recognized as the Author, center, and end of human life, and his glory is the highest human motivation (Isa 43:7; 1 Cor 10:31).
2. Humans are made in God's image (Gen 1:26–27; 9:6), so they can only be understood properly in terms of their relation to God. They flourish best in communion with him.
3. Humans, however, are now sinful and alienated from their Creator (Gen 3; Rom 3:10–18). They are damaged creatures, both in body and soul, which can lead to psychological disorders.
4. Humans require union with Christ in order to attain some measure of psycho-spiritual healing on earth and complete healing in the age to come. Through their union with Christ, believers receive many spiritual blessings from God that have the potential to significantly improve daily life and the communities in which they reside. The most important blessing is the gift of the indwelling Holy Spirit. These and other truths ought to have a profound impact on a Christian version of psychology, psychiatry, and psychotherapy.

At the same time, because of common grace—the provision of God given to all humans, irrespective of their relation to God (see Ps 104; Isa 23:23–26; Matt 5:45; Acts 14:17)—there will be overlap in the modern and Christian versions of the human sciences. For example, both communities can agree that human experience and behavior are influenced by biological and social dynamics; human memory is composed of long-term stores and working memory; and empirical research is necessary to study most aspects of humans. Indeed, these communities agree about far more than they conflict over. But those areas in which they disagree are of enormous significance and exercise a profound influence on the understanding and interpretation of humans, especially with respect to the healing of the soul.

Moreover, common grace is responsible for culture and the development of good cultural institutions such as the mental health community. Unfortunately, that institution is currently dominated by those who assume naturalism; they thus reflect that worldview orientation. The doctrines of the antithesis and that of common grace are both necessary to understand psychology, psychiatry, and psychotherapy from a Christian standpoint.

Current areas of contention between these two versions of the human sciences include the respective role of evolution and God in the formation of the human species, the area of mental disorders—the role of human responsibility and sin in psychopathology, the use and overuse of medication to treat mental disorders, questions about whether certain conditions ought to be considered a disorder (e.g., homosexuality or ADHD)—and the contemporary prohibition against sharing one's faith in session unless asked to do so by the client.

Christians currently take three basic approaches toward these three disciplines. Probably the most common approach is a relatively uncritical acceptance of them as they are currently constituted. Christians conduct themselves in these fields according to the rules of discourse and the practice of naturalism and secularism while seeking to do so with Christian integrity and remaining faithful to Christian ethics.

Second, on the other side of the spectrum are those Christians who basically reject these disciplines because of their secular, naturalistic basis. They instead practice a model of counseling based only on the Bible, treating most mental problems as exclusively spiritual in nature and remaining resistant to most psychotropic medications. This group also typically rejects professional licensure.

Finally, some Christians seek a middle way, in which they practice some measure of critical engagement and participation. Beginning with a Christian understanding of humans, and appropriating the legitimate knowledge of secular human sciences, interpreted according to a Christian worldview, they also believe Christianity offers divine resources in Christ for healing the soul. This latter approach seeks to redeem psychology, psychiatry, and psychotherapy, reordering them for the Christian community, university, and local church, while working within the secular rules of discourse and practice currently mandated within the public square.

A BIBLICAL VIEW OF HISTORY

Thomas S. Kidd

Christians believe the God of the Bible is the Lord of history. The history of everything—from an individual human life to the vast universe—is under God's sovereign control. By using the word *history*, I certainly mean the great stories of wars, kings, and political affairs, but I also mean the quieter narratives of forgotten people, those who do not appear in history books. Many are forgotten to human history, but they appear in God's view of it no matter how humble they are. Christ tells us that God does not even forget sparrows, and we are worth much more than they. Even the hairs of our heads are counted by him (Luke 12:6–7). God has never overlooked anything or anyone.

Nevertheless, God does not directly cause everything to happen in history. Most notably, he does not cause evil, for he is not the author of sin. On the other hand, nothing happens without his permission or consent, not even a sparrow's death (Matt 10:29). Critics have argued that this distinction between God's allowing evil to occur but not actually causing it is a hollow one. Christians, however, affirm that God is absolutely holy, that he directs history toward the ultimate triumph of good, and that he has permitted evil and suffering to enter the world by the agency of fallen people and the devil.

History and God's Purpose

As opposed to secular or materialistic philosophies that see no overarching point to history or human existence, Christians have a linear, purposeful view of the past, present, and future. As Christian historian David Bebbington has written in his book *Patterns in History*, Christians embrace three core convictions about history: "that God intervenes in it; that he guides it in a straight line; and that he will bring it to the conclusion that he has planned" (43). These ideas are central to the Christian belief in God's providence. God created the world with purpose—primarily to glorify himself—and since the fall of humanity in the garden of Eden, God has also been working out a plan of redemption, also for his own glory. As The Westminster Confession of Faith puts it, "God the great Creator of all things doth uphold, direct, dispose, and govern all creatures, actions, and things, from the greatest even to the least, by his most wise and holy providence."

God even plays a sustaining role in what might, at first glance, seem to be the "natural" things of history and everyday life. Hebrews 1:2–3 tells us that God the Father made the universe through the Son, who sustains "all things by his powerful word." Through Christ "all things hold together" (Col 1:17). God is, in a sense, always intervening to sustain and preserve his creatures and all creation. He has not even relinquished control of forces such as gravity or time.

But God also intervenes in special ways and particular places and times to accomplish his purposes. One could cite any number of examples. For instance, God raised up King Cyrus of Persia in order to bring about the return of the Jewish exiles to Jerusalem. Ezraa 1:1 and 2 Chronicles 36:22 speak of how God "roused the spirit of King Cyrus" to decree the return of the exiles, in spite of the fact that Cyrus probably worshipped pagan gods. In Isaiah 44:28, God calls Cyrus his "shepherd" who would fulfill all God's "pleasure" with regard to his chosen people, the Jews.

The fact of God's sovereignty over history is not just a dry philosophical proposition, but it lies at the heart of our personal trust in God's loving control over our lives. We all experience disappointments and sometimes tragedies, and in those times many are tempted to wonder where God is. What is he doing? Does he not care? Knowing that nothing takes God by surprise proves a great comfort; moreover, "all things work together for the good of those who love God, who are called according to his purpose" (Rom 8:28). We may not understand or like what is happening in the moment, but it is reassuring to know that God remains sovereign over everything—not only in our lives but throughout the entire universe.

History and Humility

A great challenge for Christians regarding history is our limited ability to discern God's purposes. Our limitations come from living in a time-bound state and having minds only partially redeemed from the effects of the fall of humankind. God, conversely, is not bound by time or space; he is infinitely powerful and holy. Humans simply do not share God's level of understanding, as he says in Isaiah 55:8: "My thoughts are not your thoughts, and your ways are not my ways." Joseph had no idea when he was sold into slavery in Genesis 37 that it would result in his elevation to authority in Pharaoh's court as well as in the deliverance of his family. Yet in Genesis 50:20, Joseph makes a statement to his brothers that reveals a humble and wonderful shift in perspective: "You planned evil against me; God planned it for good to bring about the present result."

Because of our limited understanding of God's specific purposes, we should be humble about asserting that we know exactly what God is doing in history except in matters such as those revealed in Scripture. In some cases, we may safely assert that God was moving in a certain event or in a person's life, including our own. Seminal events in church history, such as the Reformation of the sixteenth century or the Great Awakening of the eighteenth century have obvious marks of God's providence, as do heroic Christian lives such those of Lottie Moon, the missionary to nineteenth-century China, or the great revival preacher Billy Graham. Of course, signs of God's providential role never mean that the event or person in question is sinless or perfect unless the person in view is Christ himself.

Understanding God's role in other historical episodes, such as the creation of the United States, requires more reflection and caution. Many American Christians eagerly assert that America's founding was a special work of God's providence. Indeed, a number of the founding fathers saw it that way as well. We must certainly agree that America's independence from Britain, just as with any similar political transformation, happened by God's sovereign permission. But we must also remember that God's primary purpose in history is the building of his kingdom, not the building of a nation (outside of biblical Israel).

Similarly, we must be cautious about asserting that we understand God's purposes in allowing natural disasters or the acts of sinful people. In the wake of events such as the September 11, 2001, terrorist attacks, or Hurricane Katrina's devastation of New Orleans in 2005, certain Christians said these events were products of God's wrath. But other Christians contended that we are not given such direct insight into the workings of God's providence, absent the divine knowledge reserved for the Bible's prophetic authors. If New Orleans, for instance, was subject to God's judgment, then why not other American cities? And what of the godly people and churches that were devastated by the storm and floods? Does every hurricane represent God's judgment? Or just particularly devastating ones? The more we think about such questions, the harder it is for us, with our restricted vision, to know just what to make of such events from the divine perspective.

Though God does not permit us to understand the purpose for everything that happens in history, Scripture does certainly give assurance that God controls it all. It also tells us about God's most important purposes in history, especially about the redemption of believers in Jesus Christ and the building of the kingdom of God to his glory.

A RESPONSE TO EASTERN AND NEW AGE VIEWS OF HISTORY

Nathan A. Finn

According to the Bible and Christian tradition, history is linear and purposeful. History began at a particular moment sometime in the past. At some unknown point in the future, history as we presently understand it will come to an end. Historical events are not matters of chance, accident, or fate. The Lord who created the heavens and the earth is sovereign over history. He providentially guides it along from beginning to end, according to his own sovereign purposes. History has a point: to glorify the Lord.

The Christian view of history, when understood as an expansion of the Jewish approach, is the oldest philosophy of interpreting the past. The Judeo-Christian tradition of historical understanding, however, has many competitors. One of its oldest competitors is often referred to as the Eastern view of history, so-called because of its association with ancient India and China. It remains popular today in parts of East Asia. It has also influenced the so-called New Age movement in North America and parts of Europe.

Eastern Views of History
The distinguishing feature of the Eastern view is that history is understood to be cyclical rather than linear. In the Eastern interpretation, history is a series of endlessly repeating cycles. The past is repeated in the present, and the present will be repeated in the future. History has no ultimate purpose or goal; it simply happens again and again. History had no starting point, and it will have no climax. Thus, each individual cycle of history is irrelevant except insofar as it represents a particular example of repeatable patterns

that have always occurred and will continue to do so forever. Because history is not linear, it has no "metanarrative," no comprehensive meaning that transcends all of history and brings together all the individual moments in time. A revolving wheel is often the image used to visually depict this philosophy of history.

Various versions of the Eastern philosophy of history have been popular in cultures that blur the lines between myths and reality. There are at least two related explanations for the origins of Eastern understandings of history. First, each cycle of history in some respects parallels the normal pattern of a human life. Individuals grow in understanding and physical maturity from childhood to adulthood, only to experience a gradual return to physical and frequently intellectual feebleness during their final years. In Eastern historical interpretation, the individual experience was projected onto the world's historical process and incorporated into a never-ending cycle.

The second explanation for the Eastern view is related to the agrarian milieu of many ancient civilizations. History was understood to be part of natural processes. In an agricultural context, people regularly observe the yearly cycle of seasons and how they affect sowing and reaping. Year in and year out, the seasons changed and agrarian families repeated the process of planting and harvesting, understanding that their existence depended on their participation in this cycle. In the Eastern view of history, the rhythm of nature was projected onto the larger historical process; the latter, in fact, was understood to be the source of the former.

Three Types of Eastern Views

Historians point to at least three different versions of the Eastern view that have prevailed in various cultures. In ancient India, the focus was on the entire earth. All of creation participates in a birth-to-death cycle, which in turn gives way to a new cycle. This has always happened, and the pattern will continue forever. This view remains popular in Southeast Asia and is the version of the Eastern view to which this article has given most of its attention.

In ancient China, the tendency was to focus more on particular dynasties of rulers and the civilizations they governed. Each dynasty was seen as a particular expression of the wider cycle of growth-maturity-decay. This view is not widely held today.

In the third version, popular in ancient Greco-Roman and Middle Eastern cultures, the past was seen as a golden age that needed to be reclaimed.

Cultures that traditionally affirmed this third option have often been quicker to embrace a Christian view of history or some other linear understanding of the historical process. For example, in the Greco-Roman world, the Christian view became popular after the legalization of Christianity in the fourth century AD. In the Middle East and North Africa, an alternative linear approach (that borrows from the Judeo-Christian tradition) became dominant after the advent of Islam in the seventh century.

The Impact of Eastern Views of History

It is difficult to find any real personal significance in the Eastern view of history, since this approach attributes little wider meaning to history itself. For this reason, belief in reincarnation is popular among adherents to a cyclical interpretation of history, especially in the Far East. Because of the endless historical cycles, the best a person can hope for is to be reborn after death, hopefully with better prospects in the next life than those experienced in this current life. Reincarnation plays a prominent role in Hinduism, Buddhism, Sikhism, and Jainism.

In the past, many cultures that embraced the Eastern view also affirmed some form of fatalism. This was especially true in the Greco-Roman and Middle Eastern worlds. Fatalism holds that the future is irrevocably fixed by forces beyond human control. In Eastern fatalism, this historical inevitability is attributed to divine spiritual powers. Our actions do not matter in and of themselves; rather, we are acting out a predetermined plan in which we have no real freedom.

Many Buddhists affirm a form of fatalism, though Buddhist fatalism is tied to karma rather than to a god or gods. Taoism is also fatalistic. Fatalism was mostly eliminated in Europe with the rise of Christianity, though some understandings of God's providence may border on fatalism. A form of fatalism persists in Islam, even though Muslims affirm a linear view of history.

Eastern Views in the New Age Movement

The Eastern view of history has long been rejected in Western culture, largely due to the influence of the Judeo-Christian tradition in Europe and North America. Nevertheless, elements of the worldview on which Eastern historical interpretation depends became popular in North America during the 1960s.

The so-called New Age movement embraces a hodgepodge of Eastern beliefs such as pantheism, karma, and reincarnation. But these views have been combined with an evolutionary approach to history that interprets the world as becoming increasingly advanced as humanity moves toward spiritual perfection as defined by New Age proponents. Many New Agers have also been influenced by a Marxist interpretation of history that over-emphasizes social upheaval and class tensions to the exclusion of intellectual trends.

In part because of their philosophy of history, many New Age adherents are interested in retrieving marginal spiritual practices from other places besides the Far East. They believe these allegedly lost spiritual practices were suppressed by power-hungry mainstream religious traditions. Goddess worship, nature worship, gnosticism, and various forms of Native American mysticism are examples of lost spiritualities that have been recovered by New Age proponents. New Agers consider their suppressed spiritual traditions, some of which are heretical corruptions of Christianity, to be superior to traditional religions.

Many New Agers are also influenced by postmodern views of tolerance. They are in theory open to any spiritual tradition except those systems that claim to be the one true path to God. Conservative versions of Christianity, Judaism, and Islam are rejected because of their exclusive truth claims.

Christianity and Eastern Views of History

Eastern and New Age understandings of history are incompatible with the Christian worldview. Believers must look to God's Word, which has been called "the true story of the whole world," to accurately understand history's scope and purpose.

History is the staging ground for the Lord of all creation to make himself known through his mighty acts in creation, promise, redemption, and consummation. The central figure in history is Jesus Christ, and the central acts of history are his incarnation, perfect obedience, sacrificial death, and victorious resurrection. History will climax with his return to the earth to complete his work of salvation and reverse the effects of sin in the created order "as far as the curse is found."

Science

A BIBLICAL BASIS FOR SCIENCE

John A. Bloom

A popular myth in our culture says that science and theology have always been at war with each other. It may come as a surprise to learn that most historians of science believe this idea to be untrue. In fact, the Bible provided some of the key intellectual foundations for the development of the sciences in the West.

God as Master of the Universe

The first foundation is the expectation of regularity in nature, which stems from the Bible's monotheistic view of God. Polytheistic and pantheistic religions see the universe as run by committee, with unpredictable events arising from conflicts among the many supernatural personalities involved. As a result, nature is seen as capricious, without any expectation of regularity.

By contrast, the Bible presents God as the sole Master and Commander of the universe (Ps 89:11–13; Isa 48:12–13), which he spoke into existence (Pss 33:6–9; 148:5) and over which he rules (Isa 40:26). Since one God is in control of nature and has said that he does not change (Num 23:19; Mal 3:6), we can expect his universe to run in a regular way. This is more than an inference: God explicitly says that he established the heavens and earth to follow regular laws (Gen 8:22; Jer 33:20,25).

Science as a Worthy Pursuit

Another foundation is the Bible's teaching that the study of nature is a worthy pursuit in gaining wisdom and glorifying God. God's creation is good, and even though it is corrupted by sin, we are encouraged to learn from it (Ps 19:1; Prov 6:6). Psalm 104 and Job 38–39 praise God's wisdom, sovereignty, and control over creation.

Scientists such as Isaac Newton and Johannes Kepler often stated that they sought to glorify God by studying his creation. In his letter to the Grand Duchess Christina, Galileo remarked, "The glory and greatness of Almighty God are marvelously discerned in all His works and divinely read in the open book of Heaven." By contrast, many world religions view nature in a dualistic manner, regarding the spiritual world as good and the material world as evil. So studying the physical world focuses one's attention in the wrong direction.

The Complexity of God's World

A third biblical foundation for science is that God's creation is not simple to understand. God informs us that "[his] thoughts are not [our] thoughts, and [our] ways are not [his] ways" (Isa 55:8; see also Prov 25:2). Yet "the LORD founded the earth by wisdom and established the heavens by understanding" (Prov 3:19). This suggests that through difficult work we may be able to glimpse some of God's wisdom. When doing science, as Kepler quipped, we are "thinking God's thoughts after Him."

God's Contingency

The last foundation to mention here is God's contingency: God created the world as he wanted it to be; he was not bound by outside constraints like human logic or philosophical principles. God "does whatever he pleases in heaven and on earth, in the seas and all the depths" (Ps 135:6; see also 115:3). Therefore, we cannot predict how God created; we must study God's handiwork itself to see what he has done. Thus, good science is based on direct observations and experiments while theories are held tentatively until proven beyond doubt.

Tensions between Science and Theology

While the Bible is not a scientific textbook, we find that it provides the correct perspectives for viewing nature and the proper motivations for studying it. Science is arguably one of the tasks mankind is commissioned to do: Adam was to "name" the animals in the garden of Eden (Gen 2:19), and he was given stewardship over the earth (Gen 1:28), a task that required study and wisdom to do it well. Although the Bible has higher priorities than explaining how the heavens work, biblical descriptions of nature are profoundly true while simply stated. Examples are the creation event in Genesis 1:1 (see also Isa 44:24; Heb 11:3), and the heavens and the earth's wearing out over time (Ps 102:25–26), an echo of the second law of thermodynamics.

If the study of nature was historically grounded in biblical insights, how did the modern tensions between science and theology arise? The drift started in the late 1600s when the philosophers of the Enlightenment freed themselves from the shackles of Aristotle and other ancient authorities by attempting to rely only on reason and experience to establish truth claims. Newton's discovery of the laws of motion and gravity led philosophers and theologians away from a theistic view (where God is actively involved in nature) to a deistic view (where God created the universe but now allows it to operate via laws he established). In the 1800s, T. H. Huxley and others desired to ground all knowledge on physical cause and effect, removing religious authority from society and replacing it with the authority of science. This narrowed the practice of science, limiting it to purely naturalistic explanations of the world.

Thus, the issues between the sciences and theology today hinge on the religious differences between naturalism and theism. In other words, should we view the universe as purely a machine which God cannot touch, or as a musical instrument which God plays for his glory? The difference is profound with respect to the explanations we can accept for natural phenomena. For example, if naturalism is assumed, something like Darwinism must be the "scientific" explanation for how life developed because God's guidance or intervention in nature is ruled out a priori. Any naturalistic explanation must be preferred, no matter how implausible it is, because others would not be naturalistic. Unfortunately, by ignoring some possible answers, science today may be missing the truth. This is perhaps most evident in the fields of biology, psychology, and the social sciences where the abandonment of man's special place in creation in favor of explaining him as a machine or an animal has led to the devaluing of human life and personhood.

Strikingly, this philosophical shift in the foundation of science from theism to naturalism leaves people with little justification to pursue science. Better technology can earn one fame and fortune, a military advantage, or more comfortable living, but naturalistically minded scientists have no reason to expect mathematics to explain and predict how the universe behaves, no reason to expect the world to operate in a regular manner, and no explanation for what put the "material" in materialism in the first place. The ad hoc nature of the naturalistic presupposition has become more glaring with the recognition that our universe is not eternal but had a beginning and that the physical laws and constants themselves appear to be fine-tuned to allow for the possibility of complex, intelligent life. Naturalists sometimes suggest that our universe is just one among countless universes in a so-called multiverse, and that with so many universes the chances were good that at least one would turn out to be fine-tuned for life. But importantly, there is no evidence indicating that other universes exist.

Christians and Science

Is it possible for the sciences to return to a biblical basis? Certainly for Christians it is. We should look beyond the naturalistic, materialistic, and mechanistic blinders that limit the perspective of our culture, choosing to see that "the world is charged with the grandeur of God" (Gerard Manley Hopkins, "God's Grandeur"). Christians who marvel at the wisdom, power, and creativity demonstrated in God's handiwork, as the biblical writers and early scientists did, have a strong motive to pursue the sciences even if their colleagues espouse a narrower viewpoint.

The fine-tuning of our universe and the fact that it had a beginning strongly imply that Someone is behind it. So too does the dizzying complexity of life, which is becoming more evident as biochemistry unravels the secrets of life. If, through continued discoveries like these, the naturalistic straitjacket on valid scientific explanations comes to be seen for what it is—a theologically motivated restriction—perhaps science will soon shed naturalism, just as it shed its Aristotelian and Platonic straitjackets in the past. Perhaps then it will return to its theistic roots—the most fruitful perspective for viewing nature.

THE CHRISTIAN WORLDVIEW AND THE EARLY CHAPTERS OF GENESIS

C. John Collins

Traditionally, Christians, like the Jews from whom they arose, have read the story of Adam and Eve in the opening chapters of the Bible as describing the first pair of humans from whom all other humans descend. Reading Genesis 1–11 as describing actual events, Christians have concluded (1) humankind is actually one family, with one set of ancestors; (2) God acted supernaturally to form our first parents; and (3) our first ancestors, at the headwaters of the human race, were created morally innocent and neverthe-less were seduced into disobedience and thus brought sin and dysfunction into the world in general and human life in particular.

This is a standard belief in the ancient Christian writers, both those in the East and those in the West. Even though Christians disagree on so many important matters—such as exactly how the first sin affects all people, or how long ago these events happened—they have been united on this basic point, finding it fundamental to their view of the world.

Contemporary Questions

Today there are also voices, outside the church and within it, raising ques-tions about whether we should hold this ancient belief any longer. Some ask, "How could anything someone else did long ago have any bearing on my life here and now? Even if Adam and Eve really lived, disobeyed God, and were booted out of the garden, what of it? Why should that affect me?"

Second, there is the widely acknowledged conclusion that the material in Genesis 1–11 closely parallels what we find in other ancient stories, particularly those from Mesopotamia. Someone might ask, "If we do not treat these other stories as history, why should we treat Genesis as such? What makes us think the Bible writers meant to produce anything unique from those other stories?"

Third, we have the dominant theories of the modern sciences. Astrophysicists say the universe began with a "big bang," approximately 13 to 14 billion years ago. This is or is not a problem for Christians, depending on whether we think Genesis provides a timeline.

A more serious challenge comes from the science of evolutionary biology, with its narrative (as some construe it) of how humans arose through a purely natural process of evolution. Some evolutionary theories make it difficult to speak of the "first" members of a new species. Further, studies of DNA have seemed to imply that we cannot get the genetic diversity we find in the human population unless humanity began with more than two people. Many wonder whether the different people groups of humankind actually arose in separate places, independently of one another—a situation that would mean we are not a unified kind.

Worldview Stakes

What aspects of the Christian worldview are at stake in this discussion? Certainly there is the matter of whether we can trust the Bible to tell us the true story of who we are and where we came from, and of what has gone wrong—and thus of what God intends to do about it all. Then comes the issue of sin: Is it a foreign invader into God's good world, or is it an inevitable result of chance and time? And what of humans—do our capabilities, which distinguish us from the animal world, come with an obligation to rule that world wisely and lovingly? Is there a pattern for marriage and family life that all humans everywhere should follow? And finally, the Christian worldview traces our hunger for a loving community in which all kinds of people live peaceably and justly to our unified origin as members of one family.

Certainly a first-blush reading of Genesis supports the traditional Christian view: we read of how God created the first humans (1:26–27, with 2:5–25 giving a fuller description); their marriage was to be the paradigm for all future sound marriages, and it was the beginning of human families and communities (2:24). Sadly, they disobeyed God and thus brought punishment on themselves and, apparently, all their descendants (Gen 3–4). From Adam and Eve the rest of "the peoples on earth" (12:3) descended (Gen 10–11)—the very peoples who would be blessed by way of Abram and his family. The genealogies in Genesis 5; 10; and 11 bring us from Adam to Abram, the ancestor of Israel.

Many theologians have now come to realize that the Bible has an overarching story line, which unifies all the different parts. And that story line serves as the "Big Story" of the world; it is a narrative that tells us who we are, where we came from, what is wrong, and what God is doing about it. This is why Scripture's historicity matters: biblical faith is grounded in the narrative of God's great works of creation and redemption and not simply in a list of timeless principles.

The Biblical Story Line and the Early Chapters in Genesis

Good thinking about the biblical story line leads to a deeper appreciation of Scripture as a whole. In Genesis 12:1–3, Abram's family, Israel, was to be the vehicle of God's light to the Gentiles through living faithfully in God's covenant. But what does this require as a foundation, if it is to be true? It requires that all the Gentiles (non-Jews) need God's light because they are estranged from him by something that does not belong in their lives; and it requires that there be something in those Gentiles that can be enlivened to respond to that light, just as in Israel (the Jews). In other words, these Gentiles have a common origin with Israel as humans, a common set of human capacities, and a common need that stems from an invasive event.

That is, this estrangement from God is unnatural; it is out of step with how things ought to be. Something has come into human experience that produced that estrangement; that something is sin (cp. Eccl 7:29, "God made people upright, but they pursued many schemes"). It made its entry into human life at such a time and in such a way that it infects everyone, which means it came in at the beginning.

In the biblical story sin is an alien intruder; it disturbs God's good creation order. This comes through clearly in the way the Levitical sacrifices deal with sin: they treat it as a defiling element, which ruins human existence and renders people unworthy to be in God's presence. The sacrifices effect "atonement," "redemption," and "ransom," addressing sin as a defiling intruder that incurs God's displeasure (e.g., Lev 16).

The unnaturalness of sin is also evident in how Wisdom books such as Proverbs connect moral goodness with mental savvy and wickedness is a kind of stupidity or folly (e.g., Prov 12:1). That is, living in line with God's will is sensible while living out of step with God is foolish.

The notion that humankind is one family, sharing one set of ancestors—ancestors who, at the headwaters of the human race brought sin and dysfunction into the world—is behind all these factors as an unwavering assumption. The NT authors carry along this assumption. Certainly the apostle Paul spoke this way (e.g., Rom 5:12–21; 1 Cor 15:20–22,44–49), but the most notable example of this assumption comes from Jesus.

Consider Matthew 19:3–9, in which some Pharisees want to "test" Jesus, which probably means they wanted to ensnare him into taking sides in a debate between their various schools of thought. So they asked him, "'Is it lawful for a man to divorce his wife on any grounds?' 'Haven't you read . . . that he who created them in the beginning made them male and female, and he also said, "For this reason a man will leave his father and mother and be joined to his wife, and the two will become one flesh"? So they are no longer two but one flesh. Therefore, what God has joined together, let no one seperate.'"

Jesus's answer ties together Genesis 1:27 and 2:24. Since these people are now one flesh, joined together by God, they should not be separated. The Pharisees then asked why Moses allowed divorce (Matt 19:7, citing Deut 24:1–4), and Jesus explains that it was a concession: "It was not like that from the beginning" (Matt 19:8).

This conversation shows that Jesus viewed the creation account of Genesis 1–2 as setting the ideal for a properly functioning marriage; that was how God intended things to be "from the beginning." The family legislation of Deuteronomy, on the other hand, does not set the ethical norm. It has another function—namely, that of preserving civility in Israel: a function that has become necessary by some change of circumstances introduced since "the beginning." The obvious candidate for the change is the sin of Adam and Eve, with its consequences for all humans.

Specialists in the apostle Paul's writings have come to realize how firmly he rooted his arguments in this overarching narrative of the OT—just as Jesus did. From Romans 1:2–6, it is clear that Paul read the OT as the early chapters of the biblical story, which tells how God chose Abraham's family through which to work to restore what was damaged by sin. This ends with the anticipation of a new era in which the Gentiles receive the light. Paul links his key term "good news" (or "gospel") to the announcement that through the death, resurrection, and ascension of

Jesus this new era has begun (Rom 1:2–6; Gal 3:8–9; cp. Mark 1:15, see also Matt 28:1–20). As Paul tells us, Christian believers, both Jewish and Gentile, are those in whom God is renewing his image for proper human functioning in their individual, family, and community lives (e.g., Col 3:9–10; 2 Cor 3:18). There the fractured family is once again united.

When it comes to comparing Adam and Jesus (Rom 5:12–19; 1 Cor 15:20–23,42–49), Paul's argument likewise depends on a literal, historical narrative. That is, someone did something (one man trespassed; Rom 5:15), and as a result something happened (sin, death, and condemnation came into the world of human experience). Then Jesus came to deal with the consequences of it all (by his obedience to make the many righteous). The argument gains its coherence from its sequence of events; it is drastically inadequate to say that Paul is merely making a comparison here. Further, consider the notion that people are "in Adam" or "in Christ": to be "in" someone is to be a member of that people for whom that someone is the representative. All the evidence we have indicates that only actual persons can function as representatives.

The book of Revelation continues this narrative focus: it portrays the final victory of God's purposes using Edenic and sanctuary imagery to describe perfected human life in a cleansed creation (Rev 22).

Therefore, if we say that being prone to sin is inherent in being human and having a free will (rather than a horrific aberration brought in at an early stage by someone's disobedience), then we must say that the Bible writers were wrong in describing atonement the way they did, as addressing defilement as an intruder; and we must say that Jesus was wrong to describe his own death in these terms (e.g., Mark 10:45). Further, this approach makes nonsense of the joyful expectation of Christians that they will one day live in a glorified world from which sin and death have been banished (Rev 21:1–8). No Christian would want to imply that those who dwell in a glorified world will be less human because they no longer sin!

From this it follows that we do not have to know exactly how the sin of our first ancestors affects us; it is enough to say that it has done so. In other words, our intuitive sense that the world is not the way it is supposed to be corresponds to reality. Furthermore, if we acknowledge that the stories from other ancient cultures aimed to explain the world, we can see that the Bible writers aimed to tell the true story of our origins, and the Bible's story rings true.

Science and the Early Chapters of Genesis

But does not science undermine our confidence that this is the true story of the world and of God's purposes for it? To reply, we would have to consider whether "science" *could* actually do so. If we require beforehand that science conform to a naturalistic worldview, then it will thus conform; but that does not mean it will tell us the truth. If instead we ask good science to account for the whole range of evidence, then it must account for not simply our biological mechanisms but also the human moral sense and human reasoning, which assume that our minds partake of something transcending our bodily existence.

We ought further to consider how widespread among all groups of people is the craving for peace and justice and the recognition that something is amiss about human life. And finally, all humans are indeed one common family, with the same capacities and desires. These features distinguish us from the animal world, leaving a gap between humans and animals that no merely natural process can bridge. The story of Adam and Eve, created good, but who disobeyed and brought sin and misery into their own lives and into ours, answers this exactly. It also provides guidance for sound historical and scientific research into human origins and human nature.

Accepting the biblical story brings a further benefit. If we have a good explanation for why things have gone wrong, then we find that the Christian hope that God will put them right one day is a secure comfort as well—a comfort that will help us enjoy life as God's beloved people, even now.

There is room for Christians to disagree over questions of how strictly to interpret the details of Genesis 1–11, how long ago Adam and Eve lived, what kind of process God might have used to form the first man, and how the first disobedience affects us today. These are important questions that we ought not avoid; yet, at the same time, we must recognize that while we may offer differing answers to them, we all have a right to say with confidence that the early chapters of Genesis provide the true front end for the "Big Story" of the world—so long as we hold fast to these basic notions.

MODELS FOR RELATING SCRIPTURE AND SCIENCE

Jimmy H. Davis

Both the Scriptures and science have a story to tell. From the creeds and systematic theology that result from study of Scripture, we have the meta-narrative (grand, all-encompassing story) of God as Creator who prepared and sustains a pleasant world for humans. Both that world and its inhabitants have come under a curse due to sin, the Bible teaches, but history will end in the triumphant return of Christ as King of kings and Lord of lords.

The current metanarrative of science is the story of the Big Bang, drawing on evidence from physics that suggests that about 13.7 billion years ago space and time appeared instantaneously from nothing in an infinitely small and infinitely hot singularity. As the universe expanded and cooled, there appeared atoms, stars, galaxies, planets, life, and finally humans.

Concordism and Non-Concordism

The many approaches that biblical and scientific scholars have used to relate Scripture and science can be collected into two overarching approaches: concordism and non-concordism.

Concordism is derived from the word *concord*, which means "harmony or agreement between persons, groups, or things." Scholars who favor concordism believe that exegesis (interpretation) of the Scriptures reveals a message that is in harmony with correct understandings of modern science. This means that any time the Bible addresses a science-related issue, it does so with full accuracy. Concordism is sometimes expressed in terms of the two books of God (nature and Scripture), which will be in harmony when both are properly interpreted.

The non-concordist model does not see a harmony between the biblical testimony and the well-supported conclusions of science. Non-concordists believe this lack of harmony is due to the fact that in Scripture God never sought to speak in terms of literally correct science but instead chose to speak in accordance with ancient nonscientific ways of describing nature. Non-concordists who are not Christians would likely say that the Bible tried but failed to speak accurately about scientific topics. In the first approach, the Bible's failure to speak with scientific accuracy is taken as the expected result of God's speaking in a comprehensible manner to people living prior to the scientific revolution. In the second approach, the Bible's failure to speak with scientific accuracy is seen as proof that the Bible does not have a divine author—a skeptical viewpoint that unreasonably expects God to speak in accordance with his full knowledge rather than using "baby talk" when speaking to finite, historically situated humans.

Varieties of Concordism

There are many types of concordism, with a major dividing issue being the meaning of the Hebrew word for "day" (*yom*) in Genesis (1:3,8,13,19,23,31; 2:2). One group, known as creation science or young earth creationism (YEC), interprets *yom* in Genesis to mean a literal 24 hour day. This stance is closely tied to "evening" and "morning" being referenced alongside each use of "day" in the opening creation narrative. Advocates of the young-earth view attempt to find harmony between this exegesis and the narrative of science. The YEC approach requires major modification to the standard scientific understanding of the fields of astronomy, physics, biology, and geology. Australian-born Ken Ham promotes YEC through his organization, Answers in Genesis. One of their staple beliefs is that science must be submitted to a literal reading of Genesis.

Another group, known as creationism or old earth creationism (OEC), adopts a different understanding of the word *yom*, which leads them to conclude that the Genesis creation accounts refer to a period of time longer than 24 hours. According to the OEC approach, each creation day was a long period of time that involved many acts of creation by God. The nonliteral use of "day" in Genesis 2:4, where it refers to the "day" in which God "made the earth and the heavens," is a key textual basis for claiming that "day" does not always refer to a 24 hour period. The OEC approach sees more harmony with standard scientific understanding of the history of the universe than does the YEC approach, though it resists the naturalistic presuppositions that often creep into popular science theories. Canadian-born astronomer Hugh Ross is a leading promoter of OEC through his organization, Reasons to Believe. Staple beliefs of this and other OEC organizations include that science is not made futile by our fall into sin and that the Bible actually contains allusions or hints to scientific truths such as the Big Bang and an ancient earth.

Varieties of Non-concordism

The non-concordist approach results from a different exegesis of the Scriptures, which states that the Bible's intention is not to teach science but that the Bible uses the language of science and natural history to aid our understanding of spiritual truths.

The *framework view* is a non-concordist approach that proposes that the days of Genesis are literary devices used to convey important truths about purpose and ultimate origin. In this view God's creative activity as recounted in Genesis is arranged in a topical, nonsequential manner and does not intend to make any claims about the age of the universe. The six creation days form a symmetrically arranged, topical account of creation, set in two triads with similar activities in each triad. God is seen creating three kingdoms in the first triad: day 1 (Gen 1:3–5), light; day 2 (Gen 1:6–8), sea and sky; and day 3 (Gen 1:9–13), earth and plants. In the second triad, God populates these kingdoms with their rulers: day 4 (Gen 1:14–19), luminaries; day 5 (Gen 1:20–23), fish and birds; and day 6 (Gen 1:24–31), animals and mankind. Finally, day 7 (Gen 2:1–3) is a Sabbath for the Creator King. Some see this triad arrangement in the seven-lamp menorah of the Jewish temple (Exod 25:31–40).

In summary, the framework view holds that the narrative of Genesis is not meant to provide a literal scientific account of God's creative methods or the time frame in which he created. Rather, it asserts that Genesis was intended to combat polytheism and pantheism. The message is that God is the Creator of all things; questions about how or when he created are seen as irrelevant. The late American theologian and OT scholar Meredith G. Kline was a proponent of the framework view.

Another non-concordist approach is called *complementarity*, which states that science and theology complement each other to provide a complete picture of reality. Science and theology do not rival each other but, when properly interpreted, provide valid information about the same thing. Science may have a rational narrative for the history of the universe, for instance, but cannot explain why the laws underlying this narrative are fine-tuned for humans. The spiritual truth of the creation narrative in Genesis completes this picture of nature by providing a framework to understand the fine-tuning in terms of the creative and providential work of a loving God. English physicist and theologian John Polkinghorne promoted complementarity in his writings.

Summary

Each of the above models of relating Scripture and science are held by devout Christians. Some scholars even hold views that draw on several of the models. This side of eternity, we will probably never acquire enough knowledge to know indisputably the best way to relate these two great ways of knowing (Scripture and science). As Paul says in 1 Corinthians 13:12, "For now we see only a reflection as in a mirror, but then face to face. Now [we] know in part, but then [we] will know fully, as [we are] fully known."

THE CHURCH AND HELIOCENTRISM

Theodore J. Cabal

Contrary to widespread cultural myth, scientific theory and biblical interpretation have clashed in only two major, protracted ways. The first, the Copernican controversy, lasted almost two centuries and affected both Catholics and Protestants alike. The second, Darwinism, has also impacted all streams of Christianity since the publication of *On the Origin of Species* in 1859. This article concerns the history and lessons learned from the church's first debate over what appeared to be scientific undermining of the truth and authority of Scripture.

The Copernican Revolution

On the Revolutions of the Celestial Spheres by Nicolaus Copernicus was published shortly before his death in 1543. The work ignited controversy because its sun-centered theory of the universe seemed to contradict not only the Bible but also science. The received astronomy in Europe understood a nonmoving earth to be the orbital center of the universe; that had been the intellectual standard since the second century work of Claudius Ptolemy. But Copernicus, a devout Catholic, believed that heliocentrism provided a better explanation of planetary orbits than geocentrism.

Theologians were troubled that the Bible seemed to teach that heavenly bodies orbited a stationary earth. Joshua's famous "long day" was typically cited: "The sun stood still and the moon stopped until the nation took vengeance on its enemies. . . . [T]he sun stopped in the middle of the sky and delayed its setting almost a full day" (Josh 10:13). Other biblical texts also appeared to teach geocentrism (Gen 15:12,17; 19:23; 28:11; Exod 17:12; 22:3,26; Lev 22:7; and many more).

Unsurprisingly, the heliocentrism of Copernicus was largely rejected at first as unscientific and unbiblical. Luther warned that the "fool will overturn the whole art of astronomy. But, as Holy Writ declares, Joshua commanded the sun to stand still and not the earth." Theologians and astronomers typically stood together in their dismissal of this new theory.

But despite initial resistance, the attraction of heliocentrism grew as a theory with better explanatory power. A generation later the greatest observational astronomer of the day, Tycho Brahe, died. He left his understudy, Johannes Kepler, a wealth of observational data, the best available before the invention of the telescope. Whereas Copernicus had retained the circular orbits of earlier astronomy, Tycho's data enabled Kepler to determine in 1605 the first law of planetary motion: planets move in ellipses with the sun at one focus. By 1609 and 1619 he had discovered and published the second and third planetary laws describing the ellipses mathematically. Kepler's work greatly strengthened the case for heliocentrism.

The Generation after Copernicus

These astronomers believed in the Bible. Nonetheless, this generation after Copernicus suffered much greater controversy over the new astronomy. Theologians often bitterly wrangled over its implications for the truthfulness of Scripture. Some astronomers, called "semi-Copernicans," attempted reconciliation between the older and newer theories. They postulated "hybrid solutions" such as having the earth rotate daily on its axis while other planets revolved around the sun which orbited the earth.

The low point of this second generation culminated in the Galileo affair. Galileo Galilei built a telescope and became the first to train it systematically on the heavens. In 1610, he published his discovery that Jupiter has four moons, refuting the notion that all heavenly spheres orbit the earth. Additionally, he revealed that Venus has a complete set of phases rather than the expected constant crescent phase predicted by geocentrism. Galileo's promotion of Copernicanism alarmed ecclesiastical authorities; they warned him that his view injured the holy faith by making the Scripture false.

Galileo responded by noting that Scripture was not wrong; rather, the geocentric interpretation of Scripture was wrong. He explained that not all of Scripture ought to be interpreted literally, lest Scripture be made to affirm untruths. (Israel as "a land flowing with milk and honey," for instance, is poetic language to be read as such.) In his important letter to the Grand Duchess Christina "concerning the use of biblical quotations in matters of science" (1615), Galileo wrote: "I think in the first place that it is very pious to say and prudent to affirm that the holy Bible can never speak untruth—whenever its true meaning is understood." He argued that the divinely inspired Bible was written to speak "to the capacities of the common people." But he stressed Scripture must be interpreted carefully, or else it could be made to affirm obvious false propositions, contradictions, or even "grave heresies and follies."

Galileo's explanation did nothing to mitigate the controversy. Heliocentrism was condemned as a heresy in 1616, and books by Copernicus and Kepler were placed on the official index of prohibited books. Moreover, Galileo's continued advocacy of heliocentrism required him in 1633 to face examination by the Holy Office of the Inquisition in Rome. He was sentenced to indefinite imprisonment for spreading the heretical teaching that the earth orbits the sun.

Isaac Newton and the Waning of the Controversy

Another generation would pass before the heliocentrism controversy began to wane. The 1687 publication of Isaac Newton's *Mathematical Principles of Natural Philosophy* sounded the death knell for geocentrism. His discoveries, which essentially ended major scientific discussion about the debate, were (1) the three laws of motion, (2) the theory of universal gravitation, and (3) demonstration that Kepler's three laws of planetary motion follow from points 1 and 2. Heliocentric orbits were now understood simply to be the result of the same mechanics operative on earth.

Even before 1687, the new astronomy was being widely taught and believed in Puritan New England. Christian ministers played a primary role in propagating heliocentrism via scientific essays published in almanacs, the most widely circulated literary form of the period. A century and a half after the groundbreaking work of Copernicus, the scientific community and much of the American public believed heliocentrism without hesitation. By the middle of the eighteenth century, the exegetical skirmishes were fast dying out. The biblical passages that once were understood to teach geocentrism were now reinterpreted and understood in light of heliocentrism.

Looking Back, Looking Forward

Criticism regarding the mistakes made by geocentric interpreters of the Bible after Copernicus now comes easily. But it must be remembered that the best science for more than a millennium taught an earth-centered view of the universe. Moreover, astronomical predictions made from this old astronomy were just as accurate as those based on the work of Copernicus. In addition, the church had never dealt with apparent conflict between accepted scientific theory and long-standing biblical interpretation. Even now, debate continues regarding the lessons learned from the heliocentrism debate.

For instance, many advocates interpret the Bible in light of the latest scientific theories. But the Copernicus controversy had as much to do with bad scientific theory as with biblical interpretation. The Bible was not corrected by science; rather, faulty biblical interpretation and faulty scientific theory were both corrected by truth.

Claims that the Bible and science have been at war ever since—and that Scripture keeps losing this battle—lack any historical basis. Only the Darwinian controversy has risen to the level of that first Bible versus science debate in its widespread and long-lasting impact. Yet the heliocentrism issue is often presented as sufficient reason for accepting the total Neo-Darwinian package. In truth, creationists are justified in accepting natural selection as a mechanism for biological change while rejecting universal common descent—not to mention the inherent philosophical naturalism of orthodox Darwinism. The Copernican incident has nothing to teach about this issue other than the need for care in biblical interpretation and scientific theorizing.

Lessons for Today

What are some legitimate lessons learned from the first great Bible versus science debate? First, Christians should feel no compulsion to abandon their confidence in the authority and complete truth of Scripture. Believers should hold fast to the Spirit-given conviction that no conflict exists between the truth of God's Word and his creation. But scientific and theological theories, though necessary, never enjoy this infallibility. Confidence in this basic principle provides believers with patience to wait on solutions when faced with apparent conflicts.

Wise believers also recognize that not all theological or scientific debates are equally important, in spite of the claims made by those involved.

Some issues may not require believers to commit to a position until more truth comes to light, perhaps even in a generation to come. When an abundance of controversial, fluid "hybrid solutions" competes for allegiance, wisdom may dictate forestalling final commitment. Ultimately, discernment of the theological importance of a particular issue should prioritize one's commitments.

METHODOLOGICAL NATURALISM AND THE CHRISTIAN WORLDVIEW

Jimmy H. Davis

From the biblical writers to the church fathers to the Reformers until today, believers in the Judeo-Christian tradition have dealt with the question of how a believer should relate to the physical world. The Bible is clear from its first verse that God is the Creator (Gen 1:1). Not only is he the Creator, but he is also the Sustainer (Acts 17:28; Heb 1:3; Col 1:17); Governor (Pss 104:10,14,20; 135:7; Jer 31:35; 33:20); and Provider (Ps 104:27–28; Matt 6:26–30). Furthermore, Jesus stated that we observe the creation in order to understand it (Luke 12:54–56).

Today science is considered the best way to observe and understand the physical world. Modern science explains natural phenomena in terms of natural events and causes but does not entertain supernatural phenomena. The principles of science are governed by methodological naturalism.

Unlike philosophical naturalism, which states that the physical universe is all that exists, methodological naturalism is not concerned with the ultimate limits of reality but with the best methods for studying nature. Methodological naturalism provides the framework within which to study nature.

Is methodological naturalism compatible with a Christian worldview? Yes, in the sense that all truth is God's truth. The challenge is at the interface of science and faith—where both science and faith make historical statements about the same events.

Pros and Cons of Methodological Naturalism

The methodological naturalistic approach to answering scientific questions has been successful. By focusing on the physical aspects of the universe (the structure of matter, forces acting on matter, and energy changes), methodological naturalism provides effective ways of describing planetary motion, finding cures for diseases, and designing computers. Methodological naturalism has allowed science to function within all countries and worldviews and has greatly enhanced the standard of living of humankind—the dream of English Christian philosopher and scientific pioneer Francis Bacon (1561–1626), who hoped science would relieve some of the effects of the fall.

On the other hand, methodological naturalism can lead to philosophical naturalism—though it does not have to. The naturalistic approach affects the outcomes of natural theology—the attempt to uncover the attributes of God from the findings of nature—so that supernatural phenomena are excluded from consideration. The use of naturalistic explanations can create a blind spot, only allowing naturalistic explanations to exist at the interface between science and faith. A crucial issue found at that interface is the historical death, burial, and resurrection of Jesus.

Science, with its naturalistic outlook, can help us understand the resurrection events by providing a detailed description of the physiological changes that occur during a crucifixion and of what happens to a body within three days after death. But the resurrection is biochemically impossible; thus, naturalistic explanations regard the resurrection as scientifically, and therefore historically, unfounded.

Methodological Versus Philosophical Naturalism

Methodological naturalism does not, however, have to lead to philosophical naturalism. A scientist who begins with the tenants of the faith, rather than the naturalistic assumptions of science, may indeed observe the actions of God in nature. Starting with the characteristics of God as revealed in Scripture, the eyes of faith may observe God refining this fallen world through what otherwise appears to be waste and suffering. Our worldview determines what we see—a personal God shepherding his creation or an exclusively physical universe ruled by chance. As the author of Hebrews states, "By faith we understand that the universe was created by the word of God" (Heb 11:3). If it takes faith to understand that the universe is God's creation, then it takes faith to see God in the everyday workings of this fallen world.

Methodological Naturalism in Christian History

Are Christians who call for the abandonment of methodological naturalism right to do so? We ought not ignore the fact that methodological naturalism developed within a Christian worldview over centuries of thought. Augustine (AD 354–430) stated that all truth is God's truth—that secondary causes can be used to explain the natural world—though he was concerned that regularity in the natural order may lead to a loss of wonder. During the Middle Ages, Christian theologians and philosophers proposed that God's activities in nature follow the common course of nature—that he worked through secondary causes (physical causes and effects). Although this belief allowed the use of observation and experiment, in addition to reason, for studying nature, this belief put the visible activity of God outside the common course of nature. As such, one's faith decided whether an event, such as a strong wind, was produced by just another weather pattern or by God as he parted the Red Sea.

Thomas Aquinas (1225–1274) reaffirmed that secondary causes can be used to study nature, but he emphasized that all events are directed by God. John Calvin (1509–1564) reaffirmed Augustine's notion that God is the source of all truth. Francis Bacon (1561–1626) proposed that God revealed himself in two books—the book of creation (Ps 19:1–6) and the book of revelation, the Bible (Ps 19:7–14). B. B. Warfield (1851–1921) reaffirmed Aquinas by stating that God chooses to govern the world by regular cause-and-effect relationships. As can be seen, modern science's commitment to the assumption of physical cause and effect (what we today call methodological naturalism) has a long history within Christian thought.

Methodological Naturalism and Scientific Inquiry

Does a rejection of methodological naturalism cause science to grind to a stop for the premature appeal to God as causal agent? To evoke God as primary cause does not necessitate the rejection of natural cause and effect. Nevertheless, regarding God as a physical-like cause of every event can cause exploration to come to a halt. One reason modern science did not develop in the classical Islamic world was a philosophical belief that God was indeed involved this way in every event. As Al-Ghazali (1058–1111), a leading philosopher of Islam's golden age, stated that fire does not cause cotton to burn; rather, God intervenes to produce such a result. Furthermore, since God is so different from us, we can never be sure that it will always be God's will that cotton should burn.

The belief that God is the primary cause acting though secondary causes does not mean scientific inquiry should stop. The Christian worldview of a Creator provides the basis for believing the universe really exists and is worthy of study. The worldview of the scientist influences which questions are asked and how results are interpreted. Historically, we see that faith did not stifle the acquisition of knowledge; instead, it provided the insight needed to advance understanding.

Believing that God created out of nothing, Johannes Kepler (1571–1630) was inspired to search for the harmony of God in the heavens and so discovered the laws of planetary motion. Believing in the "fixed kinds" of God's original creation did not limit the research of the Swedish naturalist Carolus Linnaeus (1707–1778); rather, it led him to search for a classification system for biological species. Because Louis Pasteur (1822–1895) believed life was created by God and was not just a set of chemical reactions, he disproved the theory of spontaneous generation and made many discoveries in microbiology. The American agricultural scientist George Washington Carver's (1864–1943) belief that God gave the first humans "seed-bearing plant[s]" (Gen 1:29) for food led to his discovery of more than three hundred products that could be made from peanuts. The Belgian priest and astronomer Georges Lemaître's (1894–1966) faith in a Creator God allowed him to propose what is today called the Big Bang Model—espousing a dynamic universe with a beginning. In contrast, the German-American physicist Albert Einstein (1879–1955) at first refused to accept this model, even though it emerged from his own theory, because it clashed with the prevailing scientific view of a static, eternal universe.

Summary
In conclusion, the naturalistic methodology of science has been, and continues to be, a helpful tool for scientific endeavor. But we must be cautious of a possible reductionism that offers only naturalistic explanations of the physical universe.

ARE MIRACLES AND SCIENCE COMPATIBLE?

Douglas Groothuis

One of the secular claims against Christianity is that the modern world's increasing knowledge of the natural world through science (principally chemistry, biology, and physics) has made belief in miracles unjustified at best and positively irrational at worst. Recently, biologist and atheist Richard Dawkins has led this charge, especially in his best-selling book, *The God Delusion* (2007). Before responding to this challenge, we need to define our two basic terms: *miracle* and *science*.

Biblically understood, a miracle is God's supernatural intervention in creation, which produces an effect otherwise not possible given the operation of natural laws. Since God as Creator and Sustainer of the universe is the One who has established so-called natural laws, he is also free to act outside such laws. After all, natural laws simply reflect God's design for the way things normally occur. If he decides to act outside this normal design, he is not breaking the laws of nature since they are not "laws" for God; they are simply patterns that reflect his own will.

So why, then, do secularists think science is incompatible with belief in miracles? There are three main reasons.

First, if one believes there is no God, then there is no divine agent (or conscience actor) to produce a miracle. In other words, if you begin with the presupposition that God does not exist, then you cannot believe in miracles.

Nevertheless, there are ample reasons drawn from science and philosophy to believe that a personal Creator and Designer does exist. Cosmology indicates that the universe began from nothing a finite time ago with a big bang. Such an event requires a cause outside the universe. The best explanation is that God caused this event. From one point of view, the creation of the universe from nothing is God's first supernatural action, since natural laws do not allow something to be made from nothing. Physics also reveals that the laws and proportions of the universe are finely tuned for the support of human life. Chance and mindless natural law do not explain this adequately. God's purpose and design provide the best explanation.

Science, in and of itself, does not preclude the work of God within nature. But if scientists presuppose that God does not exist, then such explanations are dismissed. Consequently, many secularists define science in such a way as to exclude miracles. Science is seen as offering only natural explanations for natural events.

Second, scientific endeavor is regarded as the only legitimate source for knowledge about the natural world. No supernatural explanations are allowed in principle. So, even if the universe began from nothing, science cannot even suggest a Creator's involvement in it. Neither can science speak to the existence of a Designer to explain the fine-tuning of the universe. Inevitably, the result is that no one can be intellectually justified in believing in miracles.

But this claim for science is neither grounded in the history of science—many leaders of the scientific revolution were theists—nor is it philosophically credible. Science becomes a knowledge blocker if, in fact, God has left recognizable signs of his existence in the cosmos. Whether or not we can find evidence for God in the natural world should be an open question up for rigorous investigation. Furthermore, when science is regarded the *only* source of rational knowledge, it logically refutes itself. This approach, known as scientism, claims that (1) science is limited to giving natural explanations for natural events based on logical reasoning; and that (2) science is the sole conduit for knowledge (or credible, true beliefs). These two statements rightly receive the following rebuttals. First, the claim that science is the only source of knowledge is not justified by any natural event or logical reasoning. Scientism is, rather, a philosophical claim. And therefore, second, since this materialistic view of science is not supported by its own understanding of science, scientism must be false. This destroys the argument for science as the one source of knowledge about reality. It cannot be the only means of acquiring genuine knowledge.

Third, some affirm that the development of technology, especially in the twentieth century, is incompatible with belief in miracles. A biblical scholar, not a scientist, put this starkly. Rudolph Bultmann (1884–1976) said that no one who uses a transistor radio can believe in the miraculous world presented in the NT.

But the development of technology is not incompatible with miracles since these technologies depend on scientific discoveries and methods which themselves do not refute miracles, as argued above. The claim is a classic non sequitur—however often we hear it.

Detecting a miracle in human experience is a matter of historical inquiry. No hard science such as chemistry, biology, or physics speaks directly to events that occur once within humanity. That is, we cannot know through the methods of science that Caesar crossed the Rubicon. But this does not mean we have no knowledge of historical matters, such as social change within cultures, the rise and fall of empires, or biography. One's method of acquiring knowledge must fit the subject of study. History consults written and unwritten items from the past to discern what happened. While many historians simply dismiss God and the supernatural from knowable history, ignoring the Bible's claims to record such, there is no good reason to do so. If it is possible that God exists, then miracles are possible. If they are possible, we may investigate miraculous claims to see if there are any actual miracles.

While many religions claim miracles, none are as well substantiated as NT miracles. This is especially true of Jesus's miracles and his resurrection in particular. In fact, Christianity is the only religion that attributes miracles to its founder in its earliest and foundational documents—the books comprising the NT. For example, the historical resurrection of Jesus from the dead is affirmed in all four Gospels. It is also directly or indirectly affirmed throughout the rest of the NT. These documents were written by eyewitnesses (John 19:35) to the resurrected Christ or by those who consulted eyewitnesses (Luke 1:1–4).

Finally, there is sufficient evidence that miracles have not ceased to occur after the time of the NT. While they are not as plentiful as the signs and wonders of the apostolic period, many miracles performed in the name of Jesus have been documented. For a scholarly study of NT miracles and subsequent miracles, see Craig S. Keener, *Miracles: The Credibility of the New Testament Accounts*, two vols. (Grand Rapids, MI: Baker, 2011).

Christians need not fear that the advancement of science somehow undermines the rationality of their belief in miracles. Miracles are not incompatible with science. Only an unhelpful understanding of science, or of miracles, or of both generates this false impression. Both science and history corroborate the biblical teaching that God is a wonder-working God of space-time history and eternity.

Arts and Recreation

BEAUTY AS A PROOF OF GOD'S EXISTENCE

William Edgar

Scripture makes clear that God is the archetype for beauty. Psalm 27 expresses the desire to dwell in the Lord's house in order to gaze upon his "beauty" (Ps 27:4); other verses recommend worshipping God "in the splendor of his holiness" (1 Chr 16:29; 2 Chr 20:21; Pss 29:2; 96:9). Richard Swinburne says, "If there is a God there is more reason to expect a basically beautiful world than a basically ugly one" (*The Existence of God*, 150). Fyodor Dostoyevsky famously claimed in *The Idiot*, "Beauty will save the world."

Nevertheless, serious challenges can be raised which require thoughtful response if we are to defend the belief that God is the source of beauty. First, when asked to define *beauty*, we often follow Plato, not Scripture. Plato taught that beauty is an unearthly harmony or proportion (*The Symposium*, 209e–12a). This influenced Augustine, who felt that everything is beautiful insofar as it exists because of God: worms are beautiful for their purpose, even evil is beautiful when related to punishment (*Confessions*, VII, 18–19). Thomas Aquinas declared that beauty derives from the properties of God's Son. Such received beauty includes three conditions: perfection, proportion, and brightness (*Summa Theologica*, 1.39.8). Even Jonathan Edwards, when considering the beauty of God's attributes, sounds Platonic (*Works*, 17, 413).

Today the idea of beauty has become less Platonic and more subjective. Think of the relativistic dictum that says, "Beauty is in the eye of the beholder." This reduces beauty to a matter of personal taste, almost in the same way that some people love carrots while others do not.

A more sophisticated version of a subjective view of beauty is expressed by Immanuel Kant (1724–1804); he thought human sensitivity to beauty was tied to morality. More recently some have said that defining beauty is a masked quest for power. Harvard professor Elaine Scarry answered this claim by noting the parallels between beauty and fairness (*On Beauty and Being Just*).

The Bible on Beauty

Contrary to the viewpoints above, the Bible does not define beauty in terms of an otherworldly sense of harmony or subjective taste. Looking at a few words that are translated as *beauty* in various English Bible versions, we find concepts related to glory, honor, and only rarely to loveliness. The Hebrew term *tiph'arah*, which can be translated as "beauty," refers to glory or honor more than to proportion or harmony (see Ps 96:6; Isa 21:1,4–5; 44:13; 62:3). Aaron's robe, for instance, was bedecked in a "glory" suitable to his rank (Exod 28:2,40). The more common term for beauty is *yophiy*, which has a variety of meanings: these include the loveliness of a woman (Ps 45:11; Prov 6:25; 31:30) and the splendor of Zion (Ps 50:2; Lam 2:15; Ezek 16:25). The same goes for *hadar*, which means "splendor" (Ezek 16:14). Splendor, majesty, strength, and beauty characterize God's sanctuary ultimately because of his presence, but these notions are in contrast to dishonor, lack of dignity, and weakness—not to something we might call "ugly." When Isaiah tells us the Suffering Servant had "no beauty that we should desire him" (Isa 53:2 KJV), the term in view (*mareh*) means something like "an attractive face" or a "favorable countenance," rather than ugliness per se. So, when the Bible tells us that a certain sight, such as the trees in the garden of Eden, are "pleasing in appearance" (Gen 2:9), it means something like "desirable" rather than beautiful in the Greek sense. Often the terms for beauty are used about wrong desires, as in warnings against idolatry or seduction (Prov 6:25; Jas 1:11); therefore, they do not combine to give us a simple, comprehensive definition of beauty.

Another challenge comes from the confusion over a work of art and the beautiful. A particular painting, a piece of music, or a poem may possess beauty. If we listen to a Bach chorale or a Beethoven symphony, we are right to exclaim, "How beautiful!" Yet many works of art are well crafted but not beautiful. Who would call Goya's *The Third of May 1808* "beautiful" or attribute beauty to Matthias Grünewald's painting *The Small Crucifixion*? Such works are masterpieces but not because they are beautiful. The Negro spiritual "He Never Said a Mumbalin' Word" is haunting and profoundly disturbing but not beautiful in any conventional sense. Moreover, some artists and composers have tried to force some sort of beauty into subjects that do not warrant it. Think of cheap art or kitsch as examples.

Beauty and Aesthetics

Does the controversy over defining beauty mean we should abandon the concept of beauty or the belief that it points to God? No. A better way is to consider the broader notion of aesthetics in light of biblical revelation. Aesthetics includes beauty, but it is a more comprehensive term that also refers to the artistic dimension of life.

The first aspect of aesthetics is that it involves things we can create. A lovely pair of earrings, pretty chinaware, good music, portraiture, monuments, liturgies, and stage settings are all legitimate parts of the aesthetic dimension. Or it may be something more profound, more lasting, like a painting in a museum. Here, incidentally, we should be encouraged not to think of Christian art as only depicting religious subjects. Rembrandt's *Carcass of Beef* is as profoundly Christian as his *Road to Emmaus*. The arts may instruct us, challenge us, help us "see" what is less visible: the contours of a mountain, the sadness of a face, or less palpable things such as love, fear, or the holiness of God. Try to imagine a world without the arts, and you will understand why the aesthetic dimension is such an integral part of creaturely existence. The arts give expression to the human condition. And unlike Plato's immaterial realm of ideals that is forever inaccessible to humans, the arts are tangible, part of the real world.

The second quality of aesthetics is that our craft must be good. Throughout Scripture we are enjoined to be skillful in what we do. This includes governing wisely (Dan 1:17), military ability (Jer 50:9), statuary (Isa 41:7), fashion (Exod 39:24), and music making (Ps 33:3). To engage in aesthetics with mediocrity or lack of training is a form of laziness or insult. Also, a work of art may be highly skilled and yet blasphemous. One could think of Salvador Dali's *Christ of St John of the Cross* a superb painting with a heretical Gnostic message.

The third quality of aesthetics is that there must be agreement between what is artistic and what is true. Scripture tells us we live in a world created by God as "very good" (Gen 1:31; the Hebrew word *towb* means "excellent," both in a skilled way and in a moral way). In this world God called mankind to populate the earth, to cultivate, and to rule. This cultural mandate includes the aesthetic dimension (Gen 4:20–22). Our world, however, is now profoundly fallen—marred by sin, misery, and death. In such circumstances, even the aesthetic dimension of life has become corrupt. Well-crafted statues can be idols (Isa 44:13). Music can be noise (Amos 5:23). Poetry may be arrogant and vengeful (Gen 4:23–24). Here, too, is where the Bible tells us to see the difference between superficial charm or beauty and what is truly praiseworthy (Prov 31:30; see Phil 4:8–9).

Yet God is now redeeming the world, bringing his people to himself through the atonement and resurrection of Christ. The arts may now bespeak God's grace. This is why the Lord gave explicit directions for the artwork in the tabernacle, specifically calling gifted craftsmen like Oholiab (Exod 36:1–2; 38:23). To be biblically faithful in aesthetics means to tell the story of creation, fall, and redemption in art as in every part of life. This does not limit us to creating so-called religious art, although that is perfectly legitimate. If an artist only articulates the glory of creation and ignores the fall into misery, however, then that art is dishonest. If the work only depicts evil, then it lacks the hope of the gospel.

Beauty and the Existence of God

Does beauty prove the existence of God? Not without the qualifiers we have suggested: a rich understanding of the nature and limits of beauty as well as circumscribing the term *proof* so that it does not imply something as inescapable as a mathematical proof. Perhaps it is best simply to say, with the psalmist, "The heavens declare the glory of God, and the expanse proclaims the work of his hands" (Ps 19:1). The glory of God and his saving grace, rather than a Platonic or subjective notion of beauty, is central to our aesthetics.

FILM AND A CHRISTIAN WORLDVIEW

Doug Powell

Arguably, film is the most influential art form in our culture. That's not because there is something more important about film itself but because the cost of making movies ensures that film companies spend millions of dollars to drive our awareness of them through marketing campaigns. Movies are so costly to produce that far fewer of them are made than music albums, TV shows, novels, or paintings. The expenses sunk into each film, in fact, ensure that they will be marketed in a way that makes it far more likely that you will know about a movie you've never seen than a band you've never listened to or a book you've never read. Such widespread awareness makes movies an important piece of common ground in our culture. For filmmakers, they offer opportunities to convey worldviews. And filmgoers receive opportunity to interact with those worldviews, be shaped by them, and discuss them as points of common interest.

Art and Worldview

Art is a form of communication, and it always communicates the worldview of the artist. Often filmmakers intentionally share their worldviews.

To cite a few examples, the Star Wars series conveys a pantheistic view of the world. The 2005 film *V for Vendetta* is an argument for political anarchy (in the sense of self-rule). The 2012 movie *Life of Pi* portrays a Hindu worldview. Sometimes, however, filmmakers are unaware of the worldviews their movies end up expressing. Think about the 2004 film *The Polar Express*. Toward the end of the movie, the train conductor tells the boy what appears to be the moral of the story: "One thing about trains—it doesn't matter where they're going. What matters is deciding to get on." In a nutshell this is the philosophy of existentialist philosopher Jean Paul Sartre. In the face of a meaningless world, we are to assert ourselves and make meaning of the journey we choose. The movie, targeted to young kids, is probably not intended to create preschool existentialists; nevertheless, that is the message that comes across. Viewers of all ages will catch the significance of the conductor's statement, and it will shape the worldview of many.

In order to create a world believable enough to engage an audience, filmmakers must first decide what kind of world their story unfolds in. What is the world? Who and what is god? Who are we? What is the problem with the world, and what is the solution to that problem? In other words, films have to have a worldview so that the story they tell can be understood. Films may not explicitly answer those questions, and some of them make a special point to remain ambiguous. Still, the internal logic of the world the movie depicts will address the questions and provide a way of understanding the story. This internal logic of the story and how these questions are answered is why fantasy movies, such as the Lord of the Rings series, can portray a biblical worldview as accurately as a biopic like *Chariots of Fire* (1981).

Stories for Life

One of the things that makes films so powerful and popular is their ability to engage us in a story that resonates with us in some way. Just as in our own lives, on-screen stories always have some kind of tension that needs resolution. Drama requires something to be wrong, something that is not the way it should be, sins that need atonement and redemption. But we also know that the story told in a movie will usually resolve with a satisfying ending.

As people made in the image of God, we have a yearning for the day when God will set things right and resolve the tensions in our lives and in the world. We invest ourselves in movies in part because the resolution we intuitively expect is a foreshadowing of the resolution God will bring to all of our stories. And when movies don't provide the resolution we want, when justice isn't served or the bad guy gets away, we recognize that something is wrong, and we react strongly—almost as if the movie's outcome is our own. That our yearning for resolution is not satisfied in these cases points us to the only thing that can ultimately provide resolution for any and all problems—God.

Worldview and the Form of Film

The form of film itself also reflects a biblical worldview in many ways. First, the screenwriter is revealing something to the audience, giving information in the form of a story. The director never gives all the information about everything we want to know about the story, yet they share enough that we can understand the plot and process the information. The information is revealed through a story that plays out in a linear fashion and moves toward a resolution (or lack of resolution) that was determined by the filmmakers before the story began to be told.

Notably, the filmmaker is transcendent in relation to the film itself, standing outside of the film as a creator and guide exercising sovereign control over every aspect of it. Not only does the director exist, but he or she wants to be known; in fact, we can know something about each director because they reveal hints to us through the stories they shape and the way they reveal them to us. It is much the same in religions such as Christianity, Judaism, and Islam. According to each of these worldviews, God exists, wants to be known, and has revealed himself generally through what he has made and, more specifically, through special revelations collected in sacred books.

Art and the Reflection of God

Film as a kind of art justifies itself as an act of creation done in imitation of the God who created the ability to create. In that sense, all art reflects the God of the Bible because it is an impulse that is an integral part of being made in the image of God.

We shouldn't treat film, or any other art form, in a utilitarian way in which it is simply a kind of delivery vehicle for whatever message we want to share. That approach only results in bad art or propaganda. However, because film is an art form and therefore a kind of communication, it does always convey some message. From a Walt Disney fairy tale to a Woody Allen monologue, from the high drama of *A Few Good Men* to the hijinks of *Ace Ventura*, all films present worldviews and invite the audience to enter them. This gives Christians a powerful opportunity to talk about those worldviews with others. Almost without exception people love talking about the movies they've seen. Christians can engage them on the worldview themes put forward through film. By doing worldview analysis using movies, we can reveal the truthfulness of the biblical worldview in casual, everyday conversations.

Film and Christian Witness

Finally, there is an increasing awareness within the Christian community that film is an art that, though largely given over to the promotion of non-Christian worldviews in our current culture, must not be abandoned. Like music and theater, the art of film is a powerful tool for reaching people and communicating with them the big picture ideas that matter most. Christians should both watch films and create them.

By watching films, especially the ones that cut against our beliefs, we stay current with the larger conversation of our culture and provide accountability for those who would misrepresent the biblical worldview. By creating films, we can be an active part of directing conversation and bringing audiences in touch with the sacred truth that satisfies more than anything else—God exists, wants to be known, and has created a story in which we are all invited to participate through placing faith in the Son he sent to live, die, and rise again.

A BIBLICAL VIEW OF MUSIC

Paul Munson

Scripture provides a holistic way to think about music. It does this directly, through the well over 300 references to music within its pages, and indirectly, through teaching about creation, pleasure, and worship. One in six chapters of the Bible mentions vocal or instrumental music. The great majority of these verses (80 percent, in fact) describe it in positive terms, as something made or heard faithfully. Especially frequent are references to music in worship, but the Bible also affirms a variety of other uses, presumably requiring a variety of styles: for example, in courtship and marriage (Song of Songs), teaching (Deut 31:19), mourning (2 Chr 35:25), warfare (2 Chr 20:21), therapy (1 Sam 16:23), pilgrimage (Isa 30:29), and pure pleasure (2 Sam 19:35).

The attention Scripture gives to music is impressive, as is its prominence in today's society. From restaurant loudspeakers to movie soundtracks, it's everywhere. Obviously, whoever wants to love both God and neighbor in this world will want to learn from the Bible how to think about music.

Negative Uses of Music
To begin, not everything the Bible says about music is positive. Through Isaiah, God warns against self-indulgence:

> Woe to those who rise early in the morning in pursuit of beer, who linger into the evening, inflamed by wine. At their feasts they have lyre, harp, tambourine, flute, and wine. They do not perceive the

LORD's actions, and they do not see the work of his hands. Therefore my people will go into exile because they lack knowledge
(Isa 5:11–13; see also Eccl 7:5 and Amos 6:5).

Music can be what twentieth-century American pastor A. W. Tozer
called "a device for wasting time, a refuge from the disturbing voice of
conscience, a scheme to divert attention from moral accountability." When
music is used idly, as a substitute for the knowledge of God, no solid joy can
be its result, because "who can enjoy life apart from him?" (Eccl 2:25). But
the point is not really about music but about the misuse of a good gift from
God. As all his gifts can be misused, and therefore corrupted, the same can
be said of music.

Godly Enjoyment of Music

On the other hand, there is such a thing as godly recreation (Gen 24:63;
Ps 8:3; 1 Tim 4:3–4; 6:17). Moreover, God "provides us with songs in the
night" (Job 35:10). David, the man after God's heart, played the lyre and
sang; the king found joy in harps from ivory palaces (Ps 45:8). The Bible
teaches that all things were made for God's glory, and we find joy in them
insofar as we enjoy God through them. He is glorified when we delight in
his good gifts. And when we use our leisure well, it leaves our souls re-
freshed and ready for the next day's labors of service and worship. But what
makes music in particular delightful?

The first chapter of Genesis tells us that God charged the human race
to rule the earthly order for his glory. When a musician arranges tones and
rhythms to show their interrelatedness, their potential for harmony, and
their potential as materials for design, the musician is showing us the glory
of a Creator so wise that he could endow sounds with such properties. So
good that he enabled us to perceive such sounds meaningfully. We delight
to behold such wisdom and goodness. It is similar when we study the sky
and discover there a kind of "speech" that proclaims the Lord's righteousness, as mentioned in Psalm 97:6. Such discovery brings pleasure to people
of all ages and cultures, from children singing on the playground to a scholar pondering a fugue—only, apart from Christ, neither child nor scholar can
enjoy the ultimate Artist who created music and our ability to perceive it.

Music as a Gift

While music ultimately points to God's goodness, it is also a gift to all humanity. Like food, water, and sunshine, music blesses all people whether they acknowledge its source or not. It is part of God's common grace to his creatures and offers a way for us to express and identify with the human condition. All facets of human experience may be expressed through music—not only love and joy but sadness and conflict. It gives voice to feelings and experiences that words fail to express. This is a gift for our enjoyment and comfort.

But to fully appreciate the gift of music, we will recognize its source. Music can comfort us by "speaking" clearly about God's goodness. This explains how the Bible can use music as an effective metaphor for God's goodness. He himself sings (Zeph 3:17; Heb 2:12). Believers call him their "song" (Exod 15:2; Ps 118:14; Isa 12:2). Angels mark the beginning and end of history with music making (Job 38:7; Rev 5:8–9). And nature, too, sings when the Lord makes his salvation known (Ps 98:7–9; Isa 44:23; 55:12). The Bible sometimes treats music as a synonym for joy (Prov 29:6; Isa 35:2; 51:3). "Is anyone cheerful? He should sing praises" (Jas 5:13).

Music as Praise

John Newton, the poet behind "Amazing Grace," wrote a hymn that begins and ends thus:

> How sweet the name of Jesus sounds
> in a believer's ear!
> It soothes his sorrows, heals his wounds,
> and drives away his fear. . . .
> Weak is the effort of my heart,
> and cold my warmest thought;
> but when I see thee as thou art,
> I'll praise thee as I ought.
> Till then I would thy love proclaim
> with every fleeting breath;
> and may the music of thy name
> refresh my soul in death.

In these verses, Newton likens the contemplation of Christ's lordship and gospel to the act of appreciating music. The pleasures of both are derived from God's character. The divine counsel for our salvation is so harmonious, with every part of it perfectly integrated with all the rest, that the name of our Savior summarizes the greatest symphony of all: the covenant of grace, the threefold office of Christ (as Prophet, Priest, and King), his active and passive obedience, his exaltation, and our union with him.

John Newton will not be alone when he praises God as he ought. A large number of the Bible's references to music are actually exhortations for believers to sing. In the temple worship of the OT, skilled Levitical singers sang with instrumental accompaniment (1 Chr 9:33; 25:1–31; 2 Chr 5:12–14), but everyone else responded congregationally with short refrains (1 Chr 16:36; Ezra 3:10–13). In NT worship all the saints teach and admonish one another and give thanks to God the Father in song, as the message about the Messiah dwells in them richly and as the Spirit fills them (Eph 5:18–20; Col 3:16). This can only mean that God intends church music to function primarily as a means by which congregants communicate to one another and to him—and that what they communicate is God's Word, "the sword of the Spirit" (Eph 6:17). Their songs will be saturated with the message, wording, and aesthetic values of Scripture. Jesus himself sang congregationally during his earthly ministry (Matt 26:30; Mark 14:26), and the ultimate aim of his saving work is pictured as congregational singing (Rom 15:9; Rev 14:2–3).

A BIBLICAL VIEW OF ART

Steve R. Halla

Throughout Christian history, Genesis 1–3 has served as a cornerstone for constructing a biblical understanding of the arts. The first thing the Bible reveals about God in Genesis 1:1 is that he is the divine Creator, the sovereign Artisan of all creation. As part of God's creative activities, he made man and woman "in his own image" (Gen 1:26–27). Although the Bible does not provide a precise definition of the meaning of this phrase, Christians throughout history have consistently argued that human artistry, creativity, and imagination are ultimately rooted in the *imago Dei*. Thus, when humans engage in artistic, creative, and imaginative activities, they mirror the nature and activities of their Creator.

Humans are, by God's divine design, aesthetic—that is, artistic, creative, and imaginative. From the ornate visual designs of the wilderness tabernacle to John's apocalyptic vision of the New Jerusalem adorned with gold, pearls, and precious stones (Rev 21:10–21), Scripture consistently engages humans as aesthetic beings and appeals directly to their aesthetic sensibilities.

As part of humanity's role in creation, God, in Genesis 1:28, further declares that humans are to fill the earth and "subdue" it. All art making is in essence an act of subjugation; poets bring order to words, musicians bring order to sounds, and so on. An essential part of what it means to be human, then, is to serve as stewards of God's creation; this includes aesthetic stewardship. God, through his mercy and grace, has afforded humans the honor and privilege of continuing his creative work in the world. The arts are a gift from God that can and should play a positive role in the life and worship of every believer.

The Bible, therefore, presents a cautiously optimistic and encouraging view of the arts. Although Scripture does not directly address the arts, it does provide numerous examples of the use of the arts in worship and everyday life, as well as offering various principles and teachings that shed light on how God's people are to approach, think about, and engage the arts. Active participation in the arts, either as performers or spectators, contributes to a holistic enjoyment of God, his people, and his creation. In addition to the fine arts, such as painting, sculpture, music, poetry, and the performing arts, the Bible also presents a positive view of the applied arts, that is, art designed primarily for utilitarian purposes. This includes ceramics, textiles, metalwork, woodwork, and stonework of various kinds. The Bible, in its entirety, shows no ambivalence toward the arts; rather, it regards them as important features of its overall scope and message.

At the same time, however, the Bible repeatedly warns against the idolatrous misuse of the arts. Among the various forms of idols recorded in the OT are artistically executed "carved" images (Deut 7:25; Isa 30:22; 40:19; Hab 2:19). Shortly after the Israelites were delivered out of bondage in Egypt, for example, they gathered together the "gold rings that were on their ears" (Exod 32:3) and cast a likeness of a golden calf using a graving tool (32:4). When Moses returned from meeting with God on Mount Sinai and saw the people worshipping the calf, he burned with anger and rebuked them for having committed a great sin (32:15–35).

Similarly, in Hosea 13:2–3, the prophet Hosea warns,

> Now they continue to sin and make themselves a cast image, idols skillfully made from their silver, all of them the work of craftsman. People say about them, "Let the men who sacrifice kiss the calves." Therefore, they will be like the morning mist, like the early dew that vanishes, like chaff blown from a threshing floor, or like smoke from a window.

Because of sin, anything, including the arts, can be used inappropriately. As a result, the arts should always be engaged prayerfully and with great care. While the Bible clearly denounces the idolatrous misuse of the arts, it never forbids or condemns humanity's general involvement in the arts. As the Renaissance artist Albrecht Dürer (1471–1528) once wrote, "A sword is a sword, which may be used either for murder or justice. Similarly the arts are in themselves good. What God hath formed that is good, misuse it how ye will" (*The Writings of Albrecht Dürer*, 176).

Music and, to a lesser degree, dance represent the most prominent and fully developed art forms in the Bible. In terms of human origins, Genesis 4:21 identifies Jubal as the "father of all who play the lyre and the flute." Biblical music consisted of both vocal and instrumental styles and was performed using a variety of instruments, including the tambourine (Exod 15:20; Judg 11:34), lyre (1 Sam 16:23), zither (Dan 3:5), trumpet (Num 10:1–2; Jer 4:5), and flute (Gen 4:21). Notable lyrical songs include the Israelites' song of deliverance at the Red Sea (Exod 15:1–21); Deborah and Barak's song of victory over King Jabin's army (Judg 5:2–31); Israel's song of praise at the completion of the temple's foundation (Ezra 3:11); Mary's song of rejoicing at the news of the conception of Jesus (Luke 1:46–55); Zechariah's song of praise for the birth of his son, John (Luke 1:68–79); and the apocalyptic song of praise unto the Lamb of God (Rev 15:3). Closely associated with music is dance, which was among the most popular pastime activities for women and children (Job 21:11; Jer 31:4; Matt 11:17; Luke 7:32) and was performed in times of joyous national celebrations (1 Sam 18:6) and religious festivities (Exod 15:20; Judg 21:21).

The visual arts are best represented in the wilderness tabernacle (Exod 25–31; 35–40) and Solomon's temple (1 Kgs 6). The account of the wilderness tabernacle is of particular significance because God himself supplied the tabernacle's designs. A survey of these designs shows the use of both representational and abstract or decorative styles of art as well as a wide variety of colors, textures, and materials. From the gold-covered ark of the covenant (Exod 25:10–22) to the colorful priestly garments (Exod 28), God called for the making of beautiful objects of exquisite craftsmanship to aid in worship of him. To accomplish this task, God filled Bezalel, the son of Uri, with his "Spirit, with wisdom, understanding, and ability in every craft" (Exod 31:2–3) and put "wisdom in the heart of every skilled artisan" (Exod 31:6).

One of the most intimate connections between God and the arts in the Bible are the figurative descriptions involving God and the work of the potter. To make a clay vessel in biblical times, an artisan would first trod the clay with his feet, then form it on a human-powered pottery wheel, and finally heat and harden it in a brick kiln.

In Jeremiah 19:1–13, the Lord commands Jeremiah to go down to the potter's house (cp. 18:3–4), buy a clay jar, and then take it, along with some of the elders and priests of the people, and travel to the Hinnom Valley near the entrance of the Potsherd Gate (18:1). There, after proclaiming to the people a message of God's coming judgment (18:2–9), Jeremiah is instructed to shatter the jar in their presence (18:10) and proclaim that the Lord will "shatter these people and this city, like one shatters a potter's jar that can never again be mended" (19:11).

In Romans 9:21, God's sovereign power to mold human destinies is likened to a potter who has full mastery over his clay: "Or has the potter no right over the clay, to make from the same lump one piece of pottery for honor and another for dishonor?"

Likewise, the prophet Isaiah paints a vivid word picture of the relationship between God and humanity when he writes, "Yet LORD, you are our Father; we are the clay, and you are our potter; we all are the work of your hands" (Isa 64:8). As reflected in these verses and others (Ps 2:9; Isa 30:14; Lam 4:2), the arts and artistic imagery provide an effective means of communicating God's truth to his people.

FORMS OF MEDIA AND RESISTING THE SPIRIT OF THE AGE

Read M. Schuchardt

One way of understanding the history of God's people is recognizing that it is the ongoing narrative of the tension between the Spirit of the Lord and the spirit of the age. And the spirit of the age, or *zeitgeist*, is in many ways the unintended effect of new media.

Regardless of geographic location or historical time period, the people of God have largely been characterized by having the courage necessary to stand up to the forces of the majority, for the individual to stand against the many, and for the weak to stand against the strong and to know the outcome is in God's hands. This pattern is revealed in many of the major events in the history of God's people that are recorded in Scripture as well as in subsequent Christian history. We see this in Abraham's standing against his father's ways, leaving his father's land, and heading west to Canaan (Gen 12). We see it in Moses's standing up against the pharaoh and leading his people out of Egypt. We see it in Jesus Christ's inability to compromise with the Pharisees and Sadducees and in his courage in standing up against the Roman Empire when on trial before Pontius Pilate.

A significant aspect of this tension is that in each case where the people of God stand up against the spirit of the age, there is simultaneously a change in how they perceive and use media forms for acceptable uses toward the good, the true, and the beautiful. Thus, the media that create the plausibility of perception are themselves an intricate part of the history of God's people.

A brief walk through some of these key moments will be helpful in understanding how a change in the religious practices of God's people is often inseparable from a change in media form or media usage. How changes in media form and religious practices later shaped the culture where these events took place can help us understand our own places and purposes in today's cultural context.

Old Testament Examples

When, at age 75, Abraham declared he would never again worship gods made by human hands, he exchanged the medium of wood and stone (the previous media used for making idols, cp. Deut 4:28–29) for the intangible God. He exchanged man-made forms for formlessness, declaring God to be of the Spirit.

For the worshippers at the tabernacle, God said, "I will meet you there above the mercy seat, between the two cherubim that are over the ark of the testimony; I will speak with you from there" (Exod 25:22). Thus, God's own decree to man was that he should meet him in a prescribed visual space that was itself empty—what art historians call "negative space," the hidden ground between two other figures. Perceiving God as Spirit when coming out of such an idolatrous culture must have taken an impressive act of the imagination, and the concept was something Jesus Christ would have to remind the people of God about several centuries later.

When Moses led his people out of Egypt, he simultaneously crafted for them a new identity by receiving the Ten Commandments on Mount Sinai, which archaeologists and biblical scholars claim is a reasonable location for the Proto-Sinaitic script, the earliest precursor to the Hebrew phonetic alphabet. This suggests that as part and parcel of making a new people group, Moses had to give them a new communication form to supplant the previous hieroglyphic writing system they would have labored under in Egypt.

In symbolic communication terms, they exchanged a pictographic (logographic and ideographic) writing system for an abstract phonetic writing system, one in which the shape of the letters no longer resembled the things they represented. Instead, letters were symbolic of basic sounds the human mouth could make. When combined, these would make meaningful words. This was a huge advance, as it was an improvement in the media. It displaced more than 5,000 Egyptian hieroglyphic symbols with just 22 letters of the Hebrew alphabet. This media change represented not merely a massive increase in efficiency for learning the old system. It also introduced the possibility for culture-wide literacy for the first time in recorded history. Even the term *hieroglyphics* is telling in this regard, as it originally meant "sacred carvings" or "priestly writing"—which should be understood not so much as the writings priests do but as indicative of the knowledge monopoly literacy represented: only readers and writers of this complex code could become priests under the Egyptian system. So in exchanging this pictographic writing system for a phonetic writing system, it is no wonder the second commandment of the Hebrew Decalogue declares, effectively, that henceforth pictographic symbols be banned.

Moses exchanged pictures for words. As a result, the Israelites were born as a new people, and the rule of law was established. But the phonetic alphabet created a hardening of the categories, allowing 613 Mosaic laws to be created and leading the Pharisees and Sadducees to compete with each other over a definition of righteousness that equated keeping as many of these laws as possible with pleasing God. This gave birth to what would later be termed *legalism*.

New Testament Examples

When Jesus Christ came into the world, he was the Word who preached the Word and healed the sick, traveling around Israel with his followers and greatly upsetting the religious establishment of Judaism. Paradoxically, though we know about him from Scripture, Jesus never wrote anything down (at least as far as penning Scripture is concerned), never commanded his followers to write anything down, and never had among his disciples a designated secretary or epistle writer. The closest he had to this was an accountant, or money handler: Judas Iscariot.

So one of the most incredible questions the Gospels present us with is how could the man-God Christ be sure his message would spread if he did not ensure its inscription into an existing cultural medium? How did he place such confidence in word-of-mouth transmission of his acts, good deeds, and sermons? And why did he tell some of his patients, whom he had miraculously healed, to go and tell no one what the Lord had done (see Mark 7:36)?

That is a complex and endlessly fascinating question, but at least some part of the answer can be had in understanding that what Christ brought into the world was a readjustment of the imbalance between the spoken and written word. He clearly favored the living word as spoken in the moment as his preferred medium of transmission, even as he honored the OT with his many references to what "is written." He said that "an hour is coming, and is now here, when the true worshipers will worship the Father in Spirit and in truth. Yes, the Father wants such people to worship him" (John 4:23).

Perhaps we see Christ using the power of the medium of speech against the excesses of the power of the written word best when he frees the woman caught in adultery in John 8:1–11. In this astonishing legal case, Jesus frees her from the judgment of the written law by orally delivering an if-then clause to the judge, jury, and executioners. "All right," he says in effect, agreeing with the validity and authority of the written law, "but let the one who has not sinned throw the first stone!" Interestingly, this is the only event recorded in Scripture in which Christ himself does any writing, and it is in the dust; we have no idea what he wrote. This is significant because it makes clear that Jesus Christ is both fully educated and fully literate, yet he chooses not to make writing an emphasis of his ministry. When the judge, jury, and executioners all leave the scene, what is left is effectively a mistrial (in which the trial is rendered invalid because of errors in the proceedings). Nevertheless, Jesus does not, even at this point, dismiss the serious nature of the accused's sin. Instead, he says with a perfect balance of justice and mercy, "Neither do I condemn you. . . . Go, and from now on do not sin anymore" (v. 11). As a legal analysis of the case would show, this rhetorically perfect use of the spoken word to disrupt the otherwise deadly effect of the written law is only handled safely by the One whose heart is perfectly loving, yet who knows that the hearts of men are evil and lead them to cite the law to achieve their own purposes (which, in this case, was to entrap Jesus).

In his teachings Christ seems to have consistently reminded his followers and adversaries of the power of the present, living, breathing word of the speaker as a formidable power against the dead hand of the written law. Perhaps this helps explain what Paul later meant when he said the letter of the law kills, but the spirit of the law gives life (cp. 2 Cor 3:6)

Conclusion

This pattern of God's people following his will and concurrently changing their media habits runs throughout history. We see a media reformation in Martin Luther's ability to stand up to the abuses of the Roman Catholic Church at the time of his *95 Theses*. And today, in the digital age, where all our communication and social media leads to physical distance between even the closest writer and speaker, we see that Christians are called to be the presence of Christ in an age of absence. In this and many other ways, we see that attention to the Spirit of the Lord must also include attention to the details of how media effects can transform our perceptions, our thoughts, and our cultures.

TECHNOLOGY AND A CHRISTIAN WORLDVIEW

Read M. Schuchardt

Technology and the Christian worldview are mutually intertwined. *Technology* is a word that comes from the Greek term *tekne*, meaning "art" or "craft" and the word *logos*, meaning "word" or "pattern." In its oldest form the ancient Greek word *technologia* meant the systematic treatment of grammar, but then it evolved to mean the study of the mechanical arts and sciences. Now in standard usage it generally means the newest inventions themselves.

Interestingly, the Sanskrit word that later gave rise to the Indo-European word *tekne* originally meant "carpenter." In Greek we see that Jesus Christ is referred to in Scripture as a *tekton*, which shares this root. Christ is also referred to as the Word, or *logos*, in John 1:1. Thus, it is not insignificant that the primordial linguistic pattern of all our modern technology is deeply entwined with our earliest understandings of Jesus Christ as Builder, as Craftsman, as divine Word, and as Creator. In this sense we can see how all our technologies are but attempts at righting the world since it went wrong at the fall. But we should also pay attention to how much our technologies can unintentionally keep us distant, separated, and indifferent to one another.

Technology throughout History

Today technology's chief benefit is to create efficiency in motion, labor, and communication. When we think of technology, we think of it as a laborsaving device.

But the history of technology is also the history of warfare, as the winners of wars write history, and the winners of wars are always characterized by having technological superiority—otherwise they would not have won. Even in biblical cases where we perceive an exception to this rule—such as in the account of David versus Goliath, that of Pharaoh's army versus Moses and the Israelites at the Red Sea, or the narrative of Joshua and the battle for Jericho, we see the pattern revealed: what man thought was a better technology (bigger soldiers, larger armies, walled fortresses) led to a downfall. In each case, technological weakness gave God's people competitive advantage. For instance,

- David's sling launched a stone that hit Goliath on his forehead, the one portion of his body that was not protected by armor; this was the original smart missile.
- Pharaoh's armies meant to crush the escaping Israelites along the banks of the sea, thinking them trapped there. But the God of the wind and tides gave Moses temporary command of these natural forces. Not only did Israel escape through the parted body of water, but also the enemy drowned as the water fell; this was the original weather warfare.
- Joshua obeyed God's command for his army to blow their trumpets around the walls of Jericho, and the fortress fell; this was the original use of sonic warfare.

Each of the above incidents involved the application of an incredibly efficient technology that required God's people to trust God in the face of what seemed impossible odds. And as that smart missile found its mark, as weather warfare overwhelmed Pharaoh, as sonic warfare toppled that wall, man was given new evidences that God is the Master Technologist, the Master Builder, the Master Designer, the Master Engineer, the Master Craftsman, and the Master Strategist. He is so capable, so completely knowledgeable about all things, that what looks impossible to us is always possible to him.

Modern Technology
God's deployment of his technologies is always an act of love; by using them, he spares his people and saves their lives. By contrast, our technologies today are, often inadvertently, used in ways that have the opposite

effect. They are primarily used to generate weapons of warfare or to harness oil, nuclear, hydro, or solar energy—substances that are themselves the cause of great wars. As of 2014, only 11 countries (out of the 194 countries in existence) were not engaged in some form of armed conflict that killed at least 25 of their own citizens.

This physical death toll fueled by new human technologies is perhaps paralleled by the unintended emotional toll associated with our modern communication technologies. Even though sending electronic messages over digital media has great advantages, messages received in this format often have the effect of making us feel insignificant and can lead to resentment. An e-mail wishing you well is nice but not as nice as a card, not as nice as a phone call, and certainly not as nice as having a friend show up in person beside your hospital bed.

This disembodying effect of technology, in fact, encourages us to compensate for our loss by using mass media for 12 hours out of our 16-hour waking day. We overuse the technology to make us feel more connected—even as the greater use increases our feelings of loneliness. Today's Facebook user, for instance, has an average of 338 social media friends. That same user's "real friends," however, have gone down from five to two. Technology, though used as a compensation for the loss of the real thing in our lives, proves a poor substitute.

One strange thing about social media, for instance, is that it requires antisocial behavior for participation. It leads to a husband and wife sitting in the same room together, each engrossed in the screen rather than in connecting with each other through conversation. It encourages teens to withdraw from family activities in order to keep up with what their friends are doing online. This problem may explain why so many people end up taking pictures of their food and posting them as contributions to their friends' social lives. But to paraphrase Romans 14:17, "[T]he kingdom of God is not eating and drinking" and taking beautiful selfies. Humans were created to live in face-to-face community.

If you've ever had a colleague ask you to e-mail him when he could just as easily stop by your cubicle to chat, you know what depersonalization can feel like. Technology is convenient, it is efficient, and it is incredibly productive. But there is a price to pay for such convenience. Selfishness and thoughtlessness—such easy traps to fall into given our high-tech world—are the opposite of love.

Technology and the Christian Worldview

When humanity failed to listen to God's prophets, God sent his Son, Jesus Christ, as the ultimate Messenger heralding his love for us. But just as the terrible tenants in the parable of the vineyard killed the owner's son, we humans killed Jesus. When that act is viewed theologically, however, we see that this was precisely what was supposed to happen: our loving Creator God came to earth in human form in order to demonstrate that true love is willing to sacrifice self.

Technology can be an incredibly useful tool for solving immediate physical, practical, and technical problems. But as a mode of interaction between humans, it far too often sends a message of indifference rather than love. To correct the problem, and to truly love others as we love ourselves and as Christ both commanded and demonstrated, we must be willing to sacrifice the convenience the technology gives us. When, for instance, you receive the call that asks, "Are you sitting down?" you know you are about to hear information that takes your knees out from under you. When the sender of that message shows up in person to catch you as you fall, then you know you are loved. The burden somehow becomes a bit easier to bear. The intentional nonuse of technology could be the only way to show someone he is worth our time. That there is a God who really cares. It illustrates that we are willing to be inconvenienced on another's behalf, much as Jesus was willing to set aside all the ease and wonder of heaven for ours.

The ancient Israelites were called to be a people apart, worshipping God in the tabernacle and later the temple in Israel. The early Christians too were called to be a people set apart: worshipping God in spirit and in truth; replacing the ritual slaughter of animals on the altar with sharing Communion and fellowshipping together; and seeing to the needs of the poor and displaced among them. Modern followers of Jesus must pursue similar fellowship and charity, but we have a new task. The church is called to set herself apart from the surrounding culture by reembodying herself in all the ways modern technology has disembodied her. Only by using our physical bodies to do small things with great love can we combat the silent spirit of the technological age and be the presence of the kingdom of God for the suffering world around us.

The Christian's call to imitate God in his self-giving sacrifice does not require each Christian to be a literal martyr, but our technological age does greatly increase our opportunity to martyr the small self—one's own ego, a love of convenience and ease—in order to demonstrate the physicality of the love Christ first showed us. Christ's own description of such physical acts in Matthew 25:35–36 bears out their significance. "I was hungry and you gave me something to eat," Jesus said. "I was thirsty and you gave me something to drink; I was a stranger and you took me in; I was naked and you clothed me; I was sick and you took care of me; I was in prison and you visited me." In our technological time of digital disembodiment, our new calling as a people set apart must be presence in the age of absence.

A BIBLICAL VIEW OF RECREATION

K. Erik Thoennes

In the church, activities like play, sport, leisure, and recreation have often been dismissed as meaningless, worldly, and contrary to sober Christian living. On the other hand, Christians can be pulled into the idolatry of recreation as an end in itself. Many live for the weekend when we should be living for eternity. A biblical understanding of recreation is that it is given by God for his glory and our good; such an understanding will enable play to be a conduit of glorifying God.

To understand recreation in the Bible, we also need to appreciate related concepts such as laughter, Sabbath, feasts, festivals, childlikeness, dancing, leaping, leisure, sport, and music. These occur most often when God's presence, grace, and glory are most evident to his covenant people.

Defining Recreation

Recreation is a noncompulsory, nonutilitarian activity, often filled with creative spontaneity, which gives perspective, diversion, and rest from the necessary work of daily life. In light of God's sovereignty and faithful love, recreation should demonstrate and encourage God-centered hope, delight, gratitude, and celebration. In light of the fallen and cursed state of the world, recreation gives us a glimpse of the Sabbath rest Christ brings. Gospel-grounded recreation reminds us that God is always working, and because of that, his children can rest.

In order to bring the restorative benefits of recreation, the practical results of it must necessarily fade to an almost subconscious level, lest the restfulness of recreation be lost. Living with faith and hope leads to the kind of joyful discipleship that should instinctively lead to play, naps, games, and walks on the beach. But understanding the theological motive of recreation will increase the joy and freedom of it.

Among the thorns and thistles east of Eden, recreation provides needed perspective, diversion, and rest. Like the arts, recreation can afford "counter-environments" (to use a term from Marshall McLuhan) that provide freedom from dwelling on the daily difficulties of life in a fallen world. Recreation should not serve to anesthetize the Christian to life's burdens, preventing him from engaging them wholeheartedly; rather, it should provide a needed hopeful Sabbath from their relentless presence. As all other areas of our lives, recreation should fall under the sanctifying effects of the Holy Spirit's work.

For a Christian, recreation should never have a trivializing impact on life. Recreation should not be synonymous with wasting time; it should give testimony to the goodness of God. Without serious hard work preceding it, recreation loses its real power to be an interlude into the routine of making ends meet. If recreation serves as merely a diversion rather than giving hopeful perspective, it can actually prevent serious transformative engagement with a world badly in need of redemption. Those who most recognize the difficulty of life in a fallen world are best able to rest, play, and laugh. These moments of emancipation can remind the faithful of the ultimate liberation coming when Jesus makes all things new (Rev 21:5).

Creation

Recreation has its origin in the Creator himself. The overwhelming artistic variety we see in creation indicates that there is not only an intelligent Designer behind it but also a creative, playful, extravagant Artist. The sheer variety of tastes, colors, sounds, textures, and shapes in creation indicate anything but pure utilitarian motivation by its Creator. God is both skillful Architect and creative Artist. God does nothing based on his own need (Acts 17:24–25; Ps 50:9–12), so creation, like recreation, is meaningful but not necessary. In creating and sustaining everything, and in accomplishing redemption, God's pleasure and glory are his primary motives (Isa 43:7; Matt 10:26; Luke 11:21; Eph 1:5,9,11–12). Creation is a source of pleasure and delight for those who delight in the Creator and in the work of his hands.

Sabbath

When creation was exactly as God intended, he rested (Gen 2:2–3). His rest was a demonstration of the goodness and completeness of his work. As a reminder of this, Sabbath keeping became a central command for God's people (Exod 20:11). Keeping the Sabbath required God's people to disengage from providing for themselves and to remember the ultimate source of their daily bread. The Creator and Sustainer built a mandatory rest into each week so his people would put their efforts for survival into perspective. Rest in God's sufficiency and power attacks an anthropocentric view of life and demands we surrender any vestige of self-sufficiency (cp. Isa 41:13–14; Matt 6:25–33; Jas 4:13–17). As Fred Sanders says in his essay, "A Play Ethic: Play Studies in Psychology and Theology,"

> Productive work is an intoxicating thing. The temptation to base one's identity and esteem on what one produces is all but irresistible. . . . The command to rest and remember God is a challenge to human productivity. It arrests and relativizes even the most demanding and consuming work, for anything which can be interrupted is not ultimate in importance. Self-important people cannot tolerate this undercutting of their significance.

Sabbath keeping attacks any hint of human-centeredness or self-sufficiency. Lack of recreation, rest, and play can be a sign of profound hubris.

None of this is intended to undercut human effort, attentiveness, passion, diligence, or responsibility. Nevertheless, human activity must always be subservient to the overarching plan and power of God. While best-selling self-help books tell us that the universe will rearrange itself to give us whatever we want if we exercise the power of positive thinking, God condemns this blasphemous lie and frees us from the impossible role of playing God. He calls us to the freedom and Sabbath rest that lead to childlike dependence, trust, and recreation.

The Hope of the Gospel

The saving work of Christ leads to rest and recreation, for it injects freedom and healing to our broken world. In Christ we see that the human predicament is fixable. The Christian worldview recognizes the relentless difficulty of life in our dysfunctional world but also embraces the truth that it is being redeemed by the One who created it (Rom 8:18–39). By Christ's life, death, and resurrection, we have hope in the midst of our brokenness. When it is an end in itself, recreation can become a frivolous idol that keeps us from dealing with the human predicament. When grounded in the hope of the gospel, however, recreation can become one of life's greatest and most encouraging pleasures.

Recreation and the Coming Kingdom
The most stirring images of recreation in the Bible occur in attempts to express the joy and freedom experienced in the coming kingdom of God. The most vivid of these images is Zechariah 8:5: "The streets of the city will be filled with boys and girls playing in them" (cp. Isa 11:8–9; Jer 30:18–19; 31:4,13–14). Fearless childlike play, no longer inhibited by the effects of sin and the curse, is a key metaphor for Christ's kingdom.

Heaven: The Recreation of Eternity
Christian recreation is the response of those who know God as their Father and trust that he has overcome the world and loves to abundantly share the spoils of this victory with his children. God's saving power leads to great joy among God's people (Ps 126:2). This joy is possible even when life is brutal. Luke 6:21 gets at this idea: "Blessed are you who are now hungry, because you will be filled. Blessed are you who weep now, because you will laugh." Empty stomachs and tears are neither the whole story nor its end. God will bring ultimate healing one day.

Conclusion
Recreation, like everything else, should be done for the glory of God (1 Cor 10:31; Col 3:17). When we recreate as hopeful, forgiven children of the King of kings, it glorifies God and gives a glimpse of the final rest. Failure to appreciate recreation in the Christian life could easily turn piety into sanctimony, reverence into rigidity, and sanctification into stuffiness. We must take God, but never ourselves, seriously.

God invites us to approach him as his free, forgiven, secure children. We are to approach our holy God with healthy fear and hearts broken by our broken world. But God's people are also called to rejoice, sing, dance, play, and laugh because we know the Owner of all things is working out his perfect plan. It's a masterful narrative that ends with a wedding banquet, perfect resolution, and rest. This sure hope in God's sovereign power and loving-kindness enables us to rest and play with reckless abandon, even before the great wedding banquet begins.

Business and
Finance

BIBLICAL MODELS FOR BUSINESS

Darin W. White and Danny Wood

If you are a follower of Christ and work as a business professional, how does your Christian worldview influence your day-to-day life at work? The business world is founded on relationships—relationships between salespeople and customers, between employees and employers, and between peers up and down the organizational chart within a company. Most business professionals interact with dozens of people every day.

As a follower of Christ, a business professional should view every relationship as an opportunity to glorify God. Isaiah says that God created us for his glory: "Bring my sons from far away, and my daughters from the ends of the earth—everyone who bears my name and is created for my glory. I have formed them; indeed, I have made them" (Isa 43:6–7).

Since God created us so that we could glorify him, we should view our roles as business persons as opportunities to execute that calling. As 1 Cor 10:31 says, "Whether [we] eat or drink, or whatever [we] do, [we should] do everything for the glory of God." Being created in the image of God means we should reflect God's character. In other words, we should exhibit the fruit of the Spirit in our business relationships. Galatians 5:22–23 lists them: "love, joy, peace, patience, kindness, goodness, faithfulness, gentleness, and self-control."

But practically speaking, what does this look like in the business world? At least three implications guide us. First, a biblical worldview motivates us to work with excellence, giving our best effort. As Paul says in Colossians 3:23–24, "Whatever you do, do from the heart, as something done for the Lord and not for people, knowing that you will receive the reward of an inheritance from the Lord. You serve the Lord Christ."

Second, we should strive to be the best possible employees. Though the job might be difficult and the boss unfair, our response to such issues should not be one of whining and complaining or loafing. We represent our Lord; we are "ambassadors for Christ" (2 Cor 5:20). And ultimately, our performance should be for an audience of One. We aim to please God above all. The first part of Colossians 3:23 says, "Whatever you do." It doesn't say, "In certain things that you do" or "In a few things you do." It says that in whatever work you do, you are working for the Lord and serving him. Therefore, whether our work is full-time or part-time, salaried or hourly, involves management or nonmanagement, we are to work with enthusiasm and with our whole hearts.

In all our work we are to do labor "for the Lord and not for people" (Col 3:23). That adds value to what we do to earn a living. Our sense of accountability also increases because of this mind-set because it reminds us that God sees everything, and we will be accountable to him for what we did and how we did it. If we view our work from a biblical worldview, we will excel in our efforts and attitudes, thus setting an example for others to follow, bringing more value to our companies and gaining larger platforms from which to share the good news of Jesus Christ.

Third, a biblical worldview motivates us to be servant leaders having the same servant attitude as Christ. In John 13:15–16 Jesus says, "For I have given you an example, that you also should do just as I have done for you. Truly I tell you, a servant is not greater than his master, and a messenger is not greater than the one who sent him."

Jesus constantly taught his disciples to have a servant mind-set. He did not have a problem with a person trying to excel or better himself, but he reminded them that no matter their position in life, they needed to be servants. Jesus gave us a poignant example of servanthood when he washed the disciples' feet—a task which was usually the responsibility of a lowly servant. After that he provided the greatest act of service by voluntarily going to the cross to die for the sins of mankind.

As Christians we are to have the attitude of servants, remaining willing to do whatever it takes to get the job done. When there is a crisis in the business and the proverbial "ox is in the ditch," we must be willing to do anything needed—whether or not it is part of our job description—to get things back on track. We ought to look for ways to serve others regularly. By doing so, we will not only be a help to others but will also add value to the organization.

When a person adopts a servant attitude, he becomes a team player. This is the opposite of one who lives with a silo-builder or turf-protector mentality, only concerning himself with his own area and how everything affects him. Being a team player, who is willing to sacrifice and serve others, will bring a spirit of unity to the team and will increase the potential for success.

Those in a position of leadership are to embrace servant leadership even as Jesus embraced it as he led his disciples. Employees are not there to serve their Christian bosses and managers; rather, such leaders are to serve alongside their workers. Leaders who care and have a humble, servant's spirit, in fact, will find new opportunities to share about the One who motivates them to serve in such a manner.

Fourth, a biblical worldview leads us to be people of integrity. Proverbs 10:9 tells us, "The one who lives with integrity lives securely, but whoever perverts his ways will be found out." Similarly, Prov 28:6 says, "Better the poor person who lives with integrity than the rich one who distorts right and wrong."

Integrity is acting with a personal commitment to honesty, openness, and fairness. It is not merely holding a moral or principled idea or position but doing it. There is no cramming for a test of character. An exam always comes as a pop quiz, so believers must determine the qualities that will shape their behavior and live them out.

As Christians embracing a biblical worldview, we will be honest in all our dealings. We must not make promises we cannot keep. We ought not misrepresent our products or our companies. We must not lie on our expense reports or fudge sales numbers. Instead, we must routinely practice the Golden Rule: we must treat others as we would want to be treated (Matt 7:12).

Integrity is essential to good leadership. And while a charismatic personality will draw people to a person, only integrity will keep them there. The more followers that see and hear their leader being consistent in action and word, the greater their own work consistency and loyalty will grow.

What we do will flow from who we are. The outer person will reflect the inner. Who we are on the inside is who we will be on the outside.

Adopting a biblical worldview will lead us to live with integrity, granting us opportunities to make a kingdom impact on everyone we encounter throughout our careers.

CAPITALISM AND A CHRISTIAN WORLDVIEW

Walter J. Schultz

Capitalism is a term that may seem to go right along with *freedom, apple pie*, and *soccer mom*. Many, if not most, Western Christians would certainly agree. But should they?

The global financial crisis of the early twenty-first century caused many to lose trust in free-market capitalism. For example, in his book *A Failure of Capitalism*, Richard Posner, who once vigorously defended free-market capitalism, expressed serious misgivings about it.

How then should we, who believe that God owns the cattle on a thousand hills, that life does not consist in the abundance of possessions, that we are not our own, that we are not strict owners but mere stewards of talents, wealth, and grace, who will give to God an account of our stewardship—how should we think about capitalism?

Defining Capitalism

There are several different concepts of capitalism out there. We should first make sure which concept we are taking about. Then we should weigh how the biblical notions of property, stewardship, and identity come into play. Let us begin at the beginning.

Humans have basic needs and desire things they may or may not need. They take actions they believe will meet such needs and desires. Sometimes these actions succeed; sometimes they do not. Needs, desires, rational action—these notions are often taken to be the axioms of economics. Economics is a social science that studies the issues involved whenever a group of people have to decide what gets produced and who gets how much of it.

In 1776 Adam Smith shaped the world economy and consciousness of his day and even our own by claiming that when individuals pursue their own interests, men and women are together led as if by an "invisible hand" to achieve the common good. Smith's idea is that the rational and voluntary actions of individuals combine in some yet undisclosed way to answer the two questions about what gets produced and who gets what.

His claim also raises the deeper question of who owns the property and productive capacities to begin with. Under pure capitalism, all property and wealth are privately owned. Individuals decide for themselves what gets produced, how to go about it, and what to do with the profits. Under pure socialism, by contrast, everything is collectively owned and representatives of that collective decide what gets produced and who gets what.

But neither pure capitalism nor pure socialism exists in any nation. The approach of every modern nation lies somewhere on the continuum as a combination of private and collectively owned property. The United States is closer to the pure capitalism pole; China is closer to the pure socialism pole. Granting that at least some property and important economic decisions must be made by the state to provide for our roads, parks, and national defense, the crucial core of the concept of capitalism is that it is a mixed, private-property economy. This must be refined further.

Capitalism and Private Property

While some people treat capitalism as categorically undesirable, what they have in mind is really something else—no matter how closely related it might seem. Capitalism in this other sense has become a word for misuse of private property. It is a pejorative synonym for exploitation, greed, or oppression. This runs contrary to Scripture, which endorses private property in the form of individual stewardship of all the gifts of God, including one's talents and spiritual gifts. Since fallen people have these stewardship responsibilities, misuse and abuse is bound to occur and have collective effects. Therefore, a private-property economy must be viewed initially as a qualified good.

A private-property economy is a powerful social arrangement which, through the division of labor and specialization, has produced the highest standard of living in human history. To this extent, Adam Smith was right.

Of course, not everyone on the globe benefits equally, nor do they exert effort and discipline equally. There are obvious disparities on both counts.

Furthermore, some people confuse the profit motive with greed, but this is a mistake. All laborers deserve their wages—including those entrepreneurs who labor to provide a product people need or legitimately desire. Our concerns are not to focus on bad stewardship, or how to think about the disparities of wealth, or with greed or profit. Our concern must be limited to understanding the role of morality in the optimal operation of a mixed, private-property economy and to what extent it is rooted in Scripture and yet may be applied by those who reject Scripture as God's Word.

Three Concepts of Capitalism

Three concepts of capitalism as a private-property economy compete for attention in our world.

Naive capitalism holds that markets are "morally free zones" of social interaction—"spheres of sanctity" that remain separate from the intrusion of others. The idea is that morality has no role in achieving the common good. Many judges, public policy makers, economists, teachers of economics, and ordinary people take Smith's "invisible hand" to mean that morality has no place in economic interaction as long as everyone follows the coordination conventions of a price mechanism. This concept is widespread but mistaken, not only from a biblical perspective of property and stewardship but also in practice and in theory (W. Schultz, *The Moral Conditions of Economic Efficiency*).

Rational egoist capitalism is a version that works only in theory by assuming that adverse effects of unethical behavior are absent. It obviously leaves no room for a biblically grounded view of the moral conditions underlying the achievement of the common good. Christians should repudiate the attitudes and practices of rational egoist capitalism, recovering a clear sense of the biblical view of property and the responsibilities and motives of a truly Christian stewardship.

Finally, responsible capitalism holds that morality is essential to an efficient, private-property economy. Morality is effective only when people hold themselves and one another responsible. Only the latter view of capitalism is worthy of Christian acceptance—and, even then, our acceptance must be qualified. We must bring a biblical view of property and a biblical view of the motive and ends of stewardship to our economic theorizing and use of wealth. Responsible capitalism will work among any group of people advocating diverse moral or religious beliefs, providing they desire a democratic, private-property economy that consistently yields efficient outcomes of market interaction. Therefore, we all should repudiate naive capitalism and rational egoist capitalism in favor of responsible capitalism for all nations.

Capitalism Today

The turn away from theological ethics in seventeenth- and eighteenth-century British moral theory was more significant than many have appreciated. Adam Smith's deistic views effectively excluded a biblical view of property (Peter Minowitz, *Profits, Priests and Princes: Adam Smith's Emancipation of Economics from Politics and Religion*, chap. 7). Nevertheless, when agents share a biblical understanding of property and are motivated by such property stewardship, they too will possess the required internal incentive to comply with the rights that ensure economically efficient outcomes of market interaction.

While such a moral capitalism requires that agents be free to produce and purchase what they desire, providing benchmark procedures for aiding the poor, Christians are further constrained. We who belong to Jesus were bought with a price. In reality, we own nothing. What we possess and what we do for a living and how these affect our sense of identity are founded in these truths.

Our calling as Christ's followers is not to a life of self-indulgent consumerism. We are stewards of whatever talents, gifts, grace, and wealth God in his sovereign mercy has entrusted to us. Let us recommit to living our economic lives for the sake of the gospel, the kingdom, and his glory. Only then can we ensure our long-term prosperity and happiness.

PERSONAL FINANCES

Timothy D. Dockery

The Bible has much to say about money. The topic of money or wealth is addressed more than 70 times in the NT alone. How can a Christian living in the twenty-first century think rightly about finances using principles that were outlined in the first century or earlier? Think about all of the decisions you have made this year that were influenced by how much money you have or lack. Perhaps you chose between coffee at home versus coffee at Starbucks? Maybe you decided between tithing at church or paying off your credit card? It could be that there were days when you just wondered how to buy your next meal. The following offers a quick overview of how the Bible addresses saving money, going into debt, and giving.

To Save or Not to Save?
In Matthew 6:26–29, Jesus says,

> Consider the birds of the sky: They don't sow or reap or gather into barns, yet your heavenly Father feeds them. Aren't you worth more than they? Can any of you add one moment to his lifespan by worrying? And why do you worry about clothes? Observe how the wildflowers of the field grow: They don't labor or spin thread. Yet I tell you that not even Solomon in all his splendor was adorned like one of these.

Earlier in the same chapter, Jesus says, "Don't store up for yourselves treasures on earth, where moth and rust destroy and where thieves break in and steal. But store up for yourselves treasures in heaven" (Matt 6:19–20).

These verses seem to discourage a Christian from saving money, but several verses in the Bible encourage saving. Proverbs 21:20, for instance, says, "Precious treasure and oil are in the dwelling of a wise person, but a fool consumes them." The wisdom of this advice has been proven many times over, such as when the stock market and other investments lose value quickly. During recessions many people are laid off from jobs they planned to work until retirement. The Bible advocates saving in times of plenty to prepare for times like these.

So, what is a Christian to do? Save as much as possible for tomorrow, or give everything away today and trust in the Lord for future provision? Looking at the verses cited above alone, it might seem that we are given contradictory advice. But, in fact, the Bible advocates balance. It is wise to save money each paycheck for unexpected future expenses. It is wise to contribute to a retirement account each month, knowing a day may come when we are physically incapable of earning a wage. But it is also important not to hoard all of the money or talents God has given us. When we are saving, we must remember that ultimately God is the provider. Remembering that God provided the money makes it easier to give it back to him through tithing or providing for someone else in need. So, save your money for a rainy day, but don't be afraid to spend it if it rains or to give it away if you see someone else struggling in a downpour.

Should a Christian Ever Have Financial Debt?

According to 2013 statistics from the Federal Reserve, the average American household has about $15,000 in credit card debt, $150,000 in mortgage debt, and $32,000 in outstanding student loans. Many Americans rely on debt to continue their current lifestyle. But debt is a burden that allows past decisions to control our current spending decisions. It can prevent one's ability to be generous. Substantial debt can even hamper your ability to respond to God's call for your vocation. Nevertheless, while the Bible discourages Christians from going into debt, it does not categorically prohibit it (Rom 13:8).

Going into debt to purchase an item is often a poor use of one's resources. Borrowing money to buy something actually makes that purchase more expensive since you have to pay for the full cost of the item and make interest payments until the debt is paid in full. For example, if you financed a $20,000 car over five years with a 10 percent interest rate, it actually costs you $5,500 more than it would have if you'd paid cash. Avoiding debt is one way to do more with the resources God has entrusted to you.

Nevertheless, in the twenty-first-century economy there are situations in which one might have to use debt to purchase a home, pay for education, or pay for a health emergency. You can have debt and still be a good steward so long as you are only borrowing for a need that is manageable to repay. Throughout the Bible, Christians are encouraged to be generous, and we will be more likely to practice generosity if we have avoided entangling ourselves in debt.

How Should a Christian Think about Giving and Tithing?

In the NT, the overwhelming expectation with respect to money is generosity. Acts 20:35 admonishes, "In every way I've shown you that it is necessary to help the weak by laboring like this and to remember the words of the Lord Jesus, because he said, 'It is more blessed to give than to receive.'" So, how should a Christian practice tithing and generosity today?

Tithing was strictly required in OT times. All the people of Israel were required to give to the temple 10 percent of everything they earned or grew. Several tithes were required that would have made the total giving much higher than the traditional "tithe" of 10 percent (Num 18; Deut 14). In contrast, the NT does not specify an exact amount or percentage a Christian should give away, but many scholars believe the minimum practice of the OT sets the baseline. We are told to give generously as we are able in keeping with how we prosper (1 Cor 16:2). While there may not be an exact formula to tell us how to give, the admonishments to generosity are compelling. In Luke 6:30, Jesus tells us, "Give to everyone who asks you, and from someone who takes your things, don't ask for them back." In Luke 3:11 he says, "The one who has two shirts must share with someone who has none, and the one who has food must do the same."

In conclusion, God calls us to be good stewards of the financial assets he blesses us with so that we can seek his wisdom and give generously from what he has given. A Christian can practice that by avoiding debt, saving regularly, and living below his means so he always has something to give. In the end, it is the heart that matters most to God. Second Corinthians 9:7 point to this: "Each person should do as he has decided in his heart—not reluctantly or out of compulsion, since God loves a cheerful giver."

Christian Worldview and Ministry

THE CRISIS OF THE CHRISTIAN MIND

James Emery White

In 1995, Thomas Cahill released the provocatively titled book, *How the Irish Saved Civilization*. Cahill contended:

> Ireland had one moment of unblemished glory . . . as the Roman Empire fell, as all through Europe matted, unwashed barbarians descended on the Roman cities, looting artifacts and burning books, the Irish, who were just learning to read and write, took up the great labor of copying all of Western literature (p. 3).

Missionary-minded Irish monks later brought what had been preserved on their isolated island back to the continent, refounding European civilization. And that, Cahill concludes, is how the Irish saved civilization.

But more is at hand in Cahill's study than meets the eye. Beyond the loss of Latin literature and the development of the great national European literatures that an illiterate Europe would not have established, Cahill notes that something else would have perished in the West had it not been for the Irish: "the habits of the mind that encourage thought."

Why would this matter?

Cahill continues his assessment: "When Islam began its medieval expansion, it would have encountered scant resistance to its plans—just scattered tribes of animists, ready for a new identity" (pp. 193–94). Without a robust mind to engage the onslaught—and a Christian one at that—the West would have been under the crescent instead of the cross.

The habits of the mind have never mattered more than they do today. As Winston Churchill presciently stated in his address to Harvard University in 1943, "The empires of the future are the empires of the mind." Oxford theologian Alister McGrath, reflecting on Churchill's address, notes that Churchill's point was that a great transition was taking place in Western culture, with immense implications for all who live in it. The powers of the new world would not be nation-states, as with empires past, but ideologies. Ideas, not nations, would now captivate and conquer in the future. The starting point for the conquest of the world would now be the human mind (*The Twilight of Atheism*, p. xi).

But this time, we may need more than the Irish to save us.

"We may talk of 'conquering' the world for Christ. But what sort of 'conquest' do we mean?" asks John Stott. "Not a victory by force of arms. . . . This is a battle of ideas" (*Your Mind Matters: The Place of the Mind in the Christian Life*, pp. 20–21). Yet there are surprisingly few warriors. Those who follow Christ have too often retreated into personal piety and good works, or as one BBC commentator said, "Christians have too often offered mere 'feelings' and 'philanthropy.'" Speaking specifically to the challenge raised by Islam, he added that what is needed was more "hard thinking" applied to the issues of the day.

What remains to be seen is whether any hard thinkers remain to do the work. The peril of our day is that when a Christian mind is most needed, Christians express little need for the mind and, as a result, even less resolve to develop it. There is even a perception that an undeveloped mind is more virtuous than one prepared for battle. Richard Hofstadter, in his Pulitzer Prize-winning book *Anti-Intellectualism in American Life*, identified "the evangelical spirit" as one of the prime sources of American anti-intellectualism. He points out that for many Christians, humble ignorance is a far more noble quality than a cultivated mind (pp. 55–80).

Such devaluation of the intellect is a recent development within the annals of Christian history. While Christians have long struggled with the role and place of reason, that the mind itself mattered has been unquestioned until now. Even the early church father Tertullian (ca AD 160–220)—who had little use for philosophy and was famed for his question, "What indeed has Athens to do with Jerusalem?"—never questioned the importance of the mind (*On the Proscription of Heretics* 6, 3:246). Tertullian's conviction was that Greek philosophy had little to offer in terms of informing the contours of Christian thought, akin to the apostle Paul's quip to the Corinthian church that the foolishness of God is wiser than the wisdom of men (1 Cor 1:25). But Tertullian, as well as Paul, would have held in complete disdain any anti-intellectualism that celebrated an undeveloped mind.

Deep within the worldview of the biblical authors, and equally within the minds of the earliest church fathers, was the understanding that to be fully human is to think. To this day we call ourselves a race of Homo sapiens, which means "thinking beings." This is not simply a scientific classification; it is a spiritual one. We were made in God's image, and one of the most precious and noble dynamics within that image is the ability to think. It is one of the most sacred reflections of the divine image. It is also foundational to our interaction with God. As God himself implored through the prophet Isaiah, "Come, let us settle this" (Isa 1:18).

Jesus made clear that our minds are integral to life lived in relationship with God. When summarizing human devotion to God as involving heart, soul, and strength, Jesus added "and mind" to the original wording of Deuteronomy. It's as though he wanted there to be no doubt that when contemplating the comprehensive nature of commitment and relationship with God, our intellect would not be overlooked. The apostle Paul contended that our transformation as Christians depends on whether our minds are engaged in an ongoing process of renewal in light of Christ (Rom 12:2–3).

This is all the more reason to be stunned by the words of Harry Blamires, a student of C. S. Lewis at Oxford, who claimed that "there is no longer a Christian mind." A Christian ethic, a Christian practice, a Christian spirituality, yes—but not a Christian mind (*The Christian Mind: How Should a Christian Think?*, 3). More recently, historian Mark Noll concurred, suggesting that the scandal of the evangelical mind is that there is not much of an evangelical mind. "If evangelicals do not take seriously the larger world of the intellect, we say, in effect, that we want our minds to be shaped by the conventions of our modern universities and the assumptions of Madison Avenue, instead of by God and the servants of God" (*The Scandal of the Evangelical Mind*, 34).

Even if we do not lose our own minds, we will certainly lose the minds of others. This is the double-edged threat of our day; apart from developing and thinking with a Christian mind-set, we will either be taken captive by the myriad of worldviews contending for our attention, or we will fail to make the Christian voice heard and considered above the din. Either we begin to think, or we lose the fight.

It is essential to develop our minds in light of a biblical worldview that is then used to think Christianly about the world. From this we will be able to respond to the culture in which we live, and we will be better equipped to help the culture respond to the Christ we follow. This was the clarion call of the apostle Paul, who reminded the Corinthian church that "we do not wage war according to the flesh, since the weapons of our warfare are not of the flesh, . . . We demolish arguments and every proud thing that is raised up against the knowledge of God, as we take every thought captive to obey Christ" (2 Cor 10:3–5).

BIBLICAL FORMATION

Jason K. Allen

Scripture repeatedly emphasizes the spiritual status of the human heart. As the prophet Nathan observed, "Humans see what is visible, but the LORD sees the heart" (1 Sam 16:7). Jesus likened the Pharisees to whitewashed tombs, "which appear beautiful on the outside, but inside are full of the bones of the dead and every kind of impurity" (Matt 23:27). He also rebuked the church at Ephesus because their love—or hearts—had grown cold (Rev 2:1–7).

Every authentic conversion to Christ entails a change of heart, leading to a change of life. The Holy Spirit convicts of sin, calls the individual to Christ, orchestrates the new birth, and indwells the new believer. From that point onward, the Holy Spirit empowers the believer, facilitating maturity in Christ.

Though conversion and sanctification result only by God's grace, humans are responsible to believe in Christ and pursue Christlikeness. Moreover, the Christian is absolutely responsible for his growth in Christ yet entirely dependent on the power of the Holy Spirit to foster such growth. This duality, one of the great paradoxes of the Christian life, is captured in Paul's exhortation to "work out [our] own salvation with fear and trembling. For it is God who is working in [us] both to will and to work according to his good purpose" (Phil 2:12–13).

Thankfully, Holy Scripture reveals the key component, humanly speaking, for Christian growth: "[T]rain yourself in godliness" (1 Tim 4:7). This admonition is one of the most overlooked, yet profound, verses in the entire Bible. It encapsulates the key ingredient for a vibrant, joy-filled Christian life—practicing the spiritual disciplines.

The word *discipline* is commonly associated with punitive action or a laborious, unpleasant task, yet Paul commends it to be practiced. The term itself implies the Christian life is not a passive experience. Growth in Christ is an active endeavor—carried out on an active, dynamic footing. To this end, believers throughout the centuries have practiced the spiritual disciplines to facilitate godliness and engender Christian growth.

In *Spiritual Disciplines for the Christian Life*, Donald Whitney defines *spiritual disciplines* as "those personal and congregational exercises, habits or practices that promote spiritual growth. They are the habits of devotion and experiential Christianity that have been practiced by Christians since biblical times" (*Spiritual Disciplines*, 17). Such spiritual disciplines include Bible intake, prayer, worship, fasting, evangelism, giving, serving, and silence and solitude.

While all the spiritual disciplines are commended, Bible intake is the most foundational and most urgent. It is the indispensable discipline because it informs, fosters, and enables the other disciplines. For example, the Bible teaches one how to intercede, thus informing the discipline of prayer. The Bible presents the person and work of Christ, thus informing evangelism. The Bible is the Word of God, thus enabling worship through the reading and preaching of it. Likewise, the Bible similarly informs, fosters, and enables each of the spiritual disciplines, giving it a singular status.

The preeminence of Bible intake is rooted in the nature and status of Scripture itself. God chose to reveal himself to his people through his Word. God likens his Word to "a hammer that pulverizes rock" (Jer 23:29); it "will not return to [him] empty" (Isa 55:11). Moreover, the Bible makes binding, theological claims of itself, declaring, "All Scripture is inspired by God and is profitable for teaching, for rebuking, for correcting, for training in righteousness" (2 Tim 3:16).

Evangelical Christians embrace the verbal, plenary inspiration of Scripture. The word *plenary* emphasizes the totality of Scripture, and *verbal* underscores that the words themselves—not merely the authors' words or their thoughts—are inspired by God. Since all of Scripture is inspired of God, Scripture is true, trustworthy, and authoritative. As the Reformers reasoned, the voice of Scripture is the voice of God.

Bible intake, though singular in importance, is received through multiple conduits. Hearing the Bible is the most basic and common form of

Scripture intake. It occurs when one sits under the ministry of the Word, whether preached or taught, received in person or through other mediums. Jesus pronounced blessing on those who hear the Word of God and obey it (Luke 11:28), and Paul assigned the "public reading" of Scripture as an indispensable part of public worship to ensure God's people heard God's Word (1 Tim 4:13).

Reading the Bible at the personal level is perhaps the most essential form of Bible intake. For the Christian, nothing should displace daily Bible reading. This includes both the macro-level of reading through books of the Bible and the micro-level of reading passages and verses repeatedly for greater familiarization, deeper reflection, and specific application.

Studying the Bible gives the Christian depth and strengthens his knowledge of God, thus enabling him to more ably teach and defend the faith. Every believer is called to be like the Bereans, searching the Scriptures and weighing teachers and doctrines by them (Acts 17:10–12). Such is expected of a disciple—or learner—of Christ, and the most faithful disciple will "be diligent to present [himself] to God as one approved, a worker who doesn't need to be ashamed, correctly teaching the word of truth" (2 Tim 2:15).

Memorizing the Bible is another proven method of Scripture intake. In so doing, one hides God's Word in his heart, so as not to sin against him (Ps 119:11). Moreover, it follows the pattern of the Bible itself. Whether it is Jesus quoting the Scriptures to Satan, or Paul reasoning from the OT to his Jewish interlocutors, the Bible prioritizes treasuring God's Word in our hearts so that we may not sin against him.

Meditating on the Bible sounds like a mystic practice to some, but it is a biblical concept and a distinctly Christian activity. In fact, God links meditating on his Word with obedience and blessing (Josh 1:8; Ps 1:1–3). Meditating on God's Word is as simple as intentionally reflecting on a passage of Scripture, directly applying its truth to your life, and letting it settle in your heart. Time devoted to lingering over Scripture is time well spent, as it fosters the knowledge of God and enables the living and active Word of God to convict of sin and inform the conscience (Heb 4:12).

Praying through the Bible flows naturally from Scripture meditation. Giants of the faith such as Martin Luther, Charles Spurgeon, and especially George Mueller made a habit of praying through Scripture. The Psalms especially lend themselves to prayer. In the Psalter, one finds the full range of human emotion, gaining a panoramic view of God's work and encountering the full pallet of biblical truth. Additionally, praying the Scriptures helps assure that one's prayers are biblically sound and pleasing to God.

Though the Western world is largely Bible saturated, many professing Christians in the West live Bible-depleted lives. This is a tragic irony, though it is not perplexing. The answer to the problem is not hidden, neither is it difficult to understand. Christians are called to be people of the book—the Bible—and therefore must prioritize the spiritual discipline of Bible intake. Failing to do this leads to diminished spiritual maturity.

Not everyone can preach a sermon, lead a Bible study, or persuasively advocate for biblical truth, but every believer can engage in Bible intake. In fact, never in the history of Christendom has Bible intake been more accessible. Proliferating translations, electronic and print versions of the Bible, media ministries, podcasts, and the incalculable power of the Internet have brought God's Word nearer.

Why practice the spiritual disciplines? They facilitate abiding in Christ, leading to joy and spiritual growth. They help guard the believer against pharisaical attitudes, the condition of patent hypocrisy that Jesus condemned. They engender fruit bearing, which glorifies God, strengthens one's assurance of salvation, and radiates the gospel of Christ. Therefore, practice the spiritual disciplines—especially Bible intake—and fulfill Paul's charge to "train yourself in godliness"(1 Tim 4:7).

PREACHING AND TEACHING A CHRISTIAN WORLDVIEW

Michael Duduit

Craig Bartholomew and Michael Goheen define *worldview* as "an articulation of the basic beliefs embedded in a shared grand story that are rooted in a faith commitment and that give shape and direction to the whole of our individual and corporate lives" *(Living at the Crossroads,* 23). Worldviews answer perennial human questions like these: Where did we come from? What's gone wrong with the world, and how do we fix it? How should we live our lives?

The shaping of a Christian worldview is a lengthy process that blends a host of influences from one's family background and education to cultural and media influences and, most importantly, to the work of Scripture and the Holy Spirit in the individual heart. Worldviews are not overnight creations. So how, then, do we go about preaching and teaching the Christian worldview to others?

Be rooted in Scripture.

The Christian worldview is rooted in the Word of God. To "think Christianly" requires that one have a grasp of and commitment to biblical truth. Thus, it is essential that any preaching and teaching which seeks to communicate a Christian worldview must be solidly based on the teachings of Scripture.

This practice requires not only a dedication to biblical truth but also an understanding of valid hermeneutical principles so that we can be sure that what is being taught is itself faithful to the authentic meaning of Scripture. We want to teach and preach what God is actually saying to us

411

in his Word, and that means we must be able to "rightly [divide] the word of truth" (2 Tim 2:15 KJV).

This means the effective biblical preacher and teacher will have an understanding of various biblical genres and how they will require varying interpretive approaches. For example, teaching principles that emerge from Pauline texts will typically require a more literal approach, while preaching from poetic texts will require an understanding of the more symbolic and image-filled nature of those texts. We can create great distress and confusion when we seek to turn a metaphor into a doctrine.

The effective interpreter will also need to be a faithful exegete so that he is accurately presenting the truth of God's Word. This involves some awareness of biblical languages and historical background. For example, in 1 Corinthians 8 Paul warns believers about eating meat that has been sacrificed to idols, lest doing so lead new believers astray. If one interprets this as simply a prescription about the use of meat sacrificed to idols, then it has little relationship to twenty-first-century believers in the West, where we are unlikely to find such a section in the meat department at the local grocery store. If, however, this text is dealing with a more significant principle—that of conscience and how to relate to other believers who abstain from certain practices because of conscience—then this is a text that has an important message for contemporary Christians.

Be aware of culture.

The effective teaching of a Christian worldview requires a solid foundation in Scripture, but that is only part of the story. To use John Stott's image of preaching, we must also be able to build a bridge that connects the biblical world to the contemporary one. Such a bridge requires that we understand the world in which our listeners live so that we can engage them within their own context.

Thus, preaching and teaching a Christian worldview not only requires a grasp of the biblical truth that shapes such a worldview but an awareness of the contemporary culture in which our listeners live and work. That does not mean simply attacking popular culture; it means understanding the trends and events that contribute to shaping that culture. In a sense, we must learn the language of a culture if we are to communicate with those who reside within it.

Christian leaders need not immerse themselves in the negative elements of contemporary culture in order to address that world. For example, we need not watch pornography in order to understand its dangers. But those who wish to engage culture must at least be conversant with that culture through reading, study, and observation. In addition to reading the secular press, the Christian should also take advantage of excellent faith-based resources in the form of websites, periodicals, and books in order to better understand and interpret contemporary cultural influences from a Christ-centered perspective.

Be focused on application.

Haddon Robinson explains that "in application, we attempt to take what we believe is the truth of the eternal God, given in a particular time, place and situation, and apply it to people in the modern world, who live in another time, another place, and a very different situation." Through providing practical and godly counsel, we teach others to apply God's Word to daily life.

Making such application often will involve drawing general principles from the specific details of biblical texts, and that requires identifying the timeless truth that connects the ancient text with the contemporary situation. It is easy to connect "then" and "now" with certain texts, but many other texts require additional work if we are to find a point of connection between the biblical context and the world in which our listeners live. For these, we work with a ladder of abstraction that connects the two worlds. Visualize a ladder that has several spans, going to different places depending on what level you step on. We will select the level that will connect our text with the reality of our own time and culture. As we climb that ladder, we want to make sure the biblical and contemporary situations are truly similar, or comparable, at the points at which we are connecting them.

Though making application often involves offering real-life examples of putting a text into practice, there is danger at this point. It is possible for us, in the process of offering such application, to give the impression that our specific suggestions about ways to live out a text carry the force of Scripture. They do not, and we must be careful to avoid falling into the trap of legalism when we do application.

It is important to remember to keep the theological and practical elements linked. We want to share vital theological truths with listeners, but we don't want to leave them thinking that such truths are abstract ideas with no practical application; therefore, we must show them the implications of such theological ideas for their lives. Likewise, even as we talk about the practical acts of obedience and service God requires, we should work to keep that linked to theological truth—we serve and obey because of who God is and because of what he has already done for us. His grace saves us, not our acts of obedience.

If we don't keep the practical solidly linked to the theological, the result may foster a self-righteousness that depends on actions rather than God's grace. This is a danger when our sermons become so lifestyle oriented ("don't smoke, drink, chew, or go with girls that do"), that listeners lose sight of the fact that we are saved by grace—a message that must be front and center. Nevertheless, since grace does not make obedience optional, we must find a balance in our preaching and teaching to properly present both elements of biblical truth.

As we apply biblical truth in conversations and from the pulpit, we give our listeners handles by which they can grasp the implications of those truths and see how to put them into action as they live out their Christian lives in their work, family, and worship.

ETHICS OF PERSONAL EVANGELISM

Thom S. Rainer

Stereotypes of personal evangelism abound. The caricature of a Christian cornering an unbeliever until he relents and repents fits the image of many of those looking at the matter from the outside. Rarely, however, do Christian pastors, leaders, and scholars present the ethical mandate of personal evangelism. Telling people the good news about who Jesus is and what he came to accomplish is not something we merely should do. It is something we must do.

Biblical texts teach us about the ethics of personal evangelism in three broad categories. First, evangelism is mandated in Scripture; this requires an ethical response. Second, we have an ethical relationship that must be forged with unbelievers. Third, there is the ethical reality of an eternal destiny that precludes our silence.

The Ethical Response

A key component of any ethical system is a proper response to those whom we have pledged our obedience and faithfulness. A husband, for example, pledges fidelity and faithfulness toward his wife. That ethical statement is typically made in the presence of God, his bride, and witnesses present. The exchanging of vows is both a joyous moment and a solemn one. And it is no coincidence that if the husband breaks the vow, he is deemed "unfaithful." He has broken the ethical promise through an unethical response.

Christians, both explicitly and implicitly, make vows or promises to God. If he commands us to do something, our only ethical response is obedience. Any other response is unethical or is, like the wayward husband's actions, unfaithful.

Most Christians know that God through Jesus Christ gave us the Great Commission to share the gospel. The most commonly used example is Matthew 28:19: "Go, therefore, and make disciples of all nations, baptizing them in the name of the Father and of the Son and of the Holy Spirit." Acts 1:8 is yet another common example: "But you will receive power when the Holy Spirit has come on you, and you will be my witnesses in Jerusalem, in all Judea and Samaria, and to the end of the earth."

The mandates for personal evangelism are not limited to the better-known biblical texts, however. To the contrary, the mandate was so infused in the lives of the early believers that they could not imagine ignoring it. The disciples Peter and John were commanded by the Sanhedrin to cease speaking about Christ and the gospel. Yet facing further imprisonment and perhaps even more horrific punishment, the two followers responded to the august body with their ethical decision on whether to obey the mandate of the Sanhedrin or the mandate of Christ. Their response is recorded in Acts 4:19–20: "Whether it's right in the sight of God for us to listen to you rather than to God, you decide; for we are unable to stop speaking about what we have seen and heard."

The ethical dilemma was resolved. The ethical response was obedience to God.

The Ethical Relationship

Much of Scripture is infused with directions on our relationships with God and with others. Pastors and theologians often refer to the two as the vertical relationship and the horizontal relationship respectively. Perhaps no single verse of the Bible embodies this truth as well as that which is commonly called the Great Commandment:

> One of them, an expert in the law, asked a question to test him: "Teacher, which command in the law is the greatest?" He said to him, "Love the Lord your God with all your heart, with all your soul, and with all your mind. This is the greatest and most important command. The second is like it: Love your neighbor as yourself. All the Law and the Prophets depend on these two commands" (Matt 22:35–40).

The horizontal relationship is thus second only to the vertical relationship a Christian has with God. The clear ethical response to this command becomes an ethical relationship with others. What does it mean, therefore, to love our neighbors as ourselves? On the one hand, we should certainly demonstrate concern and care for their physical and emotional needs. Though the responsibility of social ministry has been abdicated by many Christians to government agencies and other organizations, it is—biblically speaking—first the responsibility of believers and the churches to which they belong.

Even more, however, Christians have been commanded to be concerned about the eternal state of others. That need far outweighs any of the physical and emotional needs people may have. Jesus made that reality abundantly clear: "For what does it benefit someone to gain the whole world and yet lose his life?" (Mark 8:36). The struggles of this life are but a blip in the scope of eternity.

The greatest way for Christians to demonstrate obedience to the second portion of the great commandment is to declare the availability of God's love through Jesus Christ. We cannot truly say we love others until we enter into that ethical relationship, a relationship in which we proclaim the gospel to others in word and deed. The great commandment demands an ethical relationship where we are intentionally and unashamedly personally evangelistic to those who are not believers.

The Ethical Reality

Perhaps the following illustration regarding the necessity of personal evangelism is trite and overplayed, but it still resonates. Imagine a small child skating on thin ice in winter. As you walk by, you see and hear the horror of breaking ice and watch the child teeter slowly toward an icy death in the water. The child reaches out for you to grab her. You have the means to do so. You have the opportunity to do so. You have the strength to do so. The only question is whether you will choose to do so.

Of course, most will respond that they will eagerly and willingly do whatever it takes to save the child in such a scenario. So let us take the same principle and apply it to the eternal reality of hell for those who do not place their trust in salvation through Christ.

If we know of persons who are not Christians, we are confronted with the ethical reality of their destinies. That means we must choose whether we will take the time and face the possible awkwardness of sharing the gospel.

The good news of Christ, of course, includes such biblical realities as forgiveness, adoption, reconciliation, regeneration, and many others. But the gospel also includes the reality of heaven and hell and the ethical reality that there is only one way to heaven. Jesus left no doubt as to the exclusivity of salvation through him: "Jesus [said], 'I am the way, the truth, and the life. No one comes to the Father except through me'" (John 14:6).

So the Christian is no longer dealing with a hypothetical story of a child falling into icy waters. He is now confronted with the ethical reality of a literal heaven, a literal hell, and the narrow way to the former.

The unavoidable question is thus basic but profound: Will we be obedient to Christ? As we would all reach for the dying child, will we reach out to those who do not know Jesus? Our response will determine whether we are faithful or unfaithful to his calling on our lives.

SPIRITUAL WARFARE

Charles E. Lawless

Spiritual warfare is a reality. From Genesis to Revelation, the Scriptures paint a picture of a cosmic battle that is largely unseen. Satan is, in fact, the "roaring lion, looking for anyone he can devour" (1 Pet 5:8). Our enemy is an accuser (Rev 12:10), a deceiver (Rev 20:10), a murderer and a liar (John 8:44). He is the "ruler of this world" (John 12:31), the "dragon" who dares to fight against the angels of God (Rev 12:7).

As believers, we wrestle against principalities and powers (Eph 6:12) that work to lure us into sin. The powers disguise themselves as "angels of light," seeking to infiltrate the church through false teachings (2 Cor 11:1–15). The enemy seeks to steal, kill, and destroy (John 10:10). Satan is not, however, the focus of the Bible—God is.

Indeed, God put in place the enmity between the seed of the woman and the seed of the serpent that would lead to the enemy's defeat at Christ's cross (Gen 3:15). God is the warrior who led his people across the Red Sea (Exod 15:3). David fought the Philistine giant, not with a sword and a javelin but in the name of the Lord whose battle it was (1 Sam 17:45–47). Jahaziel likewise assured Jehoshaphat of God's presence in the midst of battle by saying, "Do not be afraid or discouraged because of this vast number, for the battle is not yours, but God's" (2 Chr 20:15).

Moreover, Paul challenged believers to put on God's armor, not human armor (Eph 6:11). God is our shield (Gen 15:1; Ps 28:7), and he wears righteousness as body armor and the helmet of salvation (Isa 59:17). This sovereign God even allows spiritual battles to take place in our lives in order to accomplish the greater good of his will (see Job 1–2).

Because the Bible's story is about the One who will ultimately cast the devil into the lake of fire (Rev 20:10), our task as spiritual warriors is not to know Satan well; it is to know God so intimately that Satan's counterfeit becomes obvious by comparison. To know God and to recognize his sovereignty is to understand that we gain spiritual victory only through Christ, who has been raised above every power and authority (Eph 1:20–23).

Victory in Spiritual Warfare

Believers need not fear the enemy, for we have the sword of the Spirit, the Word of God, as a primary weapon in battle (Eph 6:17). The Word reminds us that Satan has been disarmed by the cross of Christ (Col 2:15), his power is limited by the will of Almighty God (Job 1:10–12), and he will ultimately be bound (Rev 20:10). Like Jesus in the wilderness temptations, we can defeat our enemy through confidence in the Word (Matt 4:1–11).

Our victory is anchored in the central story of the Scriptures: the event of the cross. Jesus took on himself the sin of the world, paid the penalty for that sin, and conquered death (2 Cor 5:21; 1 John 2:2). He ultimately broke Satan's power by his obedience "to the point of death—even to death on a cross" (Phil 2:8). Through his shed blood Christ has redeemed us (Eph 1:7) and placed us on the winning side of this spiritual battle. Indeed, we are on the offensive, daily living out the triumph of the cross.

The world sees our victory in spiritual warfare not by our strategies and techniques but by our walking in truth and righteousness. The defeat of the enemy is consequently evident by how we live. And, for many believers who face persecution today, the enemy's defeat will also be seen by how they die. What surely seems a loss from a human perspective will instead be an announcement of mighty victory in heaven.

Cautions in Spiritual Warfare

Interest in the topic of spiritual warfare today has, however, often resulted in faulty understandings of warfare strategies. For example, some "warfare" writers and practitioners emphasize demonic exorcism as a primary tactic. Scholars debate whether demon possession occurs today, but it is difficult to prove that possession never occurs—especially when considering frontier mission fields in animistic cultures. Nevertheless, the Bible does not present exorcism as a chief ministry strategy. Jesus exorcised demons, yet he did so in the context of preaching and teaching ministry (see, e.g., Mark 1:21–28). He did not adopt elaborate exorcism rituals common in his day, nor did he go demon hunting.

Jesus's approaches to exorcism were, in fact, varied. Often he spoke to the demon (e.g., Luke 8:29) but not always (Luke 13:10–17). He was not always physically present with the demon-possessed person (Matt 15:22–28). Only once is there evidence that he asked the name of a demon (Mark 5:9), and that was not to gain authority over the evil spirit. "Rebuking" language is common (e.g., Luke 4:35; 9:42) but not universal. Nowhere in the Bible is there a clear, reproducible exorcism ritual; thus, teaching such a pattern is biblically unwarranted.

Equally problematic are the implications that there are particular symptoms of possession and specific steps in exorcisms; again, such conclusions are not evident in Scripture. Demonic manifestations included, among other things, physical symptoms (e.g., Matt 9:32–33; 12:22), self-inflicted wounds (Mark 5:5), falling (Mark 9:18), and supernatural strength (Mark 5:3–4). Such diverse descriptions, however, are just that: descriptions rather than expectations.

Further, some "exorcists" assert that demons can possess believers. This conclusion is biblically indefensible. The Scriptures teach that believers are indwelt by and sealed by the Spirit of God (2 Cor 1:22; Eph 1:14), and the One in us is more powerful than the one that rules the world (1 John 4:4). The Scriptures contain no example of a demon-possessed believer.

Others affirm the existence of "territorial spirits," or demonic beings that inhabit or reside over a region. Some warfare practitioners teach that we must cast down these demons before effectively doing evangelism in an area. The biblical evidence for such demons is weak at best (e.g., Dan 10:1–14), and nowhere is there a mandate for identifying or "praying down" these powers. A process of aggressively attacking territorial demons implies that the air must be cleared before the gospel can be effective. The implication is thus that the word of the cross as "the power of God" (1 Cor 1:18) apparently needs help in some situations. Such an implication demeans the power of the Word.

Christians and the Armor of God

How, then, should we respond to the issue of spiritual warfare? We must first recognize its reality. Even those who believe exorcisms are unwarranted cannot deny the continued reality of spiritual warfare. The enemy still seeks to destroy God's people, and to deny that is to invite defeat.

Second, we must proclaim the Word of God. Potent and life changing, the message of the cross frees the blinded minds of the unbelieving (2 Cor 4:3–4) and equips believers for good works (2 Tim 3:16–17). The proclamation of the Word is, in fact, an act of warfare against Satan's kingdom. It is no wonder, then, that the enemy so viciously strikes those who stand on the Scriptures—the very Word that promises us victory even in death (Heb 2:14–15).

Third, we must teach believers how to put on the full armor of God and resist the enemy (Eph 6:11; Jas 4:7). Putting on the armor is about learning to walk in truth, righteousness, and faith. It is about reading and proclaiming the Word of God while standing firmly on the gospel. When our strategies for discipleship—a fundamental element of spiritual warfare preparation—are weak, we send new believers into a lethal context unarmed. Defeat is then almost inevitable.

As followers of Christ, we are to wear the full armor of God, proclaim the gospel to unbelievers, and disciple believers. Taking on the enemy is not about a formula or a technique. It is about a lifestyle—a Bible-saturated, God-centered, Jesus-glorifying, Spirit-filled, prayer-driven lifestyle.

THE GOSPEL AND SOCIAL MINISTRY

Mary Anne Poe

Social ministry is generally defined by its aim to provide assistance to those with physical or social needs, whether in the form of food, shelter, emotional or mental health care, family life support, and advocacy for social justice. The Scriptures and church tradition point to the centrality of social ministry as evidence of the power of the gospel at work in human lives. While the church throughout its history has debated about and vacillated between an emphasis on social ministry or an emphasis on preaching and evangelism, Jesus's teaching and his works of service suggest that both preaching and social ministries are central to the gospel. What Jesus taught, what Jesus did, and the tradition of the church attest to what has become known as the integral mission of the church.

Jesus and Social Ministry

The bookends of Jesus's teaching frame the importance and centrality of social ministry in the gospel. Jesus announced his mission at the inauguration of his public ministry in the synagogue through a reading from the prophet Isaiah: "The Spirit of the Lord is on me, because he has anointed me to preach good news to the poor. He has sent me to proclaim release to the captives and recovery of sight to the blind, to set free the oppressed, to proclaim the year of the Lord's favor" (Luke 4:18–19).

By using this text, Jesus asserted that God's purpose through Christ is wholeness and healing in body, soul, and spirit through the coming kingdom of God. Jesus announced that because of his coming the poor will be blessed, the blind will see, the lame will walk, and relationships will be restored. The worldwide impact of Jesus's coming was not only the promise of a future spiritual kingdom but an effect on the present realities of the broken human condition. Jesus said that if his followers would believe in him, even greater things would be done (John 14:12).

At the conclusion of Jesus's earthly ministry and just prior to ascending into heaven, Jesus instructed the disciples about what their mission, and the mission of all future disciples, was to be: "Go, therefore, and make disciples of all nations, baptizing them in the name of the Father and of the Son and of the Holy Spirit, teaching them to observe everything I have commanded you" (Matt 28:19–20).

Being a follower of Christ means we should do what Jesus did, commit to his purpose, and invite others to join us in observing what he taught. Following Jesus is costly and strenuous. His teaching was unambiguous as he drew a distinction between true discipleship and simple assent to a religious teaching. The gospel Jesus proclaimed from beginning to end addressed the concrete realities of the present world as well as the spiritual hope for all eternity.

Jesus teaches us to pay careful attention to all aspects of our social relationships. The Sermon on the Mount speaks to a wide range of social issues: forgiveness, anger, broken relationships, divorce, truthfulness, responses to evil, love for friends and enemies, almsgiving, use of wealth, anxiety, and social justice. All of these issues can be addressed through social ministries offered through the church or other faith-based organizations.

Much of Jesus's teaching came in the form of stories or parables that direct our attention to the fact that God cares about the everyday matters of human existence. They speak to spiritual wholeness and faithfulness, but they also concern themselves with various challenges of human relationships in the present world. Jesus describes his kingdom as a place where justice and righteousness prevail: good seed bears fruit; lost sheep, coins, and sons are restored; faithful stewardship is compensated; issues of wealth and poverty are explored; labor practices are examined; and helping the downtrodden is rewarded. The examples Jesus gave of what the kingdom would be like are not mere abstractions but concrete ways he is calling us to live. Social ministries help the church to address the concerns of human relationships in practical and tangible ways.

The example of Jesus's life and ministry reinforces the teachings of Jesus and demonstrates the significance of social ministry as a central aspect of the gospel. What Jesus did with his time and energy emphasized engagement with people, especially those who lived on the margins of society. Jesus experienced the hardships of homelessness, alienation, hunger, betrayal, and physical pain. This allowed him to be a sympathetic Savior (Heb 4:15).

The first-century world was amazed by what Jesus did. His public ministry focused on healing the sick, feeding the hungry, reconciling outcasts to the community, loving the poor, challenging the wealthy, touching the leprous, condemning religious hypocrites, eating with prostitutes and tax collectors, confronting the powerful, and restoring mental health. He defied societal and cultural structures and belief systems that created oppressive conditions. Simple conversations with people, such as the Samaritan woman, tax collectors, those with leprosy, and children violated cultural norms and aroused the antipathy of those who would keep oppressive systems in place.

Clearly, Jesus's expectations for his followers included acts of kindness, advocacy for social justice, and demolition of social barriers that marginalized groups of people. His invitation to the disciples was to do what he did, to follow him, in demonstrating the love and mercy of God—especially to people who might not otherwise experience a compassionate and hospitable world. His miraculous works served to show the consistency with his character and message confirming his teachings by meeting concrete human needs as well as bearing witness to his deity. Jesus taught that those who will be invited to inherit the kingdom are those who have demonstrated the same character and message by engaging in social ministries like feeding the hungry, visiting the prisoners, and offering hospitality to strangers (Matt 25:31–46).

The Early Church and Social Ministry

The church was notable from its inception for the radical nature of her social relationships and ministry. In Acts 2 and 4, Luke, with a sense of awe, highlights the nature of the church as a place of continual fellowship, teaching, and prayer. Participants were inspired to sell property and possessions and share with all so no one had need of anything. The resurrection of Jesus and the coming of the Holy Spirit on the church allowed the work and ministry of Jesus to continue through the lives of those who believed. The social ministry of the church in the early centuries drew attention to the transformative power of the gospel to shape relationships among people. Rather than an entirely spiritualized, otherworldly religion, the Christian faith promised eternal life that changed how people lived in the present.

The church in its earliest history became known for its array of social ministries to care for the poor, the ill, and outcasts. The Cappadocian Fathers established the first institutions of social ministry. Hospitals and other refuges provided care for those who suffered while simultaneously offering the presence and power of God for all eternity through their teaching and preaching. In the centuries following, Christians have been noted for establishing orphanages, schools, hospitals, and refuges as well as advocating for social justice for those who are oppressed.

In the twentieth century, Dietrich Bonhoeffer asserted that one cannot understand and preach the gospel concretely enough. He gave his life in the battle against the oppression of the Nazi regime much like other Christians in other times and places have done to advance the cause of the gospel in the face of social injustice. Present-day followers of Christ continue to provide leadership in all kinds of social ministry as churches and faith-based organizations around the world fight poverty and injustice in myriad ways as part of the compelling mission and message of the gospel.

Conclusion

Social ministry is not an addendum to the traditional evangelistic mission of the church. It reflects the character and purpose of God to establish justice and righteousness. Jesus considered the concrete, physical realities of this world so important that he entered into it and spent his time healing the suffering. Physical conditions did matter to Jesus—the purpose of the gospel was to break the power of suffering and to bring healing and reconciliation to all aspects of human brokenness. Jesus came for those who need help. Social ministry affords an opportunity to embrace the whole gospel and the mission of Jesus himself as announced in Luke 4.

LEADERSHIP AND BIBLICAL ETHICS

Benjamin P. Dockery

Leadership always has a moral component. Everyone knows leaders should get things done. They should be efficient and effective in their ability to accomplish tasks with and through other people. Leaders carry influence for good or ill, and effective leaders should ask good questions to set and implement their vision. This does not mean, however, that they always ask the rudimentary moral question, what ought we to do? The Christian vision for life, rooted in the gospel, infuses a life-giving ethical framework into the heart and mind of the leader.

A Leader's Ethical Foundation: Scripture

How should we ground ethical judgments in an ever-changing realm of moral opinion? The Christian leader relies on the Bible as the Word of God and the only sufficient and authoritative rule of all saving knowledge, faith, and obedience. God alone determines and judges what is good or evil (Rom 2:1-5). Leaders will be tempted to judge God, the Creator of everything, by a standard of morality they conceive to fit their particular situations. Instead, Christian leaders should be reminded that God at Sinai gave the Israelites his gracious words in the Ten Commandments and placed them in the book of the covenant (Exod 19–24). God's leader, Moses, reported the words of the Lord, and he preserved two tablets of testimony inscribed by the finger of God (Exod 31:18). God's word, delivered to his people, led to life and flourishing. This set a pattern. God's full instruction revealed in the Scriptures is the unchanging ethical foundation for Christian leaders.

A Leader's Ethical Task: Leadership

A Christian leader's task is to lead in the sphere of influence God has given him. Leadership is a gift granted to some believers according to the grace God has given different members of the body (Rom 12:8). Those called to lead ought to steward the gift they have received. When stewardship becomes the guiding perspective on leadership, the conversation is framed as delegated authority and not as earned authority. This buoys those in authority from the common abuses of coercive rule on the one hand and abdication on the other. Furthermore, it reinforces Paul's admonition in the preceding verses not to think too highly of oneself (Rom 12:3). The result is a servant's posture of outdoing one another in showing honor (Rom 12:10) that is fueled by a drive to lead because God has entrusted his people with the gifts to lead.

A Leader's Ethical Framework: Worldview

It is simple to say that a leader should follow the Bible, but it is far from simple to implement a unified biblical approach to all of life's ultimate questions. The Bible provides a Christian worldview that helps us to construct a framework for distilling the specific ethical challenges that people and organizations face (Rom 12:2), but no good leader does this on his own. The Bible calls for wisdom to be formed amidst an abundance of counselors (Prov 11:14; Rom 12:4-9). Leaders should read widely from the Christian intellectual tradition as well as from current authors who address modern moral dilemmas. The Christian worldview is a community project, but the community has boundaries (Titus 1:10-16).

Christian leaders must do the hard work to identify the worldviews influencing their own assumptions. For example, power and might have determined what is ethically "right" in some cultures. Social hierarchy or tradition have also guided leaders to set direction and policy. In other cultures, the chief values tend to be aesthetic or creative considerations, and moral behaviors submit to so-called progressive ideas. Additionally, efficiency is a chief value in many capitalistic cultures, but it is not the only determinative question—and certainly not the fundamental question—for the Christian. Christian leaders are called to filter society's ethical norms through the grid of a Christian worldview in both the church and the marketplace. They should understand the stewardship to lead in accordance with divine revelation and help shape the moral fabric of society by affecting their realms of influence (Matt 5:13-16), whether in a small business, a large church, or an international corporation.

A Leader's Ethical Dilemma: Wisdom

Christian leaders are rarely asked to make moral judgments on issues about which there is already a consensus. Instead, they get involved in decisions when those they lead get stuck in the decision-making process or when something has gone considerably wrong. Thus, leadership can be a burden demanding tough decisions. Furthermore, many amoral decisions or strategies—such as whether to have two or three sales divisions—have unintended moral consequences that also require ethical leadership. When complexities arise, Christians with the best intentions can make the mistake of applying their worldview analysis too hastily. Often, the best way to begin untying the Gordian knot is by admitting, "I don't know." As Proverbs 9:10 states, "The fear of the LORD is the beginning of wisdom." Wisdom does not find its genesis in the thoughts of any man. God gives Christian leaders wisdom and graciously invites them to pray. He invites them to pray for more wisdom because he has unlimited resources and is not stingy (James 1:5-8). No leader will get it right every time, but James is clear that humility is the way through dilemmas, for God gives grace to the humble but resists the proud (James 4:6).

A Leader's Personal Ethic: Virtue

A pattern of wise and humble decision making, rooted in a biblical worldview, produces virtuous leaders. The Bible is not interested in an ethic that only applies to decisions outside the leader; instead, it implicates the leader's whole life. The Christian worldview leaves no room for exceptions when it comes to a leader's personal integrity (Prov 10:9; 2 Cor 8:21; Phil 4:8-9). Leaders don't get a pass or a moral exemption, even to accomplish a good outcome. Instead, the leaders of God's church are qualified primarily on the type of people they become (1 Tim 3:1-13; Titus 1:6-9; 1 Pet 5:1-8). Since leaders are often forced into instantaneous decision making and judgments, their reactions will stem from who they are when there is no time for deliberation or consultation. Leaders should daily seek to be transformed by putting off the old self and constantly being renewed to a true knowledge according to the image of Christ (Col 3:1-11). When the world, the flesh, and the devil attack, a Christian leader's true virtue is revealed. His ethic must operate from the virtues birthed from a new heart, mind, and new desires.

A Leader's Ethical Leader: Jesus Christ

A Christian worldview of leadership ethics must be centered on Christ. There is no other name by which we are reconciled to God and no other name by which Christian leaders lead. Jesus, not a moralistic or therapeutic deity, is the unapologetic banner over, under, and around the Christian leader. Christian leaders must seek to become great by obeying Jesus's call to serve, by becoming first by being last. "Last" does not seem like the position of a leader, but a servant's basin and towel do not seem like the tools of a leader either (John 13:1-5); nevertheless, Christ used them effectively. Jesus gave us a way of leading that descends, not climbs, to greatness. When answering the question—How ought we to lead?—Jesus provides a picture of leaving the comfort of heaven instead of gaining the comforts of earth (John 6:38). He calls Christians to lose their lives to save them (Luke 9:24). He demonstrated his teaching by loving those he led enough to make himself nothing and to lay down his life (Phil 2:5-11).

Conclusion

When surveying the confusing cultural milieu of the twenty-first century, we must remember that the Christ of the Christian worldview still demands a leader's soul, life, and all. Even the best Christian leaders will make blunders, but leaders still lead. They lead on the foundation of Scripture, through a worldview that aims to produce wise and virtuous people committed to the cruciform way of their leader, King Jesus.

THE WORSHIP AND SERVICE OF GOD

David S. Dockery

Worship, though primary in the life of the church, is often elusive and misunderstood, even among Christians. Worship is ascribing worth to God with our voices, our minds, and our hearts. It is the act of bringing glory to God—which, of course, may be and should be applied to all of life. More specifically, though, the word refers to the act and activity of praising and glorifying God when Christians assemble in a local congregation.

If, as Christians, we are truly concerned with ascribing to God the supreme worth that he alone is worthy to receive, we must be cautious about allowing our worship to be shaped by our own felt needs rather than by Scripture and a healthy appreciation for our Christian heritage. Believers must recognize that worship is the active response to God the Father through the Son. Praise, prayer, preaching, the celebration of ordinances, confession, and giving are all Christ-centered, scripturally informed actions. The focus of the church's worship on the exalted Christ gives a Spirit-enabled depth and content to a gathering. Fitting and acceptable worship, in fact, can only be offered by and through the enabling ministry of the Holy Spirit.

Christians need to be hesitant to acknowledge one form of worship to be inherently better than another, but they should always seek to ground authentic worship in the teachings of Scripture. Perhaps, taking Acts 2 as a guide, Christians should expect variety in their worship. In that passage, some emphasize formal celebration in the temple, and others prioritize informal gatherings in homes.

Genuine worship must include the proclamation of the whole counsel of God's Word (Acts 20:27) and the primacy of textually grounded preaching. The gospel message forms the center and shape of worship. With that recognition, worship services need to seek to touch lives while creating worship experiences that simultaneously exalt God and edify his people. Anything less fails to be faithful to the NT teaching and the early church's pattern.

When genuine worship takes place, the entire body of Christ is enhanced and built up; moreover, the mission, service, and outreach of local churches are strengthened. The people of God who have worshipped him and who have been mutually strengthened are prepared to enter the world to touch lives, meet needs, counsel hurts, speak to injustices, and both bear witness to and proclaim the saving message of the gospel. Exalting God and serving others are hardly in conflict, especially for Christians who seek to understand and live out the Christian faith in a coherent manner. As a matter of fact, authentic service is built on genuine worship (see Isa 6:1–8; Matt 28:16–20) and is focused on the church, the culture, and the world.

Church

The church was inaugurated at Pentecost (Acts 2) as God's new society (Eph 2:15). It was founded on the finished work of Christ (John 19:30) and the baptizing work of the Spirit (1 Cor 12:13). The church was a mystery (Eph 3:9–11), was prophesied about by Christ (Matt 16:18), and was revealed at the Spirit's coming at Pentecost. The church was built on the foundation of Christ's apostles, with Christ Jesus himself serving as its cornerstone (Eph 2:20–21).

The true church is more than a human organization; it is a visible and tangible expression of the people who are related to Christ. As far as is possible, all Christians should involve and invest themselves in the visible, organized church of Jesus Christ. God gifts his people in the church in order to prepare them for works of service so that they will be strengthened and prepared for faithful living and ministry. The Spirit of God uses gifted leaders in the church to help bring maturity to other Christ followers. They, in turn, will be able to proclaim Christ, admonishing and teaching others with great wisdom and engaging the culture and serving the world through both word and deed (Eph 4:11–13; Col 1:28).

Culture

Many people today reject the church and the Christian faith, not because they perceive it to be false but because they believe it is superficial or trivial. People are looking for an authentic and integrated way of seeing life that brings coherence to all of life's experiences—some of which are confusing. In many ways, our post-Christian Western culture in general—and American culture in particular—resembles the pre-Christian Athens of Paul's day (see Acts 17), particularly in its focus on the new, the novel, and the world of change as emphasized by the Epicureans. Our culture is similarly enthralled by novelty.

Truth and values in our culture seem to be of minimal concern or consequence. In the address by the apostle Paul in Acts 17, we find a model for how to lovingly and effectively combat such thinking. We learn how to engage culture in meaningful and relevant ways, as well as how to communicate and live this truth in an effective manner in the midst of an incredibly superficial world. The cultural trends that shape much of our society are similarly influenced by the rise of neopaganism and various and diverse forms of spirituality. Thus Paul is an insightful guide who enables thoughtful Christ followers to respond to this changing post-Christian world.

The World

Christians live in a world where English is the new common language in most discussions of globalization. The Spanish language, however, is the most frequently spoken tongue used by Christians around the world. We live in a context that points to the movement of the Christian base toward the Global South. Christ followers in the West, therefore, must be willing to defer to non-Western opinions and ideas whenever our most basic Christian convictions are not at stake. Western wealth and isolation have at times kept us from understanding the real issues of the Majority World and those in the unevangelized belt. Similarly, we must recognize the importance that social justice plays in helping us understand and carry out the mission of God. We need to engage in the serious work that seeks to connect theology, education, justice, and missions together as partners rather than competitors.

Many Christians, particularly younger believers, comprehend the importance of providing homes for the homeless and food for the hungry. They understand that they are to work for justice while simultaneously taking the good news of the gospel to new areas of the world. We must recognize that we now live in a globally connected context, with new faces representing the various contexts and cultures of our larger global family. We must recognize that what brings Christ followers together is not our homogeneous characteristics but our deep love for Jesus Christ. Our lives are to become an offering of thanks to Jesus. This is best expressed through compassion to the least of these in our world.

Christians should assume a posture of humility, listening to and learning from one another. The current climate of fear that characterizes the world around us will likely create a strong challenge, keeping many people from participating in new opportunities. A love for Jesus Christ and a desire to understand others will help counter this fear, launching exciting global opportunities for the days ahead. We should think not only about international opportunities but intercultural ones as well. The major cities across the United States now look as if the world has moved into these places.

Poverty, homelessness, drug abuse, and violence surround us. Our cities are multiethnic and intercultural. Christians, therefore, must grapple with our own insulation. We have the privilege of locally living out the global implications of our faith, joining with others to forge relevant ties for global service. We thus seek to know and exalt God, to think seriously and coherently about all aspects of life in order to serve others and to take the gospel to the ends of the earth. Let us not shy away from this task. Let us ask the Lord to raise up and develop a new generation of thoughtful, committed, convictional, and courageous Christ followers who will go forth in wisdom, humility, and confidence to serve the church, engage the culture, and disciple the nations for the glory of the triune God.

Christian Worldview and the Global Church

GOD'S PURPOSES IN A CHRISTIAN'S PARTICIPATION IN MISSIONS

Mike Barnett

Perhaps you've heard the story of the young William Carey? In 1792, this shoe cobbler and pastor of a small church in the midlands of England wrote an inquiry and made a plea for the pastors in his region to send missionaries into the world. Carey publicly challenged his senior colleagues to mobilize their churches to go and disciple the nations. One of the leading pastors in that assembly cut Carey off, by saying, "Young man, sit down! You are an enthusiast. When God pleases to convert the heathen, he'll do it without consulting you or me."

Today William Carey is known as the "father of modern missions." He led a movement that lasted over a hundred years and laid Christian foundations around the world. Yet, the older colleague's question reflected a dominant worldview that haunts the church to this day. How dare Carey think God needed or even wanted him to participate in his mission? Indeed, what kind of God needs people to carry out his work in the world?

God's Mission

Carey discovered the biblical worldview of the mission of God as he read his Bible. He was overwhelmed with the reality that God's mission was for "all the peoples on earth [to] be blessed" (Gen 12:3–4), that God would be renowned among *all* nations. This, in fact, is the theme of the Bible. It's the central agenda behind the church, the reason for Christianity.

But what did God mean when he said all peoples would be blessed? Over and over again in Scripture, God explained this blessing to Israel. He promised Israel that if they followed him, he would walk among them and be their God (Lev 26:12). Yet Israel never really understood this agenda. God delayed his wrath on Israel in order to be glorified (Isa 48:11), repeatedly reminding Israel that his mission for them was bigger than themselves. He said, "It is not enough for you to be my servant raising up the tribes of Jacob and restoring the protected ones of Israel. I will also make you a light for the nations, to be my salvation to the ends of the earth" (Isa 49:6). But the worldview of Israel's citizens was stuck because the people focused only on themselves. How ironic that God still used them to shine the light of Jesus the Messiah on the Gentiles.

Young Carey was right. He understood the true meaning of the good news about Jesus. God's greatest desire is to be known by all peoples, even the entire creation—including "the rulers and authorities in the heavens" (Eph 3:10). The most amazing thing about this mission of God is that he uses his followers, the church, to participate in and carry out the mission.

Like the ancient Israelites, Carey's generation was self-centered about God's mission. In their minds, God had finished his Great Commission by their day. The call of Jesus to disciple all nations was not for them. After all, they had enough of their own problems to deal with. Sending their best disciples to the ends of the earth to minister the gospel to the uncivilized "heathen" was not on their agenda. William Carey's worldview, by contrast, was transformed by the Bible. He captured God's agenda and the reality that we cannot opt out of serving in God's mission to the nations.

But do we share in this mission today? Or could it be that we too have adopted a self-centered version of a biblical worldview, like Israel and like Carey's colleagues? Have we replaced God's mission to be known and worshipped by his creation with a goal of making ourselves happy, successful, and fulfilled?

The Basics

What are the basics concerning God's mission? The root of the Latin term *missio* means "sending" or "to send." What begins in Gen 1 with God sending the Creator (John 1:3) and Spirit (Gen 1:1–2) continues throughout Scripture as one sending of God after another. God sends Abraham to Canaan to establish the nation of Israel (Gen 12). The OT is the story of God's mission through Israel that culminates with the sending of God himself through Immanuel—God with us (Isa 7:14; Matt 1:23). The NT is the story of Jesus establishing the church and the Holy Spirit sending the church on mission to the nations. In Revelation we see the mission accomplished on that final day when the Lamb of God is worshipped among all peoples. This is the mission of God—past, present, and future—as revealed in his Word. The Bible teaches us about God's mission and where we fit in it.

Whose mission is it? It is God's mission. He is the One who accomplishes the mission. The Bible is his revelation to us.

What is this mission of God? It is a blessing for all peoples. Revelation 5:9 indicates it is for "every tribe and language and people and nation." This is the "mystery" the apostle Paul speaks of frequently. The God of Abraham is the God of all peoples, of all creation (Eph 3:3–6,10)!

Why is this the mission of God? Because God desires to be . . . no, God *will* be worshipped and praised among all nations. God's name will be hallowed; he will be famous; his kingdom will come (Matt 6:9–10); and he will be glorified (Isa 48:11). The reason for the mission to all peoples is God's glory.

How does God accomplish his mission? God sends (e.g., Gen 1:27; 3:23,8–9; 11:8; 12:2; Exod 6:7). God loves by sending his Son (John 3:16). He compels us to love him (Matt 22:37–38). And he expects us to love one another (22:39). Yes, God's mission is all about God's love.

God's mission strategy is people to people. He is a relational God who works relationally, and we are created in his image. There is no place for the lone-ranger Christian in God's mission. From the beginning, it has been a people-to-people mission. God worked in the past through Abraham and his physical descendants (Gen 12:2–3); remarkably, he works in the present through Abraham's spiritual descendants (Gal 3:7,29; Eph 3:6)—the church (Eph 3:10)—and in the end he will continue to work through worshippers from all nations for eternity (Rev 7:9). God accomplishes his mission through people.

What is the primary task of this mission of God? Discipling. In the well-known commission text, Matthew 28:18–20, God directs us toward this task. We are to disciple all nations; that is, we are to teach all nations to become followers of Jesus. Right there in the same command he tells us how. Jesus says we enlist them into the community of faith by "teaching" and "baptizing them in the name of the Father and of the Son and of the Holy Spirit" (vv. 19–20). We introduce them to Jesus. We engage them into fellowship with Jesus. We proclaim the good news, the gospel, and they join us in following Jesus. But we do not stop there. We teach them not simply the teachings of Jesus but how to obey them. To wholeheartedly follow everything he commanded. This is the primary task of the mission of God. Teaching one another to obey.

How can we do this among *all* nations? By following God's plan, his strategy for multiplication. We can no longer simply rely on priests to serve in a single temple in Jerusalem or employ pastors to perform the ministry of established churches. We must equip all believers to do the work of the mission of God through the church. Yes, some will be called as equippers to train church members to do the mission (Eph 4:11–12); but all are called to be witnesses (Acts 1:8) and disciple makers (Matt 28:18–20).

The Biblical Worldview

God's Word from Genesis to Revelation is the story of God conducting his mission. It reveals a biblical worldview, God's worldview, of his mission and our role in it. When William Carey read the Bible in 1792, he could not escape the reality that God commands all believers to participate in his global mission. This is God's intent. It is not a sign of a weak God who needs us. It is the reality of a sovereign God who demands for us to serve alongside him. This is for his glory, not ours. Yes, we are blessed when we embrace this mission of God. He becomes our God, we become his people, and we serve his mission. It doesn't get any better than that.

WHAT IS GLOBALIZATION?

Choon Sam Fong

Globalization is not merely an abstract notion used by economic and political analysts to make hypothetical claims about the world today. It has profound effects on the man in the street. Consider these examples from everyday life:

- An American restaurant chain has become more popular (and profitable) outside the United States.
- The latest *American Idol* winner is a global phenomenon, as is the top UK boy band, as is the most popular K-pop star.
- When you get on a subway train, you regularly hear languages you cannot identify. You learn later that these languages originate from halfway around the world.
- Your child's classmates come from many different cultural or ethnic heritages; and they are not international students.
- When you have an Internet problem and you call your service provider, the call is attended to by someone at a call center in India or the Philippines. The call is either free or charged based on your local rates.

We are regularly reminded that the physical distances that separate people have shrunk, as though the world has been compressed. We also sense that changes are taking place much faster than before. Twenty years ago, the media spoke of a globalizing world. Today we speak of a globalized world.

What is globalization?

Globalization is a continuing movement in which economic, technological, political, and cultural trends interpenetrate on a worldwide scale, moving the world toward the reality of becoming connected at every level. It is not an entirely new phenomenon. In the past, people living under a far-reaching governing authority such as the Roman Empire quickly developed a transnational mind-set and traded with people who lived far beyond their borders. What is new today is the scale and speed of globalization.

The acceleration of globalizing tendencies became evident in the 1980s when several phenomena happened concurrently: the burgeoning of international trade, mass migration of people from poorer to richer nations, and rapid improvements in communication technology—especially the beginning of the widespread use of the Internet. These soon converged with other worldwide trends such as the deregulation of international trade and developmental efforts aimed at reducing the inequality gap between rich and poor nations.

These powerful movements have created a world in which political or geographical borders have much less impact on how people live and think. Traditional boundaries that separate countries and continents are becoming less meaningful. Although immigration authorities can still prevent a person from crossing into another country, the exchange of ideas and technologies is freed from past constraints of state control.

Technological and Economic Globalization

We can speak of technological, economic, ideological, cultural, and religious globalizations. Technological globalization involves universal access to communication technology. Easier access to new means of communication has flattened traditional economic inequalities. Developing nations can access such technologies, reducing the advantage of developed nations in the global economy.

Economic globalization involves the movement of capital, production, and labor across borders. Often the main players in such movements are large companies or conglomerates rather than governments. Although there is no consensus on whether economic globalization has helped reduce the wealth gap between developed and developing nations, most economists agree that globalization has helped reduce the poverty level of many populations.

On the other hand, economic globalization is viewed by many as a threat because it is sometimes experienced as "global capitalism." This happens when those with better access to financial resources exploit the benefits of globalization, resulting in power being concentrated in the hands of large corporations.

Globalization's Impact on Culture and the Christian Worldview

Although the effects of technological and economic globalizations are far-reaching, ideological, cultural, and religious globalizing can change our lives in even more profound ways. For the first time, all the major ideologies of the world are experiencing a kind of "ideological tsunami," an overpowering wave of global trends that do not originate from any single location. While Christianity has long been assaulted by secularizing influences, the current scale of assault is unprecedented.

In the various strands of globalization, we can discern the emergence of a new public ethos that could surpass all previous ideological, ethnic, or nationalistic codes. This new ethos is sometimes called "global hyperculture," a powerful homogenizing influence that is capable of eroding local cultures, while replacing communities with individualistic consumers. This hyperculture can impact our worldview in several ways. It can lead to the fragmentation of communities since it pays scant attention to issues of ethnicity and does not promote moral responsibility for one's place of belonging. It can produce a globalized spirituality in which everything is indiscriminately accepted, and ethics is attempted without absolutes. Not least, it can propagate a utopian vision that celebrates human accomplishment—a vision at odds with the Christian view of the future.

Although the concept of globalization is descriptive rather than prescriptive, it must be assessed in light of the biblical worldview. We must avoid the denunciation of globalization as immoral, capitalist exploitation but also not embrace its full acceptance that may confuse it with the promised Christian future.

Responding Positively to the Times

While we are cautious about the homogenizing tendencies of globalization, we can also respond positively to the opportunities that it presents. Just as missionaries in the Age of Discovery took advantage of the infectious spirit of exploration that took hold of Europe from the fifteenth to seventeenth centuries, boarding the ships that were heading to Africa, the Americas,

Asia, and Oceania, Christians can find new ministry opportunities in the twenty-first century.

First, as we enjoy the benefits of local, regional, and global connectedness, we can gain a sense of human solidarity. The (re)discovery that we are one global family leads us to ponder our basic humanity under the lordship of the one God and Father from whom and for whom all things exist (1 Cor 8:5–6).

Second, we can engage with the exciting challenge of understanding old truths in new ways. For instance, what does the word "neighbor" mean in globalized living (Luke 10:25–29)? What does it mean when we pray for our debts to be forgiven as we forgive our debtors (Matt 6:12)?

Third, globalization weakens the cultural and social domination of the West since it exposes the consumer to many different cultures. For instance, informed comparison can help African or Asian Christians become less enamored of Americanized or Europeanized Christianity, which can pave the way for a more indigenized, but globally integrated, Christianity.

Finally, global culture can complement a worldwide view of missions. Unprecedented cross-cultural contact and instantaneous communication have made it possible for Christians to share the gospel and to equip workers for the spiritual harvest in new and innovative ways. We can engage in missions from everywhere to everywhere. Urban missions and ministry can gain fresh impetus, as the massive global migration of peoples presents new opportunities to do missions at your doorstep.

Conclusion

A rapidly changing world is not a runaway world that is no longer in the hands of the sovereign God. He continues to sit enthroned above the earth and has the power to reduce princes to nothing (Isa 40:22–23). What is more, the Christian faith is well suited to a globalized world because of its global missionary vision.

THE EMERGENCE OF EVANGELICAL CENTERS

Harry L. Poe

The emergence of evangelical centers around the world in the late twentieth and early twenty-first centuries is only the most recent of many shifts in Christian work since Pentecost (Acts 1). From its first center in Jerusalem, Antioch emerged as a mission-sending center. Alexandria, Ephesus, and Rome became centers by the end of the first century. With the legalization of the Christian faith in the fourth century, Constantinople became a center of faith, too. As the Western Empire faded in the fifth century, Christianity spread into the Celtic spheres of Western Europe. By the end of the tenth century, however, Eastern Orthodox Christianity also had spread to Russia, which would become its new center in the second Christian millennium. Even so, Christianity had faded in the Eastern Mediterranean and North Africa with the Islamic invasions of the eighth century.

As the gospel spread, different aspects of the gospel message addressed different local and regional spiritual issues and questions so that the local theologies reflected the aspect of the gospel that was most significant to that culture. The Eastern church, for instance, would orient its theology and worship around the resurrection of Christ who defeated death and sin, and around the Holy Spirit who brings regeneration and union with God. The Western church, both Roman and Protestant, would orient its theology around the sacrificial death of Jesus, while Protestants would add the authority of God's fulfilled Word, the Bible. For the African church during the Roman period, the coming of God in the flesh as Jesus Christ who demonstrated God's love and mediated our reconciliation took center stage in the affirmations of Athanasius. Thus, various local theologies arose even as Christians everywhere affirmed the same faith upon which these theologies are based.

The more modern emergence of evangelical centers around the world has its roots in the changing European situation 500 years before it. Coinciding with the Protestant Reformation, European powers in the late fifteenth and early sixteenth centuries ventured forth in search of nautical trade routes to the Far East. These ventures began with voyages east around Africa before Columbus made his famous voyage in 1492. That same year, Ferdinand and Isabella consolidated their kingdoms and united Christian Spain by defeating the last Muslim kingdom on the Spanish peninsula.

Catholic Spain, Portugal, and France began a program not only of extending their trade but also of extending their sovereignty over other lands. The new Protestant countries of England, Holland, Sweden, and Denmark also embarked on their own programs of expansion. The first wave of colonization resulted in communities of Catholics and Protestants in the Americas. The English, Dutch, and Swedish colonies in North America became early centers of evangelical faith out of which the First Great Awakening spread. By the mid-nineteenth century, the European powers had established global empires that controlled most of Africa, Australia, Central America, South America, and large portions of Asia.

The modern mission movement began in the context of growing British control over the subcontinent of India. William Carey went as a Baptist missionary from England. Adoniram Judson went as a Congregationalist missionary to India, but upon converting to Baptist convictions during the long voyage from New England, he went to Burma instead. Organized Baptist denominational life in the United States, known as the Triennial Convention, began as an effort to support the mission of Judson. In 1865, Hudson Taylor founded the China Inland Mission as a conservative interdenominational mission society. By its nature, this society was broadly evangelical rather than denominational in its orientation. It adopted a policy of propagating an indigenous Christianity that identified with the Chinese people rather than an imperial European power. As Britain extended its control in Africa, from Egypt southward and from South Africa northward, the Anglican Church sent missionaries into every new region that came under British rule.

While the evangelization of Asia and Africa tended to follow the pattern of colonial expansion, the spread of evangelical Christianity in Latin America proceeded in a different manner. By agreement between Spain and Portugal negotiated by Pope Alexander VI in 1493, newly discovered territories and pagan territories in the Far East were divided between the two great Catholic powers. Thus, Spain had hegemony in America west of the leading edge of South America that became Brazil. These claims extended around the globe to the Spanish territory of the Philippines. Portugal's lands extended east from Brazil to include Africa and India. Evangelical mission work in Brazil came from the United States in the mid-1800s with Methodists, Presbyterians, Episcopalians, and Baptists establishing work there once the old Spanish and Portuguese colonial power structure came to an end with the independence movement.

The gains of evangelical missions by 1900 could be called modest at best. With the dawn of the new century, however, an increasing optimism marked the gospel enterprise. The Student Volunteer Movement for Foreign Missions of the 1880s and 1890s emerged from an awakening among students at Cambridge University. John R. Mott coined the slogan of this movement: "The Evangelization of the World in This Generation." Mott organized the Edinburgh Conference of 1910 that brought together more than 1,200 missionaries from different evangelical mission societies around the world. Some declared the twentieth century to be "The Christian Century." A nondenominational evangelical gathering in Edinburgh in 1910 was the last great transnational Christian gathering before the Great War of 1914. By the end of that war, most of the great imperial monarchies of the world (China, Russia, Ottoman Turk, Austria-Hungary, and Germany) had come to an end, or their empires stood on the verge of collapse (as in the case of France, Spain, Britain, and Netherlands).

Freed from colonial and imperial attachments, the gospel spread tenaciously across Asia, Africa, and Latin America during the twentieth century in the context of civil war, revolution, famine, economic depression, and global warfare. In the midst of the social, political, and economic turmoil of the twentieth century, however, a number of spiritual awakenings took place around the world in the midst of the chaos. Beginning with the Welsh Revival of 1905, which encouraged the international mission movement and the 1906 Azusa Street Revival in Los Angeles that launched the international Pentecostal Movement, awakenings also took place in Asia, Africa, and South America.

In China, the Shantung Revival prepared Chinese Christians for the horrors of World War II, the Communist Revolution, and the Cultural Revolution. A century after the Chinese Revolution of 1911 led by the Christian Dr. Sun Yat Sen, perhaps as many as a hundred million Chinese had converted to Christianity. An awakening in South Korea following the Korean War has led to approximately half the population of South Korea converting to Christianity.

An awakening in East Africa in the context of the new independence of former British colonies has led to a sudden and dramatic spread of the gospel in sub-Saharan Africa. An awakening among the evangelical and Pentecostal churches of Brazil has resulted in a significant spread of the gospel there.

The post-World War II global awakening saw a rise in local national Christian leaders around the globe who assumed the leadership role that had once belonged to the original missionaries. The gospel issues of Asia, Africa, and South America differed from the theologies of North America and Europe, rooted as they are in the traditions of the evangelization of the old Celtic peoples more than a thousand years ago. In Korea, an emphasis on prayer through the exalted Christ is prominent. In Africa and South America where the Pentecostal Movement has been particularly strong, an emphasis on the power of the Holy Spirit over all other spiritual forces and the authority of the exalted Christ over all spiritual realms has been prominent. In China, which has had a pluralistic religious tradition for thousands of years, including the practice of Taoism, Buddhism, and Confucianism alongside traditional polytheism and ancestor worship, the reality of the one Creator God has been prominent.

The massive shift in the center of Christianity away from Europe and North America during the twentieth century after the colonial period is the kind of experience the church has not seen since the mass people movements of Celtic and Russian conversion over a thousand years ago. We watch with avid interest and rejoicing as another chapter of the gospel's spread unfolds.

A BIBLICAL VIEW OF THE NATIONS

Jason G. Duesing

In American sports culture a team's fan base is often described as a "nation." Websites and apparel are designed for the "Yankees Nation," the "Aggie Nation," and so on. The use of the word *nation* in this respect refers to something larger than just the fans that attend games or live in proximity to their team's home stadium. These so-called nations consist of all people who share a common bond of fanatic interest in a team, regardless of any geographical or ethnic boundaries. While they exist in greatest number in the region surrounding the team's headquarters, members of the team's "nation" can exist globally and can join other members in enthusiastic support.

When considering a biblical view of the nations, an American sports understanding of the term proves helpful. Within the Bible the word *nation* is often used to describe political entities defined by geographic boundaries that have kings or rulers. For example, Deuteronomy 7:1 lists "the Hethites, Girgashites, Amorites, Canaanites, Perizzites, Hivites and Jebusites" as seven nations "more numerous and powerful" than Israel. Additionally, the term *nations* is often used as a collective that describes all groups of people outside of Israel; this large and diverse group is also known by the Latin term *Gentiles* (Acts 10:45). Taking the collective non-Israel use further, *nations* is also used to describe peoples identified by ethnic commonalities such as language or customs. In the covenant God makes with Abraham (Gen 18:18), he indicates "all the nations of the earth" will be blessed through the nation that will descend from Abraham. These people are also described as "families of the earth" (Gen 12:3 KJV) and "all the families of the nations" (Ps 22:27). These phrases reflect a corporate emphasis on non-Israelites in the Bible as opposed to a mere individual focus.

The Nations in the Old Testament

The nations were first created when God broke up a unified and proud human race, all descended from Adam and Eve and then from Noah's family, during their construction of the tower of Babel (Gen 11). Previously having one language, and thus possessing the ability to enforce their will on one another and perfect their rebellion against God, the people were dispersed throughout the earth due to the fact that God confused their tongues. It was at the time he gave the people distinct languages so they would be forced to separate from one another and gather together in new communities—each with its own language. Genesis 10 lists Noah's descendants, recognizing the dispersion recorded in the following chapter. It calls the ethnic groups "nations" (10:5).

The nations, both Jewish and Gentile, are central entities in God's plan to display his glory and the work of salvation and judgment. The nation of Israel is called to declare the glory of God among the nations (Ps 96:3), and the psalmist calls on God to "let the nations rejoice and shout for joy" at his work in the world (67:4). God is sovereign over all nations (103:19), and as a part of his covenant plan brought forth from Abraham, God gave Israel to be "a light for the nations" (Isa 49:6). God judges all nations (49:24–27) and provides salvation for them (2:2–4).

The Gospel for the Nations

Into the nation of Israel, God sent his Son, Jesus Christ, as Messiah to "suffer and rise from the dead the third day, [that] repentance for forgiveness of sins would be proclaimed in his name to all the nations" (Luke 24:46b–47). After his resurrection and before his ascension to heaven, the Messiah commanded his followers to "make disciples of all nations" (Matt 28:19). This message of salvation first went forth from Jerusalem (Acts 1:8).

It is the commission of Christian churches to continue the task of taking the message of God's plan of salvation (Rom 10:14–15) to those nations who have not heard (15:21). Jesus Christ is the hope of all nations (15:12), and from the nations he will gather his people (John 10:16). This message will be proclaimed by his followers "to all nations" until the end of the world (Matt 24:14). At that time the Messiah will return to the earth, and all nations will see God's glory (Isa 52:10). They will submit to his rule and reign (Phil 2:10–11). People from every nation will worship him (Rev 7:9).

Regardless of ethnicity and culture, there is ultimately no distinction between Jew or Gentile in Christ (Gal 3:28). In him God has made Jew and Gentile "one new man" and "fellow citizens" together (Eph 2:15,19). As the body of Christ is comprised of believers from many nations (Rev 5:9), one's citizenship is permanently in heaven (Phil 3:20). This should not discourage temporal patriotism or appropriate stewardship of civic service as earthly citizens of nations; rather, it should serve as a warning against an ethnocentrism that hinders the missionary task. It should show us the folly of racial or ethnic prejudice of any kind. To hold such biases is to position one's self squarely against the revealed will of God, who has created all people and all nations and has offered salvation to everyone.

The story of Jonah illustrates one problem caused when we prioritize one ethnic group over another. When God commanded the Israelite prophet to go to Assyrian Nineveh and "preach against it," Jonah instead boarded a ship and attempted to go to Tarshish (Jonah 1:2–3). So seriously did God take Jonah's disobedience that he sent "a great storm" to threaten the ship and its crew, and he relented only when Jonah was tossed overboard by the reluctant sailors (Jonah 1:4–15). What was Jonah's motive for shirking God's command? He explains it in a prayer: "I knew that you are a gracious and compassionate God, slow to anger, abounding in faithful love, and one who relents from sending disaster" (Jonah 4:2). Likely because he despised the military might and strong-arm tendencies of Assyria, Jonah preferred to see God's wrath fall on Nineveh rather than seeing God's mercy extend to its people. This manner of viewing the nations is self-centered and does not reflect awareness that God is Lord of all peoples and offers them mercy through faith-based repentance.

Allegiance to King Jesus

When one remembers that to God "the nations are like a drop in a bucket" (Isa 40:15) and that he has the power both to make them great and to destroy them (Job 12:23), allegiance to any earthly nation should clearly not supersede allegiance to the Ruler of nations (Ps 22:28). Allegiance to him is our primary and lasting citizenship. Through faith in Christ, we are the nation of God, a kingdom drawn from all earthly nations and ethnicities (cp., Rev 7:9–10). It should be our great joy and high priority to reach both next door and overseas to spread the message of eternal hope in the Son whom God sent to pay our sin debt on the cross and to defeat death in his resurrection.

NORTH AMERICAN EVANGELICALS AND THE GLOBAL SOUTH

Mark A. Noll

The relationship of North American evangelicals to world Christianity is at once simple and complex. The simplicity concerns the character of the faith itself. All believers, in all times and places, are equal recipients of God's grace and his gifts, equal participants in the work of the Holy Spirit and as fellow heirs of Jesus Christ. In these terms North American evangelicals merely display variations on common patterns of God's merciful dealings with humankind.

The clear message of Scripture is that all believers, wherever they are found, make up a universal entity. Believers present in one local expression of Christian faith are linked to all others in their local settings because all are joined to Christ. And this linkage is much more than just a jigsaw puzzle in which the pieces touch only those other pieces that are in closest proximity. Rather, the great image from Scripture is the body of Christ where circulation (meaning assistance), a unified nervous system (meaning communication), and coordinated muscular exertion (meaning common action) are essential for all. This body of Christ anticipates the eternal reality described in Rev 7:9: "There was a vast multitude from every nation, tribe, people, and language, which no one could number, standing before the throne and before the Lamb. They were clothed in white."

Yet the relationship between North American evangelicals and the Global South is also complicated because of the history of Christianity over the last three centuries. For much of that period, evangelicals in North America were active participants in the Western missionary efforts that sought to spread Christianity throughout the world. Through the nineteenth century, Americans and Canadians followed the lead of Britain. Pioneering missionaries like Adoniram and Ann Judson went out from Massachusetts to Burma only a few years after the English cobbler William Carey pioneered British missionary work in India. Lottie Moon left Virginia as a Southern Baptist missionary to China less than 20 years after Hudson Taylor founded the China Inland Mission as the English-speaking Protestant world's most extensive outreach in Far East Asia. Rufus Anderson of the American Board of Commissioners for Foreign Missions followed the lead of Henry Venn, leader of England's Church Missionary Society, in promoting the "three-self formula" as a missionary ideal: self-governing, self-financing, and self-reproducing.

From roughly the dawn of the twentieth century, the number of evangelical missionaries from the United States, having overtaken the number from Britain, took the lead in cross-cultural proclamation of the gospel. (As a comparative note, it is worth observing that Canada, with its smaller population, long contributed a larger proportion of that population to missionary service than did the United States.) North American missionary efforts have been especially significant in promoting Bible translation. At the forefront of those translating efforts has been the Wycliffe Bible Translators, with the Summer Institute of Linguistics as its academic arm. The Wycliffe organization was founded in 1942 by an American missionary to Central America, Cameron Townsend; thousands of North Americans subsequently contributed to the more than 700 completed, and many more in-process, Bible translations created since that time.

Beyond providing people and resources for Bible translations, American missionaries have planted new churches all over the world. They have trained disciples, provided immense quantities of Christian literature, founded schools to teach basic literacy, established universities for advanced learning, set up hospitals, assisted agricultural and industrial development, and—in general—tried to provide as many dimensions of the Christian faith to others as they have experienced themselves.

Within recent years, however, the relationship of North Americans to the rest of the Christian world has entered a new phase. It is suggested by the fact that Wycliffe workers now come from all parts of the globe. Some formerly mission-receiving countries like South Korea have even contributed more personnel (as a proportion of their population) than the traditional mission-sending countries like the U.S.

Even more complications are introduced if we think of the United States as a country that receives missionaries from the Global South. In recent decades Christian missions have in fact moved from "the West to the rest" to a pattern of believers going "from everywhere to everywhere" (an insightful exposition is Michael Nazir-Ali, *From Everywhere to Everywhere: A World View of Christian Witness*, 1991). And some of those believers are now evangelizing within North America.

For the most part, Christian missionaries to the United States work among immigrant populations. As an example, Mark Gornik has documented the presence of scores of mission works in New York City alone that are offshoots of Christian communities in Africa (*Word Made Global: Stories of African Christianity in New York City*, 2011). Missionary organizations like the El Shaddai movement from the Philippines (a lay charismatic organization) and the Christian Church Outreach Mission from Ghana (founded by Abraham Bediako) are among the larger groups that also sponsor missionaries in some American locations (as well as many in Europe). Increasingly, missionaries to the U.S. are also beginning to reach beyond immigrant communities to the general population.

The relationship between American evangelicals and the churches of the Global South involves one more complicating factor. This factor concerns the type of Christianity that has been spreading so rapidly in much of the non-Western world. That type increasingly resembles the type of Christianity that has flourished in the U.S.

The distinguished missiologist Andrew Walls has explained these parallels in several helpful works (esp. *The Missionary Movement in Christian History: Studies in the Transmission of Faith*, 1996; and in *The Cross-Cultural Process in Christian History: Studies in the Transmission and Appropriation of Faith*, 2002). He first points to what happened with Christianity when it was successfully transmitted from Europe to North America. That successful transmission required giving up church-state establishments, hierarchical societies, and aristocratic or monarchical governments in favor of the separation of church and state, egalitarian society, and democratic government. European observers did not believe Christianity could survive without its traditional forms. But it did survive. In fact, from the late 1700s to the late 1800s, the United States experienced one of the most dramatic expansions of Christianity that had ever taken place in the long history of the church.

For the most part, Americans turned to voluntary, self-directed organization as the primary means for carrying on the work of the church. They practiced the faith by forming their own churches and religious agencies, generating their own financial support, and taking personal responsibility for spreading and upholding the faith. Evangelicals led in setting up churches in this pattern and then in forming missionary agencies on the same basis.

The new American pattern embodied a much more informal Christianity and pushed consistently for ever-more flexible institutions and ever-newer innovations in responding to spiritual challenges. It established an affinity between Christianity and the American social movements of the age. The connections grew strong between Christianity—based on conversion and voluntary organization—on the one hand, and fluid, rapidly changing, commerce-driven, insecure, and ethnically pluralistic society on the other. But that kind of nineteenth-century American setting now describes many of the world societies that Christian faith—based on conversion and voluntary organization—is growing so rapidly.

These newer societies tend to be competitive and not deferential, open to Christian witness but not officially Christian, allowing space for entrepreneurial activity while not restricting religious expression too drastically. To the extent that these conditions have developed, it is not surprising that styles of Christianity that flourished in North America's competitive, market-oriented, rapidly changing, and initiative-rewarding environment would also flourish when other places begin to look more like nineteenth-century America than fifteenth-century Europe.

American evangelicals continue to influence the Global South through missions. But so also has the Global South begun to do missions in the U.S. Much of Christianity through the entire world now resembles American forms of Christianity—not primarily because of direct American influence but because Christianity meets humanity's greatest needs there in ways that it has done, and continues to do, here.

WORKS CITED

Ballor, Jordan. "Avoiding Confusionism: Liberty and Civil Society." Cato Unbound. https://www.cato-unbound.org/2013/05/13/jordan-ballor/avoiding-confusionism. Cited on page 189.

Barth, Karl. *Credo*. Eugene, OR: Wipf and Stock, 2005. Cited on page 105.

Bartholomew, Craig and Michael Goheen. *Living at the Crossroads: An Introduction to Christian Worldview*. Grand Rapids: Baker Academic, 2008. Cited on page 411.

Bauckham, Richard. *Jesus and the God of Israel: God Crucified and Other Studies on the New Testament's Christology of Divine Identity*. Grand Rapids: Eerdmans, 2008. Cited on page 90.

Bauckham, Richard. *The Theology of the Book of Revelation*. New Testament Theology. New York: Cambridge, 1993. Cited on page 209.

Bebbington, David. *Patterns in History: A Christian Perspective*. Grand Rapids: Baker, 1990. Cited on page 317.

Blamires, Harry. *The Christian Mind: How Should a Christian Think?* Vancouver: Regent College, 2005. Cited on page 405.

Boesak, Allan Aubrey and Curtiss Paul DeYoung. *Radical Reconciliation*. Maryknoll, NY: Orbis, 2012.

Bostrom, Nick. "Transhumanist Values." In *Ethical Issues for the 21st Century*. Edited by F. Adams. Charlottesville: Philosophical Documentation Center, 2004. Cited on page 239.

Budziszewski, J. *Revenge of Conscience: Politics and the Fall of Man*. Eugene, OR: Wipf and Stock, 2000. Cited on pages 177, 182-183.

Cahill, Thomas. *How the Irish Saved Civilization*. New York: Anchor Books, 1995. Cited on page 403.

Cottingham, John. *On the Meaning of Life*. New York: Routledge, 2003. Cited on page 71.

Craig, William Lane. *Reasonable Faith*. Wheaton: Moody, 1984. Cited on page 220.

Dawkins, Richard. *The Blind Watchmaker*. New York: W.W. Norton, 1996. Cited on page 154-55.

---. *The God Delusion*. New York: Mariner, 2008. Cited on page 151.

Dürer, Albrecht. *Literary Remains of Albrecht Dürer*. Translated and edited by William Conway. Cambridge, UK: Cambridge University, 1889. Cited on page 370-371.

English, James W. *Handyman of the Lord: The Life and Ministry of the Rev. William Holmes Borders*. New York: Meredith Press, 1967. Cited on page 224.

Ferry, Luc. *A Brief History of Thought: A Philosophical Guide to Living*. New York: Harper, 2011. Cited on page 90.

Fuller, D.P. "Satan." In *International Standard Bible Encyclopedia*. Edited by Geoffrey Bromiley. Vol. 4. Grand Rapids: Eerdmans, 1988. Cited on page 62.

George, Robert P., Ryan T. Anderson, and Sherif Girgis. *What Is Marriage? Man and Woman: A Defense*. New York: Encounter, 2011. Cited on pages 249.

Hess, Karl. "The Death of Politics." In *Mostly on the Edge: An Autobiography*. Edited by Karl Hess, Jr. New York: Prometheus, 1999. Cited on page 185.

Howard, Thomas. *Evangelical Is Not Enough: Worship of God in Liturgy and Sacrament*. San Francisco: Ignatius, 1984. Cited on Page 68.

Hurtado, Larry. *Lord Jesus Christ: Devotion to Jesus in Earliest Christianity*. Grand Rapids: Eerdmans, 2003. Cited on page 90.

Jastrow, Robert. *God and the Astronomers*. 2nd Edition. New York: W.W. Norton, 1992. Cited on page 53.

Kidner, Derek. *Genesis: An Introduction and Commentary*. Tyndale Old Testament Commentary. Downers Grove: InterVarsity, 1967. Cited on page 68.

King Jr., Martin Luther. "Letter from Birmingham Jail." University of Pennsylvania. https://www.africa.upenn.edu/Articles_Gen/Letter_Birmingham.html.

Koyzis, David. *Political Visions and Illusions*. Downers Grove: InterVarsity, 2003. Cited on pages 174-75, 179, 191, 192, 198.

Kurtz, Paul. "Libertarianism as the Philosophy of Moral Freedom." In *Freedom and Virtue: The Conservative/Libertarian Debate*. Edited by George W. Carey. Wilmington, DE: ISI Books, 2003. Cited on page 186.

Leithart, Peter. "When Marriage Is Dying." *Touchstone Magazine*. https://www.touchstonemag.com/archives/article.php?id=14-10-020-v. Cited on page 233.

Leupold, H.C. *Exposition of Genesis.* Vol. 1. Grand Rapids: Baker Books, 1968. Cited on page 232.

Lewis, C.S. *The Great Divorce.* New York: HarperCollins, 2001. Cited on page 110.

---. *The Last Battle.* New York: HarperCollins, 1984.

---. *Mere Christianity.* New York: HarperCollins, 2001. Cited on pages 46, 276.

--. *Miracles.* New York: HarperCollins, 2001. Cited on page 67.

--. *The Weight of Glory.* New York: HarperCollins, 2001. Cited on page 12.

MacLaine, Shirley. *Out on a Limb.* New York: Bantam, 1983. Cited on page 108.

Macleod, Donald. *The Person of Christ.* Contours of Christian Theology. Downers Grove: InterVarsity, 1998. Cited on page 87.

Marx, Karl and Friedrich Engels. *The Communist Manifesto.* In Karl Marx: Selected Writings. Edited by Lawrence H. Simon. Indianapolis: Hackett, 1994. Cited on page 196.

Moody, D.L. *New Sermons, Addresses, and Prayers.* New York: Henry S. Goodspeed, 1877. Citeed on page 207.

More, Max. "True Transhumanism: A Reply to Don Ihde." In *H+/-: Transhumanism and Its Critics.* Edited by Gregory R. Hansell and William Grassie Cited on page 242.

Neuhaus, Richard John. "Seeking a Better Way." *First Things.* https://www.firstthings.com/article/2002/10/seeking-a-better-way. Cited on page 194.

Noll, Mark. *The Scandal of the Evangelical Mind.* Grand Rapids: Eerdmans, 1995. Cited on page 405.

O'Donovan, Oliver. *Resurrection and Moral Order: An Outline of Evangelical Ethics.* Grand Rapids: Eerdmans, 1994. Cited on page 90.

Reno, R.R. "Deadly Progressivism." *First Things.* https://www.firstthings.com/web-exclusives/2015/11/deadly-progressivism. Cited on page 178.

Sanders, Fred. "A Play Ethic: Play Studies in Psychology and Theology." Quoted in K. Erik Thoennes. "Created to Play: Thoughts on Play Sport and the Christian Life." In *The Image of God in the Human Body: Essays on Chrsitianity and Sports.* Edited by Donald Deardorff and John White. Lewiston, NY: Edwin Mellen, 2008. Cited on page 385.

Scruton, Roger. "Sacrilege and Sacrament." In *The Meaning of Marriage.* Edited by Robert P. George & Jean Bethke Elshtain. New York: Scepter, 2010. Cited on page 230.

Storkey, Elaine. "Sphere Sovereignty." In *Religion, Pluralism, and Public Life: Abraham Kuyper's Legacy for the Twenty-First Century.* Edited by Luis F. Lugo. Grand Rapids: Eerdmans, 2000. Cited on page 182.

Stott, John. *Your Mind Matters: The Place of the Mind in the Christian Life.* Downers Grove: InterVarsity, 2006. Cited on page 404.

Swinburne, Richard. *The Existence of God.* 2nd Edition. New York: Oxford University, 2004. Cited on page 357.

Tutu, Desmond. *No Future without Forgivness.* New York: Image, 2000.

Vander Elst, Philip. *Libertarianism: A Christian Critique.* Newcastle, UK: The Christian Institute, 2003. Cited on pages 188-89.

Whitney, Donald. *Spiritual Disciplines for the Christian Life.* Colorado Springs: NavPress, 1991. Cited on page 408.

Wright, N.T. *The Resurrection and the Son of God.* Christian Origins and the Question of God. Minneapolis: Fortress, 2003. Cited on page 221.

---. *Who Was Jesus?* Grand Rapids: Eerdmans, 1992. Cited on page 90.